"A marvelous book full of practical and sensible suggestions and advice. This volume will be of great help to parents and professionals alike and an invaluable resource for all those concerned with supporting individuals with Asperger's."

—Fred R. Volkmar, MD, Irving B. Harris Professor, director, Child Study Center, Yale University School of Medicine

"Patty Romanowski Bashe has done it again. . . . This is a compass to send you in the right direction to get the supports you may need. Thank you, Patty!"

—Jed Baker, PhD, director of the Social Skills Training Project and author of *No More Victims: Protecting Those with Autism from Cyber Bullying, Internet Predators, and Scams*

"*The OASIS Guide* has always been a go-to resource for information regarding Asperger syndrome. . . . With all the controversy regarding the conception of the autism spectrum disorders, *Asperger Syndrome: The OASIS Guide* is an even-handed treatment that emphasizes solid, empirical research. It belongs on every clinician's and researcher's bookshelf."

—Bobby Newman, PhD, BCBA, founder of Room to Grow and author of *Move with a Purpose, Behaviorspeak, and Behavioral Detectives*

PRAISE FOR THE PREVIOUS EDITION OF
THE OASIS GUIDE

"A godsend to the increasing number of families who have a child recently diagnosed with Asperger syndrome (AS) . . ."

—Uta Frith, professor of cognitive development, University of London; deputy director of the UCL Institute of Cognitive Neuroscience; and author of *Autism and Asperger Syndrome*

"Well beyond merely identifying and defining AS, the authors provide dozens of field-tested strategies that can be used at home, in the classroom, and in the community. . . . If you share your home or classroom with a child with Asperger syndrome, buy this book."

—Richard D. Lavoie, executive producer of *How Difficult Can This Be? The F.A.T. City Workshop* and author of *It's So Much Work to Be Your Friend*

"Incredible! *The OASIS Guide* contains tremendous advice, tips, and practical solutions to manage the confusion of special ed and Asperger syndrome. The new parent and seasoned veteran should read the guide cover to cover. It is excellent."

—Peter W. D. Wright, Esq., coauthor of *Wrightslaw: Special Education Law* and owner of wrightslaw.com

"If someone were to ask me to suggest the most useful resource about AS, I would not hesitate for an instant: *The OASIS Guide.* This is a must-read book for parents, educators, and individuals with AS alike."

—Brenda Smith Myles, PhD, author of *Asperger Syndrome and Difficult Moments: Practical Solutions for Tantrums, Rage, and Meltdowns*

"Rarely does one find such a wealth of quality information all between the same two covers. This book has important work to do, and it is more than up to the task."

—Carol Gray, director, Gray Center for Social Learning and Understanding

"Barbara L. Kirby and Patricia Romanowski Bashe have provided the community of Asperger syndrome with more than a rainbow's end of gold. They've opened a treasure chest brimming with understanding and support."

—Liane Holliday Willey, EdD., author of *Pretending to Be Normal: Living with Asperger's Syndrome* and *Asperger Syndrome in the Family: Redefining Normal*

Also by the author

*The Parents' Guide to Teaching
Kids with Asperger Syndrome and Similar ASDs Real-Life
Skills for Independence*

ASPERGER SYNDROME:

THE
OASIS
GUIDE

Advice, Inspiration, Insight, and Hope,
from Early Intervention to Adulthood

FULLY REVISED, UPDATED, AND EXPANDED THIRD EDITION

PATRICIA ROMANOWSKI BASHE, MSEd., BCBA

FOREWORDS BY Tony Attwood AND
Michael John Carley

HARMONY
BOOKS · NEW YORK

Foreword copyright © 2014 by Tony Attwood
Foreword copyright © 2014 by Michael John Carley

Published in the United States by Harmony Books, an imprint of the Crown Publishing Group, a division of Random House LLC, a Penguin Random House Company, New York.
www.crownpublishing.com

Harmony Books is a registered trademark and the Circle colophon is a trademark of Random House LLC.

Previous editions were published in hardcover in the United States as *The Oasis Guide to Asperger Syndrome* by Harmony Books, New York, in 2001 and 2005 respectively.

Library of Congress Cataloging-in-Publication data is available upon request.

ISBN 978-0-385-34465-4
eBook ISBN 978-0-8041-4148-2

Printed in the United States of America

Cover design by Kathy Kikkert
Cover photography by Stan Godlewski/Stone

10 9 8 7 6 5 4 3 2 1

Third Revised Edition

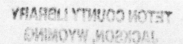

As always, for Justin Eric Romanowski Bashe

AUTHOR'S NOTE

No book, including this one, can ever substitute for the care or expert guidance of a fully qualified health or education professional who knows and works with your child. All opinions and views expressed herein are those of the author, her cited interview subjects, or the authors of the sources cited. Nothing in this book should be construed as having the endorsement of any organization with which the author is or has been affiliated. This book contains no case histories based on real persons. All examples are fictitious scenarios of common situations for individuals with ASDs. The names used in these examples are all fictitious, unless otherwise specifically indicated, and chosen at random. Any resemblance to persons living or dead is coincidental. The exception is to statements about my son, Justin Bashe. He has read and approved all references to himself herein. In the "Medication" chapter, specific medications are mentioned for illustrative purposes only.

CONTENTS

CONTENTS

FOREWORD

Tony Attwood

When I started my journey of exploration of Asperger syndrome in the early 1980s, I felt as if I was one of the first psychologists to discover a new world. It was at that time a world with no clinicians or parents' maps or traveler's guide, and there was, and still is, a sense of excitement from discovering an alternative way of perceiving and thinking. Very soon there were fellow travelers—colleagues, parents, and also those who have Asperger syndrome—explaining their world and culture in conversations and autobiographies. Patricia Romanowski Bashe and Barbara Kirby are parents, each with a young adult who has a diagnosis of Asperger syndrome. Their first *OASIS Guide* was published in 2001. It quickly became a popular and highly recommended resource for parents and an extremely valuable resource for teachers and specialists in autism. This is now the third edition, this time written by Patty on her own, to keep the reader up-to-date with our evolving knowledge of Asperger syndrome.

Over the last decade, there has been an amazing increase in the research literature on Asperger syndrome, as well as numerous books on specific aspects of Asperger syndrome, and the development and evaluation of services and resources for parents, teachers, therapists, and clinicians. It is difficult to keep pace with all this new knowledge, and I am so pleased that this third edition provides a comprehensive, unbiased, and clear description of our current state of knowledge. The text will answer the many questions raised by parents and professionals. It is almost an encyclopedia of Asperger syndrome, its wise advice based on reviewing the research literature and a personal and insightful perspective.

Patty writes in an engaging, reassuring, and informative style, as though she is your best friend who really understands your experiences, thoughts, and feelings. She originally explored the world of Asperger syndrome as a parent and by analysis of the OASIS message board and surveys. She is now a professor of graduate courses in special education. Thus, she really knows what she is writing about and has empathy for the challenges faced by parents, teachers, and those who have Asperger syndrome.

If you are the parent or teacher of someone who has Asperger syndrome and are starting out or are already on the journey of exploration of the world of Asperger syndrome, this is your guidebook and your collection of maps. Patty is your personal companion to ensure you do not get lost and that you know where you are going, and who and what will help you along the way.

Tony Attwood is the author of several books on autism and Asperger syndrome, including the classic *The Complete Guide to Asperger Syndrome*. Since the publication of his first book on AS, *Asperger Syndrome: A Guide for Parents and Professionals*, in 1998, Dr. Attwood has increased understanding of the syndrome through his writings, workshops, and presentations around the world. He lives in Brisbane, Australia, where he maintains his practice and lives with his family.

FOREWORD

Michael John Carley

When I first entered the autism/Asperger world, it was two years before GRASP (Global and Regional Asperger Syndrome Partnership) would be formed, and three years before GRASP had a website. And during that era of 2001 to 2004 (not to mention beforehand), it was very difficult to obtain information of any kind—off the internet or elsewhere—about Asperger syndrome.

People forget: In those days, Asperger syndrome was still thought of as this weird second cousin to autism. Though having been made official by the fourth edition of the *Diagnostic and Statistical Manual* in 1994 (*DSM-IV*), the diagnosis was only starting to enter into public consciousness. These were the formulative years, where parent organizations were starting to see that their kids' worlds might not be as tragic as they thought prior, where spectrumites themselves were starting to sniff the self-worth in rejecting negative stigma, and where the research community both scrambled to reassess its overall approach and simultaneously saw a goldmine in the expanded definition of autism. It was a period of rapidly emerging new ideas that carried both the promise of emotional health as well as the stark, ugly realization of how unhealthy our attitudes had been up until then. We were desirous and starving for a new world, but resources were slim.

At this crucial time, there was one—and only one—site: Barbara Kirby's OASIS (Online Asperger Syndrome Information and Support) site. The url was a mess of code, rendering it impossible to remember, and the site's graphics and layout were basic at best. But whoever's website had the second most factually based material . . . was a very *distant* second place. Barbara's essential website set the tone; for GRASP, and for everyone else, as armed with far more resources than Barbara ever enjoyed, GRASP and others soon created sites that became the new standards.

Seeing a new need even as OASIS continued growing, Barbara joined up with journalist/mom Patty Romanowski Bashe, and together they wrote *The OASIS Guide to Asperger Syndrome*, published in 2001, when few books were out there. It was a thorough read for parents: a book that satisfied both in quality and (in thoroughness) quantity. There was no need to buy nine additional books.

But those early years are gone. And in the past decade or so, the market has become saturated with books, most of which are inexplicable rehashes of what is now old information. New autism organizations pop up every week, someone creates a new Facebook group every twenty-four hours, and at least twenty times a day Googlefeed provides my inbox with media articles about the spectrum world . . . that often completely contradict one another. We now live in a community, for better or worse, where everyone assumes they are a leader.

So once again to provide clarity to a confused world, OASIS has stepped in.

Few books address anywhere near the dearth of topics as does this volume. Fred Volkmar's book comes to mind, and I may be missing one other. But in this revised and expanded edition of *Asperger Syndrome: The OASIS Guide*, Patty Bashe answers every parent concern: from the first hints of suspicion about a toddler to the day in which our children outlive us. It is that comprehensive. And because it is so thorough, there might be times when you disagree with something said. But those times will be few; and because this book is not written in an agit-prop, fear-based style, *your* opinion, in those instances, will be made more clear to you.

In addition to being an individual with Asperger's, I'm also the parent of an Asperger kid who is about to say good-bye to us for college. Like many children diagnosed around the millennium, my son has far exceeded his initial prognosis. Is it because I and other parents did a great job? Who knows and who cares? What I do know is that a large part of his success was created by the world around him becoming more accustomed to his differences. As pioneers like the OASIS team of Barb and Patty spread more and more positive iconography around a condition that once reflected as dirt in the eyes of the average Joe, my son didn't have to go through the anxieties of confusion and ostracization that prior generations endured. And in that relative calm, my boy could listen better, learn more, enjoy more, and trust the outside world a *lot* more.

The studies tell us that whether we're discussing academics, socialization, athletics, careers, sexual performance, and perhaps parenting: (a) that resources/size matter, (b) that talent matters, and (c) that work ethic matters . . . but that *confidence* matters much more. I thank the world for the confident young man he is.

The right books will provide you, the parent, with that essential confidence. Patty Bashe's *Asperger Syndrome: The OASIS Guide* will give you that. And more.

Michael John Carley is the Founder of GRASP, a consultant for the New York City Public Schools, and the author of *Asperger's from the Inside-Out* (Penguin/Perigee) and *The Last Memoir of Asperger's Syndrome* (TBD). More information can be found at www.michael johncarley.com.

ASPERGER SYNDROME:

THE
OASIS
GUIDE

INTRODUCTION

WELCOME to *Asperger Syndrome: The OASIS Guide*, the third edition of *The OASIS Guide to Asperger Syndrome*. The OASIS (Online Asperger Syndrome Information and Support) website from which this book still takes part of its name was founded, developed, designed, written, nurtured, run, and supported by my partner in writing the first two editions, Barbara L. Kirby. From its launch in 1995 until Barb chose to close the original OASIS to pursue other interests in her life several years ago, that website and message board held an important—I would even argue, historical—place as what one renowned autism expert termed "the town square" for people living with Asperger syndrome. When we met over the phone after my son was diagnosed, we shared a perspective on Asperger syndrome—that there was not enough good, accessible, reliable information out there—and a determination that only two mothers could sustain. That was 1998. The first edition of this book arrived three years later. This is the first edition that I have revised and expanded completely on my own. In some places, the editorial *we* persists, not only because it feels right but because without its original foundation, this edition could never stand.

I cowrote the first edition of this book as a journalist and mom, not as the professional in the field of autism I am today. Fifteen years ago, I went out to hunt down and bring home all the answers we needed, but more often than not, I came back with more questions than I left with. So when our son was ten, three years after his diagnosis, I did what any irrational and desperate mom might: I went back to school and changed careers. To be honest, it was not so much because I was in love with the idea of being a teacher (though it's great) but because I wanted to understand the hidden curriculum behind systems that shortchanged or failed kids like mine due to lack of knowledge and understanding about what Asperger syndrome and similar forms of autism spectrum disorder (ASD) were all about. In the decade since then, I have taught and consulted for children from age two to adulthood across the spectrum. As a professor of graduate courses in special education and applied behavior analysis, I'm not shy about offering students—most of them current or future teachers, psychologists, and district administrators—insights into how we parents see things. Having a foot in each world, so to speak, has opened the view "behind the curtain" of the Individualized Education Plan (IEP) meeting, the social skills program, the transition planning.

So at this point, you might expect some huge revelation or exposé. Sorry to disappoint. What I learned was that most of my professional colleagues care about our kids and want to do the best job they can for them. What they need—what we all need—is information, access, and time. We all need to look at each child realistically, to diagnose accurately, to assess fairly, and to advise with caution. We need to listen to each other and try to understand where a teacher or a doctor is coming from when their suggestions do not mesh with our expectations. (And that road runs both ways, professionals.)

No one can tell you for sure where your child will be in five, ten, fifteen years. No one can predict where you will be on this journey or how you will feel about special education, various interventions, your child's social challenges, or anything else this diagnosis brings your way a week, a year, a lifetime from now. The best that any of us—including the older teen or young adult with Asperger syndrome (AS)—can do is learn, understand, tolerate, and keep moving.

Even though it's been kicked out of the new *Diagnostic and Statistical Manual of Mental Disorders—5th Edition*, I do not believe that

Asperger syndrome, in the many forms that individuals may choose to use it—as shorthand for a particular ASD profile or as part of a personal identity—is going anywhere. And, as before, parents and people with ASDs will continue to make a difference. The history of autism has largely been written by parents who founded and funded the organizations, took part in the research, denounced the quacks, and supported the experts and authors committed to making this a better world for our kids. This work goes on.

Though the online community this book was originally titled after ceased to exist several years ago, the perspective and goals have not changed. *The OASIS Guide* is designed to provide parents, individuals, educators, and other professionals with comprehensive, unbiased, research-based, reliable, and objective information on living with Asperger syndrome and similar forms of ASD. The two previous editions of *The OASIS Guide* were endorsed by virtually every leading expert in the field because they were the books we set out to write. Those traditions continue to inform the book you hold in your hands (or store on your e-reader).

Today, we have not only more information and better research, we also have a perspective and a view of the future not available before. Back when our kids were diagnosed, parents were assured that as long as their children had verbal abilities, had an IQ in the average range, and were free of severe behavioral issues or other conditions, they were "smart enough" to master everything else. Kids with Asperger syndrome were so "different" from those with other types of autism that experts and parents unknowingly embraced a dangerous and, now it appears, false distinction. As the result of several important long-term outcome studies, we know that *regardless of IQ and other talents or abilities*, individuals with AS and similar forms of ASD need explicit, structured education in order to achieve mastery of basic social, self-help, and other daily living skills. We also know that individuals with AS and similar forms of ASD may need more support and more training than typical peers to whom they compare favorably in other measures of accomplishment or skill. Despite everything everyone thought they knew about AS, we find that outcomes for most individuals in early adulthood are disappointing and fall short of reasonable expectations. Even the experts were surprised at these findings.

Although *The OASIS Guide* is written for anyone dealing with

Asperger syndrome and similar forms of ASD, it speaks most directly to parents. Again, as always, parents must lead the way. Part of leading the way is teaching our children to understand themselves and the role that ASDs play in their lives. We speak freely and often of parent advocates, but there comes a time when it is both appropriate and empowering for parents to engage their kids as "advocate apprentices." Given the documented paucity of good transition information and implementation, it comes as a surprise to far too many parents that once the IEP ends or the age of majority arrives, their legal ability to represent their child's interests—at college, in job training, on the job—is virtually nonexistent. There are bright, college-bound individuals with ASDs who have never even seen their IEPs or could not name or describe their diagnoses.

Having worked with kids across the spectrum has given me a broader and deeper understanding of the rewards and the challenges we all face. Raising and loving my own son has given me something no credentialed expert ever experiences, much less can ever truly, deeply understand: the hope and hopelessness, the pride and the fall, the doing and undoing that come when a different way of seeing the world scrambles the rules of how to do everything from tying your shoes to living on your own. I know there are professionals reading this—maybe even some I work with—who will balk at this characterization. That's fine; bring it on. Most of us cannot always follow through on every intervention, plan, strategy, or intention as consistently and as faithfully as we would like. Few of us can honestly say that we do not have a private catalog of moments when we felt like the worst mom or dad on earth. Those are two of the few things we share with all parents. However, these truths endure: No one knows your child better than you do. No one will work harder for your child than you will. And no one else—no matter what their title or their role in your child's life—will care as much as you do.

The goal of this book is to help you understand your child's condition, what really works and what doesn't, and what to plan for, what to go for, and what to avoid. As my mother often counseled (as only a mother who was proud to call herself an Okie could): "You learn something new every day, if you don't watch out." When working with these incredible kids and young adults, the only way you could avoid learning something new is to believe you already know it all. What we know today about autism comes late, delayed decades by misplaced faith in self-appointed experts and profiteers. None of us will ever know it all, but we can all continue learning from one another, from true experts, and most important, from these kids. There's a lot of catching up to do.

I am humbled daily by the generous heartfelt support and encouragement I have received from readers through the years. You cannot know how much it has meant.

Now, let's get back to work.

Part One

ASPERGER SYNDROME

BEHIND every diagnosis of Asperger syndrome or related form of ASD* there is usually a story. It may be a long, painful tale spanning years and featuring an ever-changing cast of doctors, specialists, teachers, and schools. There were tests that showed "nothing," treatments and interventions that never seemed to work, and other diagnoses that failed to stick. For some fortunate families, it may be a short, relatively happy tale of the

---

*Here and throughout, when I write "Asperger syndrome," I mean the familiar *DSM-IV* diagnostic profile and any other autism spectrum disorder that shares similar characteristics, symptoms, or behaviors. Further, it is important to remember that effective, evidence-based treatments and interventions are not "Asperger syndrome specific." What works for one "variation" of ASD can be designed to work for others.

right child at the right place with the right doctor. Either way, an ASD diagnosis signals a new direction.

There are many different ways to look at ASDs like Asperger syndrome. Some consider it a devastating disability, while others accept it as a gift. Some view people who have it with pity, because they are outside the mainstream, while many believe that these individuals are part of a distinct and positive culture. Understanding Asperger syndrome goes far beyond knowing the medical diagnostic criteria. It requires careful consideration of how we as parents, educators, and others who know these children and society at large view individuals with this intriguing, mysterious, and complex disability, condition, or difference (you can choose a term to suit your view). Understanding a person with Asperger syndrome also demands that we look carefully and honestly at what it means to be "normal" or "typical."

In the course of living with any ASD, most of us find that our thinking about it changes and evolves into a philosophy that guides us and our loved ones. Some feel it important to teach our children how to blend in and not define themselves by their condition. Others are more comfortable teaching their children to accept themselves as they are while showing them how to negotiate the sometimes-foreign culture of what some of us call "Neurotypical Land." (We prefer the term *neurotypical* to the less clearly defined *normal*.) We cannot presume to advise anyone on the "best" way to approach this. We do hope to give you the information and the tools you need to develop the perspective that best serves you, your child, and your family.

Chapter 1

WHAT IS ASPERGER SYNDROME?

ASPERGER syndrome is an autism spectrum disorder character-ized by the symptoms, behaviors, and deficits that constitute one of several sets of diagnostic criteria. But it's almost impossible to extrapolate from that information what it means to have AS. For that reason, this chapter focuses on what Asperger syndrome is (or, depending on which version of the *DSM* you're using, *isn't*) from a clinical diagnostic viewpoint and how it often manifests in terms of symptoms and behaviors.

Asperger syndrome was named for Dr. Hans Asperger, a Vien-nese pediatrician whose paper describing four boys he treated in a hospital during World War II, "'Autistic Psychopathy' in Child-hood," was published in 1944 in German.[1] By then, Asperger had been working with children whom he described using the word *autistic* since the early 1930s and, in the opinion of one colleague, had treated perhaps hundreds.[2]

Asperger's paper did not become widely known until the British psychologist Dr. Uta Frith translated it into English in 1991, but it would be a mistake to say that Asperger's work was completely un-known. In fact, Dr. Bernard Rimland referred to "Asperger's syn-drome" in his *Infantile Autism*, the 1964 book that challenged the then-prevailing notion that autism was caused by poor parenting, a failure in bonding, and so-called refrigerator mothers.

Where It All Started

In 1932, Dr. Asperger began running a department of Vienna University's children's clinic. At the time, Asperger's patients lived at the clinic, or hospital. There treatment consisted of education and a range of therapies, including speech, play, and music. As Dr. Frith points out in the classic *Autism and Asperger Syndrome* (which contains her translation of Asperger's 1944 paper), Asperger's approach was not "special education" as we understand the term today. We need to step back in time, to when many professionals working with children whom we would today recognize as having ASD sought in Freudian psychotherapy both the causes for and the solutions to their patients' problems. Asperger took a different approach: what Frith terms "a synthesis of medical and educational practice, applied by inspired doctors, nurses, teachers, and therapists in a team effort."[3] The German term that Dr. Asperger used to describe his work—*Heilpädagogik*—captured the integration of several types of interventions encompassing education, the arts, and daily living skills. The children lived in a specially designed and decorated ward where the daily routine included physical education, music, drama, singing, and speech therapy, in addition to school. A bombing in 1944 destroyed the ward and killed the woman whom Asperger credited with running the program, Sister Viktorine Zak.

Postwar anti-German sentiment in many Western countries might explain why Asperger's ideas and his work remained so little known in the United States. Another possibility is that, even if his work had been translated and made accessible to English-speaking professionals, the prevalence of Freudian thinking about psychological and psychiatric issues might have made it difficult for Asperger's ideas to take hold. Asperger's work coincided with the Nazi occupation of Austria, and though the occupiers targeted his clinic because he housed and treated "abnormal" children—a population Hitler targeted for extermination, due to their "inferiority"—some might have presumed Asperger a Nazi sympathizer. In fact, he was not, and on several occasions, he took great risks to protect his charges.[4]

Reading Dr. Asperger's work makes it clear that he cared about these children. He recognized their strengths and talents as well as their struggles. It was Asperger who coined the term "little professor" to describe children with precocious knowledge and willingness to share it. It was also Asperger who first pointed out their vulnerability to being bullied and their need for special, explicit instruction in social and adaptive skills. Asperger's observation that parents and other family members might share traits has been supported by recent discoveries in genetics. His tone is compassionate, and his quest to understand these children and to help them is evident. Though many disorders bear their discoverer's name, knowing something about Asperger the man and how he understood these children sets a fine starting point for anyone who cares about these children today.

ASPERGER SYNDROME "ON THE SPECTRUM"

People have been referring to an autism "spectrum" for about twenty years now, and in 2013 *DSM-5* made it "official" by herding all autism diagnoses under autism spectrum disorder, or ASD. When Asperger syndrome first appeared in *DSM-IV* in 1994, the diagnostic criteria were neatly captured by what British psychiatrist Dr. Lorna Wing terms a "triad of impairments affecting: social interaction, communication, and imagination, accompanied by a narrow, rigid, repetitive pattern of activities."[5] Among the characteristics that are thought to distinguish Asperger syndrome from other forms of ASD are the presence of normal to above-average intelligence (although even by *DSM-IV* criteria, mild mental retardation could occur); apparently normal language development; and one or more special interests that may dominate attention, conversation, and social interactions.

Originally, the word *spectrum* nicely captured the sense that the presence or absence or degree of impairment resulting from specific symptoms could range from nonexistent to mild to severe, and that in each individual, every symptom or behavior could conceivably fall on a different point. So, for example, one could be brilliant at calculus yet unable to organize the backpack for school, or have prodigious skills in spelling and grammar and yet be unable to write a simple three-paragraph essay about summer vacation.

You may hear of AS described as a "high-functioning" form of autism. While that is an easily understood description, we agree with Dr. Ivar Lovaas and find the terms *high functioning* and *low functioning* discriminatory. This is not simply a matter of semantics or a desire to be politically correct. The fact is, individuals with ASDs each have within themselves a spectrum of abilities and challenges. We have seen young children with serious deficits in language and speech who are more independent in self-care than some older adolescents with AS who have IQs over 130. The term *high functioning* is often applied to AS because people with this diagnosis typically have a normal or above-normal IQ and many, though not all, exhibit exceptional skill or talent in a particular area, often their area of special interest. (This should not be confused with the autistic savant phenomenon, depicted in the film *Rain Man*, where a person with autism demonstrates incredible feats of calculation or memory, or a creative talent.[6])

Another distinguishing feature of Asperger syndrome is the absence of a "clinically significant delay in language." In other words, young children with AS typically have early (before age three) language development that ranges from normal to precocious, but not always. This is typically not the case with children on other points of the autism spectrum. While early language development might *appear to be normal* in children with AS, there is growing evidence that the deeper language deficits are always present. This becomes most apparent when the curriculum shifts focus in upper elementary grades from a concrete to a more abstract, conceptual understanding of material. Further, some people who had severe language delays as children do receive the AS diagnosis later on, as did, for example, Dr. Temple Grandin.

THE CURIOUS INCIDENT OF THE DIAGNOSIS THAT "DISAPPEARED" (FOR NOW)

Although there are now—and will continue to be—people whose presentation suggests a diagnosis of Asperger disorder, "officially," as of spring 2013 in the United States, there is no longer an official diagnosis called Asperger syndrome or Asperger disorder. The decision of the American Psychiatric Association (APA) to "merge" Asperger's disorder (the official name of the diagnosis), childhood disintegrative disorder, autistic disorder, and pervasive developmental disorder—not otherwise specified (PDD-NOS) all together under "ASD" has not been without its critics (among them Dr. Fred Volkmar of the Yale Child Study Center, primary author of the *DSM-IV*'s autism and pervasive developmental disorders section[7]). One of the problems with the earlier criteria, according to the APA's 2013 statement, was that "these separate diagnoses were not consistently applied across different clinics and treatment centers,"[8] and anyone working in the field can attest to that. As I spoke to medical professionals in the field in many contexts over the years, several issues of diagnosis became clear. One was that PDD-NOS did indeed become the "catchall" diagnosis. It included children who met criteria for autistic disorder (a diagnosis that might have made some professionals and parents alike uncomfortable). A second was that any individual on the spectrum who had verbal skills or a normal IQ was "promoted" to Asperger disorder, regardless of the presence of speech delay before three, lower-than-average IQ, and the absence of the telltale special interest.

Research discovered that in many ways, individuals with Asperger disorder and those some describe as having atypical or high-functioning autism really were not that different in important ways, though they were in some.[9] Further—and this is something we should all keep in mind—there has yet to emerge a scientifically based, proven intervention for any form of pervasive developmental disorder under *DSM-IV* that could not be modified to work for someone with Asperger syndrome and, conversely, no treatment that is "only good for" one particular ASD profile.

The important take-home message: Each individual with ASD is truly an individual, in every way. Not every individual comes with behaviors and symptoms that make a "perfect" match with *any* diagnostic criteria. Those who receive any type of ASD diagnosis have enough in common in terms of presentation of symptoms or behaviors outside the norm in the three key areas (social, language, repetitive behaviors or interests) that, yes, ASD is "real." And despite the word's being eliminated from the *DSM-5*'s diagnoses, these differences, deficits, challenges—whatever you decide to call them—are *pervasive* in that they touch most aspects of daily living. And they are *developmental*, meaning that they were not "acquired," but were present in some form at birth, whether anyone detected their presence or not.

Medical professionals are advised by the American Psychiatric Association not to use the old *DSM-IV* diagnoses any longer.[10] However, it seems to be both understood and accepted that those who received the earlier diagnoses will "keep" them. Because while "autistic disorder" might have been too "scary," and "PDD-NOS" might have been too "vague" and "catchall," when applied correctly, "Asperger disorder" did signal to those familiar with the criteria some important differences and characteristics.

My son has "had" Asperger syndrome since he was five years old and, realistically, since the day he was born and probably before. Not only is "replacing" AS with the *DSM-5* criteria awkward—because he would now be diagnosed with "Autism Spectrum Disorder without accompanying intellectual impairment but requiring level 1 support, without accompanying language impairment but requiring, associated with other disorders—specifically learning disabilities, dyslexia, etc.—and without catatonia"—but for most listeners, this information would be useless.

Further, in the past twenty years, despite the diagnostic confusion *DSM-5* was designed to address, countless people found something useful, valuable, even sacred in having a name for the differences and the way they understood and interacted with the world. Individuals enthusiastically embraced a diagnosis that may have "corrected" previous diagnoses or negative attributes or attitudes used to describe their behaviors and thoughts. Some even assumed the "Aspie" label with pride and a sense of community that is reflected in both online and real-world support groups and advocacy organizations. Does anyone truly expect that an organization such as GRASP (Global and Regional Asperger Syndrome Partnership, which was founded and largely run by people with ASD) will change its name or change its focus simply because Asperger syndrome or disorder no longer "exists"? I hope not.

How Do We See Asperger Syndrome Today?

Well, for one thing, we see it! The media and popular culture seem to love real people and fictional characters with Asperger-type tendencies. If they are prodigies or geniuses, or make an exceptionally good presentation, write a best-selling book, or have a cool savant skill to demonstrate, so much the better. But with this comes a different kind of misunderstanding about what it means to have an AS diagnosis.

When I said, "My son has Asperger's," in 1997, the first question was invariably, "I've never heard of it. What's that?" By 2012, the response was no longer a question because suddenly many people felt that they knew all about AS. They tend to say things like "Oh, yeah, like . . ." and then spin the wheel of "fill-in-the-blanks" possibilities that could include "that kid in *The Curious Incident of the Dog in the Night-Time*," "Temple Grandin," "the kid on *Modern Family*," "that man who used to make guitars for KISS," "the kid in Jodi Picoult's novel *House Rules*," "the guy who did the thing with pi and speaks all those languages," "Sheldon on *The Big Bang Theory*," or "Bill Gates." Please note that half the responses involved fictional characters, with the remainder split between people with ASD who are geniuses and/or prodigies and public figures whose diagnostic status remains a parlor game of speculation (such as Gates). Do any of these answers assure me, as a mother, that the speaker knows anything about how to talk to or understand my son or anyone like him? No.

WHO HAS ASPERGER SYNDROME?

We have yet to have an actual "head count" on the prevalence of AS. Currently, the Centers for Disease Control and Prevention (CDC) state that 1 in 68 children have ASD. Autism spectrum disorder is more common than childhood cancer, Down syndrome, muscular dystrophy, or cerebral palsy.[11] Authorities who focus on AS estimate that perhaps 1 in 250 present with that profile. AS is still much more common among boys than girls. Four out of every five people diagnosed with ASD are male, though new studies suggest that nine times as many boys than girls are diagnosed with AS.[12] The picture gets a little muddier when other research finds that many girls and women go misdiagnosed or undiagnosed altogether.*

Since 1997, when the prevalence of all ASDs was estimated at 1 in 1,000, the rates have clearly risen.[13] Are the statistics rising because of an actual increase in autism in general, or is it because more children are being identified? There is evidence to support either position. One can safely assume it's a combination of the two.

Theories about the cause of this rise abound, but no one really knows why ASD is more common today than five, ten, twenty years ago. We know for sure that it is not caused by childhood vaccinations or any component used in those vaccines. Scientific evidence points to a basic defect in fetal development of the neural tube, the primitive structure from which the brain evolves, occurring between day twenty and day twenty-four of gestation. Clearly, there is a genetic component to autism, but if genetics were the sole factor in determining autism, the rates of autism would be expected to be near constant (or even decreasing, since many people with autism would be presumed not to have children). There is still much scientific research needed.

WHAT DO WE KNOW FOR SURE?

Like any form of ASD, Asperger syndrome is a neurological disorder. A person with AS has no more control over how he or she views the world and interprets what is seen, heard, felt, or understood than a person who has suffered a stroke or developed Alzheimer's disease. All ASDs result from anomalies in the physical brain, not emotional or behavioral problems, although those certainly can *result* from it. Although effective interventions can help people with ASD learn to respond more appropriately, there is no way to change what the

---

*One possible reason why the 4:1 ratio of boys to girls for ASDs generally does not carry over to the 9:1 for Asperger syndrome is that even though girls make up a smaller percentage of all ASD diagnoses, girls with ASD are more likely to also suffer cognitive, or intellectual, disability than boys are.

Genetics in ASD and Asperger Syndrome

Numerous studies have established a genetic component in the development of autism. From the first papers published on autism and Asperger syndrome, by Dr. Leo Kanner and Dr. Hans Asperger, respectively, authors have noted the frequency with which parents—usually fathers—present with traits and behaviors similar to those of children with Asperger syndrome, although the parents' symptoms are usually milder. Today these family members would be considered to fall under the broader autistic phenotype (BAP). Studies have established that in cases where one identical twin has autism but the other twin does not, 90 percent to 95 percent of the seemingly unaffected twins will have language or social disturbances, as will 30 percent to 40 percent of fraternal twins. Nonautistic siblings also have a much higher rate of language and social disturbances.[14]

These findings suggest two possibilities: the involvement of more than one gene (which is the case in most genetically transmitted diseases) and the influence of other, as yet unknown, environmental factors on the development of autism. If autism arose out of a single genetic defect, 100 percent of monozygotic twins would be expected to have autism.

Studies of families of people with autism indicate a higher-than-average prevalence of autism and autism-related disorders among first-degree relatives (parents, siblings). Of ninety-nine families surveyed in one Yale study, nearly half—46 percent—reported a family history of AS or a related disorder (19 percent fathers, 4 percent mothers). Other studies have found higher rates for other disorders, several of which are frequently seen in people with AS.[15] First-degree relatives (parents, siblings) have higher-than-normal rates of social phobia, simple phobia, and major depression.[16]

world "means" for them. When we speak of "treatment" and "intervention," we are referring to methods of addressing issues, of teaching skills and strategies that will increase a child's repertoire across a wide range of domains: educational, social, emotional, and self-help. We are not talking about effecting a "cure." There is no known cure for any autism spectrum disorder, despite the alleged "miraculous breakthroughs" that draw the media's attention. Barring a true scientific advance, your child probably will always be a person with ASD.

ASD is among the most heritable of disorders. There is no question but that something genetic is going on. Scientists continue to catalog genetic anomalies present in autism and to identify a host of risk factors. As yet, however, a specific biological or physiological "marker" (as a single target gene or physical difference detectable through an imaging or blood test) or distinct, telltale "sign" eludes us.

Common Behaviors in ASD

Echolalia

Echolalia is a particular speech pattern in which the individual repeats what he or she has heard. There are several types of echolalia:

- Immediate echolalia: This is when the individual immediately echoes back words. It has been suggested that because a child with AS has poor language comprehension, he or she repeats what has just been said to buy more time to understand the question and formulate a response. For example, when one boy was asked, "Do you want dinner?" after a relatively long pause, his response was a rhetorical "Do I want dinner?" And after another pause, he said, "Yes. What are we having?" In this case, he used his echolalia as a holder to give him time to process the question and provide the appropriate answer. Another child who is asked the very same question might echo "Do you want dinner?"—in this case reversing the pronoun. However, even with pronoun reversal (common in ASD), it should be assumed that the child is still trying to understand the question.

• Delayed echolalia: There are two types of delayed echolalia: functional and nonfunctional. In *functional* echolalia, children will take a word or phrase and overgeneralize its meaning. For example, a child might use a phrase he has learned from a video or favorite movie and apply it to a real-life situation. Rather than say, "I bumped my head," a devotee of *Thomas the Tank Engine* might say "James ran off the track." In *nonfunctional* echolalia, a child may repeat entire movies, television programs, books on CD, commercials, or radio programs he has memorized. While some of us might marvel at a child's ability to repeat lengthy scenes from movies or passages of text, it should not be regarded as a "talent" so much as evidence of a problem in language processing sometimes called "chunking." Even when parents and others can "translate" the words into the child's meaning, as in the "James ran off the track" example, it is still highly irregular and warrants intervention.

• Stress echolalia: A third type of echolalia occurs when a child is under extreme stress or feels cornered. This type of echolalia involves the child repeating the last few words spoken to him, but in an intense, rushed manner that often involves echoing the word or phrase anywhere from two to more than a dozen times. For example, a child who is told, "Let's go," might repeat "Let'sgolet'sgolet'sgo" in a forced and hurried fashion.

• Pallilalia: This is the noncontexual, inappropriate, or meaningless repetition of a word, syllable, or phrase. Where you might say, "Okay, thanks," someone with pallilalia would say, "Okay, thanks. Thanks. Thanks. Thanks."

Perseveration

Individuals with Asperger syndrome who show repetitive behaviors and interests are sometimes described as exhibiting *perseveration*. One way you hear perseverative behavior described is "getting stuck." For example, the child might play with the same toy, using the exact same motions in the same sequence (for instance, crashing a toy car into a wooden block). Perseveration also occurs when a child insists that toys be played with in exactly the same place, sequence, manner, and/or with the same "narration" every time. In addition, perseveration occurs when a child begins an activity like a jigsaw puzzle and cannot leave it without significant emotional distress or a major tantrum until it is complete and/or perfect.

Children who perseverate exhibit a single-mindedness and concentration that can range from impressive to frightening, depending on the situation. In the case of perseveration of thoughts, a child might get "stuck" on a certain event or situation and be unable to let go of it. He may perseverate on a specific fear or on an event that happened long ago. She might laugh out loud in class during a test because a funny scene from a favorite cartoon is replaying, as if on a loop, in her mind's eye. Or a child who wishes to engage in his special interest may not be able to let go of it. For example, a child who is waiting for the latest superhero movie to arrive in theaters may talk and talk and talk about it, seemingly unable to change his focus to something else.

Not surprisingly, many of these children are diagnosed with obsessive tendencies. Some perseverations can be diminished or extinguished through behavioral techniques (see page 184).

Unusual Eye Contact or Gaze Avoidance

Many individuals with ASD exhibit gaze avoidance and have difficulty making "normal" eye contact. Although this behavior can be disconcerting to others because it seems as if the person with AS is not listening, many individuals with AS have described the process of making eye contact as painful, uncomfortable, and even impossible. Often when individuals with AS do make eye contact, they tend to do so in ways that are "off": either looking too long and hard or glancing so briefly it goes unnoticed. In addition to the sensory overload that direct eye contact brings some (which, if we think about it, even neurotypicals can have trouble with; consider for a moment the staring contest), it also could be troubling to children with AS because they have difficulty doing two things at once and find "looking" and "listening" simultaneously nearly impossible. This leads one to consider how important it may be to teach such children to "look at me" or "make eye contact" in every social situation.

Certainly, the child who is not looking cannot learn to imitate the actions of another or follow nonverbal cues or communication. However, many teachers have commented that children with AS seem not to be listening because they don't look directly at them, but later when they ask the child a question, they discover that he or she was indeed paying attention and did learn the material. (Later, when we discuss educational strategies, we will talk about under what circumstance kids really do need to keep their eyes on the teacher.) Other individuals with AS make appropriate eye contact when talking but look away when listening or trying to process an answer. Or vice versa. Whether a child with Asperger syndrome should be "forced" to make eye contact is a subject of some debate. In terms of social success, learning to make appropriate eye contact is important, but many believe a child should not be expected to make contact when it is so stressful. One mother suggested a compromise. She told her son to look at the cheek or chin of the person rather than directly into his or her eyes, which he found less threatening.

Stereotypies, or "Stims"*

Stereotypies are repetitive motor movements such as hand flapping, finger flicking, hand regarding, walking on tiptoe, rocking, spinning, twirling, chewing, pulling, and picking. The possibilities are limitless. You may hear them referred to as "stims" (self-stimulating behavior), but that term may be misleading, for several reasons. One is that we have no way of knowing if self-stimulation is the cause or the effect of the behavior. In some cases, obsessive-compulsive disorder or a tic disorder may be the cause of the behavior. Some individuals with such disorders will tell you that engaging in these types of movements is not

---

*Though the word *stim* is used commonly, there are a couple reasons why you might wish to "trade up" to *stereotypy* or *repetitive behavior* instead. The word *stim* takes on other associations, particularly around those not familiar with ASDs, when you are talking about behavior that might appear sexual (for example, self-touching) or that involves masturbation or any behavior that someone might interpret to be that.

so much stimulating and enjoyable as it is a necessary "release," much like a sneeze.

Most of us exhibit some type of repetitive behavior: repeatedly checking our cell phones, biting our nails, popping our chewing gum, running our fingers through our hair, licking our lips, checking our fingernails, or needlessly clearing our throats before we speak. ASD gives these behaviors a distinct quality. For one thing, the behaviors tend to be less socially acceptable and more intense, in both their execution and duration. The question of "socially acceptable" often boils down to a question of right time and/or right place. Sometimes while engaging in them a child seems to be totally out of reach. Sometimes stereo-typal behavior increases in frequency and/or intensity when the child is under stress. Whether anyone should intervene to stop a child's stereo-typies through behavioral intervention, nagging, punishing, or somehow physically preventing is not always clear. It has been suggested that the stereotypies release a child's stress and that if one is eliminated, another will appear in its place. One goal of a behavioral approach is to recognize that the compulsion to engage in the behavior may never go away and so try to change its expression (or *topography*); for instance, to substitute running one's hand through one's hair instead of pulling the hair out. Another approach is to give the child something to manipulate or squeeze unobtrusively whenever the urge strikes. Small squishy balls in a pocket, strips of Velcro placed under a desktop, and other sensory-rich objects can be used.

More often than not, outside the privacy of home, stereotypal behaviors appear odd and are socially stigmatizing. They can also be misinterpreted by others, sometimes in ways that are detrimental to your child. Some families have used behavioral strategies to reduce, eliminate, or change their child's behavior. This is always recommended when the behavior is socially inappropriate (touching one's genitals, masturbating, nose picking, screaming), socially risky (pinching, smelling, hugging, kissing, and touching strangers), or potentially harmful to the person herself (hair pulling, skin picking, self-biting, lip chewing) or others (hitting, biting, pinching, choking), or when it interferes with learning.

THERE IS NO CRYSTAL BALL

Some consider Asperger syndrome a "mild form" of autism. Certainly the prognosis for a child with a normal IQ, speech (albeit abnormal), and a desire for social relationships is somewhat more optimistic than it might be for a child with a lower IQ who lacks speech and a desire to relate to others. It is important to remember that Asperger syndrome is a serious, lifelong disability that requires individualized expert intervention and should be treated as such. As these children have grown to adulthood, researchers were surprised to discover that, statistically, the outcomes for most people with an Asperger profile are not as good as they expected (for more, see pages 148 and 456). Why this is so—and what parents and others can do to improve the odds for the best possible outcome—is what this book is about. One key finding is that academic accomplishment is often overstressed and that the ability of academic accomplishments to carry a child forward and "make up for" persistent deficits in social skills, adaptive living and daily self-help skills, and executive function is far more limited than most would expect. More about that in the chapters to come.

So while the assumption that a child who is highly verbal and more empathetic than someone else with ASD would do better than a child who is less verbal and struggles socially, no one can tell you for sure how things will turn out. However, we do know that early intervention has made an incredible difference for many children. For example, today there are children who appear at age eight or older to have AS but who at age three were nonverbal, were socially withdrawn, and tested with extremely low IQs. Through early intensive intervention, ideally before elementary school, these children were not only sufficiently verbal and socially skilled to join mainstream classrooms but also showed average to above-average IQs on retest. At the other extreme are children with highly developed language and high IQs who are struggling tremendously. When they were age three, four, five, or beyond, a professional might have "green-flagged" them, concluding that though some interesting "quirks" were observed, other things—typically good language, normal IQ, and social behavior not as "guarded" as some people expect from those with ASD—"outweighed" the possible deficits. And somewhere in the big middle are those who require supports and services, who manage to make great strides, but for whom there will always remain challenges and limitations.

Prognosis for any of our children depends less on the actual diagnosis than on the support, intervention, and care they receive. Even the most able person with Asperger syndrome may always require some form of assistance in one or several areas of life. These children also need parents and others who care to view them and their ASD completely and realistically. Gone are the days when a parent could write off major social skills deficits with the dream that a child would find a well-paying job doing something that didn't call for social skills. Everyone needs some level of social proficiency, even if only as a matter of safety.

The message is clear: any child with ASD needs timely, early, intensive intervention, regardless of what strengths he or she appears to possess. Throughout the rest of the book, we will look at the many facets of AS in more depth and explore how understanding AS can help you understand and support your child.

SEEING THE WORLD DIFFERENTLY

To begin to understand what it's like to have AS, we need to consider what it means to *not* have AS. We pride ourselves on our individuality. Our society celebrates the individual who does what he thinks is right, who goes his own way. In truth, however, one sign of being neurologically typical, or "neurotypical," is that we behave, think, and act in ways that are similar enough to how others around us behave that, in most social situations, we have a fairly accurate idea of what to expect from others; we have a fairly accurate idea of what others expect from us; and we have the ability to say and do things that will conform to those expectations. And—this may seem like "magic" to someone on the spectrum—we have the ability to understand and display the appropriate behavior without, in most cases, even thinking about it. We usually find ways to fit in, or at least not behave in a way that makes us conspicuous. One big advantage that a neurotypical person has over someone with a social disability like AS is that he moves through the world and relates to

Thinking Like Columbus (or Anyone Else)

Parents should be on the lookout for a troubling trend in education: academic success in elementary school followed by a "sudden" plateau or plummet in grades and in learning somewhere between the late elementary and middle school grades. Suddenly schoolwork requires more independence, organization, social reasoning, and abstract and conceptual thinking. The advent of the Common Core curriculum, with its emphasis on critical thinking across the curriculum, appears set to up the ante. Most kids with AS are fine with questions like "What year did Columbus sail the ocean blue?" or "What were the names of Columbus's three ships?" Trouble starts for many students when the curriculum shifts to focus on critical thinking and the questions are more along the lines of "What do you think inspired Columbus to set out on his voyages?" or "Describe what you think the Native Americans might have thought when they first approached Columbus and his men." Twenty years after AS became a diagnosis in the United States, the response to these well-known, predictable changes in fit between student ability and curriculum demands remains largely unaddressed. We explore this issue later in chapter 9.

others with the understanding that others do have expectations of his behavior and a general idea of what those are.

In fact, we're so good at this that we often meet people's expectations even when we really don't want to. If you think that makes most of us sound less like independent-thinking individuals and more like sheep, you may find common ground with some people with AS. Some with ASD literally don't understand why most people feel it's important to make small talk, dress in the current style, feign interest in people or topics they could not care less about, or tell white lies.

This degree of moral ambiguity and rule bending that we accept as part of normal social interaction is unthinkable and can be quite confusing to a person with AS. How did we *learn* when and how to tell this kind of lie? Moreover, how did we learn that it was not only okay to do but also the best thing to do? How did we learn to lie in this situation but not in another? If pressed, we can each offer a careful, blow-by-blow account of how we came to that decision, but that's just Monday-morning quarterbacking. In the moment, we did not even think about how we would respond. In less than a millisecond, we knew to say something complimentary. And the lady in the dressing room, who may have been thinking, *I know this outfit is a mistake*, replied "Thank you."

What accounts for this amazing ability? It provides the software that shapes the content and style of our conversation to fit perfectly the expectations of the person to whom we are speaking. It automatically adjusts our body posture, gestures, volume and tone of voice, word choice, and physical proximity. It tells us where and

Try This

If your friend asks, "What do you think of my new outfit?" someone with AS might guess—perhaps incorrectly—that the friend really wants to know the truth. And some friends do. However, without even thinking, most of us "instinctively" know that our friend wants—and expects—to be offered an opinion that reflects her own. If she is smiling and posing before a mirror as she asks, it's clear to most of us that the best answer is "Great!" unless we have the kind of relationship that can stand up to our honest thoughts about pink fishnet tights and a tutu-style skirt. If the person before the mirror is your five-year-old niece, the answer is obvious. But if she is a middle-aged stranger in a department store dressing room, at almost the speed of light, your brain consults an invisible multistep flow chart of social do's and don'ts, and the factors weighed behind each. In less than three seconds, you know that the "right" answer is something along the lines of a noncommittal "Wow" or "Yes, interesting . . ." Delivered, of course, with your politest smile. Congratulations! You have done the socially appropriate thing: you told a white lie—not truthful and yet not "wrong."

what to look at and for how long. It lets us know when the conversation is winding down, picking up, going slowly, or dying on its feet. It alerts us to when we are being lied to, misled, pressured, or embarrassed. It regulates how much we ask of someone else in conversation and how much we reveal.

The role of theory of mind in the "dance" or "mechanics" of conversation and purposeful social interaction is clear. What we tend to consider less often—probably because most of us never have cause to think about it consciously at all—are the other ways in which an intact and functional social understanding is so important in countless daily interactions that influence our happiness, our safety, and our overall quality of life. Being born with this ability allows us to glean accurate information about things that weren't even specifically addressed in conversation, things that we'd have no other way of knowing. It allows us to have some knowledge of what others are thinking; to predict in general terms—and with pretty amazing accuracy—what they will say and what they will do. It gives rise to having "funny feelings," "suspicions," "hunches," and "second thoughts" about a person or a situation. It convinces us to take an action that in the moment seems irrational but "feels right": avoiding a particular stranger on the street, for instance, or surprising a potential love interest with a meaningful look or a kiss.

All of this is possible because most people possess "theory of mind," which is essentially the innate capacity to understand that other people can have desires, ideas, and feelings different from our own. In addition, most of us also have an innate ability to "read" nonverbal social cues; to naturally pay attention to what most of us consider the relevant information from our surroundings (central coherence); and to instantly process all of that with little or no conscious thought.

In contrast, people with ASD do not know, automatically and instantly, what to expect or what is expected of them in social situations. They cannot always grasp the gist of a situation or instantly sort irrelevant information and stimuli that they don't need in the moment from the relevant cues that they do need. Intelligence and disposition have nothing to do with our ability to read the minds of others. Despite a high IQ and a loving, generous disposition, a person with AS may still find himself saying or doing the "wrong" thing or, even worse, not being able to defend himself against being deliberately misled by others or from being misunderstood. For now, however, it is important to understand that a deficit in theory of mind, or mind-blindness, is common to some degree in all ASDs. It lies at the heart of the disability AS entails and is often at the root of the behavioral challenges and social difficulties that people with AS face.

AS SYMPTOMS

Preoccupation with a Special Interest

Many people with Asperger syndrome are often identifiable by their all-consuming interest in one or more particular topics. In *DSM-IV*, the special interest was described as the "encompassing preoccupation with one or more stereotyped and restricted patterns of interest that is abnormal either in intensity or focus." Today, under *DSM-5*, the special interest is very similarly described as "Highly restricted, fixated interests that are abnormal in intensity or focus (for instance, strong attachment to or preoccupation with unusual objects, excessively circumscribed or perseverative interests)." Both seem to capture the same behavior, but *DSM-5* seems to offer somewhat more detail in specifying the level of severity from three choices. At Level 3, "Requiring very substantial support," the behaviors "markedly interfere with functioning in all spheres." At Level 2, "Requiring substantial report," the behaviors "interfere with functioning in a variety of contexts." At the mildest level of severity, "Requiring support," one would expect "significant interference with functioning in one or more contexts."

Though not everyone who fits the Asperger profile has a special interest, most do. The most prevalent special interests are peer-appropriate fads or interests (anime, for instance); video or computer games; works of art, movies, fictional books, or television programs; and computers. Among adults with AS, common special interests tend more toward specific concepts or ideas; computers; and works of art, fictional books, movies, or television programs. Sometimes the object of fascination is something that peers and even adults can relate to: dinosaurs, trains, cars, anime, or other trends; popular cartoons, television series, books, and movies; a celebrity or historical figure, a historical object or event such as the voyage of the *Titanic*, the space program, World War II, or 9/11; subjects such as math, physics, chemistry, or astronomy; technology such as computers, smart phones, video games, and the programs to run them; or sports.

Of course, these are areas of interest to many neurotypical people, too. But there are some notable differences when someone with an AS profile engages. For instance, if the interest is sports, the fascination is more likely with sports history, statistics, and strategy behind hires, fires, trades, plays, lineups, and calls, *not* with actually suiting up to the play the game. (That said, there are some very accomplished athletes in the AS circle.) Works of culture, particularly popular culture, tend toward those that offer a created universe in some form, and usually, if it is a book, movie, television program, or cartoon, odds are good that the storyline covers either an extended period of time or features numerous characters with clear though sometimes complex personal histories and relationships. Not surprisingly, then, *Star Trek*, *Star Wars*, *Harry Potter*, *X-Men*, *Lord of the Rings*, and *Doctor Who*—in their many media incarnations and iterations—remain perennial favorites. For younger children, *Thomas the Tank Engine* and cartoon programs such as *SpongeBob SquarePants* and *Yu-Gi-Oh!* tend to be popular, sometimes years after same-age peers have moved on to other, more age-appropriate things.

Girls with Asperger syndrome also have special interests but, as Tony Attwood points out, in talking about them they do not sound as much like "little professors" as they do "little philosophers." Girls' special interests tend toward those that might be shared by peers: dolls, animals, and literature. Whereas boys tend to be interested in how things work, girls are more likely to be concerned with how people work. It only makes sense, then, that popular interests for girls include writing fan fiction, following the exploits of favorite celebrities, and reading autobiographies. Even though many people with AS do not care much about fashion, I have met young women and young men for whom it is a special interest. Again, if there are "rules" about having Asperger syndrome, somewhere there's a person with Asperger syndrome out there breaking at least a couple of them.

More noticeable are the special interests that concern objects, people, events, or abstract concepts that, by neurotypical standards, range from peculiar to downright bizarre. Children with AS have been known to be obsessed by such things as bleach bottles, alarms and alarm systems, street lamps, lawn mowers, junipers, organs and organ music, road signs, maps, clocks, time, directions (north, south, east, west), the British royal family, telephone books, issues of *TV Guide*, sports announcing, game shows, and insects.

A person with AS might collect items related to the special interest and, as he or she grows older, collect information as well. So, for example, a child at three might collect *Thomas the Tank Engine* toy trains and play with them exclusively. Once he starts reading, he might read about trains exclusively, or collect train schedules and maps, and then feel compelled to talk about what he has learned. "Walking encyclopedia" or "little professor" often capture the amount, depth, and detail of information children can accumulate about a special interest, but not everyone follows the same pattern. Some might be content to collect model trains without learning the differences between wheel configurations, track dimensions, or manufacturers. Others may take an "all or nothing" approach. Whereas I'm fine with simply listening to a favorite Beatles album, my son's experience is not complete until he knows which guitars were played on each song, by make, model number, and other details.

Although much is written about a child's single special interest, most people with AS have more than one at a time. Special interests can first emerge as early as age two to three, though some show signs of the interest as early as the first birthday. In speaking to people with special interests, it is not unusual to discover that they cannot recall a time when they didn't have an interest. Most people who have a special interest actually have several, with the number increasing with the person's age.

What Role Does the Special Interest Play in the Lives of People with AS?

The line between a person sharing an interest in a hobby or profession and an AS-style special interest is usually immediately clear upon hearing a person with AS talk. Not surprisingly, the number one way kids with AS pursue their special interest is by talking about it. In contrast, adults with AS are more likely to read about their special interest than to talk about it. A special interest "exchange" is noticeably one-sided, run-on, and more a monologue than a conversation. Where most people would complete one point, then pause for a listener's response, someone with AS might seem to just keep going, fluently, steadily, and perhaps a bit excessively. People with AS are often unaware of the repertoire of nonverbal and verbal cues listeners may use to stop or redirect the conversation, so they may not notice that the person to whom they're speaking is changing the subject, breaking eye contact, affecting an uninterested look, turning away, or even walking away. Unfortunately, this can leave the impression that a person with AS is, to put it nicely, overbearing, self-centered, or rude. This can erect barriers to social interaction instead of building bridges, as sharing a hobby often does.

Also, immersion in the special interest may come at the expense of other, more socially appropriate experiences. The playdate that collapses under the weight of a child's insistence that his friend play only "name that freight car" or listen to him recite, by name, the launch date, destination, and fate of every military satellite since *Sputnik* is a social setback from which it may be difficult to recover.

How Parents Cope with Special Interests

Or, meet the other moms who have eight more SpongeBobs, Wolverines, or My Little Ponys—hidden in the closet.

Special interests can range from mildly annoying to intolerable. In the original OASIS survey, 57 percent of parents said that they had tried to control or curtail their child's special interest, usually by restricting access to it or placing limits on the circumstances and the length of time it could be discussed. Over a third of the parents told us that they had reduced the degree to which they would accommodate the special interest, and 21 percent refused to participate in activities related to the special interest.[17] One positive aspect of a special interest is its power to motivate or reinforce. Making access to the special interest contingent on clearly specified behavior can be very effective—for example, for completing an assigned task or spending some time with someone else engaging in *their* preferred activity. Special interests can also be used more informally as a reward for appropriate behavior, including not talking excessively about the special interest.

The Empathizing-Systematizing Theory

Renowned autism researcher Dr. Simon Baron-Cohen offers an intriguing theory to explain the almost magnetic pull of the special interest. His empathizing-systematizing theory posits that ASDs, including Asperger syndrome, may result from not only a deficit in the ability to empathize or understand others, but an "accompanying drive to analyze or construct systems."[18] There are many kinds of systems: collectible, mechanical, social, abstract, and so on. What defines a system is the presence of rules. According to Baron-Cohen, "When we systematize, we are trying to identify the rules that govern the system, in order to predict how that system will behave."[19]

While many experts have offered explanations of why people with AS may be drawn to special interests and what special interests have to offer, Baron-Cohen's explanation of systematizing does a few more things: first, it offers a way of viewing a wide range of repetitive behaviors across the spectrum; and, second, Baron-Cohen advances the argument that this represents a different style of learning about the world, not just a deficit. Another way to look at it as a parent is to understand that, neurologically, your child seems wired to experience the world in a way that is different from the way most other people do.

It is important to bear in mind that special interests do serve a function. People with AS truly enjoy their special interests. In a world that can be wildly unpredictable, the special interest is an oasis of predictability, calm, and control. The special interest can provide a sense of accomplishment, mastery, and happiness. Further, conversations about the special interest—one-sided though they often are—are socially safe in that they are, from your child's viewpoint, predictable. Odds are good that when your child talks with you or anyone else except for a fellow enthusiast about her interest, the conversation will remain steadfastly "on topic." Unless the person your child is talking to knows a lot about the special interest, there probably will not be many surprises, either. Most available conversation partners will not be "qualified" to introduce a lot of new information or ask questions that your child will find it difficult to answer.

Special Interests: There Is Something to Love

In a world where too much of our kids' education focuses on teaching to a test, where information is everywhere but understanding eludes most, people who are passionate about discovering and learning have a lot to offer. They can be interesting and engaging. Of course, this is not to suggest that everything about the special interest is positive. Especially when children are younger and the special interest is relatively "fresh," parents, teachers, and others might regard the special interest as a source of anxiety, a distraction, an obsession, or an inconvenience. Parents have changed plans, schedules, and routines; avoided specific routes, locations, activities, and people; been late to arrive or early to leave appointments and get-togethers; and have bent or broken household rules to deal with, head off, or eliminate behavioral issues related to the special interest. Make sure the special interest works for your child, not against her. Teach her the "right time/right place" rules for displaying the special interest and be sure she knows how to detect and follow social cues that signal when enough is enough.

Often those special interests can build bridges to interaction and enjoyment with others who share similar interests. By joining a club that focuses on a particular interest, the individual may have a real opportunity to interact with others. The special interest can become a common ground for friendship, recreation, and, yes, maybe someday even a career.

Some educators recommend using a special interest to help develop skills. If you and your child's teacher give it some thought, you may find many ways to base lessons on a wide range of topics on a special interest. Justin's enduring interest in World War II aircraft has yielded knowledge of geography, science, and history. Later, in chapter 9, we will explore pros and cons to redesigning a curriculum to fit a special interest.

Odd though it sounds, a restricted special interest can broaden a child's world. You can use the special interest to encourage the child to try new things. It can also be a way to spend special time with your child. If your child's interest is one shared by many others—cars, animals, railroads, or movies, for example—there are places to go, videos to watch, and books to read. Making time to include the special interest sends your child the message that you are comfortable not being "the expert" and look forward to learning new things, too. (When you think about it, daily parenting life offers few opportunities for children to lead.) It also allows you to model for your child what level of involvement and especially conversation with new acquaintances and friends is socially okay. Being engaged also offers many opportunities to each kid to be comfortable with steps outside their particular special interest comfort zone. So, yes, I would love to accompany you to the railroad museum, but it's only fair that we get to visit the aquarium down the street for a while afterward, too.

People with AS can sometimes channel their special interest into a satisfying career. Livestock management expert Dr. Temple Grandin is perhaps the most famous example of that. This is especially true if the interest can be applied to a profession that makes few social demands (i.e., it allows independence as opposed to teamwork and limited interaction with the public) and attracts people with similar traits or a generous tolerance for social differences. While professions and work situations that seem tailor-made for people with AS are frequently mentioned in the media, the truth is, every work situation is unique. Once a young man with AS was offered a job working at a New York City museum. It was a job he could have done easily. A train buff, he would have loved the daily trip into Manhattan. But even though the position had been perfect for a number of people with AS who had preceded my friend, his job coach and parents and even he deemed it too socially isolating for him.

Another reality, which will be discussed further in chapter 11, is that the fields once considered the exclusive domains of nerds, geeks, and code writers are now viewed as top career choices for neurotypicals who have the technical chops *and* career-ready social skills. The idea that every individual's special interest clears the road to a fascinating, fitting career has been somewhat oversold. Whether your child's special interest will evolve into a career depends on a number of factors, most of them beyond anyone's control (for example, the economy, local access to jobs related to the Civil War).

Noticeably Stiff, Pedantic, One-Sided Conversational Style

This is most clearly noticeable when a person with AS is talking about a special interest, but it can be observed in other situations, too. Listeners may get the impression that they are being lectured *at* rather than spoken *to* by someone more intent on showing off his knowledge in the minutest detail than in participating in a reciprocal conversation. A child with AS may have an impressive, adultlike vocabulary, often adopting an overly formal, sometimes almost old-fashioned manner of speaking. There are many possible reasons why this is so. One possibility is that among the many social behaviors children with AS do not master is that of noticing, imitating, and "acting like" others their own age. AS seems to limit the degree to which a child can absorb and model the age-appropriate behavior of peers. In addition, because most children with AS do not spend a lot of unstructured time interacting with peers, they do not get the benefit of peer feedback. Peers can be quite direct in responding to manners of speech, social behavior, or just about anything else that another kid does that strikes them as "weird," "odd," "stupid," or whatever the term *du jour* is for "not what we do." Such exchanges can be rough, or they can also be tactful and caring, but they are usually effective in influencing peer behavior. Most of our kids with AS miss this "shaping" experience because of the limited time they spend interacting with peers.

Problems in the Social Use of Language

The difficulty that people with AS have in the social use of language can range from subtle to striking. Even though your child may be sophisticated in her expressive use of language (what she says, the vocabulary and sentence structures used), most people with AS have "hidden" yet deep and pervasive deficits in their understanding of what is communicated to them, through the use of words (semantics) and the flow of nonverbal information we transmit constantly through tone, rhythm, and inflection of voice; body language; facial expression; and gaze modulation. Pragmatics is the use of language in social contexts. Even children with apparently good expressive language skills may reveal surprising limitations when in the grip of strong emotions such as anger and frustration. These deficits give rise to such common AS-related behaviors as overly literal interpretation of metaphors and images and its "mirror" deficit, incomplete understanding of oral communication that is insufficiently explicit. As a result, your child might become alarmed at such common Momisms as "I'm losing my patience" (which your child may offer to help you find).

Parents of children with AS also notice that the parts of messages they assume will be understood often are not. For example, for most children, "Get ready for school" is interpreted as "Go upstairs, brush your teeth, wash your face, put on clean underwear, pants, a shirt, shoes, and socks, gather your book bag . . ." That is not necessarily the case for a person with AS. Behaviors that we may attribute to laziness, lack of organization, or lack of skill may in fact be caused by an individual's inability to fully process language, to keep front and center in her mind what she is supposed to do, in what order. This is frequently cited as executive function deficit, which will be explored more fully later in this chapter.

People with AS also have deficits in other areas key to carrying out such a seemingly simple instruction: problems with fine- and gross-motor skills, planning, organization, and conception of time, to name a few. Most parents can recount dozens of examples when the information "inside" the message did not seem to reach its destination. For some children with AS, the process of getting ready for school must be broken down into short, clear, specific sequential oral instructions or visual reminders, often with a lot of prompting and supervision, regardless of how bright the child or how many times (even hundreds of times) you two have been through the same routine. Looking back, parents of kids with AS—and our kids— recall many instances of flaring tempers and tears over such situations that were wrongly miscast as bad behavior. As we explain later in chapter 9, there are time-tested methods that teach skills and independence that parents can use to avoid the cycle of dependence and learned helplessness that too many families fall into.

Inability to Interpret Correctly or Express Nonverbal Communication

We rarely give it much conscious thought, but most of us instinctively know that it's not what you say but the way you say it that fully communicates what you mean. Because people with AS often have deficits in their ability to interpret and use nonverbal forms of social communication, they often appear socially naive and inept. Part of this is due to the challenges of coping with spoken language, as outlined earlier. Another part has to do with an inability to understand nonverbal language. Some experts estimate that up to 90 percent of communication is nonverbal. It's easy to understand why someone who devotes the bulk of his attention only to that verbal 10 percent can miss or misinterpret the full message.

When the Eyes Don't Have It

In revealing studies published in 2002, Dr. Fred Volkmar and Dr. Ami Klin and their colleagues at the Yale Child Study Center were able to track the eye movements of people with and without AS or high-functioning autism (HFA) and compare them.[20] They showed the subjects a videotape of the emotionally charged film *Who's Afraid of Virginia Woolf?*, starring Elizabeth Taylor and Richard Burton. Interestingly, most of the "action" during this evening in the life of a toxic marriage is in the actors' words. The researchers discovered that the neurotypical viewers watched everything on the screen but paid particular attention to the faces of the actors, particularly the eyes. People with AS or HFA, however, focused on the mouth of the actor speaking, in contrast to the neurotypical control subjects, who focused on the whole faces of both the actor speaking and those being spoken to. In a related study, preschoolers with ASD watching an episode of *Barney* had their eye tracking patterns compared to preschoolers who did not have ASD. The findings were similar. Whereas neurotypical youngsters' eye movements "traced" a triangle whose "angles" were formed around the eyes of Barney and two child actors he interacted with, children with ASD were more often focused on inanimate background objects.

> Since we learn to use appropriate facial expression, body language, and gestures through observation and imitation, it's not surprising that people with AS—who are limited in their ability to notice these in others, imitate what they see, and then recall this knowledge and apply it appropriately in future social situations—would be at a disadvantage. There is also the possibility that deficits in this area may be related to problems with motor skills, specifically imitation of the expressions, gestures, and behavior of others.

Some individuals with AS have a great deal of difficulty listening and looking at the same time. They may understand the "words" but miss the context because they are unable to concentrate on the nonverbal actions and subtle cues being offered. Thanks to brain-imaging technologies, we know that the brains of some people with AS are structurally and/or functionally different. This may explain why ASDs seem to "force" or "drive" attention on things most people ignore, while causing people with AS to ignore or simply not register information that most individuals seem "programmed" and compelled to observe and act upon. At the same time, it seems clear that even individuals with AS who do attend to the verbal and nonverbal language of others do not necessarily interpret what they perceive correctly or with the degree of fluency or subtlety necessary.

Seeming Lack of Empathy Toward Others

The term *empathy* crops up a lot in ASD-related discussions. Most people assume that it means only the ability to understand and relate to the feelings of others. But there's more to empathy than that. As Simon Baron-Cohen explains, empathy encompasses two things: *cognitive empathy*, or the ability to understand the feelings and thoughts of others (in other words, theory of mind); and *affective empathy*, or the ability to know how to respond appropriately to another person's feelings and thoughts.[21]

The idea that children with AS seem to have no feelings for others or no ability to empathize is mentioned prominently in the literature. It fuels oversimplified popular media depictions of people with AS as being "emotionless," "disconnected," or "like robots." Many parents and people who work closely with our children would beg to differ with that impression. People with AS are not cold, mean, or uncaring. Their apparently limited empathy is one aspect of their problems with theory of mind (ToM), as we discussed earlier. Because of this "mind-blindness," a child with AS may literally not understand why you would be angry that he tracked mud across the kitchen floor you just mopped, why a sibling gets angry when he grabs her toy, or why his friend does not wish to share her snack. (After all, you may hear, "I told her that I wanted it.")

Educators and others who know just a little about AS often express surprise at how "nice" and "kind" our children can be. In fact, we have heard from many parents who were told, "Your child is too affectionate" to have an ASD, or "too caring," or "too emotionally connected." Children with AS can be very affectionate and loving. While they may have difficulty reading people at school or in other social situations, they can be surprisingly perceptive about the emotional states of parents, grandparents, siblings, friends, and beloved teachers, babysitters, and others. Parents of children with AS have speculated and many adults with AS have expressed that it is not that they don't "feel" at all, but rather that they feel too much. Often these feelings are overwhelming and confusing. These children feel emotion but lack the ability to modulate it comfortably, which can then lead to trouble expressing it appropriately.

Negativistic Worldview

For reasons that have yet to be fully explained, many children with AS seem to see the glass of life as perpetually half empty and, depending on their mood at that moment, dingy and cracked as well. Often their emotional responses are much more or much less intense than one might expect. For example, a child may cry hysterically over something that would seem to most people not worth the tears, and later show no emotional response to something others view as extremely sad. One mother recalls hearing her son with AS comment out loud at a family funeral, "Part of me wants to laugh and part of me wants to cry." He was clearly feeling something (in this case, sadness); he just wasn't sure how to express it. Or perhaps a child simply may not share in another's enthusiasm and lacks the social skills to fake it.

Some of these children complain, whine, protest, and argue more than most other children and often more than a given situation warrants. Many of them also have prodigious memories, but parents often remark on how vivid and persistent bad memories are, while happy moments seem somehow to fade. It's as if the child's emotional response to a difficult time or situation overwhelms whatever pleasant experiences she may have had. Parents of children who have AS and some degree of obsessive behavior know well the seemingly constant "replaying" of the unhappy moment and the memory of it that can persist for years. Add to this the fact that some children with AS simply do not express happiness or pleasure with quite the same verve and enthusiasm you generally expect, and you may get the impression that they are apathetic or uncaring.

Of course, most children with AS are neither apathetic nor uncaring. It's important to put these comments in the context of the child's daily life, which, for too many of them, is stressful. One child expressed the sentiment that a "good day" was a day when nothing went terribly wrong. Honestly, how many days like those do some of our children have? Probably not many. We know that children with AS are at much higher risk for anxiety and depression. We also know that these are children who, because of their inflexibility, literal-mindedness, and trouble dealing with the unexpected, probably do perceive that more "bad things" happen to them.

Often, a person with AS can be incredibly emotional about, say, animals, select people in his life, or an idea or cause. This sometimes leads others to make unkind comparisons along the lines of, "He cares so much about horses, why can't he just be as concerned about his classmates?" No one has a clear answer for that, except to say that there are situations in which the rules for expressing deeply felt emotions might be clearer and someone might feel more comfortable with them.

Difficulty Relating Socially with Others, Particularly Same-Age Peers

Though it is becoming increasingly apparent that children with AS probably showed some telltale, atypical social behaviors years before they were diagnosed, the extent of their social disability is rarely obvious until preschool or kindergarten, when they are faced with the increased social demands of a peer group in an organized setting where routines are set by others and there is little downtime or alone time. Before then, most playdates likely consisted of two or more children engaged in parallel play; that is, playing "near" but not "with" each other. As children get older, they typically learn and naturally seek out cooperative play with others. Children with AS, however, tend not to—or when they do play with other children, the play is one-sided and lacks the social give-and-take of a typical peer relationship.

Their difficulty interacting with peers is the culmination of all the important symptoms mentioned thus far. It's not so much that they are lost in their own world in the same way that a child with a different type of ASD might appear to be. Rather, it's that they seem not to know how to enter a conversation or a social situation. Several factors probably come into play here, among them their impoverished ability to observe and adopt socially appropriate behavior, their one-sided conversational style, and their unusual manner of speaking. Their special interest may preclude their being interested in or willing to tolerate play that involves anything else.

Unlike typical children in a play situation, children with AS seem unable to "go with the flow" or tolerate the frequent shifts in focus and activity that free social play involves. A child with AS may become upset when another child will not play what he wants to play for as long as he wants to play it or without following his special rules. Alternately, children with AS may drift off and not pay attention to the other children. Unfortunately, what constitutes fun for some of our children is not always enjoyable to their peers, and what constitutes fun for other children is not always enjoyable for ours. While many children with AS do well one-on-one with peers, most typical children by the time they reach school age are able to interact with more than one playmate at a time and are capable of playing at an activity they may be ambivalent about for the sake of playing. Sustaining attention with more than one child can be difficult and stressful for a child with AS, and feigning interest for the sake of social interaction may be near impossible.

Children with AS are often hampered in developing peer relationships by the fact that they have two built-in "outs." One, they often have no trouble playing by themselves and may actually prefer to do so. Two, they usually find it much easier to talk with and be tolerated or even accepted by sensitive older or younger children, teenagers, and adults. Our children feel more at ease socially around people who can carry the conversation, socially speaking. Despite our children's deficits in terms of social observation and theory of mind, they do sense clearly, even painfully, when they are not being accepted.

When your child seems happiest playing alone or engages in productive, rewarding activities on his own (at the computer, for instance), it can be hard to fully appreciate what he is "missing." We have noticed that parents of children who are highly skilled in some independent endeavor or who are academically exceptional may be less likely to see the value of developing peer social skills. It is important to remember that no matter what talent or skill your child has, no matter how little he may seem to miss being around other children, learning to be among peers is a critical skill. Why? Our social experiences throughout childhood teach us much about others and ourselves. Like all children, ours need opportunities—structured, brief, few, and supervised though they may be—to know others, to tolerate someone else who makes a different choice or has a different thought, and to experience what makes other people valuable, enjoyable, and worth spending time with.

As researchers, experts, and parents have had these twenty-plus years to really get to know AS and individuals with the diagnosis, several surprising facts have emerged. First, many children with AS who profess not to care about social relationships or being with their peers in the elementary school years frequently change their views by high school. Unfortunately, those who do not begin to receive any structured, ASD-specific social skills intervention until middle school or high school can have a hard time "catching up." Why? Because "learning" social skills is a crucial but ultimately small piece of the puzzle. What creates fluency and ease in social skills is the same thing that gets you to Carnegie Hall: practice, practice, practice. Further, many peers are forming their friendships and peer groups in those years. Sadly, many kids with AS who suddenly feel compelled to join something after age twelve or so discover that the groups are "set" and not necessarily looking to recruit new members.

For girls with Asperger syndrome, the picture is a bit different. Unlike boys, girls with AS seem more interested in peers. Because some typical girls enjoy looking out for or caring for others, a girl with AS might be "adopted" or taken in by a group of peers, who will teach what is expected and basically how to act. Some girls with AS are avid "students" of such tutelage, and some even go so far as to choose one or several peers whom they imitate in terms of gesture, manners, dress, and style of speaking. This can be a difficult and stressful endeavor.

As a mom of a child with AS who has spent countless hours with other parents of kids with AS and other ASDs, I know that it can be difficult to convince a child that a social skills program or outing is important. I have seen the reluctant social skills group member, the sulking playdate partner, and the movie buddy who cannot stop complaining that the snack bar has Coke, not Pepsi, or Pepsi, not Coke. As parents, it's easy to see the child's response to the situation as the problem, and it's easy to avoid the problem if you never venture outside your front door again. However, the truth is that the real problem is a deficit in developing age-appropriate skill in coping with social situations, surprises, and the age-old, ever-present reality that sometimes things do not go exactly the way any of us would like.

The often disheartening reality is that once your child decides that it's time for social skills work and practice, it may be a much more difficult endeavor than it might have been had you started earlier. Children who begin social skills training early are often not aware that they are being rejected by peers, and their understanding of why they are at sessions often boils down to its being part of the weekly routine. Older children, however, have more awareness and thus are more likely to view any intervention as an indication of something being "wrong." Older children and teens are not as easily persuaded and may even be immune to stronger attempts to influence them. While the old saw about leading a horse to water is no doubt true, it's probably best to get started while you can still at least lead the horse to the water. Even children who are not thrilled to be in a social skills group or who might not participate as much as everyone would like are still getting some helpful experience and practice in following a different set of rules and working under a different set of expectations; being exposed to information about social skills; and observing other members of the group or the professional leading the group demonstrating, modeling, practicing, and talking about specific social skills. Professionally, I have supervised social skills groups for children of all ages. Simply learning to devote a short period of time to doing something that may not be your favorite activity in the world, sitting among peers whose special interest is not your own and may strike you as boring, learning to wait your turn in a conversation or to ask someone else what they think—all have real value and are essential to even the most basic level of social competency.

BEYOND THE CORE: THE "OTHER" TELLTALE SIGNS OF AS

Complicating the already busy picture for most individuals with AS is the common presence of a legion of other deficits, disabilities, and syndromes. Having AS compromises the ability to recognize a difficult or uncomfortable situation and limits the ability to cope or create compensatory strategies for dealing with something like social anxiety, tactile sensitivity, or motor clumsiness. For example, one problem that people with AS often have is an inability to understand that other people might know something they themselves do not. A neurotypical child who experiences extreme distress over a clothing tag touching the back of her neck has the theory of mind to ask someone else to cut it out for her. A child with AS might simply fall into a tantrum, the cause of which appears inexplicable to those who do not understand how the disorder manifests in that particular child. Or a neurologically typical but physically awkward person might compensate by learning to anticipate the movement of strangers in a crowd, a feat that involves a level of social awareness to anticipate the movements of others, motor planning to get yourself out of the way when needed, and the ability to attend to numerous stimuli simultaneously—three skills that many with AS simply do not have or cannot exercise consistently and comfortably without tremendous effort.

Emotional Lability and General Anxiety

Even the happiest child with AS tends to live under some degree of stress. He may become easily and quickly upset over something that would not bother most people. Common behaviors range from general grumpiness and low-key whining to violent tantrums that may involve physical aggression directed toward oneself or others. One common hallmark of the AS tantrum is its seemingly instant onset and its supersonic trajectory from calm to complete meltdown in a matter of minutes, if not seconds.

To those unfamiliar with AS, these tantrums seem to come "from out of the blue." However, there is usually a trigger or antecedent that may not be immediately obvious. Children may be at a loss to identify, articulate, or explain what prompts the outburst. Parents find themselves playing detective to discover the culprit, then acting like Secret Service agents, casing out every situation for potential triggers. Tantrum antecedents range from extreme confusion and stress because of theory of mind and socialization problems; avoidance of touch or tactile stimulation; sensitivity to certain sounds, smells, tastes, textures, or light; or what many parents recognize as simply mental fatigue from the stress of coping or other daily demands, such as school. One result is that our children sometimes strike others as emotionally immature, manipulative, and spoiled, and we parents as overprotective or indulgent. In fact, all we're doing is protecting our kids from a world that can be too loud, too busy, too quick, or too confusing for them. Usually, though, in the moment of the meltdown, there is no time to explain.

People with AS can be extraordinarily sensitive to what they consider "criticism," which may in fact be only a request, suggestion, or mild reprimand. A child with AS may become very angry or very sad because an adult has reminded him to remove his hat inside or because there are no lemon lollipops at the doctor's office. In uncomfortable or new situations, a child's stress can prompt negative or inappropriate responses. For example, a child with AS who witnesses another child being hurt might laugh. This could be interpreted as lacking empathy, but it is more likely that the child is nervous or doesn't know what the appropriate response should be.

Some research suggests that girls with AS are at higher risk for anxiety. No one is sure why. One possible explanation is that because they tend generally to be more active in seeking out social engagement, they may have higher expectations, make more social attempts, and have more experiences of disappointment when things do not turn out.

Oversensitivity or Undersensitivity to Sensory Input

A person with AS may react strongly to touch, smell, sound, taste, and visual stimulation. He or she may be overwhelmed to the point of feeling panic or nausea by the sensation of sitting in a doctor's exam room without clothing, the antiseptic smells, the taste of the tongue depressor, the feel of the paper on the examination table. In school, the touch of chalk, the texture and scent of a new textbook, and the sharp crackle of the PA system may be unbearable. At the shopping mall, the "white noise" of a large space, the scent of several perfumes, or the bright reflection of halogen lighting on chrome and glass counters can set off panic or tantrums.

Difficulties Processing Auditory Information or Input

Many people with AS also have symptoms associated with what speech pathologists and others term central auditory processing disorder (CAPD), of which there are several forms. Behaviors typical of CAPD include the inability to follow oral directions that involve two or more steps (e.g., "When you finish breakfast, bring your dishes into the kitchen, rinse them, stack them in the sink, then use the dishcloth to wipe the table"), difficulty attending to conversation or other aural input in the presence of competing sounds or distractions, and repeatedly asking others to repeat themselves.

In the past several years, a handful of small studies have suggested some possible explanations for why auditory information seems sometimes to be ignored or "misprocessed." A 2009 study of children with autism measured the magnetic fields emitted from the children's brains. The authors found that, compared to typical children, those with autism processed speech fractions of a second slower. Dr. Timothy Roberts explained the significance of the delay like this: "If you're saying 'elephant,' they'd be stuck on the 'el' when you're on the 'ant.'"[22] A second study from the same year compared sixteen verbal children with ASD to eleven typically developing children. The authors suggest that their findings indicate that children with ASD process speech in quiet environments only about as well as typical children process it under conditions with background noise.[23]

For those who also have auditory sensitivity, the sounds of a child crying in the next room can be overwhelming; the pitch of a telephone's ring or a beeper may be physically painful. While some are sensitive to sound at high volumes, many are made uncomfortable by certain sounds and pitches, regardless of volume. A child might cringe at the sound of a distant leaf blower and yet enjoy banging loudly on a drum.

Some parents have noticed that sometimes the ability to control the noise makes it tolerable. These same children may also have difficulty regulating their own voices. They may not realize they are speaking too loudly and some find it impossible to whisper. They may speak at a very low volume and not pick up their listeners' cues that they need to speak up. Sometimes when prompted to speak up, someone with AS might reply that they thought they were talking too loudly already.

Hearing and Noise

Anxiety, depression, tantrums, avoidance behavior, crying, screaming, running, and totally shutting down to the point of putting oneself to sleep are some of the ways a person with AS or other ASDs may react to sound. For those of us whose brains process sound normally, it can be difficult to imagine the sheer panic a child might experience at something like the sound of a car starting or water running down the bathtub drain. Most of us simply assume that only loud, sudden noises might be distressing. However, people with AS who have auditory processing problems may be as unnerved by what most of us consider the near-silent hum of fluorescent lights as we would be by a loud car alarm. A surprising number of children in our survey were very troubled by the sound of other people chewing food, for example. Sensitivity to sounds tends to increase with fatigue, overstimulation, and stress.

In our original OASIS survey,[24] we found that the most frequently identified problem spots were any environments where there are many people (specifically, school assemblies and school cafeterias), sudden loud noises (such as a balloon popping), sirens and alarms, high-pitched whistles, and fireworks. The sound of a baby or young child crying bothered about 25 percent. In addition, parents indicated that their children had difficulty understanding what was said in the classroom (68 percent). Parents also noted other unusual responses to sound. Sixty-four percent said that at least half the time, their child became easily distracted by noises that most people would not notice, and more than 52 percent indicated that their child seemed to respond to questions at a noticeably slower rate than would be expected. Eighty-nine percent of the parents said they had "avoided situations in which the child could easily become overloaded."

Motor Clumsiness and Developmental Coordination Disorder

Dr. Hans Asperger wrote perceptively about motor clumsiness in his original 1944 paper. Problems with body awareness, motor planning, balance, fine-motor coordination (especially handwriting, using scissors, and multistep fine-motor tasks), bilateral motor integration, and gross-motor coordination are commonly seen among children with ASDs generally and AS in particular. Most people with AS struggle with some degree of fine- and gross-motor skills deficits. They have trouble tossing and catching a ball, dressing and undressing, tying shoes, holding a fork properly, balancing, hopping, or following directions related to physical movements (for example, "Raise your right hand over your head," "Hop up and down on your left foot"). Many individuals have an unusual gait and problems with spatial judgment; they may not know where their bodies are in space. This may account for their unusually high rate of spills, trips, and bumps into things. Many are also dysgraphic and have a great deal of difficulty with handwriting, some to the point that holding a pencil is literally painful.

A large percentage of children with ASD also have symptoms associated with developmental coordination disorder (DCD). Although you may never have heard of it, DCD has been in the *DSM* for years. The criteria are straightforward: a child's performance in "daily activities that require motor coordination is substantially below that expected given the . . . age and measured intelligence." There may be delays in reaching standard milestones for motor skills, such as crawling and walking, poor handwriting, difficulty with sports activities, overall "clumsiness," and a tendency to drop things.

Atypical Responses to Stimuli

Some individuals with AS seem to experience sensory stimuli differently. They may have difficulty describing the degree and type of pain they experience; their responses may seem out of proportion or inappropriate, overreactive or underreactive. The same person who has no problem getting an injection may scream when a doctor places a stethoscope on his skin; a child who eschews being touched lightly might enjoy jumping off the couch repeatedly and coming down hard on his knees. Recent research on girls and women with AS has found that sensory issues are more likely to last over the life span for them as opposed to males.

Attention Problems with Multitasking

Paying attention to more than one thing at a time can be challenging for people with AS. They may struggle to maintain eye contact while talking or listening, to follow a series of directions as they are being given, or to listen and write notes in class simultaneously. As mentioned earlier, a child with AS may appear not to be paying attention and yet can recall everything that was said. This seems to suggest that some people with AS can watch the teacher *or* listen to the teacher but cannot do both at the same time easily. It also may explain why so many have difficulty with team sports. Not only do they have to pay attention to what they are doing but also they have to heed what their teammates are doing.

Executive Function Deficits and Problems with Organization, Planning, and Follow-Through

Asperger syndrome compromises executive function (EF), or the brain's ability to plan and carry out the steps to complete the task or behavior at hand. Executive function also controls inhibitions (such as the ability to think before you act) and makes it possible for a person to generalize or apply knowledge gained in situation A to situation Z, regardless of how different the two are. People whose executive functioning is impaired (a 1991 study found that 90 percent of people with AS tested below average in EF tests[25]) are not adept at responding to situations or tasks in an organized, efficient way. This may be evident in a student who sits at his desk to do his homework but does not know where to begin. He may need prompting to gather the necessary supplies and books. Children with AS often seem behind their peers in doing simple things independently, such as getting their own breakfast, following a morning routine without prompting, or arriving at school with everything they need in their backpack.

Other Typical AS Behaviors

People with AS can have difficulty with transitions (e.g., moving from classroom to classroom in the upper grades), surprises, changes in schedule and routine, unfamiliar environments, and novel situations. They may be challenged, even baffled, by certain abstract concepts, such as those relating to time and future events or, from our earlier example, the "white lie." Confusion about time and sequence is often a stressor. A child with AS who is told that he may watch television or ride his bicycle before bedtime may finish his television program, then be surprised and upset when told it is time for bed. For most children, the fact that making a choice means getting to do only one thing and not the other is communicated clearly by the word *or*. Someone with AS may not glean that doing one thing automatically eliminates the possibility of doing the other one, too. That information needs to be presented explicitly.

Because AS makes it difficult to generalize information from one setting or situation to another, you may notice your child asking questions to which you would expect he would know the answer. One parent told us of her son's anxiety over where they would buy the Halloween pumpkin. She did not realize that because the store where they bought the pumpkin the year before had closed, her son did not know (because no one had explicitly told him) that other stores could also be expected to have pumpkins. The inability to generalize is responsible for much of the low-level "background" stress people with AS seem to experience. Imagine for a moment believing that nothing you know about going to your bank's local branch, for example, would apply in another branch office. Multiply this by the dozens of situations children with AS confront each day, and you get some idea of the uncertainty and anxiety they may experience.

THE "MASK" OF AS: WHEN SYMPTOMS LOOK LIKE STRENGTHS

Once you suspect that there may be a problem, it is easy to see everything in terms of that problem. Yes, especially after your child is newly diagnosed, and it seems that Asperger syndrome "explains" just about everything. However, never forget that there will also be things about your child that owe more to her being who she is than to her being a person with AS.

Particularly during the sensitive period between recognizing a problem and learning to cope, don't lose sight of your child's areas of strength, and try to put them in context. Children with AS often have impressive skills and characteristics: they may be academically precocious, uninterested in the fads that other children drive their parents crazy over, capable of amazing feats of memory and concentration, more emotionally attached to you than their peers are to their parents, and even be considered your adult friends' favorite child to talk to because they seem "so grown up." Best of all, yours is probably simply a great kid. These are wonderful characteristics that, if channeled properly, can be used to your child's advantage. There is something statistically unusual but certainly nothing wrong with reading at age two, being ambivalent about the latest cartoon craze, knowing the bird (and flower and tree and motto and per capita income ranking) of all fifty states, and being comfortable talking to adults.

The potential problems lie not in these behaviors themselves but in the reasons *why* a child engages in them to the degree that he or she does. Some parents of children with AS recall feeling blessed to have avoided the terrible twos. Looking back, before they suspected a problem, they recall a toddler who never screamed for a particular kind of cookie and never got into things as much as other kids did. One mother remarked without exaggeration, "If I had left him to crawl around in a room full of cleaning products and poisons, he would never even have touched them." What these descriptions of "good" babies overlook is that a toddler who screams for Oreos is engaged in the crucial testing of his communication and theory of mind "systems." The child who could be "trusted" in a room full of hazards can "be good" because either AS itself or the neurological anomaly that results in AS seems to short-circuit the natural impulse to explore and experiment with the environment.

It is only natural and right to count our child's outstanding characteristics as pluses. After all, this is your child. If anyone should track and tally every point of wonderfulness, it would be you. Doing this with AS, however, can be misleading. Having talked to or corresponded with hundreds of parents on the brink of diagnosis, and having lived through my own son's diagnosis, I know that in that uncertain time, when it seems like all anyone seems to notice about your lovely son or daughter is everything that is "different," "abnormal," or "wrong," it's hard to be completely neutral. Regardless of how extreme a child's behavior, no matter how certain a parent may be that, yes, something is definitely amiss, there is an almost reflexive drive to "balance the books," so to speak. Sometimes that involves citing true skills, such as an advanced understanding of mathematics or a natural mechanical ability. Other times, however, parents are unknowingly describing AS traits that sometimes manifest in what at first glance appears to be acceptable, exceptional, or desirable behaviors. The child who does not go with the crowd, the child who never demands play with someone else, the child who spins wildly imaginative tales from his private play world may also be a child with AS. The child who never lies, the child who has a rigid sense of right and wrong, the child who would never sneak a cookie from the cabinet may also be a child with AS. The child who really does not bother anyone once she gets home from school because she "prefers" to play video games online most of the evening may also be a child with AS.

Like many parents I know, I once viewed my child's unusual AS-related behaviors in terms that eased some of my personal discomfort about them. When confronted with the social problems, the tantrums, the sometimes-inexplicable behaviors, I tried desperately to balance the books, to take my son's "good" characteristics and use them to offset, to make up for, to diminish, and even to totally disregard the "bad" behaviors and the glaringly unusual deficits. I do plead guilty to not facing the situation head-on, but I know I was not alone. Doctors and friends who assured us that this was "just a phase" seemed to "get" him. The educators who were blinded by his academic strengths or unusual intellectual abilities did not know that these were really "scatter skills"—inconsistent, isolated, focused points of clarity that were often easily overrun by the withdrawal, the chatter, the flitting attention, the sensory overload. Some of us had family members who reminded us of someone else in the family (whom we might now recognize as being somewhere "on the spectrum"), "and look how well he turned out." Looking back all these years later, I realize that some of those who offered such assurances were as baffled as I was; they just did not know what else to say.

The first step in moving forward is to be realistic about how AS affects your child. That sounds simple, but it is probably one of the most difficult tasks you will have. No one truly "outgrows" AS or any other ASD. Whatever progress is made toward the goals that really matter comes from getting the right intervention at the right time, at the right place, from the right source. It is virtually impossible to do that if you have not accepted that the condition your child has comes with challenges, problems, and deficits that require attention to ensure the best outcome. The second step is learning to see deficits and problem areas for what they truly are, not what you wish they would be. Parents who are new to the parallel universe that having a child with a major developmental disorder like ASD pulls them into are frightened, anxious, and unsure. What does it all mean? In the quest for answers, we hear from experts—sometimes it feels like too many of them—who seem to have nothing but bad news. You learn quickly that that seemingly innocent habit of walking on his toes or her need to always be first have the potential to cause much more serious problems than you ever imagined. You might wonder if the experts you're talking to or reading are not overreacting a bit. It helps to learn *not* to say, "My child talks only about earthquakes and has no relationships with peers, *but* he is very bright," but rather, "My child talks only about earthquakes and has no relationships with peers, *and* he is very bright."

ASPERGER SYNDROME: SOMETHING TO HAVE OR SOMEONE TO BE?

In the last edition, we wrote: "The strengths of people with AS make them interesting, bright, inventive, curious, and capable of great accomplishments." Today, I would put that a bit differently, because all children grow up to show you that who they are is the product of thousands of details, not just their "having" one specific condition. I would say that there is a lot about having Asperger syndrome that brings certain characteristics to the fore and sets others back in the shadows.

As parents of children with AS, we are often faced with the dilemma of determining which AS behaviors to tolerate or encourage and which we should strive to reduce, reshape, or eliminate. Certainly atypical behaviors that a child with AS might engage in may actually serve a purpose. Some people with AS, for example, deal with stress by rocking, pacing, turning light switches on and off a set number of times, repeating nonsense phrases, or performing some other activity that appears odd to others. A child might insist on wearing the same shirt every day, violently resist brushing his teeth, or scream every time you start your car. Within the context of AS, these behaviors might "make sense." They might even be comforting. However, that should not stop you from objectively asking how they're affecting your child's ability to cope in less socially stigmatizing ways. As a consultant, I am often asked why it matters whether, say, a toddler stops and turns to look at you when you call her name or whether a middle-school student stares at the ground whenever walking in the school hallways. I always ask, "Would this behavior be safe or okay in the parking lot at Target at night?" If the answer is no (and it usually is), then it's something that needs to be addressed, because people on the spectrum typically do not generalize (or "carry over") behavior learned in one situation to another. And, perhaps most important to bear in mind, most of our kids do not "outgrow" AS.

While we celebrate and treasure all that our children can do, we should never lose sight of or diminish—in our own minds or in those of others—the things that are difficult for them. It's one thing for a preschool child to have a good attention span; it's something else when that attention is focused on the size, shape, and color of Smart Board markers to the exclusion of virtually everything else. Are catching a ball, having legible handwriting, or being able to sustain a brief, polite conversation with Uncle Ed essential for future success? In and of themselves, in the daily life of a child, the answer may be no. But what about when your child is seven, ten, thirteen, eighteen, twenty-five? What is the answer when you envision your child in middle school, high school, college, the crucial first job, or the first step in a chosen career? What is the answer when you think of your child as someone who would like to have friends, independence, a career, a romantic relationship, marriage, his or her own children?

As parents, we must look ahead and understand that behaviors and deficits are neither discrete nor limited. They have far-reaching implications, which for a host of reasons may result in social stigmatization, isolation, and rejection. They may set someone up to be dependent on the presence of objects, routines, and people that can never be guaranteed. Perhaps even worse, they may teach a child that because he is now, for example, dependent on a given routine or unable to get dressed independently, he will always be that way.

We will talk a lot more later on about the importance of teaching children independence in their daily lives, because this is one area in which parents do not always get the help they need. In the past several years, a number of studies have confirmed that AS provides few "hedges" against the challenges that individuals on other points of the autism spectrum face. In fact, there is some evidence that a higher IQ and good language abilities do not always result in academic, social, or vocational achievements commensurate with abilities or in line with the individual's personal hopes and desires.

THE FUTURE IS BUILT ON INDEPENDENCE

One of the most significant predictors for future success and personal happiness for people with any type of disability is not academic success but social success and independence. A child who cannot catch a ball, for example, stands to lose a lot more than the chance to be a Little League hero. He may not be invited to join in games, may become self-conscious and feel badly about himself, may experience an early lack of interest in physical activity or sports, and may believe that all of this is because something is "wrong" with him. However, the child who learns to catch—or ride his bike, play the game someone else wants to play, or dress in an age-appropriate manner—may be asked to join the group and have one less thing to feel self-conscious about.

While it would be unwise, even cruel, to force a child to do things against his will, there is an argument to be made for helping your child expand his repertoire of interests and skills beyond the boundaries that AS can impose. Some of our children need help—sometimes very intensive help beginning when they are quite young—to master many of the basic skills of life, and one of the most important of these is adaptability. Some of our children are amazingly resistant and unyielding when it comes to making changes. The math is simple: the more skills, the broader your child's behavioral repertoire, the more opportunity, freedom, and success he can achieve.

The child who always wears the same shirt because he has always worn the same shirt, and his parents believe he never could wear any other shirt, is not making a choice, even though parents and others may see it in those terms. In contrast, a child who has been taught to adapt to change, to be flexible, and to be comfortable with change not only has a better chance of fitting in but is less anxious and stressed. After all, imagine having your whole day depend on whether the "special shirt" was available. Rather than alleviating a child's stress by providing the special shirt, well-meaning parents actually may be adding to it. Life being what it is, eventually something will happen to make that shirt unwearable. Then what? Parents who are most at ease raising their child with AS are those who can look ahead calmly and honestly, and then make a plan. Here the only choices are either to find an exact copy of the shirt (which you could do, theoretically, forever, but since we know that fashions come and go and kids tend to grow, this may be impossible) or teach your child to feel comfortable living without it. Notice I didn't say, "Teach your child to live without it." The emphasis is on feeling comfortable with change.

This is not to say that introducing flexibility into your child's life will be easy. It won't, and not everything will yield to change—at least not immediately and maybe not for a very long time. But it is essential that you make the effort to expand your child's emotional comfort zone if you imagine your child—or he imagines himself—living in a larger world.

INDEPENDENCE IS NOT A CHARACTER TRAIT—IT'S A SKILL SET

Another important way to prepare a child to reach his potential is to teach independence. For children who are more seriously challenged by other forms of ASDs, professionals and parents alike share an urgency about teaching self-help, personal care, and daily living skills. In the best schools, such seemingly "basic" skills as using appropriate table manners, folding and putting away clothes, making a bed, brushing hair, preparing a simple meal, crossing the street safely, answering a telephone appropriately, and bathing and toileting are important components of a formal curriculum that is taught systematically to mastery. Ironically, even though among children with

AS, a high percentage have difficulty learning these same types of skills, most will never cross paths with a professional who can teach them (or, better, teach their parents to teach them). With changes across the country in autism insurance laws, and the growing willingness of insurance companies to reimburse for services provided by behavior analysts, perhaps this will change. For when we fail to teach the repertoire of everyday skills that together form what we call independence—and independence is the product of learning skills, not simply some mysterious, inherent personal quality—we limit our children and even define their futures in terms of what they *cannot* do instead of what they *can* do.

Though much has changed in the world of AS, some things have remained stubbornly the same. We know that there are children with AS who are missing precious experiences as well as social, recreational, and academic opportunities because they lack the "prerequisite" independence to participate. We're talking about the seven-year-old with the social skills to attend a sleepover but who must decline because he is not independent in toileting; the brilliant high school senior who cannot attend the Ivy League school so far from home because she never learned to work a microwave, manage a bank account, or cross a street safely; the twelve-year-old who is perennially on the social sidelines because no one thought someone so bright "needed" to know how to throw a ball or ride a bike.

Many concerned parents see the potentially corrosive effects of being locked in a cycle of hovering, reminding, nagging, arguing, threatening, and punishing over the same things every day but have no idea how to stop it. And if a parent feels exhausted, frustrated, and incompetent, imagine for a moment how the child must feel. Remember that no matter what your child's measurable IQ, having an ASD usually suggests an inability to learn through observation. Most children do not need to be explicitly taught how to dress; ours probably do. Most children are inherently driven to be independent and may even attempt to do things before they are ready. They will soldier through numerous cycles of trial and error to reach their goal; ours probably won't. Most important, and difficult for parents and experts alike to fully comprehend, despite our children's seeming facility with words, some skills just cannot be taught by telling someone how to do it. For most people with ASDs—regardless of where they fall on the spectrum—acquiring the skills of daily living and independence is more a "show" than a "tell" process.

THE REASONS FOR HOPE

All parents wonder, and worry, about what the future holds for their children. Parents of children with AS worry, too, but about things most other parents never have to consider. In the realm of ASDs, an accurate prognosis is possible only for those who are most severely affected. The more capable someone is, and the greater his or her capacity for learning, language, and social interaction, the less certainty there is in terms of prognosis. Yes, that is counterintuitive; it just doesn't seem to make sense. But, as you will read throughout the book, a number of dimensions of AS do not always receive the same level of intensive intervention they deserve.

Amid the uncertainty, there is hope. This generation that has just come of age was the first with Asperger syndrome to have the benefits of understanding, knowledge, research, treatment, and intervention. Twenty years ago, most experts looked at Asperger syndrome and compared it to other forms of autism that were more involved and impairing. By that comparison, kids who could count, talk, learn a lot about a few topics, and live without the most severe "autistic symptoms" seemed home free. When long-term outcome studies began to surface in the past ten years, they presented a very different—some would say even startling—picture. Given their measurable IQs and other skills, most adults with AS live lives that seem to fall short of their potential in terms of education, employment, relationships, and emotional health.[26] The message is clear: no one with an ASD diagnosis is ever "home free." While the skill sets typical of kids with AS might put them at the top of the achievement curve in more restrictive, supportive environments, or at the local model train club or medieval role-play club, such skills do little to help them when they are faced with the challenges of attending regular schools, colleges, professional training, and then becoming part of the everyday adult world with its social, emotional, and economic demands.

While no one can say with certainty what lies ahead for any

child, the small daily victories ours can achieve thanks to information, awareness, and the appropriate use of therapies and interventions are more than glimpses of promise—they are the way. Parenting a child with AS requires knowing what needs to be done and then actually doing it. Sometimes that means looking honestly at what is being provided your child at school, in private therapy or interventions, and even in your own family and community, and, when necessary, doing something about it. No single resource, organization, or agency—be it the school district, the best AS doctor or therapist, or your own family—can provide everything your child might need. But parents and families can often do a lot more than they expect, and sometimes can do it even better than anyone else can.

Chapter 2

GETTING THE DIAGNOSIS

FOR most parents, the process of evaluation and diagnosis is an emotionally mixed experience. There is the sense of relief at finally knowing what "it" is. Having a name for the collection of behaviors and issues opens new doors to information, support, and services. Being able to use that name telegraphs to others that your child's problems don't stem from poor parenting, bad attitudes, egocentricity, laziness, or guile. As a parent, you may come away from the confirmed, official diagnosis with renewed hope and purpose, a focus for your energy, a sense of a new beginning.

At the same time, it's impossible not to see the diagnosis as marking an end to other things: the hope that your child will completely "outgrow" or "learn to cope" with all of his differences; the possibility that her problems aren't as serious as you had feared or will be only temporary, self-limiting, and easily "cured." In the same moment when you feel pressured to charge down this new road with confidence and hope, you may feel lost, overwhelmed, and disappointed by the realization that you have to be there at all. We devote chapter 4 to the impact of the diagnosis on parents.

Much confusion has arisen around the terms *diagnosis* and *classification*. For the purposes of this book, we use *diagnosis* to denote the identification of a disease or condition by a medical professional with expertise in the area of developmental disability: a physician, psychiatrist, neurologist, neuropsychologist, pediatrician, and so on. The diagnosis may be reached through any combination of various tests, information on the child obtained from parents and teachers, and interviews with and observation of the child.

Classification is a term used by school districts and state education departments to identify types of disabilities for program design and record keeping. A classification is not the same as a diagnosis. Depending on the child and the state in which he attends school, he may be diagnosed with Asperger syndrome or ASD and yet not be classified under "Autism" by his school district. In another example, a child may be classified by his school district as Emotionally Disturbed and later diagnosed with a psychiatric condition such as obsessive-compulsive disorder (OCD). Federal and state special education statutes and regulations offer a limited number of classifications. So while a condition such as OCD is recognized as a disability and is a medical diagnosis, a child with OCD would probably be classified under the federal category "Other Health Impaired," or OHI. In fact, some kids with ASDs are classified as OHI. There is no specific classification for AS.

WHY PURSUE THE DIAGNOSIS?

We strongly advise that anyone whom you suspect may have AS—child, spouse, yourself—be diagnosed by a professional. For one thing, there are many behaviors and symptoms that can "look like" an ASD. Since most people with ASDs also have at least one other learning disability or psychiatric condition, teasing out the different diagnoses—how they might overlap or present differently in the presence of other diagnoses—is a complex task. If your child does have an ASD, other medical evaluations and tests might be warranted, such as an electroencephalogram (EEG) to rule out seizures, and genetic testing for any of a number of conditions that sometimes co-occur with ASD (fragile X syndrome, for example). The professional making the diagnosis might also have suggestions for specific treatments, accommodations or services at school, and other professionals your child should see.

It's also possible that your child does not have AS at all but one or a combination of disorders with symptoms that appear to the untrained eye to add up to AS (say, for example, obsessive and compulsive tendencies, social phobia, and a tic disorder). Or perhaps your child has AS along with other disorders or disabilities, each of which may require specialized treatment, such as seizures.

Having a definitive medical diagnosis is an important first step in accessing the appropriate and most effective services, supports, interventions, and treatments. Your conviction that your child has ASD is all but meaningless when you enter the realm of health insurance coverage and coding and the identification and classification necessary to access special education and/or related services. Failure to obtain an official diagnosis may cost your child coverage and services. If you live in a state that has passed what is commonly known as "autism insurance reform," your child might be entitled to coverage for certain services based on an ASD diagnosis. This is something you should check into with your employer or health insurance provider. Go to the Autism Speaks website at www.autism speaks.org and click the Advocacy tab. Also see "Health Insurance for Treatment of Autism Spectrum Disorder" on page 181.

THE PITFALLS OF LATE OR MISSED DIAGNOSIS

Some people feel strongly that "diagnosis doesn't matter"; that all it does is "label" or, in the words of one former best-selling pediatrician, "pathologize" people. We couldn't disagree more. Even without diagnosis, your child will still face challenges and present with whatever issues or problems got you thinking about this in the first place. How you, your child, and those who know and work with him perceive those problems and address them sometimes has everything to do with what we call them. As we discuss in detail in chapter 6 and throughout, virtually every evidence-based intervention used to treat ASD can be used for kids with Asperger syndrome, though in some cases, with modifications. Having a correct diagnosis not only helps you and your child find and receive the most appropriate, effective interventions, but it may also be even more valuable in terms of helping you steer clear of the wrong ones, or the right ones used for the wrong reasons (for example, a Social Story to teach algebra, or a precision teaching program to teach social skills).

For children who are entering their teen years, having a diagnosis might prove critical in terms of accessing special education services for transition from high school and/or accessing whatever accommodations are appropriate for college or career training (see chapter 11).

Regardless of which path you choose, it is important to remember that once your child graduates from high school, no matter her age or the type of diploma or certificate she receives, "free" services and many familiar forms of accommodation disappear. Whereas some students might even have been able to receive some special education and related services through means other than an Individualized Education Plan (IEP), the number of supports available after high school is dramatically smaller. Having useful supports in place and being able to plan a truly productive transition program depends greatly on having an accurate, complete diagnosis. (See chapters 6, 9, and 11 for more on the transition to adulthood.)

Comorbidities: Other Conditions That Can Complicate the AS Picture

Comorbidity is the technical term for disorders and conditions that "co-occur" with others. A significant percentage of individuals with ASD have comorbid conditions: 70 percent have one comorbid psychiatric condition, and 40 percent have two.[1]

AD/HD

Attention-deficit/hyperactivity disorder, or AD/HD, is a neurobiological disorder characterized by pervasive difficulty with or inability to sustain attention or control impulses at a level deemed developmentally age appropriate. AD/HD is one of the most common comorbid conditions in people with AS. It is thought to affect between 3 percent and 9 percent of school-age children,[2] and according to recent studies, an estimated 30 percent to 38 percent of children with AS between the ages of nine and sixteen.[3] There are three types of AD/HD:

AD/HD predominantly inattentive presentation
AD/HD predominantly hyperactive/impulsive presentation
AD/HD combined presentation

Because AD/HD and AS share similar features, it's not uncommon for a child to be first diagnosed with AD/HD and later rediagnosed with AS. In addition, children may have a dual diagnosis of AS and a form of AD/HD.

Anxiety

According to the National Institute of Mental Health (NIMH), anxiety disorders, which are the most common form of mental disorder, affect about a quarter of children under eighteen.[4] Whether the anxiety experienced by individuals with AS is a direct result of their neurobiological makeup, a response to the stresses of living with AS, or a combination of both is difficult to determine, but a significant number of children—38 percent in a recent Finnish study[5]— and adults with AS experience some form of anxiety disorder at some point in their lives. Girls and women are particularly at risk for anxiety disorders.

Some common anxiety disorders that have been known to affect those with AS are as follows:

Generalized Anxiety Disorder (GAD): Individuals with GAD suffer from chronic and pervasive worry that goes well beyond what would be considered normal responses to daily living. Those with GAD worry excessively about everything, often for no apparent reason. They have difficulty relaxing, are constantly "on edge," and may have problems falling asleep. Sometimes they experience physical symptoms such as trembling, twitching, headaches, nausea, sweating, and irritability. During times of stress, anxiety can increase; considering that children with AS experience some degree of stress throughout their day, it's not surprising that they could easily become anxious. Parents of children with

AS have frequently mentioned that their kids perpetually see the glass as half empty and tend to look at the negatives rather than the positives. A child with AS who behaves this way could possibly have GAD.

Obsessive-Compulsive Disorder (OCD): According to the National Institute of Mental Health, individuals with OCD experience "intrusive thoughts that produce anxiety (obsessions), repetitive behaviors that are engaged in to reduce the anxiety (compulsions), or a combination of both."[6] OCD is thought to affect 1 in 50 people, or 2 percent of the population, at some point in their lives. Individuals with AS who are also diagnosed with OCD experience ritualistic behaviors and a need for routines that may significantly impair their ability to function. However, not every person with compulsive tendencies, obsessive tendencies, or both has OCD. It is important to remember that one of the three "core" diagnostic criteria for ASD is the presence of "restricted, repetitive patterns of behavior, interests, or activities."[7] *This is not the same as having OCD.* Question professionals who seem unable or unwilling to tease out these important distinctions. Is it possible for someone with ASD to have OCD as a comorbid diagnosis? Yes. Is every instance of repetitive behavior demonstrated by a person with ASD a symptom of OCD? No. While the observable behavior might look the same, the causes and the treatment options are very different.

Social Phobia and General Phobias: A phobia can be defined as "a specific fear that leads to avoidance of situations in which the fear might be triggered"[8] and that disrupts an individual's life. Individuals with AS are often diagnosed with social phobia, an intense fear of social situations that results in anxiety, panic, and avoidance behavior that can be extreme and adversely affect ability to function. Individuals with social phobia may feel incapable of performing in certain social arenas and may avoid interacting with groups of people, prefer to stay with familiar people, and be unwilling or unable to seek out new social situations. Because individuals with AS may face profound social difficulties generally, it can be too easy to attribute aversive behaviors to AS. Social phobia does respond to medication, cognitive behavior therapy, or both. In addition, a 2010 study found that about a third of children ages nine through sixteen with AS/HFA had a specific phobia about an object or a situation (for example, spiders, thunderstorms, open-toe shoes, being in an elevator, on a plane, in a crowded room, and so on). That's about double the prevalence one would expect among the general population of children in that age group.[9]

Posttraumatic Stress Disorder (PTSD): As awareness of AS increases, adults who as children were either misdiagnosed or undiagnosed are being recognized as having Asperger syndrome. In addition, some of these adults (and children) receive a secondary diagnosis of PTSD. Many grew up misunderstood and, unfortunately, all too often mistreated. Individuals with PTSD often have pervasive and persistent recollections of traumatic incidents, and these memories can be quite debilitating. In addition to depression, sleep loss, and decreased appetite, individuals with PTSD often feel extreme anxiety. While many become withdrawn and avoid social contact, in the most severe cases, individuals can become aggressive and angry. Like many conditions, PTSD ranges from mild to severe. The prevalence of PTSD among all children eighteen and younger is estimated at about 4 percent.[10]

Seizure Disorders

Having an ASD significantly increases the risk of seizure disorder. It is estimated that between 20 percent and 25 percent of people with ASDs also have seizures.[11] In general, family members of children with AS also seem to have a higher incidence of seizure disorders.

Depression

Depression is one of the most common conditions affecting children and adults with AS. Teenagers who are realizing that they are different from their peers are particularly susceptible, but in fact depression can occur in a child with AS *at any age, even in the very young child.* Estimates of prevalence for children with AS and depression range from 6 percent to 17 percent (compared to about 11 percent for all children under eighteen).[12] Girls are three times more likely to experience depression, and the risk increases with age for all adolescents: from 4 percent of thirteen-year-olds to more than 11 percent of older teens.[13] Parents should be on the lookout for clues that a child may be depressed.

Keep in mind that some of the warning signs may seem like typical

AS behavior and therefore are not easily recognized. It's important to look for changes in behavior as well as specific symptoms. In addition to watching for irritability and physical complaints such as headache and stomachache, the American Academy of Child and Adolescent Psychiatry recommends that parents be aware of the following signs of depression:[14]

- Loss of interest in favorite activities
- Major change in eating and/or sleeping patterns
- Frequent sadness, tearfulness, crying
- Decreased interest in activities or inability to enjoy previously favorite activities
- Hopelessness
- Persistent boredom; low energy
- Social isolation, poor communication
- Low self-esteem and guilt
- Extreme sensitivity to rejection or failure
- Increased irritability, anger, or hostility
- Difficulty with relationships
- Frequent complaints of physical illness
- Frequent absences from school
- Poor performance in school
- Talk of or attempts to run away from home
- Thoughts or expressions of suicide or self-destructive behavior

Bipolar Disorder

Bipolar disorder, formerly referred to as manic depression, is a disorder involving episodes of mania and depression, which are cyclical in nature, with mood swings that may cycle from high to low and back again. It is caused by abnormalities in brain chemistry and function. Though it is thought to affect 1 percent to 2 percent of adults worldwide, only recently has attention been given to children with the disorder. According to the National Institute of Mental Health, bipolar disorder is estimated to occur in about 3 percent of adolescents. Though bipolar disorder typically starts in late adolescence or early adulthood, it can also begin in childhood. To date, however, there are no sound statistics on prevalence for younger children. This is in part due to fact that there remains some debate regarding the "boundaries of diagnosis" for children.[15] While adults with bipolar disorder often experience extreme changes in mood and behavior and energy, children with the condition are more likely to have a more ongoing mood disturbance that includes both mania and depression.[16]

Symptoms include the following:

- Expansive or irritable mood
- Depression
- Rapidly changing moods lasting a few hours to a few days
- Explosive, lengthy, and often destructive rages
- Separation anxiety
- Defiant behavior
- Hyperactivity, agitation, sleeping too little or too much
- Bed-wetting and night terrors
- Distractibility
- Strong and frequent cravings, often for carbohydrates and sweets
- Excessive involvement in multiple projects and activities
- Impaired judgment, impulsivity, racing thoughts, and pressure to keep talking
- Risk-taking behaviors
- Inappropriate or precocious sexual behavior
- Delusions and hallucinations
- Grandiose belief in own abilities that defy the laws of logic (ability to fly, for example)

Tourette's Syndrome and Tics

There are several different tic disorders, and all are commonly seen with ASDs. Whereas Tourette's syndrome occurs in about 1 percent of the general population, from 8 percent to 28 percent of children with AS have Tourette's or another tic disorder.[17] Tourette's syndrome (TS), the best known, is, like all tic disorders, a neurological disorder characterized by motor tics, involuntary movements, and/or vocalizations. Movements are repetitive in nature and may vary in location. Symptoms can be mild to severe and range from simple movements such as eye blinking, throat clearing, and coughing to more complex full-body movements or movements accompanied by vocalizations. This disorder occurs more frequently in boys than in girls and almost always appears by the age of eighteen. Contrary to popular belief, the uncontrollable expression of obscene language (coprolalia) is among the rarest of TS symptoms.[18]

Although children with Asperger syndrome may have a diagnosis of TS, it is also important that it not be confused with stereotypies (commonly and possibly inaccurately referred to as "stimming"). Since TS is believed to be an inherited condition, it is not uncommon to discover that extended family members of children with AS have TS or another tic disorder.

Oppositional Defiant Disorder (ODD)

Oppositional defiant disorder is a psychiatric condition that can occur with AS. According to the American Academy of Child and Adolescent Psychiatry, ODD is distinguished from normal childhood arguing, talking back, and disobedience by its persistence and the degree to which it interferes with daily functioning. Between 5 percent and 15 percent of school-age children have ODD, and it frequently occurs with AD/HD. Studies have found rates of ODD among children with ASD range between 13 percent (children three to five) to 27 percent (children six to twelve) based on parent reports.[19] When unresponsive to treatment, ODD can progress to conduct disorder, a separate diagnosis with high risk for more serious violent, antisocial, or criminal behavior. Symptoms of ODD include the following:[20]

- Frequent temper tantrums
- Excessive arguing with adults
- Active defiance and refusal to comply with adult requests and rules
- Deliberate attempts to annoy or upset people
- Blaming others for his or her mistakes or misbehavior
- Often being touchy or easily irritated by others
- Frequent anger and resentment
- Mean and hateful talking when upset
- Seeking revenge

ASPERGER SYNDROME: LEARNING HOW TO SEE

If you or others are asking, "Does my child have Asperger syndrome?" you will be looking for signs, symptoms, and behaviors that match the old diagnostic criteria or descriptions by experts. Some of the commonly used criteria refer to behaviors and symptoms that, arguably, most children engage in to some degree at some time. Many of us whose children have been diagnosed will admit, if we are honest, to having reassured ourselves or others with "Lots of kids do that."

So where does typical behavior end and atypical behavior begin?

- *Tommy never seems to look any adult in the eye.*
- *Roger is obsessed with dinosaurs.*
- *Ashley doesn't really fit in among other kids in her group.*
- *Kurt is unbelievably clumsy.*

Do these children have AS? Probably not, if they are developmentally within the normal range in other important areas, such as walking, talking, interacting with others. AS does not describe a single behavior or deficit but a specific combination or constellation of them that are present to a significant degree.

So if a single child had Tommy's inability to sustain eye contact, Roger's dinosaur obsession, Ashley's lack of social competence, and Kurt's awkwardness, would that child have Asperger syndrome? Again, maybe not. Children are very complicated little people, works in progress, with unique profiles of strengths and weaknesses. No single area of deficit "proves" AS. As you consider a child who might have AS, remember to see things in the broad and ever-changing context of the whole child. The importance of a specific skill or deficit depends on what other areas of strength or weakness accompany it. We would most likely be correct in assuming that these children, despite their areas of concern, would not have AS if:

- *Tommy does not make a lot of eye contact but has no trouble fitting in socially among his peers.*
- *Roger is obsessed with dinosaurs but will talk just as readily with his jock friends about baseball and with his grandparents about their garden.*

- *Ashley is shy in group situations but has several close friends.*
- *Kurt, though the proverbial bull in a china shop, has no difficulty with other fine- and gross-motor skills.*

However, we might be concerned about any of these children if:

- *Tommy's lack of normal eye contact also included a deficit in shared attention (he did not look at what another person pointed to) and frequent misunderstanding of basic facial expression and tone of voice.*
- *Roger's facts about dinosaurs were the first utterances he made to everyone he met, whether they were interested or not, whether he knew the person or not, and he became upset every time anyone tried to change the subject.*
- *Ashley's behavior around other children suggested to even an untrained person that she "literally didn't seem to know what to do or say," and playing with other children really consisted of playing her own game alongside them without showing any interest in them.*
- *Kurt's awkwardness was apparent across a wide range of activities that even children we consider uncoordinated on the playing field have no trouble with—handwriting, dressing, grooming, folding, using scissors, and so on—and his facial expressions and communicative gestures seemed odd.*

Do all of these children have Asperger syndrome or ASD? From this small amount of information, anyone can speculate, but no one can really say. Our point here is simply to emphasize that when you become familiar with the various diagnostic criteria and begin measuring a child against them, consider not only the presence of behaviors but their frequency, their severity, and the degree to which they interfere with other aspects of the child's life.

Learning Disorders Commonly Seen with AS

Having any ASD automatically increases the risk for one or more learning disorders. When children have difficulty learning, teachers and parents should explore the possibility of a learning disorder. While we know that ASDs can present challenges to certain types of learning, it would not be correct to say that a child "has learning disabilities" simply because that child has ASD. Again, different conditions call for different types of intervention, so understanding what's really going on is the crucial first step in getting your child the services and supports he or she needs.

Dysgraphia

Dysgraphia is a complex learning disorder of written language that affects a considerable number of children with AS, although many remain undiagnosed. There are three types:

1. Dyslexic dysgraphia
2. Dysgraphia due to motor clumsiness
3. Dysgraphia due to a neurological inability to understand space

Dysgraphia may present differently from one child to the next. One child's handwriting may be messy and impossible to decipher, and the writing of another child may be exceptionally neat with all letters perfectly formed. The first child may rush through an assignment without forming any of the letters correctly, and the second child is not actually writing in the usual sense but painstakingly "drawing" each individual letter, a process so slow that it might take him an hour to finish a one-page assignment. Another problem, especially for students who are working with the regular curriculum, is that taking notes becomes so laborious, students miss what the teacher is saying, what the teacher is doing (for instance, demonstrating a geometry problem on the Smart Board), or both, that the notes she does manage to get down are nearly useless.

Dysgraphia involves more than the speed of writing and accuracy of the formation of letters. Other processes are involved, including the following: attention; eye-hand coordination; motor planning; memory;

fine- and gross-motor skills (weak upper-body strength can make it difficult for the child to position his or her body appropriately for the task of writing); language; and the ability to process and perform multiple tasks such as listening, looking at a blackboard, and taking notes simultaneously. Proper writing demands that you be able to recall instantly the answer to a test question while forming letters, a feat some people with AS simply cannot accomplish. For someone with dysgraphia, the writing process may be mentally and physically exhausting. All too often, their resistance to projects involving writing is viewed as stubbornness, laziness, or perfectionism. Realize that a child who can draw beautifully, put together small puzzle pieces, or complete other fine-motor tasks with ease may still be dysgraphic.

Consider having your child evaluated for dysgraphia if you notice any of the following signs:

- Extreme resistance to writing, accompanied by anxiety and acting out and/or saying that writing is "boring" or "stupid"
- Difficulty maintaining a good writing posture (for example, the child slumps over the desk, props up his head with the nonwriting hand, or complains frequently of being tired while writing)
- Unusual or awkward pencil grip that doesn't improve with thicker pencils or pens or other special pencil-grip aids
- Complaints that writing is painful or uncomfortable
- Difficulty taking notes in class
- Difficulty completing written tests in the specified time frame
- Emotional reactions and temper tantrums when faced with a writing assignment
- Excessive time needed to complete written homework
- Exhaustion, crankiness, or depression after completing a written assignment
- Difficulty with placement of text on the paper (for instance, math problems either appear in one corner of the paper or are scattered everywhere on the page)
- Avoidance of tasks that require paper and pencil (for example, he or she refuses to write down a birthday wish list or Christmas list, even though he is capable of forming the letters)

- Comments from adults such as "His handwriting could be neater if he only tried harder," or "He understands the material but refuses to write down the answers when asked"

Dyscalculia

Dyscalculia is defined as difficulty performing and comprehending mathematical calculations. As many as 13 percent of school-age children exhibit difficulties in *some* area of mathematics, regardless of their IQ.[21] Contrary to the belief that most children who are diagnosed with AS are mathematically gifted, significant numbers of children struggle with mathematical computation and problem solving. Dyscalculia is indicative of one or more of the following neurological problems that are often seen in children with AS: language processing, visual-spatial confusion, difficulties with memory and sequencing, and high anxiety. A child with language-processing difficulties may not understand the questions being asked, and a child who has a weakness in visual processing and exhibits spatial confusion will have difficulty visualizing numbers and situations required to solve math problems (for example, using a number line, graphing points, utilizing Common Core's ubiquitous tape diagram). A child who struggles with the organization of information and sequencing will have difficulty remembering the steps to complete calculations.

Even though we tend to think of math and language as "different," the types of difficulties that people with AS may have in terms of language can have a profound effect on their ability to use math. More advanced curricula and approaches that incorporate more language and abstract understanding—like Common Core—may render math more challenging for your child than it might have been in the past.

Dyslexia

Dyslexia is a language-based disability in which a person has difficulty understanding both oral and written words, sentences, or paragraphs. People with dyslexia have trouble decoding and translating printed words into spoken words and struggle with reading comprehension. Fifteen percent to 20 percent of the population and 13 percent of all school-age children have dyslexia, the most common cause of reading, writing, and spelling difficulties.[22] Affecting males and females equally, it is thought to be an inherited genetic disorder. According to the Learning Disabilities Association of America, in addition to often reversing or improperly sequencing letters within words when reading or writing, individuals with dyslexia may also exhibit difficulties with the following:[23]

- Perceiving and/or pronouncing words
- Understanding spoken language
- Recalling known words
- Handwriting
- Spelling
- Written language
- Decoding
- Reading comprehension
- Learning a foreign language
- Math computation

Nonverbal Learning Disability (NLD or NVLD)

Among the least widely recognized learning disorders, NLD shares many of its characteristics and behaviors with AS and ASD. According to researchers at Yale University, many of the children who participated in its AS study fit the NLD learning profile. There are many misunderstandings about NLD. One is that it is the "same as" AS or ASD. It is not. ASD is a psychiatric diagnosis, and NLD is a learning profile. Though many people with AS can also be said to have NLD, it is possible to have NLD without AS, and AS without NLD. Kids with NLD commonly display language and social/emotional issues similar to those described for Asperger syndrome. Among the more common characteristics of NLD that are *not* shared with AS are the following:[24]

- On the WISC-III (the widely used Wechsler Intelligence Scale for Children), VIQ is higher than PIQ, but not in all cases—particularly during adolescence. VIQ, or verbal IQ, is a measure of an individual's abilities in terms of expressive and receptive language. PIQ, or performance IQ, is a measure of how an individual uses reasoning to plan and carry out actions. PIQ is determined through performance tests that assess fine- and gross-motor skills and visual-spatial and visual-motor function.*

- Excellent vocabulary
- Rote memory skills
- Exceptional attention to detail, but misses the "big picture"
- Difficulty with reading comprehension beginning in the upper elementary grades, especially for novel material, whether an early reader or a struggling reader
- Physical awkwardness is quite common
- Physical difficulties may be more pronounced on the left side of body
- Fine-motor skills may be impaired; handwriting may be poor and/or laborious
- Significant problems with spatial perception

Hyperlexia

Hyperlexia is marked by a child's precocious ability to decode—recognize and correctly identify and say—words at a level far beyond his years and/or an intense fascination with numbers and letters. Hyperlexic children may later exhibit problems with appropriate socialization skills and an inability to understand verbal language. Some may read extremely well yet be unable to retain or understand what they have read. Hyperlexia is often accompanied by a number of characteristics typical of other learning disorders and particularly AS:

- Selective listening
- Difficulty answering *who*, *what*, *where*, *when*, and *why* questions
- Difficulty learning expressive language
- Echolalia

---

*Beginning with the WISC-IV, published in 2003, there were changes that included substituting VCI (verbal comprehension index) for VIQ and PRI (perceptual reasoning index) for PIQ. A new version, WISC-V, is set for publication in fall 2014. Your child's evaluator should answer any questions you have about the terminology and where these scores fit in terms of identifying nonverbal learning disability.

- Perseverative or stereotypal behavior and rituals, such as rocking, repeating words
- Sensitivity to tactile, auditory, and olfactory stimulation
- Specific and unusual fears
- Difficulty with abstract concepts
- Difficulty initiating and maintaining reciprocal conversation

Central Auditory Processing Disorder (CAPD)

An individual with CAPD has reduced or impaired ability to identify, recognize, discriminate, and understand what he hears. A child with CAPD may be unusually sensitive to typical noises and/or unable to discriminate between foreground and background noise and may respond to each simultaneously. He or she can become emotionally overwhelmed by certain sounds and noisy environments, sometimes resulting in withdrawal or tantrums. Those with CAPD have difficulty following complex sentences and instructions despite having an average or above-average IQ. Children with CAPD often "mishear" words and sounds and will compensate by attempting to "fill in the blanks," sometimes resulting in a complete misunderstanding of what they heard.

THE "LABELING" ISSUE

Confronting the possibility that your child may have a problem is never easy. We reflexively reject the idea of giving a name—be it a diagnosis or even a description—to what we may view as his or her idiosyncrasies, behaviors, disabilities, or problems. On some level, we worry that having a label will render our child less of an individual in the eyes of others, that he or she will be thought of first as a person with a disability and second—if ever—as the person we know and love.

In just considering seeking a definitive diagnosis, we may be understandably reluctant to seek out what we fear may be bad news. In our protective-parent mode, we may deny the behaviors and issues that other family members, friends, and teachers question. Alternately, we may have known all along that the problems were real, and we now have to present this information to family members and friends. These may have been people who have told us that our child's problems were figments of our imaginations, or they themselves may be in denial or grieving the diagnosis. Many parents find the prospect of breaking the news to their child's grandparents particularly difficult and painful.

WHY PARENTS, DOCTORS, AND EDUCATORS MISS THE DIAGNOSIS

Parents who do consult professionals may find themselves on yet another circuitous path, for many reasons. Because we may be ambivalent or anxious about having our child labeled, we may be too easily satisfied with—or, in truth, grateful for—a more palatable, less frightening explanation or diagnosis. Even in the wake of extreme and troubling behaviors, some parents turn first to social workers, educational consultants, and all manner of therapists (including practitioners of alternative treatments, such as homeopaths, nutritionists, chiropractors, and energy healers). The neurologist, psychologist, psychiatrist, or other specialist most qualified to make the diagnosis too often represents the "last resort."

If you are a parent who believes an alternative approach to treatment is best for your child, you should still consider getting a sound medical diagnosis. Receiving a diagnosis from, say, a pediatric neurologist does not obligate you to follow the treatment course this doctor will suggest. Conversely, although the alternative treatment your child receives may prove beneficial to him, the practitioner providing it is probably not trained or qualified to accurately diagnose Asperger syndrome and/or its related comorbid conditions.

Despite a welcome increased awareness among professionals, you may still come across one whose experience with diagnosing is limited. The result can be a diagnosis that correctly identifies one or a few facets of the syndrome but fails to account for the big picture or the interrelationship between different aspects. Some professionals feel that an individual can be diagnosed only if he or she exactly matches the diagnostic criteria. To illustrate this point, let's look at two different doctors and their diagnosis of Johnny at age six.

Dr. A has not seen many children with AS and makes diagnoses strictly by the book. He may see that Johnny presents with severe and pervasive social impairment and an unusual, all-absorbing interest: the history of ancient Rome. However, Johnny is also very talkative, and though his conversational style seems a little bit odd, he forms full sentences, uses pronouns properly, and has an amazing vocabulary for his age. Johnny may also have fairly good gaze moderation. In addition, Johnny has other factors that help explain some of his problems. He is an only child who, because of chronic asthma, did not attend nursery school or preschool (perhaps explaining his social difficulties). As for Johnny's intense interest in ancient Rome, Dr. A finds it precocious and somewhat overwhelming, but he also suspects that Johnny is an overindulged child who is resorting to a familiar topic because he is uncomfortable in the doctor's office. Dr. A regards the one instance of literalism he observes—Johnny looking apprehensive when Dr. A's nurse remarks, "I'm running to lunch now. I'm so hungry I could eat a horse"—as mildly amusing. Dr. A sees nothing unusual in Johnny's motor clumsiness: "After all, not every child can grow up to be an Olympic gymnast," he tells Johnny's mother. "And once he's in school and starts writing and drawing more, he'll pick it right up."

Like almost all pediatricians, Dr. A likes children and appreciates their individuality. Based on what he learned during his training, Dr. A is averse to "alarming parents unnecessarily" and subjecting children to tests and evaluations they may not need. In his many years of practice, he has seen children with similar or even more troubling behaviors who grew up "just fine." He has also seen patients whose behaviors were treated inappropriately with negative results, so he tends to err on the conservative side. At Johnny's mother's behest, he reads the diagnostic criteria for ASD and admits that Johnny's behaviors fit some of them, but he says that he believes that there is enough about Johnny that either does not fit or is not addressed by the criteria that he cannot make a diagnosis. "Johnny is still very young. Let's just wait and see."

Johnny's parents believe in second opinions, so they take him to see Dr. Z.

Dr. Z trained at a major university hospital with a recognized autism center headed by a world-renowned researcher. He now treats a number of children diagnosed with AS and serves as a consultant to several local school districts on cases such as Johnny's. Unlike Dr. A, Dr. Z knows from experience that the wider-ranging diagnostic criteria as presented in DSM-5 do not tell the whole story. Dr. Z is less concerned with the individual symptoms and behaviors Johnny shows than with the overall pattern they form. In contrast to Dr. A, Dr. Z takes into account Johnny's motor clumsiness and literal-mindedness (neither of which is stated in the DSM-5 criteria but are common among people with AS). Unimpressed by Johnny's expressive language skills, Dr. Z sets up toys in his office and engages him in a couple of play activities to test his theory of mind. He asks Johnny to describe what a friend is ("Someone who does everything that I want to do and loves really old history") and what people mean when they say "Hop in the car" or, if he were older, "Kill two birds with one stone." Based on what he sees, Dr. Z makes the diagnosis of ASD and refers Johnny for further neuropsychological testing, which will expose the language and communication deficits behind Johnny's precocious use of language as well as pinpoint the nature and extent of his motor-skill deficiencies.

We all approach the diagnostic process differently. Parents whose children have already been properly diagnosed often feel that Dr. Z is the hero. However, in that twilight time between first suspecting a child has a problem and the final confirmation, some parents might find Dr. Z too aggressive, too willing to pathologize unusual but normal-enough behaviors that Johnny may well grow out of, given more time around other kids, more practice with motor skill tasks, and maturity. Some parents may actually prefer Dr. A to Dr. Z, because he seems more understanding, more accepting of Johnny as he is.

One father told us how thrilled he was when a pediatric neurologist assured him that some "extra help in reading" and "a little OT" (occupational therapy) was all his seven-year-old son needed. Looking back, this dad admits he suspected that there was much more to his boy Luke's problems, but that he was happy to cling to some of the words the doctor used, like *outgrow* and *catch up*. "If the doctor did not give Luke a 'real' diagnosis, how bad a problem could it possibly be?" he recalls telling friends. Today, he sees that doctor as his "Dr. A"—someone who was more optimistic about his son's possible prognosis than he should have been. One thing this dad remembers liking about the doctor was how "positive" he was compared to teachers, therapists, and family members—especially a cousin who phoned one night to tell his wife that she thought Luke "looked really autistic." Looking back now, of course, this dad realizes that his "Dr. A" was seriously uninformed.

In contrast, some other parents—especially those whose kids

show early, precocious intellect, speech, or other abilities—have a different experience. Even when parents openly seek help from friends, family, and professionals, those people may fail to recognize the problem and offer well-meaning suggestions to either "relax," "stop looking for problems," or rethink their approach to discipline.

Even those of us who acknowledge there is a serious problem often hope for another explanation. Sonya, whose child eluded a correct diagnosis, recalls how she subconsciously welcomed teachers and doctors who made comments to the effect that her son's problems all stemmed from her "poor parenting skills." "I don't want to say that I was pleased to hear that, because I wasn't. However, as long as I believed that, it meant that there was nothing really wrong with Stephen," she says. "Knowing that if the fault lay entirely with me, I could change, things could get better."*

Particularly in the early years, some of us may see our child's differences and idiosyncrasies as just that. We treasure our child's individuality; we celebrate the fact that there is no one else in the world exactly like her. We interpret any suggestion that she "should be more like the other kids" as misguided pressure to conform for the sake of conformity. "Whenever someone remarked on Evan's obsession with trains, I remember thinking to myself, *Well, at least he isn't into that violent* Call of Duty *stuff, like some of the other kids*," Marie recalls. "What I didn't understand then was that people weren't really commenting on Evan's preference for trains but the unusual quality of it."

---

*Interestingly, back in the "dark ages" of autism—from the 1950s through the 1980s—so-called experts told mothers that their emotional or psychological problems "caused" their children's autism. Countless mothers submitted to scientifically unsubstantiated treatment—mainly Freudian psychoanalysis—to help them admit to and correct their "flawed" personalities and psyches. This—and giving up their children to institutionalization—they were told, was the only way their children could be saved. Lest anyone think that professionals reserved this approach exclusively for mothers of the most severely impaired, I have met mothers of successful adults with AS who received the same horrifying advice back in the day. See the documentary *Refrigerator Mothers*, directed by David E. Simpson, J. J. Hanley, and Gordon Quinn (2002), Kartemquin Films, at http://www.kartemquin.com. You can also see a trailer of the film at PBS, at http://www.pbs.org/pov.

YES, IT IS ALL IN THE FAMILY

For decades, researchers and other professionals in the field have noted that a child with an ASD often has a parent, grandparent, aunt, uncle, sibling, or cousin who either is diagnosed with an ASD, displays milder versions of some traits, or has a diagnosis of one of the conditions commonly seen with ASD. Given that autism spectrum disorder is considered among the most heritable psychiatric disorders, the presence of this broader autistic phenotype (BAP)— essentially, autistic tendencies that are milder, less numerous, or have less adverse impact on the individual's ability to function than those of autism itself—should surprise no one. (See chapter 1 for a discussion of the genetics of autism.)

If you have read up on AS and started questioning some of your own behaviors or those of other family members, you are not alone. It's not unusual for a parent to be diagnosed as having AS or a related disorder in the wake of a child's diagnosis. Some experts suggest that a parent or other family member having AS traits or AS itself can be a unique source of support and understanding.

You, your spouse, or other relatives may share some of the same characteristics your child has. If your child counts among her relatives a grandfather who is emotionally distant but a brilliant mechanic, a cousin whose single-minded interest in dinosaurs landed him a scholarship and a plum job at a major museum, or an uncle with an odd yet refreshing *Monty Python*–esque take on the world, you may be less likely to be alarmed by similar behaviors in your child, or, for that matter, in yourself or your spouse.

WHEN OTHERS TRY TO DISCOURAGE DIAGNOSIS

On the other side of the table, there are professionals who may be reluctant to press you to pursue a diagnosis, albeit for very different reasons. Teachers, pediatricians, therapists, and others who have had the unenviable task of informing a parent that they believed a child's behavior or development warranted further evaluation may be reticent to broach the subject. They tell of parents who become angry, hostile, and even abusive.

There are professionals in every field who have a very hard time suggesting that anything might be "wrong." I am always surprised when a professional in the field expresses a negative view about special education, diagnosis, medication, or accommodations. I wonder how honest they are with parents when it is time to suggest that one of these things might be appropriate to consider.

Finally, there are professionals who believe sincerely that ASDs are "overdiagnosed" and "overtreated." They might feel confident in their ability to discern which from a group showing "autistic behaviors" are just passing through a phase and which among them should be considered "serious." Again, though, even if there were children being diagnosed or treated "unnecessarily," that's a debate for that professional and his or her colleagues. It should not be a consideration when it comes to any individual child, and certainly not when it comes to *yours*.

WHEN TO SEEK A SPECIALIST

Is this a diagnosis your pediatrician or family doctor should make? It depends. All medical professionals are much more knowledgeable about ASDs generally than they were a decade ago. If you have concerns about your child, resist the temptation to read your child's doctor's seeming lack of concern or her suggestion that you "wait and see" as an all-clear signal. It may not be. A physician may have concerns about a child's behavior or development, but it's hard to press for an evaluation if, for example, a parent insists that everything is going pretty well in kindergarten or that little Jessica is screaming because she just "hates" going to the doctor (as some kids do). Also remember that the doctor's office is a place that many children associate with unpleasant events such as injections and illness. Children with AS, ASDs, and sensory issues may be particularly tense, anxious, upset, prone to tantrums, quiet, loud, or generally misbehaving simply because they're reacting to the smells, sounds, lights, and textures they experience there. In this area, ironically, they may look much like lots of typical children.

If your child's doctor does raise concerns with you—even if you don't consider her "an expert" on autism—take it seriously. Some doctors will press forcefully for an evaluation at the first sign of unusual behavior. However, some doctors see things differently. These doctors may be more comfortable (some would say too comfortable) taking a "wait and see" approach. Others may feel that even some widely accepted conditions such as attention-deficit/hyperactivity disorder (AD/HD) "pathologize" behaviors that they believe should be considered within the broad range of normal childhood development. Others may truly believe that your child will outgrow a sensitivity to being touched or to the smell of vinegar or the touch of chalk. Although this is extremely rare today, another possibility is that your doctor, like Dr. A in the earlier example, simply may not have received adequate training in this particular area.

If you feel that your doctor isn't taking your concerns about your child seriously, press the issue. Insist on a referral for private evaluation, or contact your school district about having your child evaluated (see chapter 6). Change doctors, if necessary. Don't give up.

IN SCHOOL

While it is not always the case that teachers at regular nursery schools, preschools, and private kindergartens have training in special education issues, they do know what typical development should look like. There, teachers routinely deal with children who experience problems with separation anxiety, crying, tantrums, reluctance to share with peers, difficulty following directions, parallel play, and poor socialization skills. Most children will learn to adjust to a group play or early classroom environment, although there are always late bloomers, and any experienced, knowledgeable teacher will make allowances for them. Under these circumstances, many teachers are reluctant to voice their concerns about a particular child's behavior or responses, but if they do so, you should listen.

Today we know that the preschool and early school years are prime time for identifying ASDs and starting appropriate interventions. Ironically, this is also the period in a child's life when he is least likely to be viewed as having a serious neurologically based problem and most likely viewed as "socially immature" or having a "behavior problem." Young children often behave very differently at home, surrounded by parents and family, than they do elsewhere. The fact that day care, preschool, or school is for them a "new environment" makes it easy for everyone, but especially parents, to attribute any problems to that. Parents know that some children arrive at certain developmental milestones later than others, and that sometimes it just takes certain children a little longer to "grow out" of a behavior. There is also the prevailing notion that boys are developmentally and emotionally "behind" in some areas simply because they are boys. You may have seen this with another of your children or perhaps even yourself. It may be difficult to sort out which behaviors warrant further attention.

Children in public school settings have a small advantage in that even if their teachers lack special education training (which at this point, a growing percentage of teachers do have), they have ready access to special education teachers, school psychologists, administrators, consultants, and therapists within their district—and probably even within the school building—who do.

Sometimes the problems teachers raise don't strike parents as serious. One father recalls, "I remember listening to the preschool teacher and thinking to myself, *Is it really such a big deal that he hates to touch finger paints or finds the kiddie music they play during snack time so annoying he has to cover his ears?* I thought she was overreacting." Another mother says, "I knew she couldn't use scissors or write very well at age four, compared to the other kids. But my wife and I talked it over, and we thought of all the things we had done late as kids, and concluded that perhaps this prekindergarten program was a little too goal oriented and competitive for our daughter."

A veteran special educator offered this insight into why teachers may not be totally candid with parents: "For some parents, the very suggestion that their child be evaluated is enough to set off a flurry of unpleasant letters to the teacher, the principal, the superintendent, and the entire board of ed. Sometimes their attitude is 'If you were doing your job teaching, she wouldn't have these problems.' Other times, it's 'Who are you to say that there's something wrong with my child? Look at [name another child in the class] and his behavior.' One parent even said, 'How can you say that? You're not a child development expert.' And my answer to that was, 'You're right. I'm not a child development expert. And that is why I feel that your son should be evaluated by someone who is.'"

WHO PROBABLY SHOULD *NOT* BE MAKING A DIAGNOSIS

Despite their often having had years of experience dealing with ASD, teachers, administrators, consultants, therapists, and most school psychologists *should not* be offering you a diagnosis. For one thing, legally, none of them is qualified to do so. The sole exception would be a licensed psychologist, and many school districts have one or more on staff. Parents should also be aware that just because someone is referred to as a "school psychologist," it does not mean that he or she is a psychologist with a PhD and the licensure, training, and qualifications to diagnose. Many school psychologists hold a master's degree, though some school psychologists hold doctorates. My son was twelve before I realized that not every school psychologist was a "Doctor." When you first meet a school psychologist, simply ask, "Do I call you Dr. or Ms./Mr.?"

Warning Signs of Inadequate Diagnosis

Has your child been adequately evaluated? Are the results obtained and conclusions drawn about your child accurate? Here are some warning flags to watch for as you go through the process:

- *Professional lack of experience with ASDs.* Although this should be unusual these days, you might encounter professionals whose experience with children with ASDs is simply inadequate. An evaluator who fails to ask about your child's social behavior or who dismisses your concerns about stereotypies, noise sensitivity, or literal-mindedness probably will not provide the best assessment.
- *A diagnosis or description of your child that either does not fit or fails to account for certain behaviors and symptoms.* Many of the behaviors and symptoms that accompany ASDs can look like other conditions or disorders. If you believe that those evaluating your child are going off track, point out how you believe your

child's symptoms differ from, say, AD/HD, or how a diagnosis may be a comorbid condition but does not explain other behaviors and deficits. If your evaluator seems to be ignoring the symptoms and behaviors that don't fit the diagnosis he seems to have his heart set on, press him on why he believes those behaviors are inconsequential or should not be considered.

• *An attitude that reveals a lack of understanding of autism spectrum disorders generally.* Consider finding another professional if the one you have indicates that she thinks that behaviors that you know are beyond your child's control are willful ("I know he could do a better job of writing if he just put his mind to it"; "He needs to learn to ignore the noise from outside"), the result of poor parenting ("I guess he's used to getting his way at home"; "She's too old to be sucking her thumb"), or manipulative ("I guess he knows that if he screams long enough, Mom will come running").

• *Stating or indicating that Asperger syndrome or ASD is not a "legitimate" diagnosis any longer or that it is the diagnostic equivalent of "the flavor of the month."* Signs of this include inappropriate editorializing along the lines of "Thirty years ago, we never heard of this. Suddenly everyone seems to have it" or "I guess parents just like this label better than autism." If your evaluator makes these kinds of comments, find another one. True, Asperger syndrome no longer "exists" in the *DSM-5*. But I'm convinced that parents and professionals—not to mention people who received the diagnosis—will not be giving it up anytime soon. Even with an "official" ASD diagnosis, at the very least, you will continue to hear children whose profile fits the bill described in terms of Asperger syndrome.

• *Beating around the bush, pussyfooting, offering prognoses that are either extremely positive or extremely negative, or inability to describe in detail local resources (for example, schools, support, recreation, medical) available to you.* Despite nearly two decades' worth of autism awareness, there are still some who consider any form of ASD a "hopeless" diagnosis. Some will say that they don't believe in labeling children early or that as long as the problems are being addressed, "It doesn't matter what you call them." Others may prefer the "wait and see" approach. Finally, there are those who honestly feel that a child who does not ring every diagnostic criterion bell is better described as having "ASD-like tendencies" or some such nondiagnosis. Let them know that you are counting on them for the correct and direct diagnosis that will spur the appropriate treatment and intervention your child needs *now*.

STARTING THE PROCESS

Finding a professional qualified to give you an accurate diagnosis is easier today than ever before. How extensive a diagnostic evaluation you need depends on a number of things: resources, insurance coverage, and the complexity of your child's presentation. All things being equal, you might wish to consider the following:

A university-affiliated teaching hospital will probably have on staff more doctors specializing in pediatric psychology, neurology, and psychiatry than your local community hospital. Your access to these professionals and institutions may be compromised or restricted by geography, your health insurance coverage (or lack thereof), and other factors. This might be one area where it would be worthwhile to travel for a consultation or pay out of pocket for an evaluation, even if it isn't covered by insurance.

Given how much depends on an accurate diagnosis, try not to think of it simply as another consultation or doctor's appointment but as an investment in your child's future: the cornerstone upon which everything else will be built. Regardless of the diagnosis you receive, you, your spouse, your family, your school district, and the other professionals working with your child will be expending time, resources (financial and otherwise), and energy on your child's behalf. Through it all, probably no one will work harder toward those goals than your child. A good evaluation and diagnosis not only will help you visualize your child's destination, but it also can help you choose the best, safest, and easiest route to get there.

SCHOOL DISTRICT EVALUATIONS

Under the federal Individuals with Disabilities Education Act (IDEA), every school district is required to identify and evaluate every child within its jurisdiction from birth to age twenty-two who is suspected of having a disability. This includes children who are still too young to attend school and those who currently attend charter, private, parochial, or religious schools or are homeschooled. Under IDEA, autism and related disorders are considered disabilities. These evaluations are free of cost to parents, and most doctors, educators, and other professionals who share their initial concerns about your child will suggest you contact your school district.

Some parents are understandably hesitant to approach their school district's special education office. They worry that their child will be "labeled," for example, or that their child's disability will become part of her record or become public knowledge. You may opt to postpone alerting your school district and requesting a district evaluation until after you've had your child assessed privately. However, IDEA requires school districts to provide special education and related services to disabled children. Provision of such education and/or services will be determined by an evaluation that your school district performs. In other words, if you want your child to receive special education and related services, he will undergo a school district evaluation sooner or later anyway.

Initial evaluations should involve a multidisciplinary team and produce independent written reports outlining each evaluator's general impressions of your child, the tests administered, and the resulting scores. These reports will also include information on the child's behavior and demeanor during the evaluation and some general concluding remarks. You have a right to read and receive copies of all evaluations and to correct any factual errors that you find.

Parents are sometimes surprised to learn that these evaluations do not offer medical diagnoses or always outline specific recommendations. An evaluation may conclude with a recommendation that "occupational therapy is indicated," but it will not say, "Sally should have four half-hour sessions of occupational therapy with Mrs. Smith." School district evaluations are obviously limited in making determinations about a child's neurological and psychiatric issues, and they cannot produce an official medical diagnosis. Some school districts hire outside practitioners, special education schools, or other agencies to conduct their evaluations; other school districts have the evaluations done by school or staff psychologists, special education teachers, and therapists in speech, occupational therapy, physical therapy, and so on, as needed.

School districts differ on their policies, and state special education laws also vary. Your location may necessarily limit your options in terms of where your child can be evaluated initially at school district expense.

WHERE TO START

Ask the doctor, teacher, or school district administrator who is recommending that your child be evaluated for a referral to a specialist. Note their suggestions, but be prepared to research other possible candidates. Unless you're told that the person being recommended to you specializes in ASD, keep looking. This is especially important if you believe that, beyond the core ASD symptoms, your child also has problems that suggest other disorders or learning disabilities.

For many families, the issue of insurance coverage is a major factor as well. If you live in a state where health insurance companies are required to cover medical expenses for ASDs, you may be limited in terms of the practitioners you may choose from. Insurance laws do vary from state to state, however. For the information you need, contact your health insurance company, your state office of insurance, and local autism advocacy and support organizations.

When you receive a recommendation, ask the following questions:

- Why do you feel this is the best person to evaluate my child?
- How long have you been referring patients/students to this person?
- Can you tell me what you know about this person's qualifications or expertise in ASD?

Don't be entirely surprised if you find out that the person making the recommendation knows little about the professional he or she is recommending. Some doctors and school district personnel use one or a few evaluators because that's simply how they do things or there are few alternatives in your area. Your doctor may limit referrals to those professionals who participate in your health insurance plan. Your school district administrator may be obligated to provide you a list of possible evaluators but be prohibited from steering you away from those who do substandard evaluations or have less experience. If you feel confident that the professional being recommended to you is the right person, your search can end. However, even with a glowing recommendation in hand, you may still wish to seek out other options or learn more about the professional you have already decided to use. It's time to broaden the search.

Chances are, there are other parents in your county, your town, your school district, and perhaps even your own neighborhood who have a child with AS or a related disorder. Other parents are a great resource, because they've been where you are right now. Most people you will contact through disability-related support organizations, Special Education PTA (SEPTA) or a parent-teacher association, and online resources are parents of a child with a disability as well. These parents and groups can provide useful information on the different practitioners, institutions, and resources in your area. Further, they may be more forthcoming and candid than professionals in their assessments of possible evaluators.

WHOM TO SEE, WHERE TO GO

Psychologist, psychiatrist, neurologist, neuropsychologist, developmental (or developmental-behavioral) pediatrician, pediatric psychologist, pediatric psychiatrist, pediatric neurologist, pediatrician, family doctor—what they all have in common is that they are all, theoretically, qualified to diagnose ASD. Here are the players.

Pediatrician or general family practitioner. A pediatrician is an MD who specializes in the care of children from infancy through the teen years. Most pediatricians are general practitioners. In most cases, a pediatrician refers to other specialists patients who have or are suspected of having more serious or chronic problems. Pediatricians are experts in normal child development, and most do some developmental screening in the course of regular care. Ask other parents you know for recommendations; you may indeed find a specialist.

Pediatricians can prescribe psychoactive medication, but treating ASD-related symptoms can involve new medications, some of which may not be FDA-approved for pediatric use and/or may have potentially serious side effects. (For more on prescription psychotropic medications, see chapter 5.) Unless your pediatrician specializes in treating children with ASD, you might consider consulting a neurologist, psychiatrist, or other medical specialist when it comes to medication decisions.

Developmental or developmental–behavioral pediatrician. According to the American Academy of Pediatrics, a developmental-behavioral pediatrician has completed four years of medical school and three years of residency training in pediatrics, holds board certification in pediatrics, and has additional subspecialty training in developmental–behavioral pediatrics. The certification examination was first introduced in 2002. If you've never heard of this relatively new subspecialty, you're not alone. There are fewer than three hundred certified developmental-behavioral pediatricians in the United States.[25] While there are probably thousands of pediatricians with extensive experience and knowledge about ASDs, their training is not exactly the same. Odds are good that a developmental-behavioral pediatrician will be more familiar with different forms of therapy, intervention, and special education options.

Neurologist, pediatric neurologist. Neurology is the medical science devoted to the study and treatment of the nervous system (which includes the brain). Pediatric neurologists are neurologists who specialize in children. Neurology is a physical science in the sense that it is concerned with the actual "hardware" of the brain as opposed to behavioral issues and interventions. Among the specialists listed here, neurologists are the most qualified to evaluate problems involving motor skills, balance, vision, speech, cognition, and adaptive behavior, among others. They are trained in diagnostic technology, such as electroencephalography (EEG), computer-assisted tomography (CAT scan), and magnetic resonance imaging

(MRI), to name a few tools that are not yet routinely used in ASD evaluation but might be indicated to rule out other possible problems (such as seizures or tumors). A neuropsychological evaluation (or *neuropsych*, for short) can combine standardized assessment with psychological screening and diagnostic medical testing to create a multidisciplinary profile. Because only a complete neuropsychological workup can identify underlying and complicating problems (for example, seizure disorder, dyslexia, problems with motor skills, congenital neurological problems), it's considered the gold standard of diagnostic testing.

Psychologist, pediatric psychologist, neuropsychologist, pediatric neuropsychologist. In most states, a psychologist holds a doctorate in psychology or a related field. Pediatric psychologists specialize in children. Neuropsychologists focus on the relationship between the brain and behavior. Unlike psychiatrists and neurologists, psychologists and neuropsychologists are not MDs. They aren't trained to administer or interpret diagnostic medical tests, nor can they write prescriptions. Some psychologists do make recommendations regarding medication and may work with a consulting psychiatrist or physician who actually writes the prescription and monitors the child periodically. Psychologists can see children for ongoing psychological therapy and provide guidance in helping children cope with emotional issues and, in some cases, socialization skills. They can also perform psychological evaluations and administer standard assessments. Such evaluations can be very useful, and school districts commonly refer children to psychologists and pediatric psychologists. However, a purely psychological or educational evaluation may not capture the full diagnostic "picture" or identify or rule out physical neurological issues. Neuropsychologists, because of their extensive training in noninvasive means of determining neurological function, may be preferred. A neuropsychologist may perform a neuropsychological evaluation and refer the child to a neurologist if medical testing (e.g., MRI, EEG) is indicated.

Psychiatrist, pediatric psychiatrist. A psychiatrist is an MD who specializes in emotional and psychiatric disorders and mental health. A pediatric psychiatrist specializes in children. Perhaps to a greater extent than any other specialty, psychiatrists combine an understanding of the biology and the psychology behind thinking and behavior. Psychiatrists can order and interpret medical diagnostic tests and write prescriptions.

Psychotherapist, therapist, social worker, mental health counselor, family therapist, etc. These professionals all hold a graduate degree in the mental health field. Because licensing requirements vary widely from state to state, it is difficult to make a general statement about their qualifications. However, in most cases, any of these professionals can see private clients and offer counseling in much the same way that a psychologist would. They cannot order or interpret medical tests, nor can they write prescriptions. If you are considering having your child evaluated by someone in these professions, you should find out precisely what training he or she has received in conducting evaluations. Their ability to assess psychiatric and physical disorders is extremely limited. Our recommendation: see an MD or a clinical psychologist for a diagnosis.

BEFORE THE EVALUATION

It's not easy to have your child evaluated. The first, natural impulse is to do all you can to make your child look, perform, and behave as well as possible. However, there is no way to "prepare" your child for this type of testing beyond making sure that he is well rested and comfortable.

Prior to an evaluation, you may be asked to fill out forms—probably many of them—on your child's medical, developmental, and educational history. Before you complete the process, you might feel like you have answered the same question two or three times—and you probably have. It's simply part of the process. You may also be asked to complete a standard assessment questionnaire designed to elicit information on your child's behavior and development. There may be additional copies enclosed, with instructions that one be completed by your spouse and, possibly, your child's current teacher. If you and your spouse are each asked to complete separate questionnaires, do so independently, without consulting each other until you're finished. You will probably want to "compare notes" once you're done, but resist the temptation to change your answers later. Even a seeming discrepancy in your answers—say, you answered that your son's tantrums were "often violent" and your husband qualified them as "sometimes violent"—can provide useful information for an evaluator.

Your child's developmental history is important to any diagnosis. Be prepared to consult your child's baby book and perhaps your home video collection and family photographs for accurate information on developmental milestones and other behaviors. Another critical source is your child's pediatrician, who will have kept a full, contemporaneous record of your child's developmental progress, screening results, illnesses, and disorders. This is an excellent opportunity to request a copy of your child's entire file from her pediatrician. A letter or written report from your child's pediatrician is also useful. If you aren't specifically requested to provide one, consider asking your pediatrician for it anyway. Any input from other professionals who know or have worked with your child, including teachers, should be welcomed by the person or team who will conduct the evaluation.

Although you may not be asked to provide it, consider also getting letters about your child from previous teachers, if possible. Expect your evaluator to ask teachers to fill out some forms, too. Especially if your child is older, such retrospective reports from teachers or caregivers over time can give the evaluator a more detailed and perhaps more objective picture of your child's development.

You may also want to write a letter—with salient points bold-faced for easy reference—outlining your child's history and the progress of his problems as you have seen them. Unfortunately, the evaluation process is focused on identifying what is "wrong," but you can write about the positive aspects as well. Write briefly about your child's interests, successful social interactions, what he enjoys doing, his general temperament, and his personality. You may want to include a photo in the file. If your child is currently in school (including nursery school or preschool), collect in a three-ring binder copies of written work, drawings (particularly if your child seems to have motor skills issues), a list of books he's reading (if applicable), any behavior intervention plans (BIPs) or functional behavior assessments (FBAs) created by your child's school, and anything else you believe will be helpful.

You might be thinking that in the best of all worlds, evaluators would avail themselves of the opportunity to observe each child in her home and in her school or day care environment. However, the professionals conducting the evaluation are experienced. They know that their office environment is different from home or school. They depend on parents and teachers to give an accurate description of the child in their respective environments. In some instances, an evaluator might suggest that a visit to see the child in school or at home is warranted. However, in most cases, this will add substantially to the cost of the evaluation and probably is not necessary.

CONFIDENTIALITY CONCERNS

Regardless of where your child is evaluated, your child's and your family's confidentiality should be protected at all times. Under the Health Information Portability and Accountability Act (HIPAA), which applies to health care settings, and the Family Educational Rights and Privacy Act (FERPA), which applies to schools, no one can release personal information about you or your child without obtaining your written permission or notifying you first. Any communication between people at your child's school and your child's doctor or the evaluation team requires your written consent in advance.

During the evaluation process, you may be asked questions that are quite personal regarding the family history of emotional or psychiatric problems, learning disabilities, alcoholism, substance abuse, suicide, arrests and/or convictions, and so on. In most cases, these questions will concern not only you, your spouse, and your child's siblings but also aunts, uncles, cousins, and grandparents on both sides of the family. Legally, this information must be kept confidential. However, for various reasons, you may not feel comfortable revealing personal information, particularly concerning other family members' personal lives. If that is the case, or if you fear someone's reputation, employment, or insurance status may be compromised or threatened by such revelations, don't answer those questions in writing. When you meet with the evaluator, explain your concerns and be prepared to let the evaluator know orally, without giving names, if there is a history of learning disability, autism, Asperger syndrome, autism spectrum disorders, Tourette's syndrome, epilepsy or seizure, depression, anxiety disorder, obsessive disorder, compulsive disorder, obsessive-compulsive disorder, violence, alcoholism, drug abuse, or some conduct disorder.

Some parents feel more comfortable sharing this information with a private practitioner than with a school district evaluation team. One mother we know explained to a pediatric neurologist her family's history of alcoholism, depression, and violence, and that one of the child's uncles had an extensive juvenile criminal record. Having recently moved to a small community, she was concerned that this information was prejudicial, especially in light of her son's sometimes violent tantrums. In his written report to the school district, the neurologist merely acknowledged that "family history may be a factor" without offering any further detail.

PREPARING YOUR CHILD FOR THE EVALUATION

Realistically, there is no way to "prep" for this in the sense that there is anything you can do to improve your child's "scores." What is being evaluated is not so much what your child knows as how your child responds. Ideally, for everyone, your child will enter the evaluation being himself or herself. In terms of your receiving an accurate diagnosis and truly useful set of recommendations, there is nothing to be "gained" by your child being "perfect," even if that were possible.

Your child's evaluation may be conducted in a quiet room at his current school by a special education teacher or school psychologist in just an hour or two. Or it may involve several days of tests at the pediatric or child development or neurology department of a local hospital or university medical center. Your child may be diagnosed on the basis of parent and teacher questionnaires, extensive interviews with you and your spouse, and a few play-therapy sessions. Or your child may be observed at home and/or in school in addition to being tested. How the evaluation is conducted depends on many factors: who is doing it, where it will be done, and, most important, your child. Some children can be diagnosed after just a visit and a few brief assessments. Others might require a longer, more involved process. There is no "one" way, and no way is "better" than any other. It's simply a matter of what will be the most productive approach for your child's situation.

Whatever the circumstances, there are ways you can help your child and yourself to feel more comfortable.

- Double-check your appointment and confirm. When you do, ask about payment policies, insurance issues, and anything else you need to know in terms of payment.
- Ask if it is necessary to bring another adult with you. Sometimes the person conducting the evaluation needs to speak to the parent without the child present.
- If your child will have breaks during the appointment, ask what kinds of games and toys are available. Is there a place to take a short walk outside? Is there a snack machine? A snack bar or coffee shop nearby? Find out if your child will be allowed to bring water, juice, or a snack with him, if you think he may need it.
- Can your child bring games and toys from home? Are there any types that might be discouraged? While some kids love having electronics with them, it can be difficult for some to transition from playing a video game to going in to the evaluation room. Consider honestly whether the distraction will prove too much.
- Get clear directions and make a "test run" days before the first appointment to be sure you know where you'll be going. Find out where you should park.
- If you think it may help your child, arrange for him to visit the testing site ahead of time and, if possible, meet the person or people who will administer the tests.
- Find out beforehand how long each session will run, what kinds of materials your child will be asked to work with (blocks, patterns, puppets, dolls, board games, beads), and what he may be asked to do (hop, tell a story, listen to a story

or to a tape and then answer questions about it, remember words, count, read, build, and so on).

- If possible, find out the sequence of the tasks your child will be asked to perform and where the testing will occur. Your goal is not to "prepare" your child for the test; that is impossible. But you will circumvent much of your child's anxiety by being able to say, "First, you and Dr. M will work with blocks, and then she will ask you to listen to a short story . . ." If you're not sure what will happen, say so, but add, "These people are really nice, and they will show you lots of cool new things and ask you to play with them, or hear some nice stories." If your child is old enough to associate the terms *test* and *evaluation* with tests given in schools, be sure to explain that these are different because there are no right or wrong answers. You might explain that the person who gives these tests is really trying to "see how you do things in your own way."

- Find out where you'll be during the tests. In the same room? In an adjoining room watching through a one-way mirror? In the waiting room?

- Discuss with the evaluator beforehand what will occur if your child asks for you, panics, or has a tantrum. Be sure that the person conducting the evaluation understands your child's warning signs for extreme distress or meltdown. Be aware that people who conduct these evaluations have seen every behavior under the sun more than a few times.

- While you can request that your child be allowed to see you if he asks, this might not have the calming effect you expect. For one thing, having the evaluator actually witness a difficult moment can provide helpful information. Some tasks that your child is asked to perform during an evaluation are designed to identify the point at which frustration sets in. Interfering with this process by "rescuing" your child is counterproductive.

- Another possible problem is that once you appear because your child is upset, this might become a pattern. The evaluator might opt to discontinue for the day and have you reschedule if it becomes so disruptive that he feels that he cannot get an accurate measure of what's going on.

- If at all possible, schedule the testing for when your child will be fresh, well rested, and not hungry. (An exception would be certain medical tests, such as an EEG, for which your child may need to be sleep deprived.)
- For most children, morning works best. You know your child's limitations. If you know that he won't tolerate a three-hour testing session, request that it be broken into two sessions. Also be aware that even if your child is not especially stressed or exhausted by the testing (for most, it's actually fun), it's a novel situation. Consider keeping your child home for the rest of the school day or going for a special outing or treat afterward, especially if there will be further testing and he emerges from the first round a less-than-happy camper.
- Make the evaluator aware—orally and in writing—of anything that might affect your child's performance: medications (including over-the-counter products such as antihistamines, cough syrup, and, of course, prescription medication), recent or current illnesses (cold, flu, tummy-ache, etc.), chronic health problems such as asthma, or any changes in sleep schedule.
- Make the evaluator aware—orally and in writing—of your child's sensory issues: problems with noise in general, particular sounds, fluorescent lighting, or particular smells, textures, or types of environments. If your child is fascinated by or obsessed with Legos, coins, crayons; is repulsed by the texture of clay or the smell of Play-Doh or felt-tip markers; or gets panicky in large, uncarpeted, "echoey" rooms, let your evaluator know.

Plan to give yourself and your child plenty of time to arrive on the day of the evaluation with some time to spare. As anxious as you might feel, try to exude an air of casual confidence and be loving and attentive toward your child. Answer all of his questions, no matter how many times he asks. If it will short-circuit a brewing tantrum, give in to his needs, if the issue isn't a serious one. On the other hand, if your child wakes up not feeling well or having had a bad night with little or no rest, consider canceling for that day and rescheduling.

WHAT TYPES OF ASSESSMENTS WILL BE GIVEN?

There is no single standardized test for AS, though a number of scales are available for helping determine whether a person might have ASD. One of the most frequently used is the ADOS (Autism Diagnostic Observation Schedule), but there are others.

Even if there were a single test for AS, anyone suspected of having AS would still require further evaluation for common problems such as learning disabilities, graphomotor problems (having to do with the physical act of writing), processing deficits, and psychological issues, to name only a few of the possibilities. A thorough evaluation will explore every area of concern, either through directly testing or by reviewing the results of other professionals' evaluations and/or their reports and comments. For example, your evaluator will probably consult your child's speech pathologist's report rather than conduct a new speech test. The publishers of standardized assessment instruments are constantly releasing new instruments and revising those currently available. It would be impossible to list every single test that might be administered to your child. Further, different evaluators have their own preferences, based on their experience, the history and validity of the instrument, and their professional background. Your occupational therapist will not be giving the IQ test, for example. However, the tests administered should address the areas listed here. We also list a few examples of each type of test. These are not necessarily the only tests of this type, nor are they necessarily the most appropriate tests for your child. That determination will be made by your evaluator(s). Also note that most of the test examples listed are designed for school-age learners.

In assessing your child, evaluators will probably focus on these main areas:

Intelligence: an assessment of your child's ability to learn and to behave adaptively, or in response to situations of daily living. The best and most widely used intelligence tests assess and measure a wide range of abilities and deficits. Contrary to popular misconception, IQ is not necessarily a measure of "how smart" someone is, though it is reasonable to assume that someone with a normal IQ of 100 probably learns more easily and is better able to apply what he learns than does someone with an IQ of 80. It is helpful to view IQ testing and the resulting scores as an indication of a person's ability to learn, and learning requires skills in perception, memory, recall, organization, and generally making sense of what one experiences. So a good IQ test assesses and measures "social judgment, level of thinking, language skills, perceptual organization, processing speed, spatial abilities, common sense, long- and short-term memory, abstract thinking, motor speed, and word knowledge."[26] In addition, most comprehensive IQ tests generate scores in subsets, which are usually divided between those that assess verbal skills and those that assess nonverbal skills. Some subtests for verbal skills in the Wechsler test, for example, include arithmetic and vocabulary; for performance (or nonverbal skills), some examples include picture completion and geometric design.

Some of the most widely used IQ tests include the Wechsler Intelligence Scale (WISC; there are special tests designed for specific age groups), Stanford-Binet Intelligence Scales, 5th Edition (SBS-5), Kaufman Assessment Battery for Children, 2nd Edition (KABC II), and Kaufman Brief Intelligence Test, 2nd Edition (KBIT-2).

Academic achievement: an assessment of your child's academic progress, or what he has learned, skills he has acquired. Academic achievement tests can be designed to assess specific skills or areas (such as those listed here), or they can cover several academic areas.

- Reading skills: Gray Oral Reading Test, 5th Edition (GORT-5), Slosson Oral Reading Test—Revised 3 (SORT-R3), Woodcock Reading Mastery Test, 3rd Edition (WRMT-III), Test of Reading Comprehension, 4th Edition (TORC-4)
- Math skills: Stanford Diagnostic Mathematics Test 4 Screening Test (SDMT-4), Test of Early Mathematics Ability, 3rd Edition (TEMA-3)
- Written language skills: Test of Early Written Language, 3rd Edition (TEWL-3), Written Expression Scale (WES), Test of Written Expression (TOWE), Writing Process Test (WPT)
- Spelling: Test of Written Spelling, 5th Edition (TWS-5)
- Comprehensive achievement tests, which assess several

areas of academic achievement at once: Test of Academic Achievement Skills—Revised (TAAS-R)

Behavior/psychological: an assessment of your child's behavior. Hundreds of tests are available, but among those that are commonly used for individuals on the autism spectrum is the Vineland Adaptive Behavior Scales (VABS), which many experts in the field consider a required assessment. Depending on your child, she may also be evaluated for possible comorbid conditions. For example, the Conners Parent and Teacher Rating Scales is a popular instrument used to screen for AD/HD. Your child may also be asked to draw pictures, tell a story, or play with toys, dolls, or puppets.

Perceptual abilities: an assessment of your child's visual and auditory perception. There are dozens of tests in this category.

Speech and language: an assessment of your child's ability to physically create the sounds of language (speech) and to use language (verbal, nonverbal, written) effectively. Some of the more common tests include the Peabody Picture Vocabulary Test, 4th Edition (PPVT-4), Test for Auditory Comprehension of Language, 3rd Edition (TACL-3), and Goldman-Fristoe Test of Articulation, 2nd Edition (GFTA-2).

Other Areas That May Be Assessed

Even if there is no "apparent" reason to suspect a problem in a particular area, IDEA requires that your child's evaluation address not only obvious areas of concern but "all areas of suspected disability." So, for example, a child who appears to have normal expressive language should still be evaluated for speech and language.

THE RESULTS: WHAT DO THEY MEAN?

Several weeks may elapse between the completion of the evaluation and when you receive the results. You should receive a written, detailed report. Ideally, you should also have an appointment to speak with someone who took part in the evaluation. Ask to see a draft of the final report before it is submitted to your child's school district, if you choose to share it with the district or if the district is paying for the evaluation. If your child was evaluated by a team, there should be written reports from each evaluator and, in some cases, a general summary of all the reports as well. The reports should include the following:

- A general narrative of your child's history, including date of birth, complications of pregnancy or delivery, major illnesses, developmental history, relevant family history, current behaviors, and issues that prompted the evaluation.
- A narrative description of your child according to the evaluators' observations during the evaluation. Don't be offended if your child is described as "uncooperative" or "inattentive." That type of information will help those who read the evaluation to put the child's performance into context. That may be important if, for example, there is a substantial difference between your child's performance during a session in which he seemed tired and cranky and another session in which he seemed relatively content and cooperative.
- A list of all medical tests run and standard assessment instruments used (including information on which parts or subtests were used), the scores (both raw scores and percentiles), and, if appropriate, some narrative description of anything remarkable in your child's behavior during those tests. For example, an evaluator may note, "Danny performed well for the first half of the block design test, but once his concentration was broken by the appearance of a bird on the windowsill, his performance on this test diminished markedly." Interpreting the numerical scores of standardized assessments can be confusing. Ask the

evaluator to explain what the numbers mean in terms of your child.

- A narrative conclusion that gives the evaluator's overall impression of the child and further interprets the test scores. This is important, because when it comes to ASD, it is not simply symptoms, behaviors, strengths, and deficits that matter individually but their pattern. So, for example, an evaluator might note that the discrepancy found between scores on the verbal index and the perceptual index of an IQ test is "seen commonly with Asperger syndrome."

- A diagnosis, depending on circumstances. If your evaluation was done by your school district or by a professional or facility paid by your school district, you may not receive a medical diagnosis. If your evaluation was conducted by someone who could make a diagnosis, that may be included in the report.

- Recommendations for appropriate intervention. How specific these recommendations will be depends on several factors, including who conducts the evaluation and how familiar she is with special education and related services in your area. Some professionals who conduct evaluations write their reports with the understanding that they will be used primarily by educators to craft an IEP, Section 504 accommodation plan, or other education plan. (See chapter 6 for further discussion.) This type of report is often very detailed in terms of its recommendations. Others produce reports that are less specific and, frankly, not as useful to you as a parent in procuring services for your child. If you receive such a report and feel that it offers you little specific guidance, consider seeking a second opinion and/or hiring an educational consultant experienced in ASD to review the test results and make more concrete suggestions for intervention and therapy.

WHAT DO THE SCORES TELL YOU?

By the time most of us reach the formal assessment stage, we may feel we've been defending, explaining, and making sense of our kid for some time. So it can be unsettling to encounter the terminology, if not the very premise, behind the standardized assessments and the scores they yield. You would not be a parent if you could read terms such as *clinically significant, at risk, low average,* or *significant delay* about your child without your heart sinking. Perhaps understanding something about where the tests and the terms come from will help.

Standardized tests are the tests evaluators use because they have been shown to be *valid* (meaning they measure what they claim to) and *reliable* (meaning that similar test takers with similar levels of skills and deficits will come within reasonable range of the same score, regardless of other factors). These are vastly oversimplified explanations, but essentially all most parents need to know. The most important aspect of standardized tests is that they have gone through a process called *norming*. Prior to publication (and, ideally, periodically through the years to come), a standardized test is given to a carefully chosen group of individuals like those for whom the test has been designed. If the norm group is well chosen, their scores when distributed should reflect a *normal curve*, or *bell curve*. As a parent, it's important to understand that standardized test scores and the descriptive terms that explain them are neither arbitrary nor based on the opinions of the test's author or your evaluator. They don't tell you how your child scored on a particular test or subtest—that would be the *raw score*, which in and of itself tells a parent little—but how your child scored when compared with the test's norm group and, by extension, with other children of similar age, grade level, or (in some cases) disability.

Let's look at a standardized assessment most of us know: the IQ test. The normal distribution of scores for a test such as the commonly given WISC places the *mean score* (the average score, or the total of all scores divided by the total number of scores) at 100. In other words, if 5,000 children took this test, and we added all of the scores, then divided the sum by 5,000, the result would be 100. It's important to understand that this doesn't mean that most of those children obtained a score of 100; in fact, it's possible that none of them did. Another important (but very complicated) statistical concept is the *standard deviation*. The standard deviation results from a sophisticated mathematical formula and tells us how the scores are spread across the normal curve. Standard deviations are important for another reason: some states and school districts may dictate "cut-offs" for eligibility based on standard deviation scores.

For instance, IQ scores are distributed as follows:

Scores	Standard Deviation	Percentage of Scores in Range
56–70	−2 SD	2.14
71–85	−1 SD	13.59
86–100	0 SD	34.13
101–115	0 SD	34.13
116–130	+1 SD	13.59
131–145	+2 SD	2.14
≥146	+3 SD	0.13

These are the numbers that if plotted on a graph would form the familiar "bell curve," with the majority of scores clustered at the high middle of the "hump" and progressively fewer scores at each point moving away from the center toward the side edges. As you can see, most IQ scores—68.26 percent—fall within 86 to 115 points. Within that range is the normal IQ of 100 and what some may refer to as "high normal" (above 100) or "low normal" (below 100). Meanwhile, less than 1 percent of scores fall at or below 55 (severely mentally retarded) or above 146 (gifted). Another way to read scores such as these would be that an individual with a score of 146 or greater on this test scored higher than 99.87 percent of other test takers, or, conversely in the case of a score at or below 55, that 99.87 percent of test takers had higher scores than 55.

It is very common for parents to see test scores described in terms of percentile rank score. A percentile score does not tell you explicitly how your child "scored" (again, with most standardized assessments, that information is not very useful). What it does tell you is in which percentile of the population for this test your child's test score places him. So if you are told that your child's score places him in the 70th percentile, that means he performed as well as or better than 70 percent of the test takers, and about 30 percent of test takers scored higher. Percentile ranks between the 25th percentile and 75th percentile fall within the average range.

If your test results are given in standard scores, it gets a little confusing, because the average, or mean, is 100. A standard score of 70 would be at the 2nd percentile, and a score of 130 would be at the 98th percentile.

There is a lot more to tests than this. Always ask your evaluator to explain what the scores mean. For essential reading on understanding test scores, go to Wrightslaw at www.wrightslaw.com and "Measuring Progress—Tests and Measurements for the Parent, Teacher, Advocate and Attorney," at www.wrightslaw.com/advoc/articles/tests_measurements.html.

WHEN THE DIAGNOSIS IS NOT CLEAR

Sometimes, especially when children are young or when their cases seem unusually complex, the results of the evaluation and the diagnosis may be less than definitive. You may be told that your child has "autistic-like behavior," "possible Asperger syndrome," or any of several other terms. You might also learn that your child has been found to have a diagnosis or condition you did not expect and maybe never even heard of.

TAKING IT ALL IN

After you've had time to read and consider the report, make time to discuss your response and your questions with the person who wrote it. Don't be afraid to ask questions about terms you are unfamiliar with (and there may be many) and, even more important, what they mean for your child in "real-life" terms. Ask your professional to do the following:

- Explain what the skills or deficits indicate (neurological, psychological, emotional, or physical problems).
- Describe possible treatments and interventions.

- Discuss the implications of any given skill, deficit, or diagnosis in terms of possible impact now, in the near future, and in the distant future.
- Explain how possible treatments and interventions work and give you some idea which are more effective.
- Help you begin prioritizing skills to develop, deficits to address, and behaviors and other issues that may need attention.
- Offer a list of local and national resources, as well as the names of at least a few local professionals, organizations, schools, and other agencies or groups that might be helpful.

If your child has received a diagnosis, ask questions about that, too. You might want to know how the diagnosis was reached and what was first ruled out (and why). If, for example, your child's behavior is suggestive of an attention deficit, ask the evaluator to explain what results led her to conclude that attention deficit is not an issue. You may discover that despite all the testing, there remain some open questions about your child. Find out what they are and ask questions until you are satisfied that you understand why, for example, the evaluator thinks that your early, precocious reader is hyperlexic (see page 77) and has low comprehension, or what evidence led to the conclusion that your child may also have a comorbid condition, such as obsessive-compulsive disorder (see page 66).

WHEN THE DIAGNOSIS COMES LATE

If your child wasn't diagnosed until his teens or later, you may feel you've lost so much time that it's too late to help. We would like to stress what we feel is one of the most important messages of this book: it is never too late for a child or parent to seek assistance. Generally, most people who are diagnosed in their teens or later feel that finding out about their AS was, overall, a positive thing.

Even if years have passed in which your child's AS behaviors were incorrectly viewed as discipline problems or something else, you, teachers, friends, and, most important, your child himself can benefit from understanding and intervention. For example, we know of one social worker who runs social skills groups for people with AS well into their fifties and beyond.

If your child has been diagnosed at an older age, you may be more inclined to see behaviors and attitudes as "set" or inextricable from "who he really is." We urge you to try viewing it in a different light. What you see today may be "who he is," but it is who he is without intervention, support, awareness of more effective strategies, and help. Although we cannot possibly change everything about a person with AS, nor would we wish to do so, some of the changes that can occur have the power to make a world of difference in that person's future well-being and happiness. For many older adolescents and adults, the relief of finally knowing that there is an explanation for what they have felt and experienced is welcome.

SHARING THE DIAGNOSIS WITH OTHERS

Once you know your child has AS, you confront the question of whom to tell, when to tell, and what to say. There are no hard-and-fast rules here. While some choices may be obvious (grandparents, mature siblings, teachers, doctors, close family friends), others fall into a surprisingly wide gray area. Even if you feel strongly about being open and honest about your child's diagnosis, you must be realistic, too. Not everyone you think should know will use the information the way you would hope. Some people—including family members and close friends—may be insensitive or unable to fully understand the implications of ASD. One basic rule of thumb might be to consider educating anyone whose misunderstanding could cause your child embarrassment or stress. One mother told people about her son's AS only when she felt that *her son* would benefit from their knowing.

There are pros and cons to any approach. We strongly urge you to consider your child first, as an individual whose right to privacy should outweigh any compulsion on your part to "enlighten" the world at large. Particularly in this day of instant communication and social media, information that several years ago would stay among friends now has the potential to travel the world. If your child is old enough to have an opinion in this matter, it should be heeded. Obviously, with younger children, the matter is entirely up to your discretion. Remember, though, that kids do grow up. Five years from now, will your child feel comfortable knowing that the next-door neighbor you barely speak to or the dry cleaner knows she has ASD? While your child's grandparents will probably be eager to learn all about the diagnosis, the mother of the kid next door probably does not need to know much beyond the fact that your child may experience certain difficulties in play situations.

What to Say . . . or Not

First things first: You do not have to tell anyone about your child's diagnosis if you do not want to. An ASD diagnosis is a personal piece of health information about your child that is private and that is protected by law.

That said, when you least expect it, you may find yourself feeling the need to explain your child's behavior. First, decide if you really need to. If you decide it's the best idea at the moment, keep it brief and relevant to what's happening at the moment. If your child is having a tantrum in a restaurant, for instance, there simply isn't time to get into a detailed explanation. You can always choose to say nothing. You might say something like this:

"My son has a neurological disorder that sometimes makes it impossible for him to control his behavior. It's kind of like what happens when an older person suffers a stroke or Alzheimer's disease and it becomes difficult to respond appropriately to stressful or confusing situations. Right now I'm helping him by removing him from this situation [or hugging him or letting him pace for a few minutes or whatever it is you are doing]. He'll be all right in a few minutes. Thanks for your concern."

Other families have printed up business cards to hand to strangers that read, "Thank you for your concern. My child has been diagnosed with Asperger syndrome, a neurological disorder. For more information on Asperger syndrome, [list a reliable, accurate web resource such as NIH, NIMH, or Autism Speaks]."

We could all use more support, but your aim in telling others should be to increase understanding of your child, not pity for him or for you. If your words or manner reveal that you are anxious, embarrassed, ashamed, or upset about the diagnosis or your child's behavior, listeners will view AS and your child as things to feel anxious, embarrassed, ashamed, or upset about. If you can talk about AS and your child in a relaxed, confident, matter-of-fact way, you will be telling others that AS is nothing to be afraid of. Through your words and your actions, let people know that your child is a person beyond his diagnosis. Limit the amount of information you offer to what's relevant to the situation at hand and always consider your audience. Have your little "spiel" always at the ready. But, again, remember that you always have the right to remain silent, too. It is not your responsibility to enlighten everyone. In fact, you might encounter people you would rather not share the news with. Think of your—and especially your child's—privacy.

Parents often ask whether it is a good idea to tell classmates and friends about a child's AS. There are compelling arguments supporting either decision. Those who are for informing peers take the position that understanding encourages tolerance and acceptance. One expert told us a heartwarming story about a class of elementary school students who took a substitute teacher to task for not understanding the behavior of their classmate with AS. Even though every student may not become more supportive, and you do run the risk that teasing may actually increase, we have heard from many parents whose experience was positive.

The argument against informing a group of classmates or peers is equally compelling. For one thing, it's risky. No one can predict how peers will respond, and the presence of one or two domineering troublemakers may outweigh the goodwill of other students. There is also the question of whether telling simply stops harassment or truly fosters inclusion. If your child is being teased and bullied, and the school has failed to secure the environment against such antisocial behavior, revealing that he has AS may not necessarily solve the problem. If the school has created a climate in which such behavior is accepted, you should consider whether news of your child's AS might not simply become another weapon against him. Demand that your school district meet its obligation to protect your child from harassment, teasing, and bullying first. (See the box on "Bullying and Teasing," page 388.) Understanding and awareness do not always equal acceptance, and your child may feel exposed by everyone knowing something so personal. Especially in this age of social media, consider carefully who really needs to know.

SPECIAL CONSIDERATIONS WHEN THE DIAGNOSIS COMES LATER

Unfortunately, parents of children who are adolescents at diagnosis probably have no choice but to tell their children and, possibly, their school district. If your older child is planning to pursue employment or college after high school, he needs to know because there may be types of support, training, and accommodations that are available to him. The question then arises: Who else needs to know?

When your child is younger, you may tell whomever you choose, though with some consideration and discretion. Once a child reaches a certain age, however, he has the right to decide who knows. After all, this is sensitive, private information. You may not always agree with his choices, but you should certainly give them serious consideration and err on the side of protecting him to the extent possible. After all, he's the one who has to go out into the world "known as" a person with AS.

If your child is an adolescent, we believe that he should be involved in the decision-making process concerning telling his peers. Discuss the situation with him openly, and consider the unique variables of your situation: your child; the attitudes of classmates, teachers, and school administration; and the individual personalities of his classmates. While we as parents may want to shout to the world that Asperger syndrome is nothing to be ashamed of and feel that it is important for our child's peers to know and understand what it means, she may not yet be ready to share her diagnosis with others. On the other hand, your child might be thrilled to come out Aspie and proud.

SHARING THE DIAGNOSIS WITH YOUR CHILD

One of the most difficult decisions parents face is how to present information about ASD to our child. We worry that our child's self-esteem will suffer. We're concerned that our child may become severely depressed by the "official" confirmation that he is different from other children. We wonder if telling will give our child an "excuse" to fail, act out, or simply give up making the effort therapies and interventions demand in order to be effective. Although parents and professionals seem to agree that children with AS do realize that they are different from other children and are sometimes painfully aware of how much they struggle, there is no agreement on when or how to share the diagnosis with them. It is imperative that children understand that they are not "bad," and most certainly that their struggles are not their fault, but it is equally important that they be told of their Asperger syndrome or differences in a positive way.

Sixty-four percent of the families we surveyed for the previous edition said that they told their child about their AS within a year of the diagnosis.[27] Most families who have shared the diagnosis with their child feel that it has resulted in a positive impact on their child's self-esteem. One parent wrote: "My son is aware that he is not like other kids. I think it has been helpful for him to have a reason that explains why some things are hard for him. Also it gives him a greater sense of pride in his accomplishments, since he knows that he has to work harder for them because of the Asperger's." Of the parents who reported that telling their child was a negative experience, nearly all mentioned that at one time or another their child has used the diagnosis as an excuse not to do something that would be considered within his or her range of abilities. A few parents have reported that their children became depressed and angry that they were different from other children.

Later, on page 346, we talk about how mistakes that people with AS make in attribution—essentially explaining the cause or the nature of what happens to them—can result in misunderstandings and a distorted, negative self-concept. When a child who doesn't know he has AS concludes that everything that seems to go wrong in his life is his fault, the burden is overwhelming.

What Adults with AS Say About Telling Children

For the original edition, we asked adults with Asperger syndrome, "Do you feel that being told about your AS would have been helpful to you as a child?" Here are some of their responses.

"I feel that it would have been very helpful. In particular, it would have helped to have been told that it was understood that I couldn't read facial expressions or body language and that I was bothered by bright lights and loud voices. It would have been nice to be told that this is because my brain is different and it was not my fault."

"Because I was nearly four and not yet speaking, my parents were certain I was retarded. Though [I was] hyperlexic and ultimately identified as gifted, the early 'label' affected me. Because of my social difficulties (especially being bullied), I was viewed as unlikable by adults and peers. Had I been told, and had my parents been told that my problems were related to a developmental disorder, I think I and they would have been more accepting of my uniqueness. Instead, I grew up feeling inadequate, unliked, [and] odd, and was often depressed."

"Ideally, the child would be diagnosed young enough that Asperger's and/or autism could just be used casually all the time so there wouldn't be any big 'telling' at all—just natural questions and answers as they come up."

Here the experience of adults with AS provides some guidance. Nearly all of the adults with AS who completed our surveys confirmed that they would have liked to know about their diagnosis earlier. Unanimously, they recommend that parents share the diagnosis with their children. Looking back, they wish that they'd had an understanding of why they were so different from others, because most of them were terribly misunderstood or mistreated. Perhaps the most eye-opening fact was that adults with AS recognized that they were different as early as kindergarten. In fact, reading autobiographies of individuals with ASD, you see how early the authors sensed being different and recognized that not everyone else around them experienced the world in quite the same way they did. Given this, it is clear that hiding or delaying or pussyfooting around the diagnosis does not help anyone.

BE REALISTIC ABOUT THE CHANCES OF SOMEONE ELSE TELLING

Finally, in a world of autism awareness, the odds are very good that your child has a relative, neighbor, classmate, or peer who either has ASD or knows someone who does. The blissful years in which children fail to notice differences between themselves and others are over by the time most reach kindergarten. Contrary to many parents' wishful thinking, peers do see the behaviors and the irregularities in speech, writing, and other areas. They notice. And they ask questions. The odds are very good that your child will have classmates who know a lot more about ASD than he does. If they have a sibling, cousin, neighbor, or friend whose ASD status they know, they might easily identify your child as having ASD. They might decide to tell someone—maybe even him!—all about it. This is one way your child can get his diagnosis. Needless to say, it's probably not the best. You might consider how well you can keep a "secret" that at least some of the people he encounters regularly already will know.

We also discovered differences of opinion among the experts when it came to when and how to discuss a child's disabilities with him. Some believe that giving children a name for their differences will empower them and help them to see having AS in a positive light. They point to the advantages of thinking "the Asperger way" and mention the dozens of famous scientists, musicians, writers, and other creative thinkers who probably had AS. Others believe it's preferable to talk to the child in terms of his strengths and weaknesses, talents and challenges. They feel that the term *Asperger syndrome* may be meaningless to a child, and the word *syndrome* could be interpreted by the child to mean that he has "something wrong" or a "disease." Most experts agree that children need to be told *before* they approach the natural emotional and hormonal fluxes of adolescence. The combination of learning that you are "different" at a time in life when peer acceptance is so important—coupled with an AS-related risk of depression—is probably one best avoided, if possible.

The question of what and when to tell your child has no one right or wrong answer. It really depends on your child. Is your child more easygoing, or does he tend to be explosive? Is your child depressed? Do you think it is likely that your child will misunderstand what it means to have AS? Before you do anything, it is imperative that you understand the diagnosis and have reached some level of acceptance. If you aren't sure that the AS diagnosis is correct or you have not yet come to terms with the disorder, it may be more difficult to explain it to your child. If you are anxious and sad, your child may sense this and interpret those feelings as being directed toward him rather than the fact that he has the disorder.

Having an ASD is a fact of life for your child, and treating it that way can be helpful. Just as parents almost instinctively package information about sexuality, family, money, and religion into the right-size "box" with developmentally appropriate content, talking about AS should not be much different. Parents who talk about it regularly as they go along transform what for too many is a one-time "talk" into an ongoing, evolving conversation that shifts and moves depending on where you and your child are and her level of understanding. Here are some tips:

Take your child's age and developmental level into consideration. An older child will likely be more able to absorb and understand information than a younger one. Sitting down with a list of diagnostic criteria and talking about it with your six-year-old might not be the most appropriate way of bringing up the diagnosis. However, if your thirteen-year-old is inquisitive, she might wish to investigate on her own, by either reading books or looking at information from websites. Some teenagers with AS find online support, and many are very involved in their treatment and participate in educational decisions such as attending IEP meetings.

Present a united front. Even if one parent or caregiver disagrees with the diagnosis, it's important that the two of you present a united front to your child. If one parent is still dealing with denial or simply refuses to accept that there is any kind of problem, you may not be at the best point for informing your child.

Call on your professional team for advice. No one else can make this decision for you. That said, it could only help to have the input of those who know your child: teachers, therapists, doctors, and others. You may find, for example, that your child asks her teacher, "What's wrong with me?" several times a week, or someone else may weigh in with why she thinks now may not be the time.

When to consider telling your child. Your child might be ready to know about her diagnosis when:

- She starts to ask questions or express concerns such as, *Why am I different? Why do I have to go to speech therapy? Why don't I have any friends?*
- She begins making comments about other children who may have AS or a related disorder, such as, *Why doesn't Joseph look at me when I talk to him? Why is it hard for Daniel to hear the school bells? Why doesn't Cindy play with the rest of the kids at recess?*
- She seems to be attributing her difficulties to the "fact" (in her mind) that she is "dumb," "stupid," "lazy," "worthless," and so on. For the sake of her self-esteem and overall emotional health, we would say that whenever the challenges of AS take a toll on your child's sense of self-worth, you should consider telling.

Once you've decided to tell your child, try to read at least one of the several books, workbooks, and articles that have been especially created to help a child learn about her AS or related disorder.

Recommended Reading: Telling Children About the Diagnosis

This book is excellent.

Catherine Faherty, *Asperger's: What Does It Mean to Me? A Workbook Explaining Self-Awareness and Life Lessons to the Child or Youth with High-Functioning Autism or Asperger's* (Arlington, TX: Future Horizons, 2000).

Plan your talk. Think carefully about the message you want to send. Will you use the actual term *Asperger syndrome* or *autism spectrum disorder*, or speak in terms of "brain differences" and individual "strengths and weaknesses"? Will you talk about other people who have been known to have AS (including yourself or family members, if relevant), or will you focus only on your child? Will you discuss how it affects your child in school or socially or both? Whichever way you choose, it is crucial that you set the diagnosis within a larger, positive "picture" of who your child is. Dr. Tony Attwood and Catherine Faherty suggest describing the diagnosis as "something about you," like having blue eyes, a love of math and airplanes, two sisters, and a very kind heart.

Ideally, you'll plan the appropriate time to tell your child. Remove any distractions, allow plenty of time to ask questions, and have a place for your child to escape to, such as his room, if things become too intense for him. You might plan this for a weekend or holiday or other day when there are no other commitments. If possible, pick a time when things in school and elsewhere are going relatively well. Try to avoid telling your child about his diagnosis in the immediate wake of a tantrum, a difficult period, a failure in school, a social disaster, a bad reaction to medication, or any other event that could cause him to associate the news with a bad memory or stressful time.

Plan as you might, however, that ideal moment may never come, so at least have an outline of what you would like to say in the event your child beats you to the punch and asks before you are ready to tell. If your child catches you off guard, say, in the car (isn't that where everything important seems to come up?) or when you are running out to a business meeting, do the best you can. Ignoring the question will probably make your child more anxious, so try to say something that validates his question and makes it clear that you will talk to him more about it at a specific time, preferably as soon as possible. If, for example, your daughter says, "Somebody at school told me that I'm different because there's something wrong with me. Is that true?" you might respond, "In one way or another, everyone is different from everyone else. There is nothing 'wrong' with you. You sound like you might have some questions. Let's make a special time tomorrow afternoon after school, and I'll answer all of your questions."

Next, decide who will do the telling. Will you do this alone, with your partner, or as a family, including perhaps siblings, grand-parents, or favorite relatives? Will your child's doctor or therapist be involved? You might wish to include other people who you know have a special rapport with your child and with whom you know he would feel comfortable. Needless to say, anyone whose presence may be disruptive (young children, for instance) or distracting (the grandmother who still has not accepted the diagnosis) should not be included.

When you do discuss the diagnosis, pay careful attention to how your child is responding to the news from moment to moment. You better than anyone will notice the first signs of stress or distress in your child's general demeanor. Many children with AS do better if they get information gradually and informally. You may have al-ready told your child more than you realize in the course of explain-ing why, for example, the noise at the indoor pool bothers her or she has trouble catching a ball. Give your child time to absorb what she is being told and to ask questions. If you find that your child is becoming upset or doesn't seem to understand, end the discussion. Try again when your child indicates that she is ready or curious.

Trust your instincts. If you feel that your child isn't ready to talk about the diagnosis, you're probably correct. If the time doesn't feel right to you, don't be pressured into discussing the diagnosis before you *and* your child are ready. Years from now, your child may feel that he would have liked to know earlier or never know at all. This is simply a risk you have to take. You will know when the time is right.

Accept your child's response—no matter what it may be. How well your child will be able to understand the implications of his diagnosis depends on his age, level of maturity, and general awareness about the social world around him and his place in it. Give your child the time, the space, and the emotional support he needs to process the information and come to terms with it. Remember your own reaction and that of others close to your child. Be prepared to deal with more questions and a host of emotional responses, including anger, depression, anxiety, and sadness. Know that this will take time, patience, and no small dose of wisdom. While you as a parent might have reached some level of acceptance, your child might see things very differently. There are kids who do not "embrace" the diagnosis and who wish they did not have it. Think beforehand how you would respond to that feeling.

Part Two

TAKING CONTROL

INFORMATION is power. So is having the right attitude. You may discover that you have become the "resident expert" on your child and on Asperger syndrome. Becoming an expert on AS, however, is only the beginning. If you thought you were juggling too many hats before, add these: detective, advocate, ambassador, psychotherapist, education specialist, and socialization director. And wear them all proudly.

Invariably, you will encounter a professional, another parent, or a resource with information that seems to contradict what you learned somewhere else. Everyone has an opinion, and parents and experts can disagree strongly. Sometimes our kids' problems have no clear answers, and trial and error (and, we hope, success) become our way. We still lack a "recipe" that can tell you exactly how much of this intervention and how much of that therapy will produce the best result.

It is a challenge, but it is one that loving, informed parents can meet. Consider the source of your strength: your love for your child. Part Two will help you assemble the tools you need to do the best you can for your child.

It has always fallen to parents to change the world for a child with ASD. Without realizing it, perhaps, you are doing that already simply by caring and taking the time to see the world through his eyes. The therapies and interventions, the educational techniques, and the various other ways in which you help your child grow toward independence, self-awareness, and understanding are essential. But so is changing the understanding of ASD and your child for everyone your child knows, and maybe some people he or she does not.

Chapter 3

ACCEPTANCE BUILDS THE
BRIDGE TO SUCCESS

Accept the gift that is your child. Give your child the gift of you.
—An OASIS parent

Wisdom from the Journey

More than a decade ago, we asked OASIS members: "If you were to sit across from a parent who had just learned that his or her child has AS, what would you want to tell them?" The advice is timeless.

"Don't close any doors. Keep your dreams for your child and a belief that he can achieve them. Place no limitations on your child and don't let others place limits on him, either."

"Your child is no longer a problem child. He or she is now a child with problems, and you can work with those problems and around them. A better understanding of your child will lead to your child feeling better understood. And your child will be a much happier child for that. After all, we all want to be understood."

"These children are incredibly courageous and strong people. They have so much to deal with every day and almost every moment of the day. And they just keep battling. My son is one of my heroes. I have the utmost respect for him and what he has to do just to conform to our neurotypical world."

"Talk! Talk! Talk! Reach out for help, advocate for your child, read everything you can. Try to get people interested and educated about AS. Don't ever be ashamed. Try to accept what has been dealt to you. Accepting it doesn't mean you have to like it, but accept it. You will if you love your child."

"When the shock wears off—and it will—you will realize that this is the same child you have nurtured and loved since birth."

"Don't ever put yourself in a trap of wondering why your child isn't normal. Your child is as normal as your child can be. I started to get caught in that trap, and my pediatrician once said to me, 'How do you know your child is not normal?' In other words, what truly is 'normal'? You will find your own definition of normal in everyday life—your version of it."

"I might caution other parents not to hang on to the 'high-functioning' idea too tightly. The social disability may make the high IQ useless. Then again, it may not. That's the hard thing. You just don't know. Maybe the best advice would be to stay very much in the present. Enjoy the small victories. Enjoy who the child is and don't waste time on hoping for someone who is not here now. My biggest mistake was probably hoping for something that didn't happen. Imagine the message that must have given my child. Remember that building self-esteem means addressing reality, which includes dysfunction. When your child reaches adulthood, you will definitely wish you had taught him or her the meaning of limits. Don't make excuses because of AS for antisocial or negative behaviors. Our kids need to learn how to behave even more than everyone else. However, it is also important that you teach them skillfully and according to their ability. It can be a real tightrope."

"Get support and select your friends carefully. Don't be around people who will negatively impact your ability to be there for your child."

"Hang in there! Keep reminding your child that God loves him and so do you, that you will always forgive him and you will never leave him. This way he will know that no matter what, he can always trust you."

"Let yourself feel bad for a while, without showing your child. Your family is probably not going to be what you thought it would be, and you need to let yourself grieve for that vision of a perfect little family that you have to let go of now. Eventually you'll be able to see that what replaces it can give you just as much joy as that ideal in your head would have."

A PARENT'S PERSPECTIVE

One of the things that has always made *The OASIS Guide* different from some other books is that when we set out to write the first two editions together, we promised ourselves and our families that it would be a book about Asperger syndrome and ASD, not about us or our children. While I do share personal experiences and observations throughout, this is not a parent's memoir. We knew that the way we approached ASD in our own lives was not the only way to go. Since the first two editions, many things have changed, and now instead of relying on our homemade, informal surveys of hundreds of OASIS members (which were actually the first surveys of any kind to ask many of the questions that we did), parents and families can turn to concrete research for resources on understanding and dealing with ASD.

THE JOURNEY CONTINUES

Learning to accept, live with, and grow through parenting a child with Asperger syndrome is a deeply personal and at times difficult journey. There will be good days and bad days. There will be moments when you reflect happily on how things have improved for your child and moments when you angrily question why some neighbor, teachers, classmate, doctor, school, or agency cannot seem to "get" it. Sometimes those moments will happen within seconds of each other.

No matter what happens, through good days and bad, you will keep going. Not always happily. Not always easily. But because you are a parent, you will go forward. Unlike most of the people you will find yourself relying on for their expertise, you will not have office hours or a time clock. You will not have a clearly defined area of expertise that you cannot step outside of. You will be there at the end of the school year, at the end of the session, and at the end, period. You knew and lived with and were responsible for this child before anyone outside your home ever met her, and you will know and live with and be responsible for her long, long after they are gone. Even if you do not have the education, the professional training, the certifications, the degrees, or the licensure, you still know your child better than anyone else can. Will you always be right about what should be done? No. But neither will anyone else.

GETTING TO THIS

Every family's story is unique; we all arrive "here," wherever that is, from different places. For some, the route to diagnosis is pretty straightforward and short; for others, it's a longer, more circuitous trip with many detours and dead ends. The one thing most of us share is a sense that the train has already left the station, that our child is already on board heading for a stop that's not on the map and not on the schedule. Somehow, we have to catch it and if not make up for lost time, at least do our best to see that the time left between now and adulthood is spent well and effectively.

Just as no two people with AS are exactly alike, neither are any two parents or caregivers, including spouses and partners. Parents seem to fall into several different and distinct camps in terms of how they view AS and the impact it has on their lives. And how they feel—about the experience, about their child, and about themselves—may change over time, because the role AS plays in your child's life and in your own can change. The one thing that you can expect when your child has AS is the unexpected.

WHEN THE LANDSCAPE SHIFTS

All parents hold expectations and assumptions about their children. Often this seems such a natural thing to do that we give it little conscious thought. Most of us never realize how much about our children we take for granted until something like the ASD diagnosis suddenly throws all of our assumptions to the wind. Depending on how we come to understand that our child has AS, those old dreams either drift away quietly, one by one, or get blown to bits in a single hurricane. Either way, when it's over, the landscape of childhood and parenthood is forever changed.

WHY THIS "LOSS" IS DIFFERENT

Most of us are familiar with the psychological stages of coping with major life crises: denial, anger, bargaining, depression, and finally acceptance. Although usually associated with bereavement, these same responses are noted in parents of children who have disabilities. At some point, we must come to terms with the loss of the child as we imagined he would be. I never felt that I had "lost" a child, but I do feel that I have lost the ability to take many things for granted. Some experts say that what many of us mourn is the death of our own dreams for our child, the demise of the expectations we probably gave little thought to until they were threatened. Certainly, there is some truth to that, but with the passage of time, the loss we feel is in many ways far more profound and less easily resolved.

That is because Asperger syndrome seems to strike at the very heart of what we who are neurologically typical assume to be prerequisites of basic human happiness. Understanding, friendship, community, love, family, parenthood—the very fabric of life—can be taken for granted for your child, unless he has any ASD. I always think of the day Justin was diagnosed as the moment when all of the *whens* of his future turned into *ifs*.

It's only natural to grieve over the possibility that your child's ASD may stand in the way of these experiences. However, remember that your child may not see her situation in exactly the same light. Here and in almost every other aspect of parenting these children, we must—as autism educator Carol Gray (the creator of the popular social skills technique Social Stories) so wisely advises—"abandon all assumptions." There is no question that experiencing AS from the inside out, as our children do, can probably never be fully understood by those of us on the outside peering in, no matter how well we know or how deeply we love them. To presume otherwise is to risk further misunderstanding and to risk making decisions based on erroneous "conclusions."

What most of us do wish for our children is that they be graced with whatever it takes to live the lives they wish for themselves and to be comfortable being who they are. Every therapy, every intervention, everything that you will do for your child from this point on is geared toward giving her the tools, the skills, the secrets of what Dr. Diane Twachtman-Cullen describes as "the hidden curriculum" of daily life. However hopeful we may be and however successful our children may be in adapting to this world, many of us will encounter situations in which their differences remain glaringly clear. Having some philosophical and emotional "foundation" about this experience is crucial.

For parents of children with AS, the feelings of loss and sadness ebb and flow over time, depending on numerous factors. There will be setbacks, but as time passes, most parents come to feel more optimistic about the situation.

BLAZING A NEW TRAIL

Even when you feel like anything but the brave, intrepid explorer, that is really what you are, clearing the trail your child may follow to his own goals and dreams. Even during those times when the way seems clear, most of us still hear the loud humming of the wide, smoothly paved superhighway of "typical" life we have detoured from. As one mother put it, "For one day, I would just like to feel what it's like to know that my daughter will not scream if the cupcakes have pink rather than blue wrappers or that when a classmate greets her, she will respond appropriately. I see other kids going through life just being typical kids, and from where I stand, everything they do that their parents take for granted strikes me as a small miracle. I would just like to feel that my daughter would not need a miracle to have an uneventful, good day."

This process also entails revising our ideas about what it means to be a parent and a family. For example, parents of only children find themselves second-guessing themselves, wondering who will feel obligated to care for or at least care about their child with AS once they are gone. Parents of larger families may worry that unaffected siblings are not getting enough attention today and may wonder whether those siblings will be there for the child with AS tomorrow. Some of us face the prospect of having a child who will always be more dependent on us or on others, or a child whose social isolation seems the antithesis of childhood. There may be moments when we feel very much out of the loop. The "small" things we take for granted that "all" children experience mean something different when it's your child who isn't invited to the birthday parties or who has no place in the whirl of extracurricular activities that other parents good-naturedly complain of having to chauffeur their kids to. At the other end, many of us know the guilty feeling of reassuring ourselves that our child is "not as bad off" as another we saw in the doctor's office, on the playground, or at the store.

Will there ever come a time when you don't look back over your shoulder to what might have been—and who your child might have been—were it not for AS? Maybe not. However, it is important to remember that *most* parents second-guess many of the decisions they and their children make. You wonder about how your child would be without ASD. Rest assured that your neighbors wonder about how their children might have been were it not for their AD/HD, eating disorder, "wrong crowd" friends, pot smoking, bad grades, OCD, reckless driving, the sibling they can't stand, their parents' divorce, illness, or death, and the list just goes on and on. Not to compare disappointments, but it is safe to say that no parent's every wish for their child comes true.

Coming to a point of resolution or acceptance doesn't necessarily exclude a continuing sense of loss, nor does it require you to deny the very real disadvantages this disability confers. Resolution may entail living with a more fluid attitude and the freedom to embrace both the positives and negatives. As mentioned previously, one of the insidious things about AS is how easily its strengths give rise to weaknesses and vice versa. A skill or tendency that served your child well in elementary school (such as an encyclopedic knowledge of *Yu-Gi-Oh!*) may spell social disaster in his teen years; on the other hand, the obsession that drives you batty in middle school may be the foundation for the career of your child's dreams. When you do look back—and you should—keep your eyes on the path you and your child have traveled, not the one you left behind. Gauge your child's progress—and your own—by where you have come from, not by how far you may have yet to go or where you might have been had you taken that other road.

Start sketching your own map, knowing there will be many false starts, dead ends, trails erased and retraced. Our advice: Don't go it alone. Find support and never hesitate to take advantage of someone else's willingness to listen, advise, or console. Try to be there for the next parent who follows you.

How to Find or Start a Local Support Group

There are support groups all over the world dedicated to helping parents, families, and individuals coping with ASD. An internet search of "autism" or "Asperger," "support," and your community name will probably yield something. Barring that, contact your school district's special education department, your local special education PTA, your child's doctor or therapist, and the local chapters of any state or national organizations.

Starting Your Own Support Group

If local support is nonexistent where you live, consider starting a group yourself. Although this may seem a daunting task, you should know that most of the existing local support systems were started by parents just like you.

Your local support group can be whatever you want it to be: small or large, formal or informal in structure, devoted to fund-raising and awareness-raising efforts, or simply a place to offer parents a true community of understanding. An initial meeting can be held at a local bookstore or coffee shop where a few parents share coffee and swap stories, or it could be held in a local church, library, or mall meeting room. Starting a support group doesn't require a great deal of special skill or talent. Once you've chosen a location to meet, the next step is to advertise for either an informal get-together or an organizational meeting. Put up a web page or create a social media account. Contact your local newspaper and ask to have your meeting time and place listed in its Community Service section. Call your children's doctors and ask them if they'd be willing to post a notice in their offices or share the information with other families of children with AS. Notify the special education department of your school district and ask if it would be willing to pass along information about your meeting. Once people start to hear about your group, you may be surprised at how quickly the word travels and how supportive people can be.

Once you have several families gathered, you'll be able to determine the course you would like your group to take. Some groups have expanded into state or regional support networks and hold regular monthly meetings, sponsor conferences and workshops, and provide services such as social skills training or play groups, while other groups remain informal and meet only a few times a year to socialize.

In addition to contacting parents, you might want to talk with one of the professionals working with your child and ask if he or she would be willing to help sponsor a local support group. If you believe it would be helpful, consider inviting doctors, therapists, teachers, and others who are knowledgeable to join your group, perhaps as advisors or regular speakers.

Most important, give yourself time, space, and a break. At one point or another, most of us feel we haven't lived up to our own expectations. There may be moments when, as one mother told us, "Despite the fact that I loved my daughter so much I would die for her, there were times when I began to question if I could ever love her enough to get us both through the tantrums, the obsessions, and the compulsions. I never could give myself credit for long stretches of patience, for the days when I managed to deal with every potential crisis 'by the books.' In that one moment when my patience snapped, I knew that I was the worst mother on the planet and feared that all the good I'd put forth until then had been totally undone."

THE CHALLENGES FOR PARENTS

You are not the only parent in the world who has spent over $1,000 on your child's obscure special interest, questioned your ability to parent your other children effectively, or felt that coping with AS has stressed your relationship with your spouse or partner. Recent scientific studies confirm what we discovered from OASIS members fifteen years ago: parenting a child with AS impacts the family in numerous ways. Subsequently, numerous scientifically designed studies have found that parenting a child with any autism diagnosis is highly stressful, typically more stressful than parenting children with other disabilities, including Down syndrome, cystic fibrosis, and mental retardation (now referred to as intellectual disability[1]). Although it is often said that parents of children with ASD have a higher rate of divorce than the general population, that has not proved true. However, there is no denying that dealing with a child having ASD takes time, energy, and other resources. In our original survey, our 327 respondents were split almost fifty-fifty on the question of whether their relationship with their partner had grown stronger since their child began displaying symptoms of AS.

THE IMPACT ON OTHER CHILDREN IN THE FAMILY

It's not uncommon to hear parents say that their other children are the "best thing to have happened" to their children with AS. True, AS demands much of a parent's attention and energy, and children with less immediate and pressing needs can sometimes be overlooked. However, often it is the siblings who help teach and reinforce much-needed social skills for their Aspergian brothers and sisters. It is also important to realize that the lessons learned are not mutually exclusive—it's not just a matter of what the neurotypical child teaches the AS child, but also what the AS child teaches the sibling. Though many sibs of AS children do at times feel left out, embarrassed, or humiliated, many of those same children grow up to become caring and compassionate adults. In fact, I've encountered a number of adult siblings who work professionally with individuals like their ASD brothers and sisters as doctors, psychologists, teachers, social workers, and behavior analysts.

Although parents aren't generally comfortable talking about it, many do find their parenting skills validated when there is more than one child in the household. Not only do they have "proof" that they are in fact good parents, they also have a frame of reference to measure what is "normal" development. This seems to be particularly true if the AS child is not a first child. It's also reassuring to look to the future and know (or hope) that there will be "family" who will care for our AS children if this becomes necessary.

There is no question but that siblings of children with AS are often required to make sacrifices and assume responsibilities most other children do not. From convincing a sister to give up the last waffle for the sake of the peace to rushing out of a brother's basketball game because of an AS sensory meltdown, in ways great and small, other children feel—and, in truth, sometimes are—cheated. They may be teased or made to feel uncomfortable about having a sibling who's "different," whom they may be forced to defend. Understandably, siblings can feel that the child with AS "gets away with" more than they do or doesn't receive equal discipline or punishment.

These issues should be discussed with the siblings of children with AS, and just as the child with AS requires assurance that it isn't his or her fault, so does the sibling. As time needs to be set aside for parents to nurture adult relationships, time should also be allotted for siblings of children with disabilities. Parents also need not feel guilty if they fully enjoy the successes of their neurotypical children. One mother expressed that it took her several years to accept strangers' compliments about the behavior of her younger, neurotypical daughter. Every time someone said something nice about how well she behaved in the grocery store, she was reminded that these same sorts of people were the type to judge her parenting of her son with AS.

HOW PARENTS SEE THEMSELVES

It's common for parents of children with AS to question and doubt their parenting skills. We were surprised to learn to what degree that shaken confidence extended to parenting their other, neurotypical children. In our OASIS survey, more than half indicated, "At times I have difficulty determining what are 'normal' childhood behaviors." This is made even more difficult by the fact that it's not at all uncommon for a sibling to have what has come to be known as a "shadow syndrome"—a disability or condition but in a "milder" form—and in some cases there may be a sibling who is diagnosed with AS, autism, speech delay or other language disorder, NLD (nonverbal learning disability), or a related disorder.

FINANCIAL MATTERS

Having a child with AS can have a profound effect on a family's financial picture. Some families discover there's literally no end to the amount of money they could spend on treatments, interventions, special programs, and professional services. In addition to the obvious costs for medical care and therapies, AS has its own "hidden" costs in the form of purchases related to special interests; special-needs camps, day care, and after-care; special clothing (Velcro closures on shoes, all-cotton clothing); and specialized legal counsel for matters related to special education and estate planning.

Compounding the financial stress for a significant number of families is the fact that having a child with AS either prevents one parent (usually Mom) from working or restricts where and how much she can work. Conversely, having to meet the added expenses has also forced a number of mothers who would rather be at home back into the workforce.

DAY-TO-DAY PARENTING STRESS

Often by the time most parents learn about AS, their competence has been questioned, if not undermined, by family members, friends, educators, doctors, and strangers. We all want to be "good parents." Sometimes parents doing their best for a child with AS don't look like good parents to those unfamiliar with AS. Sometimes they don't feel like good parents, either. An Australian study found that mothers of children with Asperger syndrome experienced being stigmatized in their communities, even when their children were not present. They felt that community members were most critical of them in circumstances under which their children failed to "fit in" or meet expectations: first, in school, and then in the general community, particularly if their children misbehaved.[2]

You will strive for the consistency and the "right" response prescribed by experts (most of whom, it is only fair to point out, do not live with children with AS). You will live out the little secret few of us would ever admit to our child's teachers, doctors, or even ourselves: sometimes moms and dads melt down, too. Tempers flare, despair crashes down, and patience shorts out. Through all of that, however, you can still be the best parent for your child if you remember that no one is perfect. Look around and see how other parents behave around their children, then ask yourself whom you know who could do a better job of understanding, fighting for, protecting, and loving your child than you. Chances are, no one.

AS dramatically raises the parenting stakes. Just being the "good enough" parent of reassuring child psychology books will never be good enough again. Nothing about your child having AS will magically make you more patient, more tolerant, more understanding, or more forgiving. However, having a child with AS certainly will give you far more opportunities to develop these qualities and practice these skills than most other parents get. By the same token, you also will have more opportunities to fall short. Whether you believe that this experience results from the will of a higher power or a biological fluke, there will be lessons learned.

MORE REASONS FOR HOPE

Even if you feel that your world has ended, it does begin again. Now, however, it is a new world. You may be surprised to discover how well prepared you already are for this journey. As one mother told us, "You will understand that basically you have been coping pretty well with a difficult situation. When you look back, you will find that over the years, you have instinctively developed coping mechanisms and have been doing the right things." For example, you may have "learned" not to tell your child the specifics of an upcoming outing, because you know how he will react if the plans change, or you may have naturally developed a way of speaking in short, direct sentences. Many of us look back and see that the things we did that most often drew criticism and derision were in fact the right things to do.

Yes, there is much to gather from "outside" in the form of information and support. Always remember, though, that you have several resources that can never be replaced and that in the end will mean more to your child's happiness than any other: your love, understanding, and acceptance.

BUILDING THE FOUNDATION FOR SUCCESS

No intervention or therapy is 100 percent effective or appropriate for every child. No one has yet devised the guaranteed, one-size-fits-all treatment and intervention plan that takes into account all of your child's needs, your family's values and lifestyle, and your resources. What works for one family and one child may not work for another.

You may be facing situations like these:

- Your child's school has a general education plan for him but expects you to provide most of the socialization training.
- Your child's occupational therapist has the right approach for attacking those motor skills problems but not a lot to offer in terms of guidance for adaptive physical education.
- Your child's psychologist or psychiatrist has some attractive suggestions for reducing classroom anxiety, but your school district lacks the personnel, the experience, or the will to implement them.

You, the parent, may be the bridge between what should be done and what does get done.

WHERE TO FIND INFORMATION

Ironically, though it may seem that vast deserts of ignorance dominate the landscape, once you find one or several good resources, you could drown in the amount of information there is to read, absorb, and apply. It's important for you to determine for yourself (1) what you *need* to know versus (2) what it would be nice to know or (3) what is out there to know. These three categories of information are different and have different values to different people.

The amount of information available today can be overwhelming. And amassing a unnecessarily large amount of it can become a stressor of its own. It takes time to find, time to read, time to file, time to consider. Although it may not be obvious, the fact is, anyone can write a book, put up a website or blog, create a social media presence, or show up at a conference with a PowerPoint presentation. Some of this is useful and good, but some of it is not.

All these years later, it is disappointing to see that the news media still have trouble sorting out who is an authority in terms of having accurate information from someone who is just an expert at getting on TV. There is no guarantee that anything you read or see will be accurate or even helpful. In fact, there is a chance that much of it will not be. Our advice is to be selective and ask questions. Read critically. Guard your time. Better to find five tried-and-true sources you feel you can return to as you need them than to deluge yourself with dozens of sources, none of which is "complete" or even accurate.

Ten and twenty years ago, it made some sense for parents to say, "Well, if no one seems able to give me firm answers, why not try [fill in the blank]." Things are vastly different today, though you might not know it by the endless parade of crackpots and quacks who sometimes threaten to dominate the media discussion on ASD. Yes, it's true that you will probably never learn what definitely "caused" your child's ASD. That puts you in the company of most parents of children who have physical and intellectual disabilities. It is important to remember, though, that not knowing the cause does not mean that you cannot sort out effective, evidence-based treatments from those that do not meet those minimal standards.

Another major, and welcome, change is that doctors, scientists, and other experts have studied and evaluated some of the therapies and interventions that are commonly used. In some cases, the objective professional opinions—from the American Academy of Pediatrics, the US Surgeon General, and similar entities—have affirmed the treatment's value; in others, they have pointed out consistent flaws and lack of proof of effectiveness. We will get into this all more in chapters 4 and 6. For now, suffice it to say that it is not necessary for parents to wade neck-deep through every swamp of information to find what they need. There are good, reliable sources that can give you useful, accurate information.

BE THE EXPERT ON YOUR CHILD

If your child is newly diagnosed, you have only begun to amass what can easily become a mountain of reports, letters, and other important papers. It is wise to start laying down the paper trail you will need when dealing with your school district, your health insurance company, and just about everyone else who comes into your child's life. And do not throw anything away. As your child approaches late adolescence and adulthood, you will be surprised how much history you might need to apply to various institutions, agencies, or programs.

- Set aside one place in your home—perhaps a desk tray, basket, or large manila envelope taped to the wall—for all important papers, including receipts for therapy, medication, and transportation to and from appointments. Periodically sort through it and file or discard.
- Check with your tax professional or contact the IRS, which has a special publication, "Tax Highlights for Persons with Disabilities" (Publication 907), on expenses that are deductible and other tax considerations.
- Set up a filing system that makes sense to you. You can use a file cabinet, a file box, or a large loose-leaf binder. The loose-leaf binder has the advantage of being portable enough to travel with you to doctors' appointments and IEP meetings. Use clear plastic sheets to hold smaller papers or anything you refer to or copy often.
- Consider scanning and converting to PDF or similar format documents you know you want to keep on your computer and refer to often. It makes them very easy to send, when needed.
- Start keeping important phone numbers in your personal address book, home address book, organizer, cell phone, and anyplace else you might need them. Program the most important—your child's school and doctor—into your phones, if possible. The inside cover of your binder is also a good place for phone numbers.
- If you find a good comprehensive article or pamphlet that

you think explains your child well, consider getting several copies made to hand out to grandparents, teachers, coaches, babysitters, and others you believe need to know.

• Consider making a second "general information" binder to share with your child's school and teacher. This binder will include a few pamphlets and general information papers on Asperger syndrome, a list of recommended reading, and a short description of your child and his needs. (See page 423 for the "Letter of Introduction.")

FINDING HELP: YOUR CHILD'S TEAM

Why Have a Team?

Not all parents feel that they need a "team" of professionals to help them. Each child with AS is unique. Some may not require special education classification or services, or need to have an ongoing relationship with a child psychologist, psychiatrist, or mental health counselor.

When you're just starting to get your bearings and adapting to new approaches for school, behavior, and other important issues, it's a good idea to have a trusted professional in your corner. For most children, AS changes, so it's wise to look ahead. Many parents recall behavioral tactics and interventions that worked like magic for a while and then lost their power—and sudden, inexplicable changes, for better and for worse. It's not unusual for a very young child with AS to become moody and difficult once she realizes that she is different from other children or that socialization is difficult for her. Any life event that can trigger problems for a typical child—emotional trauma, moving, loss of loved ones or family pets, divorce, an old friend who suddenly "outgrows" the relationship, the arrival of a new sibling, an unsympathetic teacher—can have equal but unpredictable effects for the child with AS. That moment of crisis may not be the best time to start looking for a professional. It may be wiser to meet with or at least have recommendations of a doctor or therapist you could turn to in an emergency.

Beyond that, there are often more mundane situations that call for a professional's guidance. One of the most common is school, particularly when it comes to making decisions about placement, the most appropriate classroom situation, and the need for other supports, such as one-on-one aides or paraprofessionals.

Who Is on Your Team?

Your team may consist of just one person whom you and your child trust and feel comfortable with, or it may include three, four, or more. Either way, you must be the "captain," the person who makes sure that each team member gets relevant test results and other important information from the others. There's no hard-and-fast rule about what kind of professional is "best" in every case. You may find a teacher or a counselor who has a great rapport with your child and an instinctive understanding of AS. On the other hand, you may find that your local ASD expert is someone whose advice is invaluable but who does not see patients regularly. You may need to patch together what you need from an array of sources. Your child may see a counselor or therapist for socialization work and an occupational therapist for sensory integration issues weekly, while she sees an MD for medication management monthly or several times a year.

One of the biggest challenges for parents in some areas of the country is the lack of access to professionals with extensive experience with ASD. Often the solution is to find a sympathetic doctor or therapist and help that person become as well versed in AS as you are. If you and your child can build a relationship with such a professional, particularly one not averse to consulting with other specialists outside your immediate area, all the better.

WHEN PARENTS AND PROFESSIONALS DON'T AGREE

It happens. You might find yourself disagreeing with recommendations or observations, even from someone with whom you feel you have an otherwise good rapport. As much as we wish it were not so, the fact is that everyone who deals with your child has the potential to make a mistake. As a parent, of course, you should question the professionals working with your child. Don't feel compelled to follow outside recommendations solely because they come from professionals. This sword cuts both ways, however. A potentially successful intervention is just as easily undermined by the parent who opposes a particular behavior intervention plan "on principle" as by the teacher who halfheartedly trains the paraprofessional she doesn't believe your child truly needs.

Professional training, federal mandates, state regulations, and best-practices standards of treatment are only as good as the people charged with applying them. You may feel that you have more than enough to juggle without having to worry about how the people who are supposed to be helping your child feel about you or your partner personally. In a moment of frustration or disappointment, it's not always easy to think beyond the immediate problem. However, try to remind yourself that with each encounter (or confrontation), you are laying down a piece of road that you and your child may be traveling for years to come. This is not to say that you should simply go along to get along, or be more concerned with being liked than being listened to. It does mean, however, that approaching advocacy as a form of negotiation can be more effective and less stressful for everyone involved.

There are times when you may have to temper your natural parental response to become your child's most passionate, most vociferous, and most aggressive advocate. We parents often feel like we're "fighting" for our child, but in fact we're really negotiating—for services, for understanding, for support from those who may not agree with our decisions. Ultimately, we are working toward building, brick by brick, a place in the world for our child.

When most of us think about advocacy, we immediately think of school and special education services. But advocating for your child with AS often means laying the groundwork for understanding, becoming your child's ambassador to the world. You may find yourself asking others to make allowances and accommodations for your child that can range from asking a neighbor to turn down a radio to demanding that your school district hire a consultant to help your child's teachers help her do better in class. Learning the basics of negotiation can ease your stress, build goodwill, and, most important, get you and your child where you want to go.

TRY TO SEE THE OTHER SIDE

If a professional recommends a strategy or treatment for your child, try to understand why he or she is doing so. Ask. And listen when a professional tells you why what looks like a minor problem today has the potential to become a big problem tomorrow. While it is true that no one knows your child better than you do, you may encounter (if you are fortunate) at least one professional—be it a doctor, a teacher, a therapist—who has seen dozens, even hundreds of children who share at least some behaviors, traits, deficits, or skills with your child's.

While every child with ASD is unique, there is enough known about any ASD and any person with ASD that is reliable, consistent, and, yes, predictable, that good professionals can make suitable recommendations. I recall, fifteen years ago, feeling taken aback and offended when the speech pathologist evaluating my son said, "I may not know your son that well yet, but I know autism." *Who do you think you are?* I thought as I fumed, speechless. Over the next five years, she would prove to be one of the most knowledgeable, able, and valuable professionals in my son's life. As a teacher myself, I would never say those exact words to any parent, but I understand now what the speech pathologist meant.

Like parents, good teachers and other professionals also see our children as individuals, but they do see them differently. However, it is a history of experience with a number of individuals and professional knowledge of the disorder that gives them this alternative viewpoint. Good teachers—and doctors and therapists—want to see children and their families grow and succeed. What they are (that most parents are not) are witnesses to the big picture of how the disorder and its challenges may play out in a child's life, both today and tomorrow. They also have the advantage of professional distance to suggest and even carry out interventions, behavior plans, and therapies that a child may be less than happy about. If we are honest, we know that sometimes other professionals can teach or coach our kids through things that we know we could never do on our own. You owe it to your child—and yourself—to give them that chance.

As a parent myself, I am reluctant to state the obvious, but here it goes: Parenting a child with a disability often demands being more protective and more defensive than we might be of a typical child. By the time you've received a diagnosis or come into contact with professionals, you may have had a lot of practice in feeling that it's just you and your child or you and your family versus the world. Yes, it hurts to hear someone speak of your child's deficits, and it's not unusual to feel you're being criticized when even the most well-meaning professional suggests things we might do differently. It's difficult to push a child you feel needs protection. It's almost impossible to expose to risk and possible failure someone you believe has not gotten a fair shake. After all, you might wonder, if so many things are so hard for him, is it really right to demand that he learn to do things that may be difficult or at which he may fail?

The answer is yes. Remember, your child is not a "done deal"— not by a long shot. You do not know everything he is capable of achieving or overcoming. No one does. One thing that professionals may have a clearer view of is a child's potential or the value of trying, of taking a chance. Where a parent might see the possible pain of total failure at, say, participating in a gym class or learning to ride a skateboard, a teacher might see instead the value of a small victory in the attempt, the pride that follows the one little step that works.

As parents, we have to face the fact that we probably are not the most objective observers of our children. We can't be. And, in some ways, that is what makes our relationship with them so valuable. That said, it is critically important that we learn to listen calmly and rationally to what professionals say. Before thinking or saying, "Not my child," or "He doesn't really need that intervention," ask the professional what the recommendation is based upon, why she is making it, what results she hopes to see, and what present or future problems she hopes to solve.

SETTING THE AGENDA

No matter how young your child is when you realize he has AS, you probably worry over the time you've both lost, the signs you missed, the opportunities for intervention that seem to have passed. This is natural but ultimately unproductive. If you're looking back, and we all do it, do not overlook the things you did right as well. All that you can control, and all that really matters, is what you can begin doing today.

The big question many of us confront is not so much "Now what?" but "What first?"

For Extra Help Teaching Independence Skills

The Parents' Guide to Teaching Kids with Asperger Syndrome and Similar ASDs Real-Life Skills for Independence is the "companion" book to *Asperger Syndrome: The OASIS Guide*. It is the step-by-step, hands-on how-to for parents who want to take charge of ensuring that their children and young adults step into the world with confidence in their ability to live, work, and play with all the independence we expect and they deserve. The strategies are all evidence based and have been "test driven" by real parents and real kids. Why a separate book? For one thing, teaching these so-called basic skills is often difficult and frustrating—for parents and kids—because it is always difficult teaching someone else to do something you do not recall being actively taught yourself. Just take a moment and write down how you would explain folding a sheet, cracking an egg, or tying your shoes, and I think you'll see what I mean. Further, having an ASD comes with differences and deficits in a range of areas that are essential to learning: fine- and gross-motor coordination, sensory sensitivities, executive functioning, and ability to imitate the movements and gestures of others easily. *The Parents' Guide* not only helps you recognize and understand the "roadblocks" but also explains the specific behaviorally based strategies and techniques you can use to "detour" around them and make teaching these skills quick, effective, and—most important—less time-consuming and stressful for everyone.

Chances are, your child will receive more than one form of intervention. For example, if your child qualifies for special education, some of the following may be provided in the course of the school day: academic help, occupational therapy, and speech and language therapy, for instance. Even so, many parents feel the need to do more. Special education is designed to help students with issues that pertain directly to their ability to learn. You may be surprised to learn that socialization therapy isn't always a top priority for school districts, even though it is probably the single most important intervention for AS. In recent years, the glaring deficits in self-help and other independence skills have emerged as major concerns. Though the role of schools in teaching and supporting these skills might be (depending on whom you ask) debatable, the importance of children learning the basic skills of independent living is not. Many parents find that they need extra help in this area or end up doing it on their own.

Outcome Studies: A Guiding Star and a Warning

Outcome studies attempt to answer the question "What happens when people with Asperger syndrome and similar ASDs near or reach adulthood?" They typically explore questions about employment, emotional health, education, independence, psychiatric issues, and social engagement.

Several studies of outcomes for older teens and adults with AS present a puzzling picture. First, some background. For most people with any type of developmental disability, there is typically a strong relationship between IQ and the development of adaptive daily living skills. Simply, the higher someone's IQ, the more easily he or she could learn and apply independence skills.[3] So researchers were surprised to discover that for people with Asperger syndrome, there seemed to be no correlation between IQ and adaptive daily living skills. In fact, individuals with Asperger syndrome often scored surprisingly low in the realm of adaptive behavior when compared to control groups matched for age and IQ.

In a 2007 study, Dr. Ami Klin, then of the Yale Child Study Center, and his co-authors summarized earlier research on adaptive behavior functioning by saying, "Quite often, standardized instruments testing cognitive and language functioning and attainment are used to measure outcome, and yet, outcome studies of individuals in the higher end of the cognitive spectrum of autism . . . seem to indicate that higher intellectual potential and academic achievement cannot be seen as an assurance of better outcome in adulthood."[4]

When earlier studies through the 1990s found low rates of employment and independence among those with AS, it was logical to wonder if the real problem was not that these individuals had grown up before awareness and treatment of AS. Maybe they had been misdiagnosed and ineffectively treated. Maybe opportunities to live more independent lives simply did not exist for them. So shouldn't awareness, intervention, and earlier and more accurate diagnosis make a difference? The answer seems to be a cautious "Yes, but . . ."

Mats Cederlund and colleagues followed seventy males with Asperger syndrome (mean age 21.5 years) and seventy males with autism (mean age 24 years) over a period of five years after diagnosis. In their 2008 study, 26 percent of the Asperger's group had what the researchers defined as a "poor" or "restricted" outcome in terms of employment, independence, and acceptance by peers, despite 92 percent of them having an average or above-average IQ. The authors' conclusion: "Given their good intellectual capacity, the outcomes must be regarded as suboptimal."[5]

Contrary to popular belief—and a big surprise to many professionals and parents alike—is that many aspects of adaptive daily living skills, play skills, and other skills needed for independence do not necessarily depend on intelligence. In fact, while IQ is usually associated with greater adaptive skills in children with other ASD diagnoses, in children with AS, average or high IQ was not associated with even average adaptive daily living skills.

SETTING PRIORITIES

Which is more important? Socialization skills taught and practiced in a group or one-on-one therapy? Participation in a small group that shares your daughter's special interest or having the experience of being part of a modified or regular Girl Scout troop? Which behavior should be addressed first: the tantrums or the refusal to do homework? How much time should be spent on OT to strengthen handwriting muscles? How much on structured playdates? How much on academic work?

Through it all, remember that you can effectively target and address only one behavioral issue at a time. Inevitably, some problem behaviors or issues will have to wait their turn. In some cases, change will come slowly, and that can be frustrating for everyone. Now is a good time to talk with your partner and perhaps your child's doctor and teachers to pinpoint the most pressing needs. While it would be nice if handwriting were easier for Max, it may be more important that he learn to ask for help in class. Bear in mind that your priorities may not be the same as his teacher's or your partner's. Talk it out and reach a compromise. Especially if you're working on changing behaviors, it is essential that everyone be on the same page. Do your best to present a united front and be consistent. Parents' conflicting demands and changing expectations coupled with their child's struggle to change are a recipe for frustration, low self-esteem, and less willingness to "get with the program" in the future.

Even if your child hasn't been told of his diagnosis, if he is old enough, he should be included in your plans for intervention. One great thing about children with AS is that it is often easy enough to discover what will motivate them: access to the special interest, an opportunity to participate in something they enjoy, a chance to talk about a topic they really care about. Still, every person is different. Knowing that occupational therapy may make handwriting easier or that speech therapy will simplify listening to directions can give the child a goal, a reason for the many hours of hard work ahead. In a loving, nonjudgmental way, discuss the areas in which you will all be working toward improvement, and specifically how you will help your child. Have a plan that involves you, your partner, and others close to your child, so that he doesn't feel he's going it alone.

And never miss an opportunity to praise your child specifically, lavishly, and generously for his efforts.

BE A DETECTIVE

One sound strategy is to begin with an inventory of challenges, problems, and deficits that you and your team believe should be addressed. It is relatively easy to pinpoint the necessary prerequisite skills for academic success. If, for instance, a child was struggling in most of his subjects and was behind grade level in reading, we would almost automatically focus on improving his reading. Unfortunately, identifying the pivotal prerequisite skills or compensatory strategies for an individual whose profile may be complex is not so simple. Start by talking candidly with a select group of those who know your child well; this may include professionals, family members, and other people you trust. What do they see as the most pressing issues? As a parent, you may have become inured to, say, constant run-on special interest talk or tantrums. For example, many of us have lived with—and learned to accommodate and "live around"—tantrums for so long that we may not fully appreciate the negative impact they have on your child's social opportunities among his classmates or their disruptive effect on others. Of course, the final decision as to where you will concentrate your efforts is yours, but getting input from others can be very helpful. If, for instance, your spouse, your child's teacher, and her socialization therapist all consider improving frustration tolerance job one, then you can proceed as certain as you can be that you're on the right track.

You might want to spend a week or two collecting data on your child's behavior. See page 437 on how to do this. It might help to list the behaviors or challenges and then note which of these are self-contained or isolated (for example, frustration over missing a favorite television program before going to school) and which have a strong negative effect on other areas (such as sensory sensitivities or problems with social skills). As you learn more about AS, it will become easier to trace problems back to their not-always-obvious root causes. For example, difficulties with transitioning and changes in routine are not behavior problems in the usual sense. They often result from a basic anxiety and misunderstanding that can be allayed with visuals such as calendars, pictures, and schedules; Social Stories (see chapter 4); and routines.

Sometimes the most pressing problem is obvious—frequent outbursts, for instance—but the best intervention may not be. Though three children's meltdowns may look very much the same, they may each have a different cause. For one child, it may be an anxiety disorder; for another a sensory issue; for a third, simple fatigue and stress from the classroom environment. Determining the true cause often requires detective work. For parents, that means never taking any behavior at face value and never projecting how you or anyone else would feel in your child's situation. Think back to all of the times you responded to your child's crying or smiling with a remark that essentially told him what you thought he was feeling: "I'll bet you're mad that your bike tipped over," "You must have had a great/rough day at camp," and so on. Some of us do this because a child lacks the ability to express himself or herself, and such observations can help open up a conversation. However, particularly with a child who has AS, the emotion behind the expression is not always easy to read. Children with AS who have had a good day at school may become difficult once home simply because they *can* be difficult at home, where people are more understanding. It's always better to ask questions or otherwise get to the crux of the issue before offering "guesstimated" observations.

Once they know about AS, most parents can look back on specific incidents and behaviors with new eyes. You may realize, for instance, that your daughter's screaming fit at the department store makeup counter had everything to do with the bright lights, the crackle of the store PA system, and the ambient noise of a crowd of people talking in a large space with marble floors. Once you learn how to pinpoint the underlying problems, it becomes easier to see how large a role what some call sensory integration disorder or the basic inability to process social information may play in behaviors or responses that otherwise would be easily misread.

NEVER LOSE SIGHT OF WHAT'S GOING RIGHT

Often, we and the professionals we consult are so focused on what is "wrong" that we lose sight of what goes "right." This is especially true when you're tracking the precursors to undesirable behaviors and reactions. However, you can learn almost as much from paying close attention to situations and moments in which your child functions the best. It might help to begin keeping a journal that also includes incidents that occurred in the past. Let's start with a particular behavior: for example, a seeming inability to hear when spoken to. List on a piece of paper when and under what circumstances you notice the behavior most frequently and/or in its most extreme form. Include in your notes details about the environment: the size of the room, the number of people, the noise level, what kind of noise it was, the reason your child was there at that particular time, what else was going on (whether he was engaged in a pleasurable activity, for instance), and so on.

Also think back on the day: Was there another incident or situation that preceded this incident, even if it occurred hours or days before and seems, on the surface, unrelated? Was your child rested, ill, or coming down with something? Did the place or the situation have a "history" for your child? For example, the doctor's office where she got a shot, or the mall where he heard a fire alarm go off? Did your child have expectations of what it would be like there? Were there unexpected changes?

Next, list the places and situations where the behavior does *not* occur. What do they have in common? How are they different from the problem situations? Consider your child's mood, time of day, environment, and so on.

GATHER INTELLIGENCE

Ask teachers for their input, too. Each person who deals with your child will have his or her own opinions on the causes and the possible interventions. For some children with AS, environment is an important factor in their behavior, and different environments can prompt or discourage different behaviors. In addition, as Dr.

Asperger noted decades ago, some of our children can be extraordinarily sensitive to different personality types. Your child's doctor or teacher may not observe behaviors or reactions that you consider serious. One child we know had a fairly serious motor tic involving his hands, yet a pair of occupational therapists never saw it once in nearly a year of twice-weekly sessions. Another child, whom his teacher considers "a joy to have in the classroom," drives his mother to distraction with his constant whining and frequent outbursts. Conversely, teachers may report behaviors that parents never witness, including some that they simply do not believe their child capable of, such as hitting, screaming, and acting disrespectfully.

Children with AS often respond differently to different situations. The classic example is the child who manages to hold it together during the school day only to come through the front door upset, on edge, or furious. Or, because she cannot apply to one situation what is learned in another, your child may have wonderful table manners at home but not at her grandmother's. This is one reason that parents should listen to professionals with an open mind.

Not everyone will understand the influence of AS on your child. Not everyone who makes an observation or a recommendation about your child will be correct. Sometimes educators, doctors, and other professionals bear news that is disappointing or makes us feel self-conscious about our child's condition or our parenting skills. However, if your child hit someone in school, you'll help yourself and your child by focusing on solving the problem behind the behavior rather than arguing about whether it happened or whose fault it was.

MANAGING THE DAY-TO-DAY

Be Your Child's Protector

If you are neurotypical, you are probably better able to anticipate problematic situations and trouble than your child with AS can. As a result of their inability to rapidly process many bits of social information around them, people with AS are often easy to intimidate, take advantage of, or otherwise hurt. Parents of children with

AS are usually instinctively protective, even overprotective. To a greater degree than most people can even comprehend, much less understand, we are our children's shelter.

Sounding more like a Secret Service agent assigned to protect the president than a mom, one mother of a child with multiple sensory sensitivities describes a typical outing to the local ice cream shop. "Before we even park, I look at the parking lot and try to determine how crowded it is inside. If there are too many cars, we go someplace else. Once inside, I automatically run through what we call the 'Eric Inventory': loud music, crying babies, balloons that threaten to pop, blenders, what Eric calls 'noisy' air-conditioning—most of which none of us can hear. Before the waitress seats us, I'm scanning the room for the 'right' table or booth: far from the hub-bub of the kitchen and the front door, away from the cash register, out of the full sun, and away from birthday parties or other noisy groups. I also make it a point to get a look at the dessert case, just to be sure I limit Eric's choices to flavors that are available that day. They know Eric at this place, so I let him place the orders, because it's good socialization practice.

"Once our orders arrive, I ask for the check immediately and pay it, just in case we have to suddenly rush out of the place when one of the hundred things that could possibly go awry does. I enjoy Eric's company so much, and I love taking him places. But from the moment the front door closes behind me, I feel like we're all on high alert."

A large part of helping our kids cope with AS is anticipating problems that might arise and having a plan for avoiding, containing, or escaping the fallout. As time goes by and wherever possible, though, we want to focus on teaching our children to improve their own detection systems and their coping skills. For most parents, necessity—and a few memorable scenes—forces the development and constant refinement of our ace troubleshooting skills. That living "on high alert" has become second nature doesn't make it any less stressful or tiring. "I had no idea how much thought I put into just going out with Lisa until my sister-in-law Becky offered to take her out for the day," one mother said. "My 'little list' of do's and don'ts ran fifty items long and included everything from 'avoid the candy aisle at the supermarket' to 'no ice in cold drinks.' When

Becky saw it, she made some comment to the effect, 'Don't you think you're overdoing it?' When she brought Lisa, who had had a wonderful time, home that night, however, she said one of the nicest things anyone's said to me since Lisa was a baby: 'I don't know how you do it.'"

Looking back, most parents report that as their children grew, their ability to cope with difficult situations improved. Sometimes the change occurs as a result of deliberate, intensive intervention; other times, children seem to "outgrow" certain sensitivities and reactions. In the meantime, it helps to have in place your own personal protocol for potentially volatile situations. Avoiding or protecting your child from overwhelming or uncomfortable situations or stimuli is not babying, coddling, or spoiling. It's being smart and caring. Depending on the circumstances (where, when, with whom), an instance of sensory overload or acting out can be devastating for your child. Forcing him or her to tough it out—which may be appropriate for a neurotypical child and may be okay in the right time and place—probably won't help and, if anything, might be counterproductive, giving rise to future fears, anxiety, and avoidant behavior. We know firsthand the remarkable staying power of unpleasant memories, and there is substantial evidence that a history of stress and anxiety is a precursor for anxiety, depression, and even posttraumatic stress disorder (PTSD) in later life.

Sometimes an older child will be willing to attempt a historically difficult situation—a noisy mall, for instance—if he knows for certain that he has a way out. The child who tells you, "I think the noise is starting to make me nervous" or "It's too crowded here for me" is not whining, nor are you "spoiling" him by responding. He is learning to monitor his own behavior and to advocate for himself. As an adult, he alone will be responsible for his own crisis avoidance and rescue. You can reinforce that behavior by responding appropriately. If he needs to leave this time, you leave, though it would not be unreasonable the next time to encourage him to stay a little bit longer. Personally, I always found that by letting my son know that he will be taken out of a situation if he needs to be resulted in his willingness to venture into new situations.

While some AS behaviors may remain unpredictable, a lot of what strikes us as inexplicable and bizarre is actually easily explained. If you can predict or anticipate a reaction, you may have the power to avoid or ameliorate its consequences. Of course, life is full of surprises: the car alarm that sounds two feet from your child's ear, the scent of fresh-baked apple pie that leaves him gagging in the bakery. Some parents balk at having to put so much planning into simple activities such as grocery shopping or buying new clothes for school. Try to remember, though, that AS compromises your child's ability to feel comfortable and in control. Structure, scheduling, and routines help address some of that. But out there, in the world, your child depends on you or another caring person to foresee the potential trouble spots that she cannot and to establish a "zone of control" where none exists.

Be Your Child's Teacher

True, every parent is a teacher. But what we're talking about here is looking at what you can do for your child in a slightly different light. Even those children whose schedules are full of interventions and therapies still have a lot of "downtime" outside the therapeutic "net." While it would be impossible for a parent to spend every waking moment expressly teaching, there is a comfortable middle ground. In later chapters, we discuss specific actions parents can take to help teach social skills, among other things.

While you can never ignore the fact that your child is your child, when you decide to teach a particular skill—let's say better table manners or how to follow a schedule—it can help to adopt a more neutral posture than what might be natural to you as a parent. If you have decided that you are going to teach your son to get up, get dressed, and arrive at the breakfast table within twenty minutes of being awakened, consider beforehand what will most effectively teach him the independence you wish to instill. Doing most of the things that come a little too easily to some of us as parents—making multiple trips upstairs to "check" on his progress; reminding and nagging from downstairs; and, finally, lecturing him sternly, venting your frustration, or punishing him when twenty minutes pass and he's still under the covers—do not constitute teaching, nor do they encourage independence. After all, if they did, you wouldn't have this problem in the first place. Instead, you might take a more teacherly approach:

- Make your demands and the consequences (for both completing the task and not) crystal clear beforehand.
- Be sure your child has all the skills he needs to accomplish the task in the time allotted. (Can he manage his buttons and zippers? Is he showering independently? Are there distractions in his room that sidetrack him and should be removed?) If he does not, teach him those skills *first*.
- Remove yourself as a prompt or cue. Instead of you personally monitoring him, set a timer for twenty minutes and let it run. Say nothing and let the timer determine whether your child has accomplished the task. Another strategy: make a list of the tasks your child needs to accomplish and break them into realistic "chunks" of five minutes each. Then set a timer for every five minutes. This way, your child will know if he's working at the right pace to be ready in the twenty minutes allotted.
- If your child succeeds—bounces downstairs completely and neatly dressed, hair combed, teeth brushed, and so on— praise him and reward him as promised.
- If your child fails, leave your anger, frustration, and nagging out of it. As calmly as possible, outline the consequences for the failure to complete the task (no video games after school, perhaps), ask your child what might help him to do better tomorrow, and work on that, if necessary. Then move on.

Be Your Child's Advocate—and His Ambassador

One of the hardest parts of dealing with AS is learning to handle some of the behaviors and reactions that come with it—including our own and those of others. Ideally, school district personnel, doctors, friends, family members, and strangers should always treat him—and you—fairly and with respect. Unfortunately, not everyone is capable of or interested in rising to the occasion. Some situations are sadly common: the friend who loses interest, the family members who refuse to make allowances, the stranger who asks loudly, "What's wrong with him?"

We will probably never escape the persistent belief that somehow the parents are at least to some degree responsible for who their children are or how they behave. No matter what you're doing, there may be someone in your child's world who feels that you should be doing something more or something less, something different or something the same. It's also human nature, it seems, to offer up those opinions—whether they are solicited, informed, or fair. There also seems to be some cultural compulsion to talk at or about anyone who appears somehow different as if they weren't there or were incapable of understanding what was being said. If you have ever returned from an outing wishing you could never leave your house again, you are not alone.

BUILD YOUR CHILD A ROAD TO THE FUTURE

Of all the people in your child's life who might help you build that road, you and your child are the only ones who will have to travel it, and your child will be traveling a good part of it without you. Plan for that. The good news is that as you learn more about AS and more about your child, the unhappy scenes and the stressful moments become easier to avoid and easier to cope with when they do occur. With information and understanding in hand, you can become empowered. Though we may be veterans of show-stopping tantrums, nasty glares, and racing hearts, few of us ever become hardened enough. It may be that you will still spend many occasions trying to locate the quickest route out of a department store, but you'll also have many opportunities to see your child experience a great success. Throughout all of this, you may find that you are a much stronger and steadier person than you ever imagined. Develop the right combination of understanding, patience, and courage to try something new, for you and your child.

It may be difficult for you to believe that things may not always be this way, and that one day your child may be able to go to a movie without panicking, enjoy having a friend over to play, or attend a high school dance. We—and our children—are shaped by our experiences; and failure, disappointment, and fear can make it difficult to push ahead and to try again. We know firsthand how hard it is to instill confidence in a child when deep inside you fear the worst. It also takes practice to recognize the factors that contribute to success.

So what is the secret? In working with and getting to know many teens and young adults, I have observed that no parent whose child exceeded early expectations or found a comfortable place in the world did it by playing it safe. The parents took some risks. They ventured—and helped their child venture—outside their comfort zone. They learned to handle—and taught their child to handle—disappointment. They viewed every aspect of AS and weighed each for both what it could bring to their child's life and what it could take away. They never stopped learning. They valued independence. They celebrated not only their child's accomplishments but also who their child was.

The rest of the book presents a map of the landscape ahead. Let's go.

Chapter 4

OPTIONS AND INTERVENTIONS

THE first question most parents ask once they know their child has Asperger syndrome is, "What do I do now?" The answer, of course, depends on your child. Although experts and practitioners in different fields may disagree, the fact is, no single intervention, treatment, or therapy works every time for every child. Nor will a single intervention, treatment, or therapy* address every concern. That said, there are some interventions that can deal with a wider range of symptoms, challenges, and deficits.

THE NEW FOCUS ON EVIDENCE-BASED TREATMENTS

What do we mean when we say a treatment is evidence based? Typically, it means that the treatment has been evaluated by investigators using standard, scientific research methods and that the research has

---

*Many practitioners use the terms *intervention*, *treatment*, and *therapy* interchangeably, though *treatment* typically applies to medical or data-based interventions. Here, *intervention* can apply to anything done deliberately and purposefully to address an issue or create a change.

been reviewed by professional peers before publication in what is called a peer-reviewed journal. In addition, that research has been conducted more than once and by other investigators. Ten years ago, few interventions or therapies listed here (with the exception of applied behavior analysis) had been held up to such careful study. That has all changed. As you will read, some therapies that parents and professionals alike have traditionally just accepted as part of the "ASD treatment menu" are now prompting more questions—from the school districts and government agencies which provide them and from the health insurance companies which might cover them.

Parents should be asking questions, too. The challenging aspects of ASD are stubborn; they do not give, move, or improve easily. Most of our kids will need more time, more practice, more specialized instruction than other kids do in at least one area and, most likely, in many. This takes time, energy, and other resources. And no matter how much time you think you have, believe me when I tell you that every parent is at least a little surprised to wake up and find a young adult at the breakfast table where their baby used to sit. Which of the following deserves a place in your child's treatment plan? And what should you reasonably expect from each?

The question of how good a "track record" an intervention has takes on a whole new meaning in light of two recent developments: the passage of autism insurance reform in many states and the new standards set by the most recent reauthorization of the Individuals with Disabilities Education Act (IDEA 2004). New language in IDEA mandates "the use of scientifically based instructional practices" (Section 1400[e]). And in Section 1414(d), IDEA specifies that an IEP (Individualized Education Plan) include a statement describing the student's "special education and related services and supplementary aids, based on peer-reviewed research." As a parent, I can't help but ask—especially given the growing focus on the Common Core, standard assessments, and high-stakes testing for all students—why this was not a cornerstone of special education from day one.

Several popular interventions have been studied intensively over the past decade or so. Aside from applied behavior analysis and the dozens of techniques developed from it, there are few big winners in terms of evidence and effectiveness. However, researchers and special committees reviewing research on behalf of the American Academy of Pediatrics, the US Surgeon General, the National Research Council, and respected nonprofits such as the National Autism Center have identified interventions that not only lack evidence of effectiveness but also might be considered to have little or no demonstrable therapeutic value.

What does that mean to you? For one thing, even if your insurance company does cover treatment for ASDs, it may not cover non-evidence-based treatments, as those are considered ineffective by, among others, the American Academy of Pediatrics. Second, school districts should be expected to take a harder look at how much time and money are spent on interventions found to lack scientific support. See the box on page 181 ("Health Insurance for Treatment of Autism Spectrum Disorder") for more details.

"BUT WHAT IF?"

Being a parent with a fresh new diagnosis in the mid-1990s, I recall thinking, as many parents do, "Nobody can tell me anything for sure about my son's condition. No one can predict for me what will definitely work and what definitely won't. Let me do everything I can that might possibly help my son, no matter what the science says." That way of thinking made more sense back then, when research in autism treatment was still playing "catch-up" after decades of neglect. And this line of thinking still drives most parents to try as many interventions as they can. On some level, I believe that many of us fear that we will one day look back and wonder if we "failed"; if maybe the intervention we did not try was actually the one with the power to turn everything around. Years later, we have a much clearer picture of what works and what doesn't.

NON-EVIDENCE-BASED AND ALTERNATIVE
THERAPIES: A MIXED BAG

Surely, you know the expression "Been there, done that, got the T-shirt." Our situation could be described as "Been there, done that, got the Irlen tinted overlays, the DMG, the weighted vest, the expensive 'special supplements,' the casein- and gluten-free products, the trampoline, all the books that told me all about them, and the receipts for the thousands we spent." To be fair, the fact is, every single one of these things "works" for someone. It might work a little for a long time, a lot for a short time, or somewhere in between. And some of them can and do work for a number of people over the long term. The problem with non-evidence-based and so-called alternative treatments is that they either do not work "as advertised" or promised and/or that they produce the desired result for only a very small percentage of those who try them. In fact, one of these "alternative" therapies was incredibly effective for my son, but of the dozens of kids I've met who tried the same thing— and whose parents paid the same several thousand dollars—I've met only one who had the same outcome. So my son's experience was an anomaly.

Does this mean you should never try a non-evidence-based intervention? No. But it does mean that you can probably find a reasonable approach that addresses your major concerns without racing to leave no stone unturned. And the fact is, there are some stones out there that are better left where they are. There is no magic cure hiding under any of them. You will never "fix" everything an ASD brings your way, because none of us can ever be made "perfect." If you do decide to venture into more alternative, controversial areas, do so after you have run through the interventions that are the most established and that have a solid record of effectiveness over large numbers of people over a reasonably long time. Further, be sure to check into the safety of what you are considering. It is beyond the scope of this book to address every one of the hundreds of alternative interventions used to treat symptoms of ASD. However, the suggestions that follow apply to all interventions you might consider.

Your first concern should be safety. Vitamins and nutritional supplements, forgoing or delaying vaccinations, cranial and spinal manipulation, chelation, hyperbaric chamber treatment—the list goes on and on—all present real risks far more serious than simply being ineffective. For example, there's been at least one hyperbaric chamber on display at every autism fair I've attended this past decade. Why? In 2013, the Food and Drug Administration (FDA) issued a stern consumer alert about hyperbaric oxygen therapy (HBOT).[1] The therapy is approved for thirteen other conditions where a boost of oxygen is essential; autism is not one of them. Risks of HBOT include embolism, paralysis, and fire; eighty people worldwide have perished by fire while undergoing HBOT. Children have died while receiving chelation therapy and suffered preventable disease and death due to not being vaccinated. You should know the risks of any intervention before you begin. Start your research where the research is: on the websites for the FDA, the National Institute of Mental Health (NIMH), and the National Center for Complementary and Alternative Medicine (NCCAM), part of the National Institutes of Health (NIH).

Evidence-Based Practice and Autism

In 2009, the National Autism Center, a national nonprofit research organization, completed the National Standards Project. Its goal: to "establish a set of standards for effective, research-validated educational and behavioral interventions for children on the spectrum."[2] The resulting reports provide the most comprehensive, thorough evaluation of the treatments available. *A Parent's Guide to Evidence-Based Practice and Autism*, as well as a "companion" report, *Evidence-Based Practice and Autism in the Schools*, are both available as PDFs from the National Autism Center's website: www.nationalautismcenter.org. More recently, another report, *Evidence-Based Practices for Children, Youth, and Young Adults with Autism Spectrum Disorder*, was released by researchers at the Frank Porter Graham Child Development Institute at the University of North Carolina.[3] This, too, is available online (see

Endnotes to this chapter). It also contains a helpful "Fact Sheet" on each intervention, which includes a basic overview as well as a list of relevant research studies. Not only are these reports good resources when you are weighing the pros and cons of different treatments, but they might be helpful if, let's say, you find yourself being asked to support your request for a specific intervention.

The National Autism Center's reports evaluated and divided treatments for autism into three categories:

1. Established Treatments (meaning established as effective),
2. Emerging Treatments, and
3. Unestablished Treatments.

The authors use the term "package" to encompass several components related to the main treatment. So, for example, the treatments that make up the Antecedent Package can include such strategies as choice, prompting, and environmental modification of task demands, or some combination of several others.

Established Treatments

The authors point out that two thirds of the Established Treatments come directly and exclusively from the "behavioral literature (e.g., applied behavior analysis, behavioral psychology, and positive behavioral supports)," and that 75 percent of the other third of treatments derive most of their research support from the behavioral literature. In the following list, please note that except for the Peer Training Package and the Story-based Intervention Package, *all* of the strategies have their roots in applied behavior analysis. The authors also note that in the studies reviewed, both the Peer Training Package and the Story-based Intervention Package included key elements from behavioral treatment packages.

Antecedent Package
Behavioral Package
Comprehensive Behavioral Treatment for Young Children
Joint Attention Intervention

Modeling
Naturalistic Teaching Strategies
Peer Training Package
Pivotal Response Treatment
Schedules
Self-management
Story-based Intervention Package (including Social Stories)

Emerging Treatments

The report defines "Emerging Treatments" as those "for which one or more studies suggest that intervention may produce a favorable outcome" but which still require "additional high-quality studies that consistently show these treatments to be effective. Based on the available evidence, we are not yet in a position to rule out the possibility that Emerging Treatments are, in fact, not effective." This list is long, so I've condensed it to include the interventions most frequently suggested for AS.

Cognitive Behavioral Intervention
Developmental Relationship-based Treatment
Exercise
Massage/Touch Therapy
Multi-component Package
Music Therapy
Scripting
Social Skills Package
Technology-based Treatment

Unestablished Treatments

"Unestablished Treatments" includes interventions "for which," according to the study's authors, "there is little or no evidence in the scientific literature that allows us to draw firm conclusions about [their] effectiveness . . . There is no reason to assume these treatments are effective. Further, there is no way to rule out the possibility these treatments are ineffective or harmful."

Academic Interventions
Auditory Integration Training
Facilitated Communication
Gluten- and Casein-Free Diet
Sensory Integration Package

A MIRACLE? A CURE?

Sooner or later, most of us hear or read about the child who was miraculously "cured" and today shows absolutely no trace of ASD. We welcome the long-overdue surge in public awareness of ASD, but there's no denying the sometimes underinformed, biased, and sensationalistic package many of these stories come in. Understandably, parents are drawn to reports of the child who is dramatically improved, even "cured" of ASD. How did they do it? When hope clings by a thread, it's difficult to hear such stories without wondering, "If that child, why not mine?"

Remember, no one knows *the* cause of AS or any other ASD. Further, there is no single "core deficit" or "core disorder" that once "fixed" magically erases every facet of an ASD. If that were the case, you wouldn't need this book.

It is possible that ASDs, like allergies, come in many forms with many different causes, or even a combination of causes for each individual. We know that ASDs have a strong genetic component and that ASDs affect numerous neurological components and processes. That genetic difference might also have some effect on other body systems and functions. Just because your child and my child both have a special interest or engage in hand flapping does not mean that they do it for the same reasons or that the same intervention will produce the same result for both. There is no question that many children have benefited from following a casein- and gluten-free diet. Does this mean that some deficit in how the body handles these molecules "causes" autism in everyone? No. There are children whose attention has been improved by auditory integration training (AIT) or sensory integration therapy (SIT). Does that mean that auditory processing deficits or sensory integration difficulties "cause" AS? No. What is possible is that something about these interventions made the child more comfortable, less distractible, and better able to engage.

It falls to parents to weigh the options and make the hard decisions. Most parents would do anything for their child. Unfortunately, few of us are in a position to do so, no matter what our hearts tell us. Most of us encounter the service the school district denies, the doctor your insurance company will not cover, the therapy that is literally five hundred miles away. There is also the matter of time. Our children will not remain children forever. The sooner they begin to learn to be independent, to monitor and regulate their emotions, to understand and make themselves understood by others, the better. For that reason alone, it makes sense to start off with the interventions that are the most widely used and promising, and save the less established for somewhere down the road.

WHAT NEXT?

Step back, take a deep breath, and remember that even though time is of the essence, you don't have to decide anything today. Listen carefully to what everyone who has done his or her research or who has had direct experience has to say. When it comes to making intervention decisions, not every opinion is useful. Learn to think critically about the options. Learn to trust your judgment. Anything that sounds "too good to be true" probably is. In most cases, when something works, you will be able to see a difference. Positive changes that result from some interventions (for example, social skills therapy) may not be obvious until your child has been on the program for several weeks or months or years. If, after giving an intervention a fair trial, it doesn't seem to make much difference, exacerbates old problems, or sparks new ones, talk with the therapist or practitioner, and then consider taking a break from it or stopping altogether. (The one important exception, of course, is any kind of medication. Never taper or stop a medication without first consulting your child's doctor.) You can always try it again at another time (say, over the summer vacation rather than during a busy school year) or with another practitioner.

WEIGH THE OPINIONS, THINK CRITICALLY

Practitioners, educators, and parents can be enthusiastic and persuasive about treatment options they believe in or have been trained to use. They can also be equally opinionated about those that they do not believe in, those that they are unfamiliar with, or—let's be honest—those that encroach on what they consider their professional turf. We've heard from many parents who are troubled and confused by the sometimes strong, even emotional, opinions expressed by the professionals they would like to feel they can rely on for unbiased, factual information. Finally, even if the best autism doctor in town diagnosed your child, assuming that he or she is well versed in every possible treatment (with the exception of medication) might not always be wise.

It is smart to question anyone—professional or layperson—who makes sweeping generalizations about any form of treatment, pro or con. It's important to discriminate between a statement like "Vitamin B6 really reduced my son's tendency to have tantrums" and "Everyone knows that vitamin therapy is the only way to go" or "There's no evidence that vitamins do anything; don't waste your time."

Sometimes the less orthodox, least studied interventions are those that seem safer, less invasive, less expensive, or just generally more attractive than some others. We all have our own internal scales on which we rank potential interventions from "first resort" to "last resort." Understandably, most parents have no qualms about occupational therapy, for example, but they may be conflicted about the prospect of their child walking the hallways of middle school wearing a weighted vest. We have to recognize our own biases to evaluate what's best for our child. You may have a hard time coming to terms with the idea that your child requires a self-contained special education classroom (see chapter 9) or that he may benefit from medication. Try not to waste time in seeing the solution or the intervention as the problem. The real problem is what brought you to this potential solution. Grieving the intervention might result in you or others not truly seeing when something works and perhaps giving up too soon on what could have been effective over time.

It would be unconscionable to suggest that parents "get over it," "get with the program," or "move on" while we're learning to negotiate this new world. You may never become totally objective about your child's diagnosis or its implications for his life. However, you can work toward separating those strong, complex, and understandable emotions from the important decision making you must do.

How we view our child's treatment reflects not only our experiences and beliefs about AS and the role of intervention but also our ideas of what a childhood should be and how AS affects it. You may find it helpful for you and your partner to discuss and establish at least a tentative framework for your approach to intervention. In two-parent families, some couples are equally involved in researching options and communicating with the professionals involved. Most, however, find it more practical for one parent to assume most of those responsibilities, although they make important decisions together. Yet others find that one parent, because of other demands or an emotional difficulty with accepting the diagnosis, is essentially uninvolved. If you're a single parent, you may have to assume this responsibility alone. You might consider involving a caring, trusted family member or a close friend. It's always good to be able to bounce ideas off someone. Depending on your situation, you will also have to consider access to professionals and services, financial resources, insurance coverage, and other details.

Remember that how AS manifests in your child will change over time, sometimes dramatically and suddenly. Try to gain at least a basic knowledge of *all* the intervention options, including those you have filed under "last resort" so that you'll have a head start in making important decisions you may confront in the future.

QUESTIONS TO ASK

Later in this chapter, we'll review the interventions that are most widely used in ASD. In considering these or any other therapy, ask professionals and practitioners the following questions:

What specific symptoms or behaviors does this therapy address, and how? No one therapy or treatment can address every issue your child might have. Applied behavior analysis offers the widest range in terms of the different developmental domains it can address. But no single intervention can butter every biscuit. ABA cannot influence brain chemistry, as medication can; conversely, medication that improves your child's attention cannot teach him to spell. Sometimes parents are disappointed when they learn that a promising intervention helps them manage problems one through six but stops short of eliminating or reducing number seven. Ask your professional to describe the limitations of what a specific therapy can achieve. Also ask:

- What is the theory or the research behind this approach?
- Does that theory make sense scientifically?
- Is it based on science or on established, accepted knowledge about how things work?
- Does the research seem credible?
- If there is little or no research available, ask why.
- If a professional truly believes that the disorder or dysfunction his or her approach addresses is at the root of most if not all AS symptoms, ask why. And be very cautious. If someone really knew *that*, every child would be cured.

What kind of evaluations will you be conducting and what kind of data will you collect? It seems it would be obvious, but it can't be stressed enough: Determination of progress and decisions regarding the direction, continuation, cessation, or form of treatment should be made based on data—numbers that quantify behaviors that demonstrate learning, skills acquisition, behavioral changes, and anything else that would indicate "progress." Not all professionals conduct standardized evaluations, run a baseline, or collect data over time. Well-designed evaluations and carefully analyzed data can yield essential information on the effectiveness of the intervention and other aspects of your child's progress. This information can be used to refine and improve the intervention and, ideally, make it more effective. It can also give you the early heads-up that maybe this intervention or this provider is not the right fit for your child right now. Subjective evaluations of progress or assurances based on vague statements like, "He seems to be more comfortable than he was six months ago," or "She's definitely doing better," are fine for art class, but they are inadequate for most interventions provided by licensed or certified professionals. Demand concrete evidence that supports (or does not support) the effectiveness of the treatment.

What does that mean? Effective treatments for AS come from a variety of disciplines, each with its own terminology. Sometimes jargon can be helpful, as when it describes a novel concept or process or when it takes something most of us understand in an "everyday" way and frames it to be more specific. Other times, however, the overuse of highly technical terms can confuse. Since you probably will be called upon many times to explain your child or the treatment course you have chosen, it's important to be comfortable in your understanding of it.

You might want to bring a notebook to therapy sessions or appointments, at least in the beginning. Write down questions you have, terms you'd like explained, and anything you've observed in your child that might be relevant. Request any print material that is available and ask for recommendations of books, articles, and websites. Don't be shy. If you have a question, ask. If the answer you get doesn't clarify the matter, ask again or ask for an example of how a particular problem may manifest in real life for your child.

How long do you expect this treatment to last? There's no single quick fix. Except for therapies with a specific timetable (such as auditory integration training), treatments are open-ended in the sense that they continue until improvement results. Further, kids with ASDs are typically so far behind in one area or another that most experienced therapists will be able to identify not just "the next step," but more likely the next dozen. No one will be able to predict how long your child will need it. For many children, speech and language therapy, occupational therapy, social skills training, and other interventions continue for years. Considering how many different issues can impact on others (for example, how sensory issues may affect dysgraphia or attempts to eat a healthy diet), it's not always easy to sort out what's working and what's not. In some cases, the improvement can be dramatic and quick; in others it may be more like a steady series of nearly indiscernible changes that culminate in what may appear—weeks or months later—as a newly acquired skill or a reduction in an interfering, or problem, behavior. Having good data can help you to see progress that is slow but steady and headed in the right direction or complete stagnation or reversals and regression.

What can I do at home, and what can his teachers do at school, to enhance and reinforce the work you are doing with my child? Once you have a basic understanding of what an intervention is supposed to achieve and how, you can help your child expand, build on, and generalize what he learns "in session." For example, in occupational therapy, nine-year-old Sari is working on handwriting. Every evening, Sari's mom asks her to make a list: groceries they need, items that have to go to school the next day, her favorite cartoon shows. Little tasks throughout the day provide extra practice and keep the skill "working" in the real world, outside the session. Four five-minute writing tasks throughout the day equal about one session with a professional, in terms of practice time.

Most professionals working with school-age children are well aware of the challenges their clients face in the classroom. While special education teachers probably will be aware of steps they can take in the classroom to help your child with specific issues (for example, assigning the child with attention difficulties the seat nearest her), most will welcome reasonable, practical suggestions conducive to a more positive, productive classroom experience. Therapists, doctors, and other professionals can have great suggestions. Unfortunately, solutions and strategies that are easily implemented in smaller specialized classrooms or the local weekly socialization class may not always be possible or effective in the regular classroom. No one knows the classroom or your child in the classroom better than his teacher. Strategies that make perfect sense to your behavior consultant or your child's psychologist, for instance, may simply not be possible at school (as much as we all wish that they were). Do what you can to help set up situations for everyone's success. An intervention that is too intrusive, time-consuming, not fully understood, or difficult to implement in other ways will not be applied, no matter how "perfect" someone thinks it is. Better to advocate for the smaller class size or the extra help your child's teacher may need to implement the behavioral program or the one-on-one support your child needs to protect his emotional health.

Help everyone to see beyond the obvious. Ten-year-old Leo always became upset and sometimes even verbally aggressive when the teacher had the students split up and work in small groups. Because Leo's teacher knew that he knew the material, she interpreted his reluctance to join the group as a matter of noncompliance and a behavior problem. When Leo refused to join the group, he received time-outs and, if necessary, lost recess. The mystery of Leo's "bad" behavior was solved when his speech pathologist explained that he had difficulty listening to more than one person speaking at a time. The team decided to try to let Leo begin working with just one other classmate. Once he seemed comfortable with that, a second classmate was added. The speech pathologist used her sessions with Leo to help him practice attending when two people were talking; the teacher praised Leo's classmates when they spoke more slowly and waited their turns so that they were not talking over each other. In the end, the whole class benefited.

The more that children on the spectrum move into mainstream and inclusion classroom settings—and away from the constant presence of educators with special education backgrounds—the greater the need for suggestions and strategies from "outside" therapists and related service providers. Therapists may suggest classroom activities that will reinforce skills, such as assigning a child who feels he is not valued by peers the task of showing a new class member the ropes, or giving a child who is developing better motor planning skills the job of pouring juice at snack time. A child who seems to benefit from short breaks outside the classroom might be used as a "messenger" between the classroom and the principal's office or as an "escort" for other children.

PARENTS AS "THERAPISTS"

Not all interventions lend themselves completely to a do-it-yourself home approach. However, you should be ready, willing, and able to provide whatever "follow-through" a professional requests. Remember that one of the major roadblocks virtually everyone with an ASD encounters in acquiring essential skills and helpful behaviors is a deficit in the ability to generalize—to "translate" or apply something learned from one situation to another. Further, our kids typically require many (sometimes many, many, many) more opportunities to practice a skill or behavior before it "takes hold" and goes on what I like to call "autopilot." You can learn enough about Comic Strip Conversations, Social Stories, social skills training, and certain aspects of applied behavior analysis to use them effectively at home and employ the strategies throughout the day. Occupational, physical, and speech and language therapists can show you tips and tricks to help your child practice new skills and behaviors. Take them and use them. Rather than view them as "more work" for your child to do, recognize that most kids with ASD do need "more work," and for most, the more practice offered in the shortest period of time produces the strongest result.

As any trained therapist or professional will tell you, though, there's a lot more to it than knowing the information or the technique. Professionals are trained to be objective, and the success of some kinds of therapy depends heavily on their ability to remain calm and keep the child "on track" regardless of what occurs. Parents, on the other hand, are, well, parents. We are emotionally invested in both our kid and the outcome. It is a rare parent who can achieve a totally "professional" demeanor, and it's probably not desirable in every case, anyway. To work successfully with your child at home requires patience, tenacity, and an ability to check your emotions. It may be difficult to stick to a program if your child becomes easily frustrated or emotional. And, to be honest, it does take time and commitment to implement any program effectively. Some parents believe that most moments spent with their child are "therapy" oriented enough as it is and prefer not to add to that burden. But if a specific approach seems suited for you and your child, we urge you to give it a try.

AVOID BURNOUT—BOTH YOURS
AND YOUR CHILD'S

Parents whose children receive several types of intervention, concurrently or over a period of time, report experiencing "intervention burnout." No matter how effective or helpful a course of treatment may be, there is no denying the practical toll it can take on you, your child, and the rest of your family. Whatever treatment you choose, learning about it, implementing it, and keeping appointments all take time.

Expect to have some mixed feelings about some of the therapies and interventions your child receives. Watch for signs of ambivalence and burnout in your child, other family members, and yourself. A child who is chronically cranky, tired, overwhelmed, and on edge may be doing too much. Speak with your practitioner about this. Chances are, he or she can suggest techniques for getting around it. Changing the time of the appointment or the order of activities within each session can make a surprising difference. Also keep in mind that some interventions can be counterproductive if your child is tired, uncooperative, or completely resistant. That said, you are the parent, and you should presume to have better judgment about what is best for your child than your child does. Sometimes kids just have to work through learning to live with interventions. Any professional working with your child has certainly seen all of this before and should have suggestions for you.

Remember, parents burn out, too. You may find yourself criticizing the therapy or the therapist, downplaying your child's progress, and/or exaggerating the lack of it. Your first step with any intervention is to take data: write it down, every day, or even several times a day. If you find yourself discussing the effectiveness of the therapy using words like "it seems," "it feels like," and so on, you probably don't have all the hard information that you and your practitioner need to make a good decision.

First, discuss your concerns with your practitioner. Ask others who know your child well—grandparents and other family members, teachers and other professionals, adult friends—if they see any improvement or progress. This is particularly important when your child is having trouble accomplishing the goals you and his practitioner have agreed on. Most children enjoy doing things they have some degree of mastery over and may naturally avoid those they do not. One result is that children and their parents are more likely to drop out of therapies that address the areas in which the child needs the most work. Before you decide to discontinue a therapy, try to be objective. The kids who cannot take turns, who cry when they don't get their way in a board game, or who cannot stop talking over others *need* that social skills program even more than do the kids who look happiest bouncing into the session room.

When therapy becomes stressful, for whatever reason, you risk reaching a point of diminishing returns. Rather than stopping altogether, ask the therapist to consider cutting back on the least essential intervention, if only temporarily. Consider the "therapeutic" benefits of activities that are not interventions per se. For instance, you might weigh the socialization benefits your son derives from participating in a flexible and understanding scouting or church group against what he might gain from joining a more formal socialization group. Or you might opt for a weekly swimming lesson that includes all the children in your family over a second or third weekly occupational therapy session. We are not suggesting that there are "nontherapeutic" substitutes for effective interventions, or that less specialized activities are of equal therapeutic value. Realistically, however, parents may find themselves forced to make choices.

THE STAR OF YOUR TEAM: YOUR CHILD

Finally, remember that the person who is working the hardest in all of this is not the parent racing from one appointment to the next or the therapist with the patience of a saint. It is your child. Even when something is really working and the improvements are obvious, it can be challenging, sometimes frustrating work for your child. During a period of "therapy rebellion," my then-eight-year-old son asked, "Why do I have to do all these things that are so hard for me?" Good question. Once children reach a certain age, they may realize that not everyone has to forgo ice cream, take medicine, or have several appointments a week. Children are smart enough to realize that you don't have to fix what's not broken. They may get a sense that they are doing these things because something is "wrong" with them and they may feel, justifiably, that it's not fair.

When you consider the emphasis that parents and professionals place on rewarding improvement, as we should, it's easy to see how a child might wonder how we feel about him when he cannot do things as well. It's important to recognize, encourage, and reward accomplishments and new skills. But it may be even more important to acknowledge the process, the little steps, the time, the effort, and, yes, the heart. Most of all, remind him of what you love about him that has nothing to do with that improved pencil grip or better frustration tolerance. This includes particularly AS behaviors that may be rechanneled, reduced, or "repurposed" but probably never eliminated, such as stereotypies, problems with sensory stimuli, and mind-blindness. Remember to praise your child liberally and lovingly for the abilities and talents that he values within himself. That may be a natural ability with math, music, or photography; an encyclopedic knowledge of streetlights; a prodigious memory; a kind heart; or a willingness to try.

FINDING AND PAYING FOR THERAPY

Most of our kids are identified and receive their initial treatment through their school districts, so it is perhaps only natural to assume that your school district will be a good source for finding additional help. However, for many reasons (namely, school district personnel have all they can do just to keep up with matters related to school), that is probably not your best source. For one thing, experts in education tend to be experts in education. Period. For another, many school districts and their employees are either forbidden or strongly discouraged from recommending outside services or providers. Finally, though most parents believe it would be a wonderful world if every teacher were an expert on autism, that is not possible. (Besides, some of the most effective teachers I've seen working with our kids lack "autism credentials" but are just great teachers with an accepting attitude and a willingness to listen.) So certainly ask your district for any leads or guidance, but don't stop there.

Other parents can be a fantastic resource, individually and in groups. Contact your local autism or AS support group, in person or online. Some professional organizations can also provide guidance. For example, if you are seeking a Board Certified Behavior Analyst (BCBA), the Behavior Analyst Certification Board website (www.bacb.com) provides a registry that can be searched by location, proximity to your home, and so on. And don't forget your child's physicians, especially whoever made the diagnosis.

Interventions can be costly. If you cannot afford treatment, be honest with your practitioner. Inquire about the possibility of paying a reduced fee based on your income. Look into other places that may offer the treatment at reduced cost or free through teaching hospitals, colleges and universities, training programs, research centers, and studies. If you know of other children whose parents might be interested in, say, social skills training, consider forming a group and then approaching a practitioner about working with the group for a reduced fee. Contact your local AS-, autism-, or other disability-related advocacy or support group. Sometimes these organizations offer treatment and intervention programs and training for parents in topics such as behavioral interventions, advocacy, how to access local services, and so on, at reduced fees or free of charge.

Finally, contact the office or department in your state that handles programs for people with disabilities. Those new to the scene tend to think of these agencies as working primarily with adults or those more severely affected. In fact, state disability or mental health offices often provide funding through grants and other arrangements to agencies, universities, hospitals, and other providers to implement programs that serve a wide range of individuals. Because most recipients of these funds are nonprofit or small organizations, little or no funding goes into publicizing them. You might find among them some of the best-kept support, advocacy, respite, crisis, and intervention programs in your area.

Health Insurance for Treatment of Autism Spectrum Disorder

As of this writing, thirty-six states and Washington, DC, have adopted some form of autism insurance reform, and by the time you read this, there will certainly be more. This usually consists of legislation that regulates the services that health insurance companies cover, under what conditions, and with what limitations, or "caps." In many states, going hand in hand with insurance reform, some regulatory or legal measures have been enacted to address the qualifications required for professionals to treat clients with ASD. In some states, that has resulted in licensure for Board Certified Behavior Analysts, for example, or specific rules regarding which credentials a social worker or mental health counselor should have to bill insurance for treating a client with ASD.

Since every state's version of autism insurance reform is different, and because the regulation of health insurance companies comes under the purview of the state government, we will be sticking to the most general basics. In 2013 Autism Speaks—a major presence across the country in helping local groups fight for insurance reform—launched its Legal Resource Center, which functions as a source for the legal community involved with protecting the rights of families under the new insurance laws. The Autism Speaks website (www.autismspeaks.org) features excellent, authoritative articles, blogs, and Q&As on dealing with insurance laws, as well as information on contacting the governing agencies in each state.

If your insurance plan covers autism, be sure to find out exactly what is covered and under what conditions. You will want to know what kind of professional can provide the service, for example, as well as any limits on coverage. There might be a cap on number of treatments per year, the age at which certain services will no longer be covered, and the type of symptoms or behaviors that are covered. In most states, insurance coverage for autism has opened up a whole new world, for both consumers and the professionals who serve them. Expect to encounter some kinks in the works if autism insurance reform is new to you or to your state. The following advice will help ensure that your child receives all of the coverage she is entitled to:

- Request and keep a written copy of the whole health plan contract, not just the benefits overview. This is available from your employer or directly from your insurance company.
- Contact your state insurance commission. This is a governmental agency or department responsible for regulating health insurance providers in your state and addressing concerns. Find out if autism insurance reform has occurred in your state, when it goes into effect, if it applies to the type of insurance policy you have (autism insurance reform might not apply to every type of plan offered in your state, for example), and any other information you need.
- Talk with your human resources or benefits coordinator at work. He or she should be able to speak in detail about your specific plan.
- Contact your health insurance company and confirm that your understanding of how insurance coverage for ASD treatments works in your state for your particular plan is correct. Take notes on your conversation and always include the names of those you speak with.
- Before you begin treatment, be sure that you have followed whatever requirements are set forth by the law in your state and your health insurance company. What specific credentials or licensing must a professional hold to provide this service in your state? Does the treatment require a written prescription from a physician? Can the professional who diagnoses your child also provide treatment? Is the professional you are working with credentialed and part of your plan's provider network? Will the professional bill the insurance company herself, or will you pay for the services and then seek reimbursement on your own?
- If your insurance company denies your claim, request a written response from them that explains the basis for the denial. Sometimes part of a claim is accepted and covered, but another part is denied. For example, occupational therapy to address problems with coordination might be covered, but activities related to sensory integration might not.
- Find out directly from your state insurance commission what

steps you need to take to exercise and protect your legal rights. If you are contesting a denial of coverage, there are probably some deadlines and steps you must follow.

- Most important, be sure that you fully understand the law as it applies to your child and the policies of your insurance plan. If you require legal assistance, contact an attorney familiar with health care insurance issues. Autism Speaks is a fine resource, as is your local chapter of a national autism organization such as the Autism Society of America.

- Autism Speaks offers an app to help families navigate the laws in their state: Autism Speaks Insurance Link. You can access this interactive tool at http://www.autismspeaks.org/advocacy/insurancelink.

- Some of the services that families seek—such as speech and language therapy and occupational therapy—might be available to your child through his school district. Some states have issued laws or regulations that make clear that the presence of insurance coverage for ASD-related services does not relieve school districts of fulfilling their obligations under IDEA. In other words, the fact that speech and language therapy might be covered by your personal health insurance does not mean that your school district can decline to provide those services.

INTERVENTIONS AND TREATMENTS

Listed here are the interventions that are most commonly prescribed for kids with ASDs. We cannot emphasize enough that no treatment is guaranteed to be effective for every child. Much depends on the child, the expertise of the practitioner, and parents' willingness to carry through and reinforce these approaches in all environments, not just a practitioner's office or the classroom. Our purpose here is simply to help you make informed decisions.

APPLIED BEHAVIOR ANALYSIS (ABA)

What It Is

Applied behavior analysis is the science of the behavior of living things. Although most people first learn of ABA through its role as the most evidence-based treatment for autism, it is important to remember that when B. F. Skinner, the psychologist considered the father of radical behaviorism and ABA as we know it today, put forth his ideas in the 1930s, he did not invent a new way to teach skills or change behavior. Through years of scientific study, he simply provided us a scientific understanding of the principles of learning that apply to everyone, and then made it possible for practitioners to apply those principles in a consistent, evidence-based repertoire to improve the skills and overall quality of life for their clients.

According to Dr. Bobby Newman, a New York–based psychologist and Board Certified Behavior Analyst, "ABA assumes that behavior is determined, and that there are laws of behavior that we can study. Once we understand the laws of behavior, we can make certain predictions about what kinds of behavior will occur in certain circumstances. If we can manipulate some of the variables, then we may be able to bring about some behavioral change."[4] ABA systematically identifies target behaviors and skills and then teaches them by breaking each skill down into small steps that are mastered individually, and by reinforcing desirable skills and behaviors through rewards (bits of food, tickles, hugs, enthusiastic praise) that are known to be motivating for that particular child (these are called reinforcers). At the same time, ABA ignores undesirable behaviors or corrects them in a neutral manner that ignores the behavior without ignoring the student—although to the untrained eye, it may appear that the therapist is doing exactly that.

Behavior analysts also do not believe that people do things because they have this or that disorder or because they suffer from complexes, issues, or any of a number of unobservable mental phenomena (such as low self-esteem, a superiority complex, or narcissism). As a parent, I found this refreshing. Finally, the focus had shifted to the issue at hand—what the team needed to be doing for my child—instead of what someone was guessing might be "wrong" with my child.

Behavior analysts know that there are numerous factors in any environment and any situation that can be changed in some way, and that it is possible, with sufficient study and analysis, to determine what specific changes will serve to either increase desirable behaviors that are good or necessary to have, or decrease behaviors that are not working for that person in some fashion. ABA's emphasis on data collection is crucial to helping the behavior analyst see and understand what's going on and what factors are either encouraging (reinforcing) or discouraging (*punishing* is the technical term, and all it means in ABA is that it is reducing the likelihood that a behavior will occur) the behavior.

Unfortunately, we live in a world where the word *behavior* has almost a pejorative association. That's not the case in ABA, where everything a person does that can be observed or that produces change in the environment is considered "behavior"; my blinking, my typing, my yawning right now—these are all behaviors. Good behavior analysts do not make judgments about "positive" or "negative" behaviors. They see things less judgmentally and always in terms of how a given behavior or skill serves the child or client. Again, is the behavior working for you or not? Professional behavior analysts are bound to an ethical code that demands that the benefit to the client comes first. Of all available interventions, ABA is the only one that can be used to teach socially appropriate behavior, self-help skills, academic skills, and speech and language through promptly and appropriately reinforcing desired responses and behavior. Contrary to another popular misconception about ABA, the point is not to teach students to "parrot" behaviors but to "learn how to learn" and generalize the skills they do acquire, two things that most people with ASDs cannot always do naturally on their own.

The past ten years have seen a major shift in the understanding and acceptance of ABA. For one thing, it is literally everywhere. Many of the techniques and best-practices approaches to education have their origins in ABA: token systems, positive behavior support, fluency training, natural consequences, time-out (the real term is "time-out from reinforcement," which tells you a lot about how it should be applied), reinforcement schedules, response cost, "Grandma's law" (as in, first your dinner, then dessert), direct teaching, functional behavior assessment, and behavior intervention programs (when written correctly, we should add).

Yes, there are some arguments against ABA, but most of these are in response to the use of discrete trial teaching (DTT), which is only one tool among dozens that behavior analysts employ. Yes, discrete trial teaching can appear to be repetitive and rote. However, for learners who need that level of intensity and repetition to learn, it is a godsend. If your child is fortunate enough not to need it to learn, say, basic language or how to use a spoon, thank your lucky stars. In fact, though, DTT is an excellent method for teaching independence skills (like shoe tying or folding clothes) as well as some academic skills that kids really do need to have down pat, on "autopilot," so to speak, such as basic math facts (multiplication tables).

Catherine Maurice, the mother of two children with autism whose progress through ABA therapy is recounted in her book *Let Me Hear Your Voice*, urges behavior analysts to do a better job explaining to parents what the method is *not*. "It is not training for compliance. It's not turning kids into robots. It's not feeding them candy all day so that they behave." These are, Maurice says, "negative stereotypes,"[5] and, to the untrained or uneducated eye witnessing some types of ABA sessions, the technique might appear to be any or all of those things. If you are a parent interested in ABA for your child with AS, you may hear others describe ABA in similar terms, or worse. Some people have a problem with behaviorism generally, because they believe that there is "more to" why people, including children, do what they do than just what behaviors are reinforced or discouraged. Yes, it is true that the underlying principles of behaviorism and ABA were first observed and demonstrated through work with animals. But that does not make ABA "animal training for kids," as we have heard critics call it. Actually, as more people are learning more about ABA, they recognize that the principles of behavior are at work throughout our lives, from local Weight Watchers meetings to the casinos of Las Vegas. Further, behavior analysts work in sports training, human resources, rehabilitation, geriatrics, addiction treatment, and many other areas.

What ABA Might Look Like

To help explain the larger context and the principles underlying the approach, let's look at a very simple case. Four-year-old Lisa cannot watch a favorite DVD without jumping up and down on the couch. This behavior is not only disturbing to others but also potentially dangerous. You might find some parents and even some professionals who would argue that this is okay because Lisa craves some form of sensory stimulation, and she should be allowed to engage in this stereotypy in the privacy of her own home. Mom might believe that it would be "cruel" to take away the DVD. The last time she tried, Lisa "screamed for twenty minutes and hit me several times" before Mom gave in, put her on the couch, and turned on the DVD. After Lisa started jumping on the couch, she "really calmed down," Mom says.

Enter the behavior analyst. Remember, ABA concerns itself with observable behavior. From an ABA perspective, we have no way of knowing with certainty why Lisa is jumping on the couch, but here's what the behavior analyst sees (and records): Lisa is watching the DVD; Lisa is jumping. So what we know is what we see (and perhaps take some baseline data on):

- Lisa prefers this DVD (she chooses it every day).
- The DVD is acting as a reinforcer (a consequence that increases the likelihood that the behavior will occur).
- Lisa has access to this reinforcer while engaging in the jumping behavior (which occurs only with this particular DVD).
- Lisa has also learned that she can obtain the DVD by engaging in other inappropriate behavior (the screaming and hitting).
- From observing Lisa and collecting data for a few days, the behavior analyst knows that the shortest period of time Lisa sits appropriately is now thirty seconds. This will be the minimum interval for the treatment.

The behavior analyst wants to teach Lisa appropriate behavior while watching the DVD by systematically manipulating the situation and establishing reinforcers for appropriate behavior. This could be done by allowing Lisa access to the DVD once a day, asking her to sit on the couch and, using the remote control, not starting the DVD until she is sitting appropriately. The therapist could then start the DVD and perhaps offer praise, pats on the back, and a preferred edible (in that case, strawberry Starburst Fruit Chews) every thirty seconds that Lisa watches TV appropriately (every thirty seconds would be considered a "discrete trial" in this context). The second Lisa starts to stand on the couch, the therapist might stop the DVD, remind Lisa to sit down, perhaps physically prompt her (briefly, lightly touching her shoulders in a downward motion, for instance), and praise her when she is again seated. The DVD goes back on, and the process continues for a previously determined period (perhaps, to start, ten trials of thirty seconds each). The therapist would record data for each trial, and when Lisa had demonstrated an ability to watch appropriately for nine or ten out of ten daily trials, the period might be increased to forty-five seconds or a minute. When that criterion was met, on to ninety seconds, two minutes, and so on, until Lisa could watch her DVD appropriately for its thirty-minute length.

Notice how every judgment in terms of the treatment is based on the data—not just on what the behavior analyst or Lisa's mom or dad remember happened, or the fact that "she seems to be doing better," or "she seems to be doing worse" (whatever either of those vague descriptions means). Also notice that the choices made about the timing, the delivery of the reinforcer, and deciding what constitutes progress are carefully thought out and quantifiable. I can count nine good trials out of ten. I don't have to depend on my memory or my impression of how Lisa is doing: I—and anyone else—can see it.

Now here come the aspects that some parents might find unfamiliar or, as I often say, counterintuitive. In other words, everyday common sense tells you something else. Although Lisa's parents certainly did not set out to do so, they inadvertently reinforced inappropriate behavior. How? Because every time Lisa did something that they did not want her to do—jump, cry, and so on—they reinforced that behavior by giving her the DVD to make that behavior stop. So it was certainly "effective"—Lisa did stop doing those things. For that moment. In the meantime, though, a relationship between those behaviors and the wonderfulness of that DVD has been established. The current situation is not the fault of Lisa or of her parents. It's simply the laws of behavior doing what they do.

Still, no parent likes hearing that she has contributed to the problem behavior by responding to her child. The fact is, most inappropriate or interfering behavior has a history of reinforcement that was purely accidental. In other words, in the course of everyday interactions, a reinforcing consequence just happened to get linked to a behavior. Kids don't "plan" or "manipulate" this; it's the result of the laws of behavior in action. If Lisa's mom believes that "Lisa jumps for sensory reasons" and that Lisa deserves some fun watching her DVD, the connection between the screaming, the jumping, and the DVD probably isn't obvious.

Parents sometimes find it difficult to see (or hear) their children crying, screaming, or having a tantrum. We want our kids to be happy; if something makes them unhappy, our first impulse may be to make it go away. Unfortunately, these noble motives can reinforce behaviors that range from mildly inappropriate to dangerous, especially for children on the spectrum, who do not learn in the same ways that typical children do. Children have tantrums and protest for many reasons, but generally they do so to achieve escape from an undesirable situation, attention from adults (both pleasant and unpleasant), or access to desired objects or activities. In the ABA world, when Lisa has a tantrum over her DVD, the way to extinguish it is either to not give her the DVD or to ignore her behavior (and we mean *really* ignore; no reprimands, no explanations, perhaps not even a glance, provided the child is not in danger), or both. For as long as this behavior has persisted, every time Lisa's mother gave in to a tantrum, she demonstrated to Lisa that tantrums "worked" as an effective strategy for getting her desires met. (No wonder Lisa's preschool teacher is reporting that Lisa now hits her classmates.)

In Lisa's mother's case, following through with the behavior analyst's recommendations may be uncomfortable (if she believes that Lisa's primary issue is sensory) and trying (what parent wants her child screaming and hitting?). However, consistency and follow-through are essential, not optional, if you are looking for the best result for your child. There may be other conditions of this particular intervention: for example, Lisa may not be allowed access to the favorite DVD outside of the ABA therapy until she has learned to watch appropriately. If, say, Starbursts are the preferred edible reinforcer, the therapist may ask Mom to deny Lisa access to Starbursts anytime except during their sessions. This might mean that Lisa's brothers do not get to have Starbursts, either, when Lisa is around. If Lisa's mother feels that Lisa's behavior is tolerable, that it's "unfair" or "mean" to deny Lisa her DVD or her Starbursts whenever she wants them, that not giving in to Lisa's demands for the DVD is "cruel," and that—despite Lisa's observable behavior—she's "smart enough to understand why her behavior is inappropriate," even the best ABA program will not produce the outcome Lisa and her family deserve.

However, if Lisa's mother followed through with the ABA behavior plan consistently, the odds are very good that within, say, a month (though with the right plan and good follow-through, in a few days), Lisa would no longer be jumping on the couch or having a tantrum over the DVD. In fact, when Mom learns how to handle Lisa's tantrums in this situation, she may be able to apply this new skill—and new way of looking at Lisa's behaviors—in other problem areas.

Why Are We Talking About ABA?

To date, this remains one of the few books on AS to recommend ABA. And my book *The Parents' Guide to Teaching Kids with Asperger Syndrome and Similar ASDs Real-Life Skills for Independence* is the only one to explain ABA strategies for teaching kids with the AS learning profile crucial independence skills (though the strategies are applicable to any learner, including neurotypical learners). Why is that? For one thing, misunderstanding among professionals regarding ABA persists. You should know—even if other professionals you work with do not—that ABA is not psychology, nor is it "only for low-functioning learners." It does not create "robots" or "one-trick ponies." It does not produce "rote learners"; instead, it uses a wide range of teaching techniques to produce learners who can function with independence and, yes, spontaneity and fluency. In short, most anti-ABA bias is at best out of date, and at worst uninformed. If someone describes ABA as "a system of rewards and punishments," move on. After hearing from countless parents whose children's choices and potential are limited by deficits in the types of skills ABA is so effective in teaching—not to mention the parade of outcome studies verifying that deficits in these areas slam the door on the opportunities that our kids' strengths and skills open for them—we feel strongly that parents should at least understand what ABA is about and consider it if their child's needs warrant it. My view as a behavior analyst and as a mom is simple: If there's a skill that ABA can teach you that you don't have right now, you cannot be "too smart" for ABA.

A few years ago, few parents of children with AS ever heard the terms *ABA* or *applied verbal behavior* (AVB, discussed in the next section). One reason for that was that most children with AS were diagnosed during their school years. Now that pediatricians, teachers, and other professionals are more aware of the early signs of autism, children with AS are being diagnosed earlier. If your child is identified and classified before age three (when he might receive early intervention services) or from age three through kindergarten (when he might receive preschool services), the dominant therapy available will probably be ABA or AVB, in addition to speech therapy, occupational therapy, and physical therapy, if appropriate.

When ABA May Be Appropriate

Theoretically, ABA can be used to address problematic behaviors (including perseverative behaviors, stigmatizing behaviors, and some types of tantrums and outbursts), and teach a wide range of skills (including some that other professionals do not: self-help, toileting, safety, and so on). Before putting any ABA program into effect, you, your child's behavior analyst, and any other professionals working with your child should be sure to rule out other possible causes of problem behaviors, such as medical issues, comorbid disorders, neurological problems, sensory issues, and so on.

How It Works

Any behavior can be expressed in terms of ABC: *antecedent* (what occurs before the behavior), the *behavior* itself, and the *consequences* (by which we mean the response the behavior elicits from others, not a punishment). A crucial part of an effective ABA approach to any behavior is determining the function of the behavior; in other words, why does Janie panic whenever she hears the family car start? What purpose does that panic and the reaction it prompts serve for her? What is it about the response to her panic that reinforces the behavior and increases the likelihood that it will recur and/or increase? What alternative consequence will decrease the likelihood that Janie will express panic? And so on.

Another important aspect of ABA is the understanding of reinforcers. Essentially, any behavior that is reinforced will be more likely to recur and become more prevalent than one that is not reinforced. It is important to understand that in ABA terms, a reinforcer is not necessarily what most of us would consider a "reward." Rather, it is a consequence of an individual's behavior that increases the likelihood that the behavior will recur. For one child, an effective reinforcer might be a tiny bite of a favorite food; for another, it might be the chance to look at a book about trains for a few moments, or a high-five, or a big smile and behavior-specific praise: "Great job reading that passage," "Nice job folding your pants." Once the reinforcer is identified, the behavior analyst determines how and when that reinforcer will be offered (every time, as is often the case when a learner is acquiring a new skill; or intermittently, as it might be once the learner has mastered a skill and we are trying to thin or fade the reinforcement). Ideally, reinforcers are thinned as the skill is mastered and then removed once the learner demonstrates the skill across different environments and situations. (This is called *generalization*.) For example, to encourage a child to turn and look at you when his name is called, you might reinforce him every time. As the response becomes more consistent and independent, you will gradually fade the reinforcement until it reaches the level or the form available in the natural environment. So, for example, you want to scale back gradually and systematically from a Skittle every time Joey ties his shoes correctly, to praise and a hug every fifth time, to just praise. And even then, you would probably be fading that praise until it reached the frequency that matches what we find in the real, regular world. Which, when you think about it, may one day be zero for someone for whom shoe tying is no big deal.

You should find ABA at the core of good behavioral interventions in school. Let's look at a familiar scenario that has the potential to lead to school disciplinary issues, changes in educational placement, loss of learning time in the classroom, and poor relationships with school staff and peers. Even though the factors that determine behavior can be complex, the effective use of ABA can produce an elegantly straightforward solution. (Bear in mind that the factors determining behavior can be extremely complex.) If Gianni kicks his desk every morning "for no apparent reason," a behavior analyst would study the situation to determine what function Gianni's kicking was truly serving. Since the consequence of his kicking to date has been removal from the classroom, and every time Gianni kicks, he is removed from the classroom, then the removal is viewed as a possible reinforcer. We also cannot ignore the fact that even though the teacher regards this as a "punishment" and should serve as a disincentive that discourages the kicking, it does not. How do we know that it does not in Gianni's case? Simple: Gianni is still kicking.

A behavior analyst would study the situation, analyze the data, and try manipulating variables that might be serving as antecedents to help answer the question "What is prompting Gianni's kicking?" This may take some trial and error: Is it the noise of the PA system from the morning announcements? The packet of worksheets that is placed on his desk? A general need to escape the classroom? The therapist tests each hypothesis by analyzing every aspect of the behavior. If one day Gianni's teacher does not place a packet of worksheets on his desk and he does not kick, then it would be reasonable to formulate a plan based on the premise that Gianni is kicking to avoid schoolwork. Gianni may not be thinking of it in exactly those terms, and he may never have "planned" to get out of doing his work by kicking, but once he kicked and was removed from the classroom, he accidentally happened upon a behavior that produced a consequence that achieved what he considers a desirable outcome. Like Lisa, he's hit on what is to *him* an effective means to a desirable end.

The next step is to look at the consequence of Gianni's kicking—

removal from the classroom and from the work—as the reinforcer that is driving this inappropriate behavior. The behavior analyst might advise one of several possible alternate consequences:

- The teacher could ignore the kicking (which may be difficult) or have Gianni removed from the classroom to a place where he would still have to complete his work.
- In addition, the therapist might introduce other reinforcers— such as an immediate reward for doing the work in the alternate setting, and then for doing the work at his desk, and then for doing the work at his desk without kicking—to increase the likelihood that the acceptable behavior would occur again.
- The ultimate goal would be to fade the reinforcer (a sometimes complicated matter) as Gianni gains the ability to control his kicking. The important thing to remember, however, is that the teacher and everyone working with Gianni must be vigilant in ensuring that the inappropriate behavior not be reinforced by their responses—and, equally important, that they provide prompt verbal praise and other known reinforcers for the desired behavior. "Catch them being good" should be every parent's and teacher's mantra. In the beginning, it might be advisable to praise Gianni as often as every few moments for staying in his seat and doing his work.

What We Know About ABA and Asperger Syndrome

The bulk of research done on ABA and autism spectrum disorders focuses on individual case studies of persons whose diagnoses are more indicative of what we once called autistic disorder or PDD-NOS. Still, there are increasing numbers of peer-reviewed single-subject or small-group studies demonstrating ABA's efficacy in treating problems with academic skills, executive function, self-help and daily living skills, social skills, play skills, and relationship and sexuality training in AS.

Depending on where you live, odds are good that most behavior analysts you encounter might have spent most, if not all, of their time working with such children with different learning profiles. Because of ABA's scientific foundation (and, in the case of Board Certified Behavior Analysts, a strict ethical code), behavior analysts do not employ non-evidence-based strategies or programs. With its focus on helping people acquire skills and develop independence to the greatest extent possible, the treatment priorities of a behavior analyst might seem "less forgiving" of things like stigmatizing behaviors such as noncontextual vocalizations in public or a lack of personal care skills in a college-bound teen. Although you may read experts' warnings that ABA is not a quick fix for teaching and reinforcing appropriate behaviors, that is precisely how some parents of children with AS have used it, with positive results.

Discrete Trial Teaching Has a Place, Too

First, don't confuse ABA the science with certain ABA techniques that have come to define it. Discrete trial teaching is just one technique: a highly structured sequence of exchanges between a teacher and a student consisting of a teacher-directed antecedent, or stimulus; the learner's behavior or response; and the consequence. For a student learning simple motor imitation, a discrete trial might look like this:

1. The teacher establishes a readiness response: saying the student's name, "Get ready," "Let's start," establishing eye contact, or any other exchange that the student recognizes as a signal that it's time to attend and that the teacher knows that the student is paying attention.
2. Here's the discrete trial:
    - The teacher then gives the direction (or S^D): "Clap hands" (antecedent, stimulus).
    - The student claps his hands (behavior, response).
    - The teacher reinforces the behavior with praise, smiles, a piece of a preferred food, or access to a favored activity (consequence).

3. If the student errs or does not clap his hands, the teacher corrects the error in one of several possible ways, depending on the student's abilities, past performance, and other factors. She might model clapping hands, clap the student's hand in a hand-over-hand prompt, and so on. If the student is learning to clap hands, she might teach errorlessly and, for instance, clap his hands hand-over-hand right after saying "Clap hands," and then offer reinforcement and praise.

Discrete trial teaching often occurs in practice-rich massed trials. That means that this student would be asked to "clap hands" in five, ten, and fifteen regularly scheduled trials (for example, once every school day or session day). More complicated responses, such as setting a table or completing a sheet of math problems, might call for fewer trials. It is important to note that because of motor planning, executive function, and fine- and gross-motor deficits, someone with AS might benefit greatly from a modified approach to an endless list that might include hanging up clothes on hangers, tying a necktie, starting a zipper, buttoning, cracking an egg, using a calculator, touch typing, throwing or catching a ball, riding a bike, hair washing, twirling spaghetti on a fork with one hand, handwriting, shoe tying, cutting with scissors, folding clothes, or dressing independently.

ABA is distinguished by the scrupulously detailed written records that behavior analysts keep to track and quantify the frequency, duration, and intensity of specific behaviors and the detailed teaching procedures used. Careful attention is paid to the systematic use and fading of prompts. The direction of the therapy is determined by the data collected, not by a teacher's or a parent's impressions or "feelings" about how a child is doing. If the teacher determines that mastery for cutting a straight line is 80 percent (eight of ten trials, or four of five, or sixteen of twenty) accuracy over three (or four or five) days, and *accuracy* is defined as the line being cut straight within one-eighth inch (or one-sixteenth inch or no margin) on either side, Sidney will not move on to cutting an *L* until he has met that criterion. This reduces the chances that Sidney will start working on cutting *L*s without the required skills. Such systematic teaching is geared toward creating conditions under which the student can most quickly and accurately learn the correct responses and skills.

Before you consider ABA therapy for your child, consult with other professionals who work with him. Ask them about their experience with ABA (though you may find harsh criticism of the method; not all professionals truly understand ABA) and whether they know of any other children with AS who have benefited from it. If they do, ask specifically what types of behavior it addressed and, alternately, any behaviors for which it proved ineffective. Don't be shy about asking for references, from both former supervisors and employers and clients.

Generally speaking, the professional consensus is that children with AS do not need ABA therapy as urgently as they need social skills training. However, depending on your child's behaviors, it may be wise not to view this strictly as an either/or question. "No matter what the problem is," psychologist Bobby Newman says, "my basic question is, 'Okay, the student is functioning in this particular setting. Is he functioning as well as he could? If not, what do we need to teach him to do to help him function better? And if he is functioning adequately in that setting, what does he need to learn or what behavior does he need to eliminate in order to move to the next less restrictive setting?' I believe ABA gives choices. If I don't have a skill, I don't have a choice. If I can't leave the house without having the television set on a certain channel without feeling anxious, I have no choice. I have no freedom. But if I have the skill to be able to leave the house without the television on that channel, now I have a choice."[6]

Where to Find ABA

Mastering ABA requires years of training. No one can be considered a behavior analyst, behavior therapist, or behavioral consultant on the basis of taking a single course or seminar, reading a few books, or working under the occasional supervision of an ABA expert. Improperly applied, ABA can reinforce undesirable, even dangerous, behaviors and exacerbate underlying comorbid psychiatric or emotional disorders. We caution parents to refuse to submit their child to any ABA program or treatment that does not include the direct hands-on involvement of at least one BCBA who has experience with AS. You should know that national certification of behavior analysts through the nonprofit Behavior Analyst Certification Board began only in 2000. For a long time, there was nothing to prevent anyone, regardless of training, from presenting himself as qualified to provide ABA. In some states now, there are laws against that. Realistically, however, laws do not always stop people from doing what they shouldn't, especially if they have gotten away with it or it was not prohibited before. Demand to see credentials.

If your child has complicating issues or the behavior has potential for serious self-injury or injury to others, the behavior analyst should also be a licensed psychologist. (See "Recommended Resources" on page 199 to find BCBAs.) Your school district's special education administrators and teachers, or a local AS- or ASD-related support group may be able to put you in touch with ABA-trained therapists in your area. You might also want to contact local special education schools or programs, including those that provide early intervention and preschool services. If a college or university in your area offers course work in applied behavior analysis, it might also have some students who are seeking supervised practice and looking for clients. Some organizations, universities, hospitals, and adult education programs offer training in ABA for parents.

Issues to Consider

If you do go forward with ABA, be sure that everyone who works with your child is aware of the behavior you are addressing and the appropriate ABA response. Consistency of response in every setting is key to the therapy's success. So, for instance, if Nancy's therapist has determined that the appropriate response to her snapping her fingers as she speaks is a particular gestural cue or a touch on the shoulder, everyone—parents, teachers, grandparents, babysitters—should be doing it, every time the behavior occurs.

Recommended Resources

Books

Patricia Romanowski Bashe, *The Parents' Guide to Teaching Kids with Asperger Syndrome and Similar ASDs Real-Life Skills for Independence* (New York: Crown, 2011).

Bobby Newman, *When Everybody Cares: Case Studies of ABA with People with Autism* (New York: Dove and Orca, 1999) and *Graduated Applied Behavior Analysis* (New York: Dove and Orca, 2002).

Website

Behavior Analyst Certification Board: www.bacb.com.

Includes a current listing of Board Certified Behavior Analysts (BCBAs) as well as university programs that provide course work and training for students working toward obtaining BCBAs. Sometimes through university practicum programs, you can find students working under strict supervision of a BCBA.

VERBAL BEHAVIOR

You might hear someone refer to verbal behavior (VB), or verbal behavior analysis (VBA), or applied verbal behavior (AVB) as a "new" therapy or something "different from" ABA. Some refer to it as NET (for Natural Environment Training, a component of VB that focuses on working with the child in his natural environment and using his interests and activities to shape the teaching) or "the Carbone method."[7] Technically, VB should not be separated from ABA, since it is a teaching method that uses the principles of ABA, and, most important, the theory behind it was articulated by B. F. Skinner, the father of ABA. Skinner's 1957 landmark work, *Verbal Behavior*, set forth the argument that verbal behavior—what we say and why—is really no different from any other kind of observable behavior. Skinner contended that language is learned through a series of interactions in which behavior is either reinforced or punished, and that we can analyze different types of language in terms of their function. Skinner and other behaviorists focused only on observable, external behavior: what a person said (or signed or wrote).

Skinner was interested in how the conditions in the environment—including what others say to us—make it or more or less likely that we will use words in a specific way.

What It Is

Verbal behavior uses the principles of ABA to promote expressive language; in other words, to encourage children to speak, by manipulating the environment to set up natural antecedents that will promote language by establishing associations between objects, actions, and anything else we have a word for with the actual object, action, quality, and so on. VB has its own jargon, invented by Skinner as well. A request is a *mand*, a noun is a *tact*. In VB, then, "ice cream" could be both a mand (when it is requested) and a tact (when the child correctly identifies a photograph of ice cream). In VB, learners are said to be *manding* and *tacting*.

When It May Be Appropriate

For a child with Asperger syndrome who might not have an expressive speech delay, there may be a place for VB. Though for learners on other points on the spectrum it is used to elicit basic language and establish imitation skills (usually not issues for children with AS), it can also be effective for teaching more complex and higher-level forms of language such as answering "Wh"—who, what, when, where, and how—questions and fill-ins; what AVB terms the *intraverbal*. Intraverbal exchanges do not depend on imitating what someone else has said but may require prompting or modeling to elicit a response. The reinforcers are natural and social. Intraverbals require the child to attend and respond to another person's language, a crucial component in developing natural conversation skills.

VB's emphasis on teaching to mastery, fluency, and spontaneity may be a welcome alternative to less structured approaches or those that do not adequately recognize or reinforce learner initiative.

How It Works

VB in action can look quite different from ABA, especially its discrete trials. For example, in teaching manding in VB, the teacher would follow the child's lead, determine something the child would want, set up a situation in which it would be visible but not readily available (say, a juice box on a shelf the child could not reach or a cookie in the teacher's hand), then use very specific techniques to elicit the word *juice* or *cookie* (or approximations, and, in the case of children who are nonverbal, perhaps signing). The reinforcer here would be the actual object the child requests, as opposed to what sometimes occurs in ABA discrete trials, which is the presentation of a cookie for the child saying something totally unrelated, such as *cat*. VB also emphasizes allotting working in the natural environment (the NET), where the teacher would appear to be following the child's lead and seizing upon any and every opportunity to reinforce verbal behavior. For example, if a child were to walk toward the bubble wand on a table, the teacher would hold it up and repeat the word *bubble* three times, each time moving the bubble wand closer to the child. If the child makes a vocal approximation or says the word *bubble*, he receives the wand immediately. Proponents of VB also argue that because language is taught in ways that make it always functional, it helps to promote more natural prosody (the tone, volume, and rhythm and other "nonword" qualities of speech) and learner initiative.

What We Know About VB and Asperger Syndrome

We know very little at this point, but as more teachers, speech pathologists, and other therapists are trained in it, and as more children with AS are diagnosed younger, research will certainly emerge. For now, however, you should make your decision based on your child's needs and discussions with potential therapists. If your child receives early intervention or preschool services, and the only form of therapy available is ABA, you should consider requesting that language objectives be addressed using VB rather than discrete trial ABA. For further information, such as where to find VB, questions to ask, and what parents can do to help, see the preceding section on ABA.

Recommended Resource

Christina Burk's website features a number of brief, informative pages on all aspects of ABA, including verbal behavior, at http://www.christinaburkaba.com/AVB.htm.

AUDITORY INTEGRATION TRAINING (AIT)

Auditory integration training is one of the more controversial interventions here. Unfortunately, research on AIT is neither plentiful nor definitive. In fact, the American Academy of Pediatrics has adopted a position that pediatricians not recommend the use of AIT. The American Speech-Language-Hearing Association (ASHA)—the largest "professional, scientific, and credentialing" organization for speech-language pathologists and other speech, language, and hearing professionals—has issued a statement not supporting AIT, as well. Although there are several highly complex theories behind AIT, it is unclear precisely how it changes auditory perception or behavior.

What It Is

There are several forms of AIT. The two that are most associated with ASDs were developed independently by two French doctors. More than forty years ago, Dr. Alfred Tomatis introduced his audio-psycho-phonology approach using predominantly high-frequency sounds as well as the voices of the patient and his mother, songs, and stories. The therapy involves about one hundred hours of listening. Critics of Tomatis say that his claim that problems in hearing and auditory processing may be rooted in emotional problems and experiences (thus the use of the mother's voice in the therapy) is outdated, to say the very least. Among those critics is Dr. Guy Berard, who developed his method for AIT in the 1960s. Berard's approach is less psychologically oriented than Tomatis's. Based on the results of extensive audiological tests, the therapist programs a special sound amplifier to modify music from regular CDs (so a patient might be listening to Hank Williams or the Beatles) by selectively eliminating specific high and low frequencies. AIT providers stress that patients are not just "listening to music," but are listening to music that has been sonically altered according to the individual sensitivities revealed through prior testing. Berard's AIT usually involves two half-hour sessions, spaced a minimum of three hours apart, every day over the course of ten days. Both Berard's and Tomatis's AIT can be administered only by a trained professional, usually an audiologist.

In addition, there are a number of other listening programs—among the better known are Earobics and Fast ForWord. Earobics, which was originally promoted as an in-home therapy for central auditory processing issues, is now marketed by educational publishing giant Houghton Mifflin as a program designed to "have a direct impact on student achievement" in literacy.[8] Earobics is used in thousands of school districts across the nation, and its maker claims that 97 percent of students who used it "achieve significant improvements in their literacy skills." There is no mention of autism or auditory integration. Scientific Learning's Fast ForWord, which has been around for thirty years and is used in schools, clinics, and homes, also claims impressive results in improving learners' literacy and auditory processing ability.[9]

When It May Be Appropriate

Some experts assert that auditory processing disorder has a high prevalence among children with AD/HD, dyslexia, and learning disabilities (one study found that more than 95 percent of children with LD also had auditory processing disorder). Generally, informed estimates find hearing sensitivities in all forms among people with ASDs (not just those diagnosed with CAPD) to be somewhere around half. More recent research has discovered that children with autism process sounds microseconds more slowly than typical children. When you consider that most of us speak at a rate of 250 milliseconds per syllable, a child who has a 50-millisecond delay in detecting speech would quickly fall behind. There is no evidence, however, that AIT can remediate this particular problem.

Children who are diagnosed with central auditory processing disorder (CAPD) (also referred to as auditory processing disorder, central auditory disorder, auditory perceptual problems, or central auditory dysfunction) exhibit the following symptoms:

- Extreme responses—pain, anxiety, panic—to everyday sounds and noises
- Hyperacute hearing and processing difficulties
- Difficulty attending and focusing or other behaviors that suggest AD/HD or other learning disabilities

We know that people with ASD generally frequently have difficulty with auditory stimuli. (See page 78 for a fuller description of AS-related hearing problems.)

How It Works

Scientifically speaking, it is not clear precisely how AIT works, though proponents have their theories. Essentially, every AIT program attempts to address some form of auditory processing disorder. (For more information, see "Central Auditory Processing Disorder [CAPD]," page 78.) There are highly technical explanations of CAPD, but for most parents, it is enough to think of a child with CAPD as a child who can hear normally but whose brain cannot sort or make sense of what he hears. Normal *hearing* does not equal normal *listening*. In other words, a child with profound CAPD issues may well pass a typical hearing test with flying colors. The problem is not *what* is heard but *how* it is heard and how the brain responds. As one handout on the topic available online put it, "The child can hear, but listening is the problem. Think of the problem you would have if you suddenly found yourself in England at the time of Shakespeare. The speech is English, but in a strange, accented style with different constructions and meaning."[10] The goal of AIT is to help people with AS understand what they hear.

Our hearing also can affect the ability to focus and attend; modulate sensory stimulation; accurately perceive balance and movement; and develop appropriate speech and language skills. In addition, some therapists view CAPD as another form of sensory integration disorder.

Diagnosing CAPD is a challenge, because hearing is so subjective and also because there is still some disagreement among professionals regarding exactly what CAPD is. People with CAPD have nothing against which to compare their "distorted" hearing. A child with CAPD, for example, cannot possibly know that the sound of water running in a sink should not be physically painful to hear. He does not know that the sound of other students walking quietly outside the closed classroom door should not be as loud as the voice of the teacher speaking directly to him. Yet that's the way some people with CAPD hear the world. It's not surprising, then, that they may respond with confusion, anxiety, and what appears to be an inability to pay attention. Children who find what they hear at times physically painful or unusually frightening may become nervous, anxious, avoidant, whiny, or physically aggressive.

What We Know About AIT and Asperger Syndrome

Beyond a handful of first-person accounts, little is known about the effectiveness of AIT to treat CAPD in kids with ASD. Interestingly, a comprehensive review of research on auditory processing in children published in a peer-reviewed journal does not list AIT as a recommended strategy.[11]

Where to Find It

Only an audiologist should be diagnosing CAPD (although speech pathologists and other therapists may recognize signs and suggest evaluation by an audiologist). Many CAPD- and ASD-related websites post lists of practitioners and organizations that provide AIT.

Questions to Ask

- Ask the practitioner about his background, his experience with the methods he offers, and his experience with children like your own. How many children has he treated? Roughly what percentage showed significant improvement?

- Ask, Which norm-referenced assessments will be administered before and after the treatment? What changes in the results will indicate improvement? Are these assessments ones that your child's speech pathologist or other professional would be familiar with?

  - Provide the practitioner with any evaluations and reports you have on your child (speech and language, neurological, psychological, occupational therapy, etc.). Be sure that you have thoroughly discussed your child's particular challenges before the training begins and that the practitioner has a good idea about your child's basic temperament, sensitivities, and usual behaviors.
  - Your practitioner should know about any medication your child is taking, including over-the-counter and "natural" alternative products and supplements.
  - If the practitioner is not an audiologist, find out if there is an audiologist with experience in the method of AIT you will be using available to do the pretraining diagnostic testing and the posttraining follow-up evaluations.
  - Be sure you have a clear idea about the schedule of treatment.
  - Ask specifically about what happens if, for instance, your child cannot complete the training because of illness, family emergency, adverse reaction, and so on.
  - Ask the practitioner what time of day he would prefer to see your child during the training. Generally, most children are best early in the day, before school.
  - Find out about what to expect during the training sessions. Ask to visit the room where the training will occur. Will you be allowed to stay with your child? Can your child have drinks or snacks in the room during the training? If your child can have

snacks, try to avoid overly sweetened treats or foods
and drinks containing caffeine.

- Ask about possible changes in behavior during and
after the training. Agitation, hyperactivity, mood
swings, aggression, nausea, and changes in eating
and sleeping patterns may occur.

- Inquire about the cost. Most insurance companies
will not cover AIT because it is considered
experimental. Depending on your coverage, it
may be possible to receive reimbursement for
the diagnostic testing and evaluation. Costs vary,
depending on the method used and the practitioner,
but may range as high as $1,000 or more.

- Once your child has been evaluated and/or treated,
ask the practitioner or audiologist to explain
the test results to you in plain English. Ask for
specific information on what you can do at home
and what teachers can do in school to help your
child. If you believe that hearing issues are causing
problems in school, also ask that the practitioner
prepare a written report for your child's school that
includes specific suggestions for helping him in
the classroom (for example, being seated near the
teacher's desk, or being excused from loud, noisy
activities or places, such as school pep rallies).

What Parents Can Do to Help

If your child has been diagnosed with CAPD, you can do many
things to make his environment, at home and in school, more comfortable. Be patient, understanding, and accommodating. To the extent possible, avoid noises and sounds that provoke panic responses.
Try to be more conscientious about the "noise environment" wherever your child is, but don't be afraid to test your child's ability to
cope with troublesome sounds whenever you can do so safely and
you can leave the situation immediately if there is a problem. Do all
that you can to "clear the field," so to speak. To expect your child

to understand you as you talk over the stereo, radio, television, or another conversation is asking for frustration. At home, be sure you have your child's attention before you start speaking. Use a code word or a gesture, such as a light tap on the shoulder or pointing to your ear, to indicate that it's time to listen. Speak clearly and slowly, using shorter sentences, and give one- or two-step (as opposed to five- and six-step) directions or explanations. Gradually work on building up the number of steps your child can follow. Check with your child to see if she heard and/or understood what you said, and teach her to recognize when she may have missed or misunderstood something, and how to ask the speaker to repeat or clarify what was said.

Work closely with your child's teacher to ensure that her hearing difficulties are recognized and accommodated. Keep in mind that many classrooms are, acoustically speaking, not the most conducive environments for learning. Your child might require seating away from other auditory distractions (the air-conditioner, the open doorway to the hall, the class computer and printer station). Some students have benefited from using a sound system whereby the teacher speaks into a small wearable microphone and the sound is conveyed to a headset the student wears. You can learn more about such devices from your child's audiologist or speech pathologist.

Notes and Comments

Despite reports that children who listened to regular, untreated music through regular equipment and headphones showed similar improvements to children who underwent AIT, only an audiologist who specializes in AIT can determine what may be effective for your child. And only an audiologist can conduct the type of assessment needed to determine what improvement may occur.

SOCIAL STORIES AND COMIC STRIP CONVERSATIONS

Social Stories and Comic Strip Conversations are two different but related approaches to helping people with AS and other PDDs develop a clearer understanding about a wide range of social information. Though each uses a different technique, and one may be more effective in a given situation, they both do essentially the same thing: make explicit—through words, drawings, or both—the kind of information about social behavior, routines, goals, and academic skills that people with AS have difficulty picking up. Both methods are based on the premise that inappropriate or undesirable behavior arises from a lack of understanding of what's appropriate or desirable in a given situation. Social Stories may be applied to a wider range of situations; Comic Strip Conversations, on the other hand, are graphic illustrations of conversations—past, present, or future—and "systematically identify what people say and do, and emphasize *what people may be thinking.*"[12] Carol Gray, an educator and expert on autism who created both Social Stories and Comic Strip Conversations specifically to address the types of problems children with ASDs face, says that there are no firm "rules" regarding which method is best suited to a given situation, but she has made some general observations about each.

Social Stories tend to be more accessible to younger children, who can read the stories themselves or have them read to them. Writing a Social Story does require that its author (you or another adult) fully understand the issues from the child's perspective. Writing a Comic Strip Conversation, in contrast, demands a fact-finding effort on your part. Unlike a Social Story, a Comic Strip Conversation is a collaborative effort between you and the child (or you and several children). Part of the process involves asking questions and "drawing" the conversation to reflect the child's answers.

The beauty of both methods is that anyone can learn how to create them or work with the child to create them. As long as you have paper and pencil handy, they can be created anywhere; they are portable; they can be referred to as many times as necessary. Notebooks containing the Social Stories and Comic Strip Conversations about skills, fears, and issues that a child is working on or has mastered offer a great opportunity for him to see concrete evidence of his progress.

What We Know About Social Stories and Comic Strip Conversations and AS

Both Social Stories and Comic Strip Conversations have been in use since the early 1990s. They have gained wide acceptance from authorities on AS and ASDs, who view them as an effective way of overcoming social difficulties resulting from problems with theory of mind and social understanding. Because they were created by an educator and designed to work with students in the school environment, they are practical as well.

SOCIAL STORIES

What They Are

A Social Story is a brief (100- to 500-word) narrative that describes a situation (who, what, where, why, when), explains the feelings and/ or thoughts of everyone involved (including the child for whom the story is written), and gives some direction regarding appropriate responses. Although a Social Story may seem "simple," it's important to remember that it must reflect the child's perspective, and that may require some detective work. If a child is nervous about going to a movie theater, and you write a Social Story based on your assumption that the issue is the hubbub around the snack bar, it won't work if the real problem is the child's fear of the restroom's self-flushing toilets.

Nor can you use a Social Story to prescribe or dictate desired behavior without offering an adequate description of the situation or of the feelings, thoughts, or actions of others. It may help to remember that the primary purpose of a Social Story is not to dictate appropriate behaviors and responses but to increase a child's awareness and understanding. Ideally, this understanding will make it easier for the child to demonstrate the desired behavior. After writing and reviewing thousands of Social Stories, Carol Gray developed the "Social Story Ratio," which is the key to a story's effectiveness. In her formula, for every directive sentence ("do this" or "say that"), the story must include two to five sentences that are descriptive and/or offer perspective on why someone might do, say, or think something.

Here's a bit about how it works. This is an example from the "Social Story Kit," by Carol Gray. For illustrative purposes, we have indicated the type of sentence that follows in italics. In a real Social Story, the text in regular type would run as a full paragraph without the descriptive terms at the left.

Descriptive: Sometimes a person says, "I changed my mind."

Perspective: This means they had one idea, but now they have a new idea.

Descriptive: There are many situations where a person may say, "I changed my mind."

Perspective: It is safe for someone to change their mind or want to do something else. Sometimes the new idea or the new thing they want to do is better than the old one.

Descriptive: I will work on staying calm when someone changes their mind.

Perspective: It is important to try to stay calm.

Perspective: This keeps everyone safe.

Word choice is also important. Obviously, the story must be written at the child's level of understanding. In addition, the writer must avoid terms and expressions that may be interpreted too literally. Words such as *always*, *never*, and *every* may cause confusion or distress. For example, you would not write "Every day I ride my bicycle to school," even though most people would understand that implicit in that statement are such mutually understood exceptions as days when there is no school, days with inclement weather, days when the child might be home from school ill. In a Social Story you would write "*Sometimes* I ride my bicycle to school."

It is wise to exercise extra caution in phrasing the directive sentences in such a way that they don't create an atmosphere of unrealistic expectations and inadvertently set the stage for failure. "I can," "I will," "I should," or "I must" statements have no place in a Social

Story. Not only may a child not be able to comply with the directive, he may be hindered from doing so by circumstances entirely beyond his control. Instead, begin directive sentences with:

"I will try to . . ."
"I will work on . . ."
"I may [do something] . . ."
"I can try to [do something] . . ."

and so on.

Be sure that directive sentences are positive and focus on the appropriate, desired response or behavior, not on the problem behavior the Social Story is designed to address. Remember that for many of our children, simply having the understanding necessary to make the effort is a victory unto itself.

When They May Be Appropriate

You can use a Social Story to help a child with AS:

- Learn a routine, such as how to get dressed or how to set the table.
- Prepare for an event or situation that is either unfamiliar or difficult, such as attending a birthday party or the first day of school.
- Foster understanding of behaviors and identify appropriate responses, such as what to do when one feels angry or afraid generally or in specific situations.
- Recognize social cues and respond appropriately, such as "Why and How I Show People I Love Them."
- Learn how to achieve a goal using step-by-step instructions, such as "Going to McDonald's."
- Understand how to identify fictional, inappropriate interactions and events in movies, videos, video games, and other forms of fiction and media.
- Learn how to apply knowledge, such as how to make change or tell time, to practical situations.

Notes and Comments

Although the Social Story technique is easily learned, there are specific guidelines crucial to applying it successfully. These are found in Carol Gray's *The New Social Story Book* (Arlington, TX: Future Horizons, 2010), which comes with a free DVD of templates for Social Stories.

COMIC STRIP CONVERSATIONS

What They Are

A Comic Strip Conversation is exactly what it sounds like: a hand-drawn comic strip (or a single panel) that illustrates social communication. A parent or teacher may draw the conversation, but it is best approached as a joint project in which the child is an active partner. It can be used to help a person with AS understand an exchange or event that occurred in the past or to help that person prepare for a future interaction. For example, you might use a Comic Strip Conversation to explain to a child with AS why his sister cried when he told her that her games were all "stupid," or how to greet a friend.

You don't need to be an artist to draw Comic Strip Conversations; stick figures will do. The technique is fully explained in Carol Gray's short book, *Comic Strip Conversations: Colorful, Illustrated Interactions with Students with Autism and Related Disorders.* Comic Strip Conversations use the same visual vocabulary as comic books: text bubbles with tails that point to the speaker for spoken words and cloudlike bubbles for thoughts. Overlapping text bubbles signify what it "looks like" when someone interrupts: for instance, large letters spell out words spoken loudly and smaller letters indicate words spoken softly. Different emotions may be indicated by colors. Carol Gray has developed a "color vocabulary," but you can change these to suit your child's preference. Just remember to use the colors consistently (for example, blue will always mean happiness; red, anger; and so on).

When They May Be Appropriate

Comic Strip Conversations usually illustrate communication and social interaction. They've been shown to be effective in helping some people with AS better understand the thoughts, emotions, and words of both themselves and others. They provide a "map" of how conversations "work."

What Happened

Often in social skills training, we remind people to pay attention to the topic others are discussing. While that advice is good, it is not always enough information to help someone like Julie here from making a social faux pas. While, yes, the subject is smartphones, we learn that what Julie is interested in about smartphones and what her classmates care about are two different things.

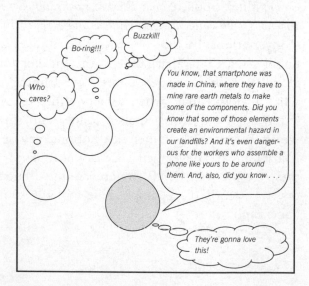

Next Time

This time, Julie notes not only what the others are talking about but how they are talking about it. All the comments so far share a common focus: the look of the phone. Though Julie knows a lot about phones, she pauses to choose her words. She has learned that not everyone needs—or wants—to hear everything you might have to share. She keeps her comments short and to the point.

How They Work

The comic strip format helps a child with AS because it "freezes" the action (which makes postevent analysis possible) and because it offers insight into the thoughts and feelings of others. A Comic Strip Conversation takes the many levels of social communication—emotion, facial expression, tone of voice, speech—and breaks them

A Comic Strip Conversation as Social Autopsy

This Comic Strip Conversation is based on a true story. Justin became upset when he "read" Sean's playful invitation to join him according to the literal meaning of Sean's words and a noncontextual interpretation of Sean's actions. Justin interpreted Sean's playful "Ha-ha-ha-ha" as "He was laughing at me" and Sean's "You can't catch me!" as an insult rather than an invitation. When Sean turned to run (expecting Justin to follow), Justin saw that as a sign that Sean did not want to play with him. The Comic Strip Conversation in panel 3 is designed to give Justin some insight into what Sean really meant and expected. Panel 4 demonstrates how to ask for clarification when someone's meaning is not clear.

down into discrete components. Once the strip is drawn, a child can revisit or become familiar with a situation at his own pace without the distraction and stress of actually being in the situation. For example, using both a text bubble and a thought bubble, you can effectively illustrate another person saying "You can't catch me!" while thinking "I really want Justin to follow me because he is my friend and I like playing with him." This level of understanding is often simply not accessible to a child with AS. For Justin, who interprets "You can't catch me" as an insult or a taunt, a vivid, visual representation of the "thought behind the words" may be the difference between being able to play comfortably among peers or not.

What Parents Can Do to Help

If you do decide to try Social Stories and Comic Strip Conversations, consult one of Carol Gray's books or work with someone who knows the technique and follow Gray's guidelines completely. Even if you don't write a Social Story or sketch out a Comic Strip Conversation for every problematic situation, it is well worth the time and effort to familiarize yourself with the approach. Simply thinking through a situation and breaking down the ideas as you would to write a Social Story can help you learn a simpler, clearer way of communicating orally with your child.

One mild caution: In the field, most professionals refer to any multisentence written instruction, to-do list, or verbal, written prompt as a "social story." It's not. It would be more appropriate to describe these works as "social narratives" or, as I call them, "elaborate visual prompts that use words." Carol Gray trademarked the term Social Story, and she has repeatedly revisited and refined the criteria of what makes a Social Story a Social Story; the latest version is termed 10.0. When you consult studies that use Social Stories, they typically indicate that they are following Gray's guidelines. If the guidelines are not followed, the story might not work like a Social Story is designed to work.

Recommended Resources

Carol Gray, *Comic Strip Conversations: Colorful Illustrated Interactions with Students with Autism and Related Disorders* (Arlington, TX: Future Horizons, 1994).

Carol Gray, *The New Social Story Book* (Arlington, TX: Future Horizons, 2010).

OCCUPATIONAL THERAPY (OT)

What It Is

Occupational therapy is a health care specialty concerned with developing, strengthening, and restoring the patient's ability to perform the tasks of daily living. It emerged as a specialized field in the wake of World War I, which left millions of survivors who were physically and/or neurologically disabled. Disabled people who were taught to regain some degree of ability with OT had quicker and more satisfactory outcomes than those who remained inactive. The term *occupational* refers not simply to paid work but to any goal one wishes to achieve.

OT recognizes and addresses nervous system (brain- and nerve-related) dysfunction that may give rise to challenges in all areas of life—intellectual, personal, social, psychological, emotional, and vocational. Occupational therapists treat patients whose problems arise from a wide range of causes: physical injury, birth defect, aging, psychological disability, illness, and developmental disability. This aspect of occupational therapy has a long, strong evidence base.

However, in terms of evidence base and research, the picture is less clear when occupational therapy is used to treat sensory integration disorder, also known as sensory integration dysfunction. Sensory integration disorder is the inability of the brain to effectively and efficiently process sensory stimuli. There is no question that sensory issues are a real and common problem for people with ASD. One recent study found that while 33 percent of typically developing children had what it termed "sensory symptoms," about 90 percent of those with ASDs did.[13] And, in fact, Dr. Hans Asperger noted unusual sensitivities to sensory stimuli, including sound, in his original

1944 paper. That said, a large review that looked at twenty-five major studies on sensory integration therapy (SIT) found that only three suggested that it was effective, eight had mixed results, and fourteen reported no benefit. The authors also noted that even the three studies that found SIT effective were flawed, and so possibly not reliable.[14] In 2012, the American Academy of Pediatrics issued a policy statement: "Because there is no universally accepted framework for diagnosis, sensory processing disorder generally should not be diagnosed."[15]

When It May Be Appropriate

For children with AS, OT may address many different types of problems. Because many children with AS have two or more of these problems, OT can make a positive difference in several areas, including problems with handwriting, learning, fine- and gross-motor skills, motor planning (dyspraxia), and general clumsiness. There is evidence for this treatment for these problems.

It is not unusual for a child with AS to have problems in more than one area and to receive OT for each. In many cases, the causes and the corrective therapy overlap. In fact, determining which disorder gave rise to which disability often comes down to a chicken-and-egg question. Is Aaron averse to handwriting because he lacks fine-motor and motor planning skills? Or is it because he has always shown general tactile defensiveness when touching crayons? Or did his development of fine-motor and motor planning skills stall out because his tactile defensiveness made him less likely to pick up a crayon and scribble?

Occupational therapy should be considered for any child who:

- Has deficits in or seems to be behind his peers in mastering skills such as feeding, dressing, and grooming himself; bouncing, catching, and throwing balls; writing, drawing, coloring, painting, working with clay or Play-Doh; or jumping, hopping, running, skipping, and climbing.
- Seems unusually sensitive to touch, sound, smells, or visual stimuli; for example, a child who goes to great lengths to

avoid being touched or hugged, covers her ears and becomes distressed at certain sounds, reacts violently to particular scents, or appears to become disoriented or distracted during tasks that require tracking a moving object or copying material from a blackboard.

- Is unusually averse to certain places, situations, or experiences: for example, a child who has a tantrum upon entering a department store for "no apparent reason" or who is unusually whiny and picky about the clothes he wears.
- Is unusually active or inactive for his age.
- Seems clumsy or uncomfortable even when performing simple tasks such as walking, opening a jar, or following simple directions such as "Put your left hand on top of your head."
- Gives the impression of "not knowing what to do with himself" by being unable to sit or stand still; or he assumes unusual postures while sitting, standing, or walking.
- Generally appears, to borrow a title from an informative book on the topic, "out of sync."

A complete list of the symptoms and behaviors that may suggest sensory integration disorder could include over a hundred items, some of which are polar opposites. So, for example, any of these children could have sensory issues:

- A child who is averse to spinning and a child who craves it.
- A child who seems to hear "too well" and a child who seems to hear poorly.
- A child who seems to smell and react to everything and a child who seems to have no sense of smell.
- A child who grasps objects too tightly and a child who grasps objects too loosely.

Your child may enjoy or avoid messy activities such as finger painting; he may seek out deep-pressure types of touch like hugs or become distressed at merely being brushed up against; he may have a stiff, rigid posture or appear overly relaxed, loose, even "floppy." We include these examples because few professionals know much about sensory issues. Sometimes parents may hear that a child who overreacts to pain "is sensory" and conclude, erroneously, that their own child, who underreacts to pain, is not. In fact, both might be.

How It Works

We know that from the first moments of life, children learn through their senses. Typical neurological development is the result of a complex and constant exchange of sensory information. Just as a child must sit up before crawling, crawl before standing, and stand before walking, healthy neurological development depends on mastering a specific sequence of tasks. Learning a discrete skill, such as writing, is actually the result of having learned and mastered countless other skills over a child's lifetime.

Key to that is the brain's ability to accurately process sensory information and to organize it in such a way that a child is capable of responding appropriately and comfortably to his environment. Proper sensory integration is a major component of neurological development. It sets the stage for emotional security, behavioral self-regulation, and learning. When dysfunction occurs in one area, it produces a ripple effect through the entire learning chain. So, for example, a child with tactile sensitivity may avoid touching objects and exploring her environment. As a result, she will not spontaneously seek out other experiences and activities that foster further sensory integration. A child who avoids exploring her environment is depriving her brain of the sensory stimulation necessary for healthy development.

According to its proponents, sensory integration therapy (SIT) addresses sensory dysfunction through activities that both stimulate the various senses and require that a child organize those stimuli to respond appropriately. Neurologically typical children do this naturally; as they play, they receive the sensory stimulation and refine the appropriate responses that compel them to try other activities and seek out other sensory experiences. Children usually find these activities fun. Bouncing a ball, swinging, and doing "wheelbarrow walking" are just a few of hundreds of standard but very playlike SIT techniques. OT may also involve working with puzzles, games, and objects that are manipulated (like stringing beads or digging small "buried" objects out of a ball of putty or clay).

The theory behind sensory integration disorder and the methods used to treat it were first developed in the 1960s by Dr. A. Jean Ayres, an occupational therapist and educational psychologist. Dr. Ayres's assertion that sensory integration is key to the development of the mind, the brain, and the body was initially rejected by the occupational therapy community. Although still controversial, it has found broader acceptance in recent years.

Dr. Ayres also believed that therapy can essentially "retrain" the brain to integrate sensory input normally. *Sensory integration*, a term she coined in the late 1960s, refers to the brain's ability to organize sensory input, or information, received not only through the five "far" senses (taste, touch, sight, smell, and hearing) but also through the so-called near senses. These are the following:

- The tactile sense, or what is felt through the skin (touch, temperature, movement);
- The proprioceptive sense, or what is felt through the position and movement of the muscles and joints (essentially where our bodies are in space, where we are in relation to gravity); and
- The vestibular sense, which is what our inner ear conveys to our brain about balance, body position, gravity, and movement.

The impact of any dysfunction in the far senses is easy for most of us to comprehend. However, the role of the near senses is more abstract and difficult to conceptualize. Some examples of dysfunction in the near senses may help illustrate the point. Examples of tactile dysfunction include being repulsed, extremely distracted, or uncomfortable, even nauseated, by the feel of a particular fabric against the skin, the texture of glue or finger paint, or a pat on the back.

One form of vestibular dysfunction that many airline passengers know well is that feeling of being slightly disoriented as a result of pressure in the inner ear. For children who live with vestibular dysfunction, the feelings may be constant and more extreme.

As mentioned earlier, one child may crave intense spinning, while another may panic at even turning around to walk in a different direction. Observing a child with vestibular dysfunction may give the impression that his left hand doesn't know what his right hand is doing, and that would not be far off the mark. These children will not automatically use their hands or bodies to "help" them execute tasks. For instance, there will be no coordination between the hand that wields a scissors or a pencil and the hand that moves or steadies, as the case may be, the paper. Children with vestibular dysfunction may also experience gravitational insecurity, which manifests in a fear of jumping, swinging, hopping, or any other activity that takes their feet off the ground.

Dr. Ayres viewed the vestibular system as the "unifying" system and believed that problems there led to "inconsistent and inaccurate" processing of sensory input through other senses. The vestibular sense signals the brain to relax or contract muscles throughout the body to adjust for movements as seemingly minute as sitting in a chair or as obvious as running. It makes it possible for us to hold our heads upright, coordinate the actions of both sides of the body, and maintain our balance during activities as simple as walking up a flight of steps. Deficiencies in this system may manifest in a range of problems with motor planning, auditory language processing, visual-spatial processing, muscle tone, balance, movement, and bilateral coordination. Vestibular problems may explain why one child seems to constantly "melt" into his chair or lean his upper body against his desk. A child who has not established a dominant hand by kindergarten or who has trouble putting together simple puzzles may have vestibular problems.

For most people, proprioceptive dysfunction is perhaps the most difficult form of sensory integration disorder to conceptualize. If your brain processes and organizes proprioceptive information, you are receiving sufficient sensory feedback from everything you do to keep your mind alert. You don't need to stop and consciously think about (or look to see) where your hands or your feet are, for example. You position your body without consciously thinking, and you move without consciously noticing, say, the distance between your arm and the wall, or your foot and the steps you're climbing. Your brain instantaneously "calculates" the correct angle, speed, and muscle force needed for every movement. As a result, you don't bump into objects or accidentally crush an egg when you pick it up.

What We Know About Occupational Therapy and AS

There is no question that kids struggling with fine- and gross-motor performance, coordination, motor planning, and other "visible" difficulties can benefit from occupational therapy to address those problems. How effective OT can be in addressing sensory issues is another matter. While educators, doctors, and other professionals who deal with ASDs usually understand the role of OT, you may encounter professionals who are not as well informed. This is particularly true with sensory integration disorder, which is not widely recognized outside the disability community. Though there are standard instruments for diagnosing deficiencies in individuals, it is difficult to measure some of the results of OT objectively: for example, increased gravitational security or decreased sensitivity to a particular stimulus. That said, there is no harm in trying such commonsense "interventions" as offering a child who is old enough to chew gum safely some hard, old-fashioned bubble gum to reduce tooth grinding or chewing on nonedible objects.

Over time, some children become less sensitive or less averse to certain sensory experiences, but it would be inaccurate to say that these problems can be outgrown completely. Some parents do find success incorporating a "sensory diet," which provides different levels of stimulation with controlled exposure to materials and activities. You can find more information on sensory diets in the books listed on page 228.

Wherever the science falls on sensory integration disorder and treatment, the fact is that many of the "treatment" activities are fun, and the time you spend doing them can promote a range of other skills, such as turn taking, executive function, and so on. But do be on the lookout for inappropriate behavior (say, screaming) that gets "addressed" with a sensory intervention (access to a trampoline or "downtime" with toys) that then evolves into a reinforcement for the inappropriate behavior and thus creates a whole new problem.

Sensory Safety

Interventions for sensory integration disorder are familiar to most professionals who work with children with ASD in early intervention, preschool, and occupational therapy settings. Although none of these techniques is evidence based, they are all three very commonly used, especially with younger children. Here are some commonsense pointers and precautions.

- **"Brushing," or the Wilbarger Technique.** Typically, this entails brushing the child using a special soft brush used by surgeons for scrubbing up before surgery. Theoretically, the stimulation from brushing the arms and legs in a particular fashion helps to stimulate the nerve endings. It seems easy enough, and the "how to" of it is often passed down from one professional—not all of them OTs—to another. What you should know that they might not:

  1. It is never an appropriate treatment for tactile defensiveness.
  2. The back, inner thighs, groin area, stomach, chest, and face should *never* be "brushed." (The stimulation from brushing can prompt physical reactions such as vomiting or urinating.)
  3. The condition of the child's skin should be monitored carefully. Though it is a soft brush, some kids can be sensitive.[16]

- **Deep Pressure or Joint Compression.** This is another method developed by Patricia Wilbarger, a psychologist and OT. Like brushing, it looks easy enough, and that probably explains why so many professionals (again, many of them not OTs) are doing it. It involves, according to the informational website OT Innovations.com, "a very specific pattern of application, using a ten-count repetition of light pressure" to the major joints, typically shoulder, hip, and sometimes knee. Do not permit anyone who is not an OT to perform joint compression on your child. Occupational therapists do promote the use of the technique by non-OTs, but only with training by an OT.[17]

- **The "Sensory Bin."** A three-year-old child sitting in a giant plastic storage container up to his tummy in raw, dry oatmeal as part of his sensory diet. What could possibly go wrong? In this case, it was instantly clear why his asthma had just started acting up again: the dust from the oatmeal that was being "churned" by his and his therapists' scooping and spilling it using their hands and various containers. Most "sensory bins" are smaller plastic containers typically filled with the sensory diet standbys: dry rice, dry beans or peas or lentils, or dry oatmeal, as well as shredded paper and other things you can literally sink your hands or feet into. The problem with the food items should be obvious: even in their "dry" state, they are perishable and capable of growing a nice crop of mold, mildew, or bacteria. Even nonfood items, such as sand, Play-Doh or therapy putty, and paper, can get nasty, given time. If you use these items, they should be changed regularly, and the bins that contain them thoroughly cleaned and dried before refilling. If moisture enters dry materials, discard them immediately. Wet sensory materials, such as shaving cream, water, gels, and so on, should be used once and then discarded. It's probably not a bad idea for your child and his therapist to thoroughly wash and dry their hands before starting sensory diet play.

- **Sensory Diet Activities.** That these should be engaged in with all safety precautions in place goes without saying, but sometimes when we see something as being helpful, it's easy to overlook the risks. Trampolines, for example, are widely recommended as a sensory activity (for one thing, jumping up and down on them does provide joint compression), but according to the Mayo Clinic, they also "pose a high risk of injury . . . In fact, the risk of injury is so high that the American Academy of Pediatrics (AAP) says that trampolines should never be used at home or in outdoor playgrounds [and] supports limited use in supervised training programs, such as gymnastics."[18] Balance boards, "scooter boards" you sit on, and other devices should be used only with supervision and a spotter. Question any professional who is not an OT if they suggest you use them or incorporate them into your child's treatment.

Where to Find It

Occupational therapists can be found in private practice and/or working in schools, hospitals, therapy centers, and doctors' offices. Occupational therapy is considered a related service under IDEA and is sometimes covered by health insurance.

What Parents Can Do to Help

Whenever your child is evaluated, be sure that he's tested by an occupational therapist for possible deficits in skills and that sensory issues are carefully evaluated. Sometimes responses that look like sensory integration problems have their true roots in learning problems or behavioral issues that can be addressed more effectively in other ways.

Occupational therapy issues may be "invisible" to others, so you may find yourself explaining it many times to family members, teachers, babysitters, and even strangers. These problems tend to be greater than the sum of all their parts. It's discouraging to hear a parent say, "So my four-year-old daughter doesn't like to swing or color? What's the big deal?" The "big deal" is that the four-year-old who doesn't swing or color could become the second-grader who is still struggling mightily with printing letters, cutting shapes with scissors, and participating in age-appropriate playground activities.

Second, remember that sensory sensitivities are real and may even be terrifying for your child. Telling your child to just "ignore" how uncomfortable his shirt feels not only is ineffective but communicates that you don't appreciate the difficulties he faces. Parents sometimes find themselves prodding a child into an activity he is averse to in the mistaken hope that if he only goes down the slide enough times or only chews meat enough times, "he'll get used to it." In fact, what you'll often get is a child who continually feels insecure, anxious, and afraid. If simple exposure were the answer to sensory integration problems, they would not exist in the first place. At the same time, do not rule out different therapeutic approaches (behavioral and cognitive behavioral) to desensitize children to certain uncomfortable stimuli. It may not be worth the discomfort and effort to teach Sally to tolerate the feel of chalk; however, when you consider the implications for safety (not to mention hygiene) of an oversensitivity to splashing water on one's face, additional intervention may be in order.

Questions to Ask Your Occupational Therapist

- What problems does my child have? And can you please explain them to me in plain English?
- How do these problems affect my child's ability to carry out daily activities?
- How do the activities you'll be doing with him as part of therapy help him? What are the goals of this therapy?
- What can I do at home and what can his teacher do in the classroom to help address these issues?
- What kinds of activities can have therapeutic value for my child?
- What are the elements of a good "sensory diet" for my child? How often should we have him engage in these activities?
- Are there any activities he should avoid for now?
- Are there any other types of evaluations or professionals you believe we should consider? If so, why?
- Who else on my child's team can be trained to implement your suggestions safely and correctly?
- Are there any safety or health issues we need to consider?

Recommended Resources

American Academy of Pediatrics, "Sensory Integration Therapies for Children with Developmental and Behavioral Disorders," online at http://pediatrics.aappublications.org/content/129/6/1186.full.html.

Carol Stock Kranowitz, *The Out-of-Sync Child: Recognizing and Coping with Sensory Integration Dysfunction* (New York: Perigee, 2006) and *The Out-of-Sync Child Has Fun, Revised Edition: Activities for Kids with Sensory Integration Dysfunction* (New York: Perigee, 2006). The first is the original on the subject.

Brenda Smith Myles, Katherine Tapscott Cook, Nancy E. Miller,

Louann Rinner, and Lisa A. Robbins, *Asperger Syndrome and Sensory Issues: Practical Solutions for Making Sense of the World* (Shawnee Mission, KS: Autism Asperger Publishing, 2000).

SPEECH AND LANGUAGE THERAPY

What It Is

The term *speech and language therapy* encompasses a wide range of therapeutic practices involving patients of all age groups and addressing problems that range from difficulty swallowing to regaining the ability to speak and understand following trauma or illness. When working with children with ASD, speech and language pathologists or teachers may engage in many different exercises to address different aspects of the deficit. However, the ultimate goal is to help children with ASD develop, through explicit teaching, the social communication skills they cannot learn through "social osmosis," as most other people do.

When It May Be Appropriate

Because every ASD so profoundly affects the social use of language, most children with it will need some form of speech and language therapy. Though you will probably hear the two types of therapy referred to simply as "speech," there are differences between speech therapy and language therapy. Speech therapy usually addresses issues of basic speech, namely correct articulation. Language therapy deals with problems in understanding (receptive) or expressing (expressive) words, both verbal and nonverbal. Children with AS usually experience difficulty in the areas of semantics (the use of words to express literal meaning), pragmatics (the social use of language), presupposition (the ability to recognize and tailor communication to a conversational partner's understanding, beliefs, and relationship to the speaker), and social discourse (essentially, the ability to initiate, maintain, and end a conversation in a socially appropriate manner).

There is some confusion in this area, because one of the older diagnostic criteria that distinguishes Asperger syndrome from other pervasive developmental disorders is the absence of speech or speech delay before age three. Some have interpreted this to mean that children with AS have "normal" speech development. In view of the many language problems children with AS often have, some authorities have begun to question whether early speech development should not be more accurately characterized as "normal appearing." As Dr. Diane Twachtman-Cullen notes in her book on students with ASDs, *How to Be a Para Pro:*

> At the more able end of the autism spectrum continuum . . . one finds individuals who often *appear* to understand and use language at a rather high level. In fact, individuals with Asperger syndrome are thought by many to have *normal* language. This, however, is not the case. Thus, it is important to note that even though students with AS may appear to have *superficially* normal language expression (in terms of grammar and syntax), and even though they may evidence advanced vocabulary usage, they nevertheless manifest difficulty in *social communication*—that is, in the *comprehension and use of language for the purposes of receiving and sending messages.*[19]

We learn what we are taught and express what we know through language, written and spoken. Even though most of us take it for granted and never even consider it, we use language when we think about something, even if we never speak or write about it. It is possible for a child who has kept pace academically through the early elementary grades to encounter difficulty later when schoolwork requires greater independence and understanding of abstract concepts. Also bear in mind that difficulties with language may also manifest as problems in mathematics and social skills. Your local school district may resist even evaluating a child with AS for speech and language problems because he may be extremely talkative and have an impressive vocabulary. You should know that IDEA specifies that one goal of evaluation is to identify *all* of the *possible* deficits a child may have and to test specifically for those known to be related to a specific disorder. The prevalence of speech and language disorders among people with AS is well established; indeed, some consider speech and language therapy the most important intervention.

Your child should be evaluated for speech and language therapy if he or she:

- Misinterprets or misunderstands the words and actions of others.
- Has difficulty understanding nonverbal aspects of communication (facial expression, gestures, body language, tone of voice).
- Often interprets oral and written language literally.
- Has difficulty using and maintaining appropriate speech volume and intonation (for example, has a "flat" tone).
- Has difficulty initiating, maintaining, repairing, and ending a conversation in a socially appropriate way.
- Fails to appreciate the listener's level of interest in and/or understanding of a topic, causing him to provide too little or too much information.
- Has difficulty understanding or talking about abstract concepts, such as time ("yesterday," "next week"), states of mind, and ideas, particularly those of other people.
- Seems to take an unusually long time to respond to questions and statements from others, and may seem not to be hearing.
- Often seems to miss the larger message or the theme of conversation, stories, books, movies, television programs, and other forms of storytelling.

How It Works

It is impossible to cover all of the different techniques and methods a speech and language therapist might employ. Creative speech and language pathologists tailor their approach to address the needs of the individual. Sessions may include elements of social skills training, listening training, occupational therapy, and play. To encourage more appropriate communication, role-playing, videotaping the child, and group sessions may be used. Group sessions in speech tend to be full of opportunities to socialize with peers.

What We Know About Speech and Language Therapy and AS

When designed for a child with AS and carried out correctly, speech and language therapy can help children improve their social communication skills as well as their ability to listen, attend, ask and respond to questions, and comprehend written and spoken language. Because atypical speech and language development is the core defining deficit in all autism spectrum disorders, speech-language pathologists usually have some training and/or experience in this area, if not with AS specifically. There is a large and growing body of literature on speech and language therapy and AS and related language-based disorders, such as semantic-pragmatic language disorder (SPD) and nonverbal learning disability (NLD or NVLD).

Where to Find It

Speech and language therapy is considered a related service under IDEA, and most public and private schools have speech-language pathologists on staff. Speech-language pathologists also practice in a wide range of medical and educational settings; some are in private practice.

Questions to Ask

- What is your experience with children with ASDs and AS specifically?
- Please explain the deficits you'll be addressing and give me everyday examples of how each deficit affects my child, both at home and at school.
- What can we do at home and what can his teachers do in school to support the work you'll be doing with him?
- From what you have observed working with my child, would you recommend further evaluations for other, related conditions, such as central auditory processing disorder, sensory integration disorders, or reading or other learning disabilities? Would you recommend occupational therapy?

What Parents Can Do to Help

Ask your child's speech pathologist for any "homework" that might be appropriate. He or she may recommend computer programs, videos, books, or techniques for home.

Recommended Resources

Sabrina Freeman and Lorelei Dake, *Teach Me Language: A Language Manual for Children with Autism, Asperger Syndrome, and Related Developmental Disorders* (Langley, BC: SKF Books, 1997) and *The Companion Exercise Forms for Teach Me Language* (Langley, BC, Canada: SKF Books, 1997).

Michelle Garcia Winner, *Inside Out: What Makes a Person with Social Cognitive Deficits Tick?* (San Jose, CA: self-published, 2000), online at www.socialthinking.com.

SOCIAL SKILLS TRAINING

What It Is

Just about everyone agrees that children with AS need social skills training. Some contend that it is the single most important intervention. However, not everyone agrees on what that training should include or how to teach it. And, ironically, there is not a lot of research to support any one approach. As a parent, I'm a veteran of about a dozen different social skills interventions. What I have learned might be surprising. First, the sympathetic, talented leader of your local scout troop, coach, or local theater director who "gets it," or, for teens and young adults, the group of peers with ASD who have no problem telling it like it is can be as effective as—and sometimes even more effective than—a psychologist, social worker, teacher, or therapist. When it comes to teaching social skills, holding academic credentials is less important than having the ability to make a connection that fosters in your child trust and willingness to venture out on the limb. After all, it's out on that limb that social growth occurs.

What do parents want from social skills training? As a mom, I totally understand the most common answer I hear: "To have a friend." Yet having supervised a social skills program myself, I also understand—and do my best to help parents understand—that the first goal is acquiring specific social skills: taking turns, conversation, sharing, joining a group, being polite to or at least tolerant of others, working with others toward a common goal, understanding facial expressions, tone of voice, and so on. Next, social skills training must provide a safe and supportive place in which to practice those skills. A talented group leader or therapist should make the group sessions fun.

As your child grows, she should also come out of social skills with an age-appropriate understanding of what it's all about. Remember, it is not enough for your child to learn how to greet a new acquaintance appropriately. He also needs to acquire that skill in an environment that is positive and reinforcing and will leave him with the impression that other individuals are worth the time and trouble to get to know. And if he can't get to that for some reason, he needs to learn to at least be polite about it. As kids get older, they also need to understand why what they are learning is important to practice outside the session.

Ideally, a social skills group contains three to six children. It will vary, based on the children's ages and the type of issues the group will address. It is large enough to give each kid a number of other members to "practice with" but small enough to allow for critical individual attention. The group should be led by someone who is enthusiastic, understands the skills that matter most, and is working from a plan, be it a packaged curriculum or a series of activities he has designed. There should be a logic behind the program, even if it isn't apparent to your child. Group facilitators or leaders can have a background in child development or psychology (social worker, psychologist, psychiatrist, therapist) and experience teaching this skill to kids with ASD. These people can be teachers, behavior analysts, school psychologists, and others. Social skills therapy is also used for children who have emotional and behavioral issues, as well as those with other specific disorders (such as AD/HD).

It is important that a child with AS be placed with peers who are in the same "range" in terms of age and verbal and cognitive ability. Some groups include only children with ASD, while others also bring in "coached" neurotypical children to model appropriate peer behavior. In one social skills group, the children rehearsed and then ordered their own desserts at an ice cream shop, role-played appropriate responses to teasing and bullying, practiced making telephone calls to one another, and worked together as a group on a play, which was videotaped and shown later to parents at a "premiere." In another that used trained peer models, members used their weekly sessions to go on outings to restaurants, stores, and other places, and each location came with its own social skills "mission." For example, a trip to Best Buy required the kids with ASD to find a clerk, request an item politely, and pay for it. In yet another program, eight of twelve weeks follow a carefully designed behaviorally based curriculum and four weeks are left "open" to address issues the group members raise, such as bullying, how to act at a school dance, or what to do when classmates gossip.

The idea of social skills training is neither new nor exclusive to spectrum disorders. It has been a key component in the education of individuals with a wide range of issues, diagnoses, and challenges. A number of popular general social skills curricula (for example, Skillstreaming, which is designed to help students of all ages), although not specifically designed for use with students with spectrum disorders, are widely used programs in schools.

There is such a need for good social skills programs and no real means of regulating them that virtually anyone can hang a shingle and offer a program. The problem with this is obvious. We recently heard about a so-called social skills program where the leader (a special education professional) had the group of elementary school children (whose diagnoses ranged across the spectrum) sit in a circle and answer the question "How do you feel about being here today?" For most kids with ASD, this would be a nearly impossible question to answer without specific instruction. The techniques and objectives of a social skills program developed for, say, children who have AD/HD, whose parents have recently divorced, who are dealing with grief, or who have problems with garden-variety shyness might not be very effective for a child with AS. All types of professionals can and do offer social skills training: psychiatrists, psychologists, social workers, school counselors and school psychologists, teachers, and others. There is no accrediting body for social skills training in the realm of ASDs. Perhaps the most important "credential" for working with children who have AS is experience working with children with AS.

When It May Be Appropriate

Most children with AS can benefit from some form of structured instruction and practice in social skills. According to special education authority Richard Lavoie, "Social skill development is one of the greatest challenges that parents of special needs children face. The social competence of a child will determine his self-esteem, friendships, and adjustment to school life. Most important, social competence will determine his ultimate success and adjustment in the adult world."[20]

While Lavoie was speaking of children with special needs generally, the need to acquire, practice, and master social skills is even more urgent for the child with AS, whose disability is often invisible and whose words and actions may easily be misinterpreted. Contrary to the impression they may sometimes give, most children with AS are interested in their peers, and many of them long for companionship. The problem is that in social situations, a child with AS does not know "automatically" how to behave in a manner conducive to creating and sustaining relationships. Few would disagree that friendship is an important part of life, and a source of satisfaction and joy. Most of us would find it impossible to imagine our lives without friends.

How It Works

Social skills training makes it possible for the child with AS to do what the disorder prevents him from doing automatically, naturally, and fluently for himself: observing, processing, and imitating appropriate social behavior. Social skills training takes a social activity—say, answering the telephone or initiating a conversation with a classmate—and, in Dr. Tony Attwood's words, "freezes the action," breaks down the steps of the activity, and clearly explains the applicable social rules. The crucial element of social skills train-ing in a group is the sheltered practice with peers, something that one-on-one therapy with an adult cannot provide.

What We Know About Social Skills Training and AS

There have been few studies on the efficacy of social skills training per se. What does exist are many studies that examine the effec-tiveness of individual components that, in the real world, would be incorporated into programs. (For example, looking at how video modeling and Social Stories might enhance conversation skills.[21]) Even though a review of studies proclaimed that "empirical sup-port for social skills training for children with HFA/AS is in its infancy . . . [and] has yet to be firmly established,"[22] most experts agree that social skills training is one intervention every child with AS should have, in one form or another.

Using Commercial Programs

Many companies offer videos, computer programs, and apps de-signed to increase social skills, with more released almost every week. It's impossible to provide a comprehensive overview. To find apps, go to the ratings page of Autism Speaks: www.autismspeaks .org/autism-apps. Here you can learn what is available, which for-mats it comes in, and the current state of research on it. Some other good sources for videos are Coulter Video (www.coultervideo.com) and Model Me Kids (www.modelme.com). Skillstreaming (www .skillstreaming.com) is among several of the more general skill-building programs that are popular, especially in schools. Finally, Michelle Garcia Winner has been at the forefront of developing books, DVDs, posters, and even board games that teach what she terms Social Thinking. You can find more information about her work and her many helpful products at www.socialthinking.com.

One of the more innovative, research-based tools to address one aspect of social skills training—recognition of emotions—comes from Dr. Simon Baron-Cohen and colleagues at Oxford Univer-sity. *Mind Reading: An Interactive Guide to Emotions* is a CD-ROM or DVD computer program that presents 412 distinct human emotions, grouped into twenty-four categories, each with facial expression, tone of voice, and inclusion in a brief, simple story. The faces are those of professional actors—both American and British, which offers a wide range of different accents—including Daniel Radcliffe, aka Harry Potter. In the Emotions Library section, each of the 412 emotions is accompanied by several video clips, each showing different types of people (male, female, young, old, of different ethnic backgrounds) and audio clips, in which an actor speaks, conveying that emotion. The Learning Centre section contains lessons and quizzes tailored specifically to meet the needs of people with ASDs. You can test-drive and order this program at its easy-to-use website: www.human-emotions.com.

Where to Find It

Ask your child's doctors, therapists, and teachers for recommendations. Other parents, however, are also a good source. Social skills groups are run by private practitioners, hospitals, universities, and nonprofit organizations, including religious institutions. If you choose a group that is run by a licensed physician or therapist, some or all of the cost may be covered by health insurance.

Questions to Ask

- How long has this group been meeting?
- Who is the group leader? What is his or her experience working with children with AS?
- What do you consider the primary goals of the group? What specific skills will you be working on? Can you give me some idea of the activities you'll be doing to help teach those skills?
- How do you evaluate progress?
- Tell me about the actual meetings: When do they meet? How often? How long are the sessions? What is the cost? Do you break for summer or continue year-round?
- How many children are in each group?

- What are some things we can do at home and his teacher can do at school to reinforce what he learns here at group?
- What are the rules of behavior for the group?
- Is it possible for me to observe a group in session? If not, are there other parents I can call to ask about their experience with the group?

More Thoughts on Social Skills

Formal social skills training is important, even crucial, for children with AS. However, one of the biggest mistakes parents and professionals make is to think of each social skills training program as an end unto itself. Nothing taught or practiced in session will "stick" or grow into your child's everyday behavioral repertoire or understanding without constant practice in the course of everyday life. Going to session without practicing in real life is like wearing your glasses only when you go to the eye doctor. For social skills training to be effective, parents, teachers, and others who work with our children need to take advantage of every possible moment to teach, reinforce, and expand it every day. If learning to use the telephone is a current objective, let your child make that routine call you make to your spouse to remind him or her to pick up milk on the way home. If your child is learning to ask for assistance, send him to the neighbor's house to borrow a cup of sugar or a blank CD (after you call and set it up first). In school, ask your child's teacher to send him on a daily errand to another classroom or the principal's office. We talk more about this in the chapters that make up Part Three.

Recommended Resources

Also see "Recommended Resources" on pages 218 and 233 for other related resources.

Jed Baker, *Social Skills Training for Children with Asperger Syndrome, High-Functioning Autism, and Related Social Communication Disorders: A Manual for Practitioners* (Shawnee Mission, KS: Autism Asperger Publishing, 2002).

Michelle Garcia Winner, *Inside Out: What Makes a Person with Social Cognitive Deficits Tick?* (San Jose, CA: Think Social Publishing, 2000). Although Garcia Winner has written many more books, this is the "starter."

Patricia Howlin, Simon Baron-Cohen, and Julie Hadwin, *Teaching Children with Autism to Mind-Read: A Practical Guide* (Chichester, UK: Wiley, 1999).

Jeanette McAfee, *Navigating the Social World: A Curriculum for Individuals with Asperger's Syndrome, High Functioning Autism and Related Disorders* (Arlington, TX: Future Horizons, 2002).

My Favorite Social Skills Book for Older Kids

Comic Sense, by Nancy Mucklow, is the only social skills book I've ever described as "delightful" to parents and professionals. Interestingly, Mucklow herself states on the first page, "[This] is not a social skills book. But if you figure out how to think with common sense, you'll find social skills much easier to learn and much more natural to use." Highly visual and innovative, it tackles common topics in a fresh and sometimes funny way. For example, one section titled "Deposits in a Relationship" uses the metaphor "A relationship is like a bank account," explains what constitutes a "deposit" and a "withdrawal," and then compares two "accounts"—"Bank Account with Your Friend" and "Bank Account with Your Boss"—using friendly, homey, hand-drawn line graphs and arrows with brief captions describing the high points on the "Goodwill" scale ("Employee of the Month award!") with bottom-of-the-scale events ("Boss had a firm talk with you"), and lots of things in the middle ("Making an effort but bored"). Much of the action throughout the book is illustrated with simple cartoons featuring two talking worms. (Take my word for it: they are really cute.) Mucklow has a gift for analogy ("A Conversation Is Like an Engine," "Safety as a Flashlight," "Perspective Is Like a Lens") and incorporates checklists, boxed comparisons ("How People Read You" has one column for "What They See" and a second for "What They Assume"), to-do lists, lots of great line drawings, and some hands-on activities. (My personal favorite: "Rate These Apologies: Good or Bad?")

Nancy Mucklow, *Comic Sense* (Kingston, Ontario, Canada: Michael Grass House, 2010).

Brenda Smith Myles, Melissa L. Trautman, and Rohna L. Schelvan, *The Hidden Curriculum: Practical Solutions for Understanding Unstated Rules in Social Situations* (Shawnee Mission, KS: Autism Asperger Publishing, 2004).

PSYCHOTHERAPY

When we say "psychotherapy," we mean individual, one-on-one cognitive behavior "talk therapy" that is designed to help change, modify, and/or replace dysfunctional behaviors and inaccurate perceptions and self-perceptions. Freudian-style psychoanalysis, psychodynamic therapy, family therapy, group therapy, and most other psychotherapeutic approaches are not recommended for children with AS. Also inappropriate are the following:

- Any therapeutic philosophy that is confrontational, is aggressive, or holds the patient entirely responsible for all of his feelings and actions;
- Any therapeutic approach that considers AS and related disorders to be the product of poor or incomplete maternal bonding, early emotional trauma, the "choice" of the person with AS, and so on;
- Any therapeutic approach that views AS as anything other than a neurological anomaly or disorder; and
- Any therapeutic approach that dismisses or fails to accept as valid professional diagnoses of other, comorbid conditions (AD/HD, OCD, Tourette's syndrome, anxiety disorder, depression, and so on).

When It May Be Appropriate

It is important to understand what cognitive behavior therapy can do and what it cannot do for the child with AS. Its purpose is not to "treat" Asperger syndrome itself but to help the child deal with the specific emotional difficulties that result from having AS or the neurological anomaly that gives rise to AS. A psychotherapist who understands AS can also teach social skills, self-monitoring, relaxation, stress management techniques, and a repertoire of appropriate behaviors. Because people with AS are at high risk for depression, anxiety, and suicide, especially consider psychotherapy for your child if he meets any of the criteria for depression (see page 67) or anxiety (see page 65).

These criteria are the typical symptoms of anxiety and depression; however, youngsters with AS may exhibit other behaviors instead of or in addition to those listed. A person with AS may begin devoting more (or less) time to or talking more (or less) about his special interest. He may have more emotional outbursts and tantrums or seem more emotionally sensitive than usual. Another possibility is that behaviors that are common to your child may change in frequency, intensity, or duration. Or you may see new behaviors that are not usually associated with depression and anxiety but that are known to arise in people with ASDs. Some of these might include echolalia, repetitive motor movements, rocking, spinning, or a desire for light touch or deep pressure.

What It Is and How It Works

Cognitive behavior therapy is a type of psychotherapy widely used as the primary or secondary treatment for many disorders. It is based on the premise that emotional disorders arise from dysfunctional or distorted thinking. Cognitive behavior therapy teaches patients to recognize and monitor their emotions, evaluate the validity of their perceptions about people and situations, and develop appropriate, functional responses. This can be accomplished through talking with a therapist, role-playing, games, and other therapeutic activities.

Given the challenges that boys and girls with AS face in understanding other people's thoughts, feelings, and intentions, as well as their own, typical cognitive behavior therapy has proved somewhat limited in helping effect change. The main stumbling block is that people with AS may lack the basic level of self-awareness, social understanding, theory of mind, and linguistic ability (particularly when discussing abstract concepts such as emotions, thoughts, feelings, and intentions) necessary for effective cognitive behavior therapy. Parents whose children have undergone some form of cognitive behavior therapy prior to their Asperger diagnosis often report that it was ineffective, confusing, or stressful.

What We Know About Cognitive Behavior Therapy and AS

In the hands of a therapist who is familiar with AS and willing to work with your child, cognitive behavior therapy can be very effective. However, it is crucial that you and your child's therapist understand the need to tailor the therapy with an eye to explicitly teaching the basic social, emotional, and linguistic skills most of us assume we never actually actively "learned." You might want to consider cognitive behavior therapy for your child if you lack access to a good social skills group.

Where to Find It

Psychotherapists work in a wide range of settings: in private practice; through public and private agencies; in schools; and in hospitals, clinics, and other health care settings.

Questions to Ask

- What is your experience working with children with AS?
- What do you feel are my child's specific problems and how do you think they should be addressed?
- What activities will you be using in therapy?
- What specific skills will my child be learning in the course of therapy?

ASPERGER SYNDROME: THE OASIS GUIDE

- What can we do at home and what can his teachers do at school to reinforce and support what you'll be doing?
- Are you knowledgeable about and taking into account my child's other, comorbid conditions?
- What other therapies and/or interventions would you recommend that we explore, and why?

Recommended Resources

Tony Attwood, "Modifications to Cognitive Behavior Therapy to Accommodate the Cognitive Profile of People with Asperger's Syndrome," at www.tonyattwood.com. Look under "Archived Papers." Required reading for any parent or mental health professional working with a child who has Asperger syndrome.

Angela Scarpa, Susan Williams White, and Tony Attwood, eds., *CBT for Children and Adolescents with High-Functioning Autism Spectrum Disorders* (New York: Guilford Press, 2013).

"ALTERNATIVE" THERAPIES

Several research studies have confirmed what we discovered with our OASIS Surveys more than ten years ago: parents of kids with Asperger syndrome or a similar profile were much less interested in alternative therapies than were parents whose children fell on other points of the spectrum. It is beyond our scope to delve into each one here; there are literally dozens.

Special Diets: Casein- and Gluten-Free

The use of special diets that eliminate casein (found in dairy products) and gluten (found in wheat, other grains, and processed foods) has long been an area of interest in the autism community. The explanation for the need for such diets in ASD is complex but boils down to the theory that when inadequately digested, the protein molecules in casein and gluten result in amino acid chains (called *peptides*) that adversely affect neurological function. There is no doubt that some individuals on the autism spectrum do suffer from gastrointestinal and digestive problems, including celiac disease (intestinal damage caused by malabsorption of certain nutrients) and dermatitis herpetiformes (a skin rash that is often accompanied by tissue damage in the intestine). Constipation and/or diarrhea are other common problems in kids with ASDs. (See more in chapter 10 on health.) These are not typically food allergies in the usual sense. Even if your child's test for allergies for milk or wheat comes back negative, it does not necessarily mean that he might not benefit from eliminating casein or gluten.

The interest in these diets has been spurred by the anecdotal accounts of parents who claim to have seen marked success with them and the professionals who market them. Only recently, however, have research studies on the diets and their effectiveness in ameliorating or eliminating autism-related symptoms and behaviors been conducted. To date, no scientifically conducted study has found a causative link between diet and autism. On the other hand, more people every day are adopting these types of diets for ethical, political, or other health reasons. Some people claim that they simply "feel better" after eliminating one or both.

We have heard from parents whose children's AS symptoms were considerably reduced through a wheat- and dairy-free diet, but these approaches seem to have a higher rate of success in children whose symptoms are more involved than those with an AS profile. One possible reason why these diets might "work" is that in the process of eliminating wheat and/or dairy, you essentially remove every trace of preservatives (such as monosodium glutamate, to which many people are very sensitive); artificial colors, sugars, and sweeteners; and virtually all of the foods that are too starchy, too fatty, or too rich in empty calories. That alone can make a big difference, especially if your child tends to stick to a limited diet: the white starches such as breads, pastas, and potatoes; or high-fat and/or high-sugar "healthy" snacks like cheese and yogurt. Many kids on these diets, at least in the beginning, are consuming more fruit and vegetables, complex carbohydrates (in the form of whole grains), and high-quality, lean protein than they did before.

On the positive side, it can be argued that a dietary change is a lot less intrusive than some other therapies and carries less risk of side effects than just about anything else. Such dietary restrictions may be very difficult to adjust to, however, and the cost of special foods and lack of convenience are considerations, even though these products are more widely available and less costly than before. Families who have found them helpful say they learn to cope and it is well worth the effort. Consult a health professional or nutritionist when you begin to ensure that your child gets all the nutrients necessary. Also be prepared for your child not to like everything you present. For your child's sake, especially if she is not old enough or able to understand why the rest of the family gets to keep eating her old favorites, consider switching everyone's diet, at least at home.

Resources on Alternative Therapies

The following organizations and websites provide reliable information on alternative therapies and numerous links to other resources.

Association for Science in Autism Treatment (ASAT) at www.asaton line.org.

National Autism Center, *A Parent's Guide to Evidence-Based Practice and Autism*. See the box on page 165.

National Center for Complementary and Alternative Medicine (NCCAM) at www.nccam.nih.gov.

A FINAL WORD

Do your research. Only you can prioritize your child's and your family's needs and decide how best to spend your time, energy, and financial resources. It makes sense to begin with the most widely used interventions (they got to be that way for a reason), which are best supported by research and/or endorsed by people, organizations, or agencies with a great deal of experience in this area. Being human, we often make choices based on reasons that may have nothing to do with the actual proven efficacy of an intervention. That's especially easy to do in an area where even some widely accepted methods have so little hard research behind them.

Once you embark on an intervention course, shift your focus

from all the reasons why you like or chose that method to the results it is—or isn't—producing. Be a consumer when you make your initial decision, but be a scientist once the therapy is under way. Is it working? Is it producing any documentable, obvious improvement? If so, how much? If Jason had tantrums twelve times a day before the treatment, and a month later he's having a tantrum once every four days, you may have a keeper. Count. Keep written records. Ask others who know your child. Yes, some therapies do take time. But for certain problems—violent, self-injurious, suicidal behavior, for instance—there might be no time to play around or experiment with a new diet or special "natural" supplement.

Chapter 5

MEDICATION

DECISIONS about using psychotropic (or psychoactive) medication are among the most difficult and confusing that parents of children with ASDs confront. The use of medication in children to address problems with behavior, concentration, depression, tic disorders, sleep problems, repetitive behaviors, eating disorders, anxiety, aggression, violence, and other psychiatric symptoms is complex and in some cases controversial, regardless of the diagnosis. Add in the mysteries of any ASD, and the decision becomes even more daunting. Nonetheless, it is a decision that at some point many parents—including those who ultimately decide not to use medication—will face.

Many individuals with ASDs will be taking a prescribed psychoactive medication at some point in their lives. A 2012 study found that 27 percent of children ages two to seventeen were taking one or more psychotropic medications, 7.4 percent were taking two, and 4.5 percent were taking three. For adolescents from age twelve to seventeen, the percentage taking one or more was 66 percent. The presence of disorders such as AD/HD, OCD, anxiety, depression, and bipolar disorder were associated with a higher rate of psychotropic medication use.[1] As the research has grown with our kids, we have learned a number of things that were not known even a decade before. First, anxiety is a major problem for most children with ASDs, and its "legacy" endures long after the original experience. In fact, Dr. Tony Attwood has spoken and written movingly of adults with AS who live with what he terms posttraumatic stress disorder due to having suffered uncontrolled anxiety as children and teens. We also know that untreated anxiety places a child at greater risk for depression. Second, therapies that do not employ medication—behavioral interventions, cognitive behavior therapy, and so on—can be helpful and in some cases should definitely be the first approach. However, these can take time, and depending on your child, the resources available to you (e.g., good psychologists and other professionals experienced in working with kids like yours, ability to pay, insurance coverage), the immediate severity of the problem, and the risks of not resolving it as quickly as possible, more immediate action might be required. What we do know is that psychotropic medication is never as effective "by itself" as it is when used with whichever of these other interventions are deemed appropriate for your child. So it is really not an "either/or" question. That said, for some serious conditions, such as bipolar disorder and schizophrenia, prognosis and outcome depend heavily on the right medication being used as quickly as possible.

THE MEDICATION QUESTION

In talking to parents over the years, I have learned that there is nothing many of them feel more "definite" about than this. Surprisingly, they are sometimes "for" or "against" medication even before there is any indication that it might be suitable for their own child. Sometimes, it's because they know a friend of a friend, or the child of a friend, who tried a certain medication that "did not work." Or they read some side effect horror story on the internet or in the news. (Please steer clear of anything about psychotropic meds and kids that does not come from one of the websites listed under "Recommended Resources" on page 287.) Or they are concerned about side effects, drug abuse, and other possible problems. Rather than place these questions and issues into a larger context of understanding what these medications are, how they work, and what they can—and cannot—do, they simply "just say no." Some parents who find themselves faced with a serious problem that essentially forces the question seem surprised when the prescribed medication actually does work and improves their child's ability to function comfortably in the world.

Individuals with ASDs are not prescribed psychotropic medications just because they have ASD. They are prescribed medication to help to reduce or relieve symptoms or behaviors that are causing major difficulties in their ability to function in their daily lives; and/or to reduce or eliminate symptoms that pose a risk of physical or emotional harm to themselves or to others, now or in the future. Neurologically speaking, people with ASDs are very complicated. In fact, 70 percent of all people with ASDs have a second psychiatric disorder, and about 40 percent have two or more.[2] In other words, they have conditions for which psychotropic medication might be indicated *even if they did not have an ASD.* Having an ASD makes countless aspects of daily living more difficult for our kids. No one should be surprised that living with and managing a separate psychiatric disorder would top that list and present major—even overwhelming—challenges and stress. A recent study found that externalizing symptoms (e.g., severe behaviors, aggression, self-injury, threatened or attempted suicide) were the leading reason for children with ASDs to visit the emergency room. In fact, among pediatric visits to the ER, having an ASD made it nine times as likely that the reason for the visit would be psychiatric in nature.[3]

Many parents—far too many, in my opinion—are forced to face a decision about medication in moments of crisis: a total emotional breakdown, violent episode, suicidal ideation or attempt, self-injury, and so on. Parents may not have time to gather all the information they would like; they may not feel that they are making a truly "informed" decision under the circumstances. Another common scenario is children wanting to make their own decisions about the medications they take. This can go two ways: those who currently take something and want to stop, change, or cut back; and those who currently take nothing and want to try something to see if it helps with anxiety, attention, or other problems. What do you do when you "don't believe" in medication but your brilliant child who is failing physics begs you for the AD/HD meds he has read on the internet can help him? What do you do when you know that without that daily dose of Risperdal or Abilify, your twelve-year-old daughter's rage zooms from zero to sixty in seconds, but now she is refusing to take it? For better or worse, the dates on which these issues arise will not be penciled in on your calendar. Again, none of these situations lends itself to optimal decision making for the unprepared.

So the purpose of this chapter is not to "advocate" for one position or the other but to prepare you with information. Regardless of what your feelings are today about this issue, I urge you to read this chapter through, if for no other reason than to get a basic background and understanding of what medication is used for and when it is considered an appropriate choice to think about. It would be impossible to include in this chapter everything there is to know about every possible medication (and medication combination) now used for children with ASDs. Providing the in-depth, detailed, medical information you should be receiving only from a licensed physician is beyond our scope here. Every parent, teacher, and therapist should have Dr. Timothy Wilens's excellent *Straight Talk About Psychiatric Medications for Kids* on their shelf. Authoritative, concise, and balanced, *Straight Talk* provides an excellent factual background on the issue and important medical advice for any parent faced with this decision. In addition, anyone who works with children who might be using medication should at least know what these various drugs are designed to do and what the side effects might look like, if only to help ensure a child's basic safety.

PSYCHOTROPIC MEDICATION FOR PEOPLE WITH AS

Many people with AS have taken or are taking medication. One study found that over 68 percent of 109 respondents had taken some psychotropic medication at some point.[4] Although many children with AS will go through life without needing it, there are those for whom medication will be indicated, either to support the child through a difficult time or a crisis or on a long-term basis to address chronic problems such as depression, anxiety, obsessive-compulsive disorder, bipolar disorder, seizure disorder, attention-deficit/hyperactivity disorder, sleep problems, eating disorders, or tics. Some situations and developmental phases can present more challenges and create more stress, such as adolescence. Because many of our children are attending regular schools and plan to pursue college or professional training after high school, grades can be very important, so issues with attention might warrant intervention if learning is affected. We also know that people with AS—including even young children—are at higher risk than others for anxiety, depression, seizure disorders, tic disorders, and suicide, and medication can help address these problems.

WHAT CAN THESE MEDICATIONS DO?

When doctors prescribe psychotropic medication, they are not "treating" ASD the same way we think of "treating" diabetes with insulin or pain with morphine. There is no pharmacological "cure" or remedy for ASD. A number of medications have been shown to be effective in addressing certain specific common ASD symptoms as well as separate comorbid conditions that may exist alongside it (see chapter 2).

Comorbid Conditions Commonly
Seen in People with AS

Attention-deficit/hyperactivity disorder (AD/HD), see page 64
Anxiety, see page 65
Bipolar disorder, see page 68
Depression, see page 67
Eating disorders, see page 466
Obsessive-compulsive disorder (OCD), see page 66
Psychosis (Note: People with AS who make inappropriate comments or respond to stress in certain ways may be misdiagnosed as "psychotic" when they are not)
Seizure disorders, see page 67
Sleep disorders, see page 470
Social phobia, see page 66
Tourette's syndrome and tics, see page 69

WHAT MAKES THE MEDICATION
DECISION SO DIFFICULT?

Even when medication is clearly indicated, parents may hesitate, wondering if it isn't possible that their son or daughter might "just grow out of it" or not need it if they made certain changes at home or at school. Some would argue that except in those cases of psychiatric crisis (a child becoming a danger to himself or to others, threatening or attempting suicide), it's reasonable to try addressing difficulties through changes and accommodations in your child's life. Learning what works and what doesn't can also give you and your child's doctor additional insight into the problem. Others believe that it makes more sense to take a proactive approach long before a child's emotional state becomes a crisis.

There are legitimate concerns over the fact that the long-term safety and efficacy of some psychotropic medications for children have not yet been established. In fact, in many cases, even the pharmaceutical companies that make them cannot say with certainty precisely how many of these medications work. Later in this chapter, we address questions about FDA approval, off-label usage, and other related matters.

Whatever the reason, most parents agree in theory that medication is not the "best" first choice, and that alternative approaches (such as behaviorally based intervention, cognitive behavior therapy, social skills intervention, changes and accommodations at school and at home) should be tried first. In most cases, this is a reasonable approach. However, there are conditions for which medication is the first-line treatment and sometimes the most effective or only effective treatment available. This is particularly true when dealing with a child who is deeply depressed or suicidal, or if allowing a behavior or mood to persist would pose a danger to the child or to others or be detrimental to the child's emotional well-being. That said, there is no such thing as a "magic bullet": a medication that can resolve your child's issues single-handedly. In virtually every case, medication along with other supports and interventions are most likely to be effective.

THE CRISIS IN CHILDREN'S MENTAL HEALTH CARE CONTINUES

Contrary to what many people believe, anxiety disorders, depression, eating disorders (anorexia nervosa, bulimia), disruptive behavior disorders, schizophrenia, tic disorder, obsessive-compulsive disorder, and bipolar disorder can begin in early childhood. Psychiatric disorders in children are not just "junior" versions or less serious versions of adult disorders. They are serious conditions, and the short- and long-term outcomes are often determined by how early the condition was diagnosed and how effectively it was treated. As in almost everything else, the earlier the condition is recognized and addressed, the better. This is not just common sense talking. Studies show that individuals whose mental disorder is treated have less risk, in both the short term and the long term, of delinquency, illicit substance abuse, violence, school failure, poverty, and suicide. Further, for those who would justify not providing adequate mental health care because of its cost, there is no question that adults whose mental disorders are not treated exact a heavy toll on health care, social services, and the criminal justice system—and incur costs that far outstrip those of adequate, timely care. And this does not even begin to measure the immeasurable pain and suffering of individuals, families, and communities.

Although professionals in the realms of health care, education, and government know this, children with mental health problems are still underrecognized and underserved. The National Alliance on Mental Illness (NAMI), citing the landmark 1999 US Surgeon General's report on mental health, states that four million children and adolescents live with a "serious mental disorder that causes significant functional impairments at home, at school, and with peers." Twenty-one percent of kids ages nine to seventeen have a "diagnosable mental or addictive disorder." (As do 1 in 4 adults, according to NIMH.[5] In addition, 1 in 5 adults takes a prescribed psychopharmaceutical drug.[6]) Though 1 in 10 children and adolescents suffer some level of impairment due to mental illness, only about 20 percent of them are diagnosed and receive treatment.[7] Half of students over age fourteen who have a mental illness drop out of school.[8] In addition, there is concern that when children are diagnosed and treated for these disorders, they don't receive the long-term treatment they should, because of limitations imposed by health insurance companies, a lack of health insurance, or difficulty finding a qualified specialist. Another problem some families face is the high cost of certain psychopharmaceuticals. A 2004 study conducted by the Pharmaceutical Research and Manufacturers Association found that prescription drugs were the "least insured of major health care services." Whereas private insurers covered more than 90 percent of hospital inpatient costs and about 70 percent of physician costs, only 60 percent of prescription drug costs was covered, leaving consumers to pay about 38 percent of these costs out of pocket.[9] Even on good plans, monthly copays for some medications can exceed $100.

WHEN THE "NEWS" ON KIDS AND MEDICATION OVERSHADOWS THE FACTS

The facts cited here seem to fly in the face of the popular perception that children today are being "overmedicated," or given psychotropic medications unnecessarily. This should not be read to mean that children who have real, confirmed diagnoses are taking such medication "unnecessarily," although that might occur in rare cases. Rather, there is evidence to suggest that one contributing factor to the rise in psychotropic medications in children is misdiagnosis. For example, one 2000 study of 5,000 children between ages nine and sixteen who were receiving stimulants (such as Ritalin, Dexedrine, Adderall, or Cylert) to address symptoms of AD/HD discovered that only 34 percent met the diagnostic criteria for AD/HD; another 9 percent were diagnosed with AD/HD-NOS.[10] In other words, over half of the children in the study who were receiving stimulants for AD/HD did not have the disorder for which they were being treated.

On the other hand, many children who would meet the diagnostic criteria either are never diagnosed or, if diagnosed, are "undertreated," meaning they could benefit from medication but don't receive it. And then there are children who are never seen by a professional or diagnosed, whose problems are attributed to "emotional" or "behavior" issues. More recently, if you throw into the mix the news stories of students with no diagnosis obtaining psychoactive medications, especially those in the stimulant class, to churn out lots of last-minute assignments or improve their focus for high-stakes testing situations, it's easy to form an opinion. Clearly, inadequate treatment and abuse are bad for kids for all kinds of reasons. But while one may feel strongly about a subject like this, it's important to keep in mind that the problem of teens popping Ritalin the morning of the SAT or doctors making sloppy diagnoses has *nothing* to do with *your child's* situation.

It's equally important to bear in mind some other facts. Perhaps because it has been on the market since 1955 and is among the ten most frequently prescribed pharmaceuticals, Ritalin continues to be the stalking horse for the antimedication faction. Critics argue that AD/HD is not a "real" disorder but just "kids being kids," and point to discrepancies in the rate of AD/HD diagnosis and Ritalin use along geographic, ethnic, and socioeconomic lines. And there *is* evidence that in some areas of the United States and among some groups, doctors may be prescribing medication for AD/HD more often than they should. However, when you consider that, according to *DSM-5*, between 3 percent and 7 percent of school-age children meet criteria for this diagnosis, but girls are routinely underdiagnosed[11] and that, according to the US Surgeon General and other credible authorities, only 1 in 5 children with a mental disorder is ever diagnosed, and a smaller percentage of that number is ever treated,[12] the "overdiagnosis" story quickly loses air. Amid all the misinformation, it's important to bear in mind that Ritalin is the most widely tested and safest psychotropic medication on the market today, an established fact that is often drowned out by sensationalism. And the long-term risks of untreated AD/HD— substance abuse, problems with school, work, and relationships— are well documented. Further, it is estimated that up to 75 percent of children with AD/HD also have at least one other psychiatric disorder.[13]

Given the furor that persists around a medication with five decades of safety and efficacy behind it, the controversy and confusion that surround newer, and in some cases stronger, agents isn't surprising. But when we question or challenge trends in psychopharmacology for our kids, we should be sure we're asking the right questions and not limit them to issues of safety and efficacy.

Many factors contribute to the rising rates of psychotropic use among our kids. Better-qualified physicians making more accurate diagnoses no doubt play a role, but ironically so do less-experienced physicians making inaccurate diagnoses, educational settings that fail to provide appropriate supports and services, and professionals whose interventions and advice fail to address problem behaviors. Add to this the statistical increase in diagnosed psychiatric disorders in children and adolescents, growing awareness of the dangers of untreated psychiatric disorders in children, and the relatively recent availability of pharmaceutical agents (including the SSRIs, atypical neuroleptics, and nonstimulant medications to treat AD/HD) that target their symptoms. Clearly, there is more to the "overmedication" story than simply anxious parents and pill-pushing doctors.

THERE IS NO "UNIVERSITY OF GOOGLE"

Some parents and professionals (usually those who are not medical doctors) take a stronger view against medication: they simply "do not believe in" medication and may even view those who use it as taking an "easy way" out. Remember, much of what people who lack MDs know about psychotropic medication may be incomplete or inaccurate. In 2004, the Institute of Medicine reported that "nearly half of all Americans do not know how to use basic health information." The authors of the report pointed out that "health illiteracy" was common even among the most highly educated.[14] Understanding the intricacies of ASDs, comorbidities, brain chemistry, and how any medication works goes way beyond what most would consider "basic health information."

Here's a special word about the books, website content, and public statements of some self-styled "authorities." And, yes, I specifically include former Playboy Playmate turned "warrior mother" Jenny McCarthy here, though she is hardly alone. Clearly, the people who publish McCarthy's books and the producers of programs who repeatedly have rolled out the red carpet for her impassioned but scientifically incorrect (and, some would argue, dangerous) views on autism treatment and vaccines could not be bothered or chose not to perform the most basic due diligence to corroborate the scientific accuracy of her claims. That does not make them right.

The scientific facts are available through the credible sources listed at the end of the chapter. After that, talk to your doctor and other credentialed experts who do know the facts. For your child's sake, and for your own, you can never have too much sound, credible information. See "Recommended Resources" on page 287 for sources you can trust.

EVERY CHILD IS UNIQUE

Whatever one's opinions on the matter—pro or con, informed or not—will seem irrelevant when it is your child who is depressed, suicidal, anxious, phobic, obsessive-compulsive, oppositional, aggressive, violent, self-injurious, hyperactive, or unable to attend school or socialize to a degree that he cannot tolerate, or that you believe may ultimately be more damaging to him in the long or the short term than the possible risks of medicating. Suddenly, it just comes down to one thing: What is the best decision right now for my child? And let's be honest: untreated comorbid conditions and behaviors like those listed earlier have their own "side effects," their own "risks."

Even when you make the "right" decision, you may still wonder what else you could have done to avoid facing these risks, or what the fact that your child needs medication says about you as a parent. Remember, then, that many of the behaviors, symptoms, and disorders that respond to medication arise from physical problems in the brain—namely in the neurotransmitters, the chemicals that facilitate communication between neurons. As we are learning, neurotransmitters can determine not only how we feel (in terms of mood and emotion) but also what we are able to do (focus, attend, function). Medication works by chemically "normalizing" a process or reaction in the brain, by either raising or lowering the amount of neurotransmitter available—a power beyond that of parenting, therapy, and other interventions.

That said, you should begin by asking questions, gathering good, sound scientific information, and talking with professionals, and you should continue doing that all the way through. There might be times when even a successful medication protocol needs reviewing and possibly modifying. Over time, you might identify a better set of accommodations at school, a better way to interact at home, a more appropriate set of social expectations that might reduce or eliminate the need for a specific medication. Please see the two excellent resources from Autism Speaks in "Recommended Resources" at the end of this chapter.

MENTAL DISORDERS ARE PHYSICAL, TOO

Debates over children and medication inevitably elicit analogies along the lines of "If your child had diabetes, you wouldn't think twice about giving her insulin." Although the comparison seems apt, it actually misses the point. After all, stabilizing blood sugar levels does not change or affect how the person on insulin thinks or feels emotionally. It might make them feel better physically, but it doesn't touch the essence of who they are. Psychotropic medication, however, is different. While we may recognize the improvements it can bring, parents are often left to wonder about immediate and long-term side effects. And by "side effects," we mean more than simply those listed on the package insert. Even when the outcome is positive, a parent may still wonder: How is this making my child feel? How is it affecting his physical, emotional, and intellectual development? Parents whose children take medication may find themselves wondering whether the medication reveals or masks who their child really is.

BRING IN THE EXPERTS

Finally, this is never an easy decision. Be sure that your child is seen by the best-qualified and most experienced doctor you can find. We recommend a psychiatrist or neurologist who specializes in pediatrics and, if at all possible, ASDs. Your family general practitioner or pediatrician can prescribe these medications, but you should consider consulting a specialist. In his book *Taking the Mystery Out of Medications in Autism/Asperger Syndrome*, Dr. Luke Y. Tsai, an eminent physician and researcher and the father of a child on the spectrum, writes: "I appreciate that it is often difficult for parents to find a physician who has adequate training and experience in ASD and related disorders. I wonder, however, how many parents would want a physician without adequate training and experience in cancer treatment to treat their child's leukemia or any other form of cancer. I also wonder how many family physicians and general pediatricians without [that training] would prescribe cancer medications for children with the disease."[15]

Pediatric psychopharmacology is a constantly evolving field in which a single pediatric psychiatrist may be seeing and treating more children with a particular medication than the number included in the largest study on that medication. For many children with ASD who take medication, finding the right one (or ones, as it is not uncommon for two, even three to be taken simultaneously; see below) is a process of trial and error. In fact, finding the correct psychoactive medication for *anyone*—child or adult, ASD or no—is always a trial-and-error endeavor. It is an area where professional experience is everything. Do your research and ask as many questions as you need to, as many times as you need to, until you're satisfied that you understand the medication your child will be taking and what you can expect.

POLYPHARMACY: WHEN MORE THAN ONE MEDICATION IS PRESCRIBED

An emerging trend is toward prescribing more than one psychoactive medication at a time (known as *polypharmacy*). Often this involves using medications from different classes: for example, a neuroleptic such as Risperdal in combination with a stimulant such as Ritalin. Other times, your child's doctor may prescribe two medications from the same class. Because many children have more than one disorder (comorbidity), they may require polypharmacy. Sometimes a second medication may be added to offset a troubling side effect in an otherwise "perfect" or very necessary first medication. In addition, some medications work better in combination, which is known as an additive effect.

One reason polypharmacy is so common is that many newer

medications are designed to be much more finely targeted in terms of how they act in the body (which does include the brain). Where an older drug might have treated tics by being heavily sedating, a newer drug might just treat the tics without that side effect. If there are symptoms for which a calming, sedating, or anxiety-reducing approach is indicated, a second drug would need to be prescribed. One of the best things about some newer drugs is that they "do less," which means that their effect is focused and limited. As we said before, most individuals with ASD have more than one disorder for which medication might be a viable approach.

INFORMATION YOU SHOULD HAVE AT ALL TIMES

Which information about your child's medication is important? All of it! This basic information should be typed up, printed out, and "on hand"—which means where whoever needs it can literally put their hands on it: not in your file cabinet, on your computer, or locked in the safe-deposit box. Be sure you always know and/or have written down (perhaps in your datebook, on a slip of paper in your wallet, or in your cell phone) the following information:

- Correct name and spelling of each medication, both its trade name (brand name) and its generic name. For example, the generic sertraline (always lowercase) is marketed under the brand name Zoloft (always capitalized).
- Be sure that you have the medication's full name. A growing number of medications are being released in new forms. There's a big difference between Prozac and Prozac Weekly (as the name suggests, one dose lasts a full week), for instance, or Risperdal and Risperdal Consta (the latter is an injection given only once every two weeks).
- Diagnosis, condition, or specific symptoms for which it is being prescribed.
- How the medication is dispensed from the pharmacy (e.g., 1 milligram tablets), a description of what it looks like ("white, oval tablet with the name JANSSEN stamped on one side"), and how it is given to the child: tablet, capsule, liquid suspension, transdermal patch, injection.

- Daily dosage, including the daily total (for example, 1 milligram of Risperdal) as well as the schedule of medication and how it correlates to how the medication is dispensed from the pharmacy. (For the sake of clarity and safety, when you have quantities less than a whole milligram, place a zero before the decimal point.) For example:

  - 0.5 milligram (one half of a 1-milligram tablet) of Risperdal at bedtime
  - 0.25 (one quarter of a 1-milligram tablet) with breakfast
  - 0.25 (one quarter of a 1-milligram tablet) at 4:00 PM

- All possible known side effects.
- Information on how your child responds to the medication (for example, "is a little drowsy the first half hour after a dose"), and any activities or situations that should be avoided.
- Any other medications, foods, supplements, or vitamins that are strictly contraindicated for use with this one (consult your doctor, pharmacist, and the *Physicians' Desk Reference*).
- Anything special someone might need to know. For example, do you refer to the medication by its name (Ritalin) or do you call it something else ("your attention medicine")? Does your child prefer to take it with a specific food or beverage? Are there any routines you follow regarding the medication?

Make copies of this information available to the school nurse, your child's other doctors and dentist, babysitters, any relative or friend who might care for your child in the event you are unavailable, and anyone else who may need to know (camp counselors, parents hosting a sleepover, and so on). Have copies readily available in case your child requires emergency treatment. Keep a copy in a sealed, clearly labeled envelope in your glove compartment(s), on the refrigerator, or anyplace it will be handy. Have this information with you and/or your child at all times, especially when you go on vacation or your child is away from you.

MEDICATION AND ASPERGER SYNDROME

Categories of Medications

Psychotropic medications are grouped under categories such as "antidepressants," "neuroleptics," and "stimulants." Many people find these confusing, because a particular medication may be prescribed to treat a range of symptoms and disorders that seem very different from those for which the medication was first created. For example, guanfacine, the active ingredient in Intuniv, was approved originally to treat high blood pressure; it is classified variously as an antihypertensive, central adrenergic inhibitor, or central alpha-2 adrenoreceptor. As Intuniv, it is prescribed to address inattention, impulsivity, and hyperactivity.[16] Just remember that simply because your child's doctor prescribes an antipsychotic (also known as a neuroleptic) or an antidepressant, it does not necessarily mean that your child is psychotic or depressed. Certain neuroleptics (or antipsychotics) are used to treat depression, bipolar disorder, tic disorders, stuttering, OCD, and anxiety, for example. Some antidepressants also work well against OCD.

FDA Approval: What Does It Really Mean?

Many people assume that to obtain Food and Drug Administration (FDA) approval to market a medication in the United States, manufacturers must prove its safety and effectiveness in every population for every conceivable use. That is not the case. Pharmaceutical companies are required only to demonstrate a medication's effectiveness and safety when used to treat the particular condition for which it will be marketed. Once the medication is on the market, physicians may prescribe it however they see fit. FDA approval does not limit the drug's use to the condition for which it is indicated, nor does it in any way limit which conditions it may be prescribed to treat. So, for example, an SSRI that has been approved to treat depression may be prescribed to treat premenstrual syndrome (PMS). However, in order for a company to market it for that use, it would have to seek additional FDA approval based on data from studies of that medication for PMS. Most companies choose not to reinvest in further research because it is expensive and time-consuming. But others might choose to do so because a new approval to treat another condition extends the life a company's patent and exclusive right to market the drug.

How Are Medications Tested to Receive FDA Approval?

Most often the process goes something like this: A pharmaceutical company develops a promising new medication to treat a particular condition. Over the course of several years, the new drug is subjected to a series of four different types of studies, each designed to elicit different types of data on its safety and effectiveness. It is first studied and tested in the laboratory and/or in animals to establish its general safety and how it works in the body (preclinical testing), then to establish its safety in humans and to determine the maximum safe doses and schedule of administration (phase I). Next, researchers establish the medication's effectiveness and monitor side effects (phase II). The final phase (phase III) compares the effectiveness of the new agent against currently available and accepted treatments and monitors adverse side effects that may result from long-term use.

Many of the final-stage studies run for a relatively brief period, sometimes as short as several months. Most new medications reach the market lacking data on potential long-term effects. This is why it can be helpful to know when a medication was first approved, the indications it was approved for, how long it has been used by adults and by children, and its general safety record.

What Is "Off-Label" Use?

When a new drug receives FDA approval, the manufacturer must provide detailed information on virtually all that is known about it, including its chemical composition, dosing, results of clinical trials, side effects, and contraindications (conditions under which the drug should not be used or used with caution). Under "Indications and Usage" you will find the conditions, disorders, or diseases for which the manufacturer has established the drug's efficacy and safety. In the case of Risperdal (risperidone), for example, in late 2004, it was "management of the manifestations of psychotic disorders." Any other use, such as to manage repetitive, aggressive, or violent behavior—for which it is commonly prescribed for people with ASDs—was technically off-label. However, as the result of further clinical trials, in 2006, the FDA approved the manufacturer's request to include "irritability associated with autistic disorder" as an indication for use.[17]

Prescribing drugs off-label is not illegal, nor is it uncommon. As a drug becomes widely used among the general population, physicians and researchers sometimes notice unexpected therapeutic benefits. Some drugs developed and marketed to treat purely physical conditions turn out to have psychoactive properties. For example, Tenex (guanfacine), a drug originally approved to treat high blood pressure in 1986, had been widely prescribed by doctors looking for a nonstimulant alternative to treat tics and Tourette's syndrome, as well as aggression, hyperactivity, sleep problems, and agitation. All of these uses were, technically speaking, off-label. In 2009, a reformulation of guanfacine emerged as a "new" AD/HD treatment called Intuniv. Although it was tested and frequently prescribed for children, the product label contains the following:

> The safety and efficacy of INTUNIV™ in pediatric patients less than 6 years of age have not been established. For children and adolescents 6 years and older, efficacy beyond 9 weeks and safety beyond 2 years of treatment have not been established.[18]

In another case, Abilify (aripiprazole), approved for adults with schizophrenia, was found in the mid-2000s effective in children with bipolar disorder. In 2007, the FDA approved Abilify to treat schizophrenia in those ages ten to seventeen; in 2008, to treat patients with bipolar disorder, ages thirteen to seventeen; and in 2009, for use in patients ages six to seventeen to treat irritability related to autism.[19] Psychotropic medications may also be found effective in treating a wider range of symptoms than originally intended. Zoloft (sertraline), a drug originally indicated solely for depression when first approved in 1991, has since been approved for obsessive-compulsive disorder in adults (1997) and in children age six and up (1998), and for posttraumatic stress disorder (1999). However, it is not indicated to treat children for any condition but OCD.[20]

If your doctor is recommending a medication that will be prescribed "off-label," do not be alarmed. Instead, ask her to review with you why she thinks that this medication might be helpful and what evidence she can offer to support that. Do not be surprised to learn that there have been good studies supporting the efficacy of the medication or a history of widespread use that may speak to safety concerns. Not every pharmaceutical company goes through the expense of conducting a new set of clinical trials every time a potential new use for the drug arises.

FDA Approval for Pediatric Use: Why Is It So Rare?

For a drug to be approved for use in children, it must be studied in children. A placebo double-blind study—one in which half of the participants receive the medication and half receive a placebo, or sugar pill, and not even those conducting the trial know who receives which until the end—is considered the platinum standard in clinical trials. However, few are conducted on children, for several reasons. Parents' reluctance to expose their child to any medication without cause, and their unwillingness to risk getting only the placebo when their child might benefit from the medication, play a role. Legally, patients enrolled in studies must give their informed consent, and some doctors and medical ethicists question whether and at what age children can be considered capable of giving such consent. Finally, the number of children with AS or ASDs is relatively small, and not all who share a specific diagnosis share the same symptoms. The frequent presence of comorbid disorders may complicate attempts to discern the effectiveness of a given treatment on a given symptom.

Testing psychotropic medications on children raises many of the same questions about short- and long-term side effects parents face when considering these treatments. Understandably, pediatric volunteers for a premarketing study are rare. The result is, as Dr. Dianne Murphy, associate director of the FDA's Center for Drug Evaluation and Research, told the *New York Times* in 2000, "up to 81 percent of all products used on children have not been studied or labeled for infants and children. We're treating our children without studying the medicine to the degree that we require these drugs to be studied in and understood in adults."[21] Fortunately, things have changed. Beginning in December 2000, the FDA required that any new drug that might be used by children undergo pediatric study and that manufacturers provide information on correct doses for children. In addition, under certain circumstances the FDA can require pediatric studies on a drug that has already been approved. Introduced in late 2002, Strattera (atomoxetine) was one of the first psychopharmaceuticals for which children as young as six were included in the preapproval randomized, double-blind, placebo-controlled studies. As the off-label use of psychotropic medications increased, officials at the National Institute of Mental Health created a model for testing medications that were already in use by children but for which there were insufficient data on safety and efficacy. The resulting Research Units on Pediatric Pharmacology (RUPP) began conducting clinical trials in several cities. Because of its wide off-label use in children with AS and other PDDs, Risperdal was among the first medications studied under this program and it later became the first drug specifically indicated to treat certain symptoms of autism.[22] In the years since, as one expert put it in 2011, "There have been more studies in children conducted in the last five years than in the previous thirty years combined."[23]

What Every Parent Should Know

Every medication, psychotropic or not, presents risks as well as benefits. FDA approval is based not on a "guarantee" of safety, only on the fact that the known benefits of using a particular drug outweigh its known and most common risks. No one—not even the most experienced expert in pediatric psychopharmacology—can predict how *your child* will respond to a given medication. Generally speaking (although there may be exceptions depending on the severity of your child's symptoms), your child's doctor will opt for what is known as the "first-line" treatment, the medication that has the highest probability of being effective with the lowest level of known risk. Unfortunately, the first-line treatment isn't always the one that works for your child.

Of course, there are always individual exceptions, and because of differences in metabolism and health considerations, some medications are prescribed for children in doses that are equal to or even higher than those for adults. With most medications, however, it is wisest to start low and build slowly, increasing the dose only after you have established that your child is tolerating it well.

Before you leave the doctor's office, be sure you have in writing (written by you or the doctor) two sets of instructions: how to start the medication and how to stop it, if necessary.

Things to Know for Starting a Medication

- What the prescription is for. It should be sufficiently clear and legible so that you can read and understand it. If it's not, ask your doctor to please rewrite it. A surprising number of medications have similar-looking and -sounding names, and mistakes do happen.
  - The names, both brand and generic, of the medication.
  - Whether your doctor thinks a generic, if available, is acceptable. According to Dr. Luke Tsai, some doctors are reluctant to prescribe generic versions because of concerns about quality and dose. Consistency and reliability of a medication may be essential for some children, depending on the drug and its purpose. In fact, generics are not always simply cheaper versions of the same drug marketed under its trade name. Dr. Tsai notes that the FDA does not recognize every generic "as equivalent to its brand-name counterpart." You can find out if the generic your doctor prescribes or your insurance company insists you accept is truly equivalent by checking the FDA's so-called orange book, which is available online at the FDA's website.

- What the medication looks like. Ask your doctor to show you its picture in the *Physicians' Desk Reference*, at PDR.net, or on the manufacturer's website.
- What form the medication will come in (pill, tablet, suspension, transdermal patch, etc.).
- The dose as it will be dispensed by the pharmacy (important because your child's actual dose may be half or less of a pill or tablet).
    - The dose as it will be given to the child.
    - The dosing schedule.
    - The schedule for gradually increasing the dosage up to a target level (called *titration*).
- Anything you need to know about how the medication should be taken: With meals or on an empty stomach? Can it be crushed and mixed into food or juice? Are there any foods or drinks that the medication should or should not be taken with? Can the pill be crushed or broken? (Some time-release medications, such as Concerta, can be ineffective if not swallowed whole.) As Dr. James Snyder put it, it's like "chopping a radio in half and expecting each half to work." Others, like Strattera, can cause mucosal irritation if taken broken or crushed.
- What to do if you miss a dose.
- Any types or classes of medications—including over-the-counter medicines, herbal remedies, homeopathic remedies, vitamins, nutritional supplements, and so on—your child should avoid. Many "natural" substances—including vitamins and minerals—react with medication, either reducing or amplifying its effect. Be sure your doctor is aware of *everything* your child takes, and be sure to check with your doctor before you give your child anything new, even if it sounds "safe" and "natural."
- Each of your child's other health professionals—physicians, dentist, optometrist or ophthalmologist, occupational therapist—should know what your child is taking as well as the pertinent data listed previously.
- Any activities that should be avoided or that require extra caution. For example, some medications may cause skin reactions with sun exposure or disrupt the body's ability to cope with heat.

- Date of your next appointment with the doctor.
- Schedule for future follow-up visits. Some states have specific rules about how often a physician prescribing certain types of medications to children must see the patient. Some doctors decide on their own that they require office visits at a certain frequency before they will write prescriptions or refill orders for certain medications.
- Procedure for refills. Some can be called in to your pharmacy, but prescriptions for controlled substances—which include Ritalin, Concerta, and some other frequently prescribed stimulants—require the submission of a three-part prescription form that must be delivered to the pharmacy. This is especially important if you plan to purchase the prescription through an online pharmacy in the United States.[24] You may have to allow extra days for processing the paperwork. In addition, some states have regulations regarding the frequency of doctor-patient contact when certain types of medications are being prescribed and/or when patients are under a certain age.
- Side effects that warrant a phone call to your doctor.
- Side effects that warrant an appointment with your doctor.
- Side effects that warrant emergency treatment, including signs of overdose.
- Side effects that would necessitate stopping the medication.

KEEPING ACCURATE AND USEFUL MEDICATION RECORDS

Ideally, your doctor should provide, or you can create, a form for charting your child's response. It's very easy to lose track of when a dose was increased or when a response first appeared. This information is important for you and for your doctor in making informed decisions. A sample form appears on pages 290.

Keep a daily log for each medication, or combination of medications, that your child takes. Communicate with the prescribing doctor. Some side effects weaken or disappear over time. The potential benefit of a medication may warrant giving the body extra time to adjust before stopping. Supplement this with a long-term summary that provides your child's entire medication history, including the following:

- The medication taken
- The date your child began taking it
- The dose and how it was given throughout the day
- The date your child stopped taking the medication
- General response
- Side effects
- Why the medication was stopped
- Your child's behavior after the medication stopped

Things to Know for Stopping a Medication

- Circumstances under which you might have to consider stopping this medication.
- Side effects that warrant a phone call to the doctor.
- Side effects that warrant an appointment with the doctor.
- Side effects that warrant emergency treatment, including signs of overdose.
- Whether this medication should be stopped suddenly or be slowly tapered.
- If it should be tapered, exactly what the doses, over the course of how many days, would be.
- What to expect once the medication is tapered or stopped.

MEDICATION AT HOME

All psychotropic medications can be dangerous, even lethal, if misused or taken by anyone other than the person for whom they were prescribed. They should be handled with caution at all times, from the moment you pick them up at the pharmacy until you dispose of any "leftovers" in your garbage. (Do not flush unused or expired drugs down the toilet or sink!)

- Try to fill all of your child's prescriptions—for everything, including antibiotics—at a single pharmacy that keeps good computerized records and has a knowledgeable pharmacist you feel comfortable talking to. Be sure that your child's prescription history is reviewed and considered when any prescription is filled, so that the pharmacist will be on the lookout for possible drug interactions. In addition to consulting your child's physician, talk to your pharmacist before using any over-the-counter medicine.
- Before leaving the pharmacy, read the label and make sure it's correct: your child's name, prescribing physician, medication, dosage. In the presence of the pharmacist or other employee, open the container and make sure that the medication is in the form, size, and color you expect. Pharmacies do make mistakes, and once you open a container outside the pharmacy, they have no obligation to take it back or issue a refund. The bigger concern is that you accidentally offer or your child takes on his own something that was not prescribed for him.
- Keep all medicines in their original, child-resistant containers, in a safe, secure place, out of reach of all children, including the child for whom it is prescribed. Consider keeping your medication in a locked box.
- Have a daily routine for dispensing medication and stick to it. As much as possible, try to link taking the medication with an event that occurs every single day at about the same time. Bedtime is usually an easy one, but parents sometimes fall off schedule with weekend morning doses or afternoon doses that were given by the school nurse. At least for the first several weeks—and beyond, if you need it—keep a chart on the refrigerator or someplace else convenient and mark off each dose as it is given.
- That said, don't let your routine become "so routine" that you or your child forget when and if the medication was taken or your awareness of safe handling begins to drift.

One day when talking on the phone to a client while I was dispensing my son's medication and my own vitamins, a lapse in attention resulted in my son staring confusedly at my calcium tablet as I realized that I had just swallowed his Risperdal. Don't be that mom!

- If your child is taking pills that have to be cut, ask your pharmacist to do it for you. If you do it yourself, do an entire prescription all at once. Pill cutters are handy, but they don't work for pills with unusual shapes. Try using an X-Acto artist's knife, and change the blade often, after every twenty cuts or so. Try cutting on a gel-type plastic cutting board. If your child is taking half a pill in the morning and a quarter at night, ask the pharmacist for extra bottles with child-resistant caps. Clearly label one bottle, for example, "Klonopin, 0.5 mg, morning" and the other, "Klonopin, 0.25 mg, night." Always keep the medicine in the same safe place.

- Always check with anyone else in the household who has access to the medication before giving it to your child. In the bustle of daily family life, it sometimes happens that one parent gives a dose and forgets to tell the other, who then repeats it. This can be extremely dangerous. Asking your child may not always help. One solution might be to put one adult in charge of the medication. Another solution is to say, "Whoever reads the bedtime story does the medication," or "Whoever makes the coffee in the morning gives Joey his pill." Whatever you do, find something that works and stick with it.

- Have a backup plan in case you forget a dose. First, find out how to handle the missed dose. That information is usually available on the printed patient information sheet that comes with the medication. If unsure, ask your pharmacist or your doctor. In a safe, clearly labeled, child-resistant bottle, stash a couple of doses and put it in the glove compartment of every car and perhaps one in your purse. If the child is a frequent visitor at Grandma's or Uncle Jeff's, consider keeping a dose or two there as well, just in case.

- With all current Transportation Safety Administration (TSA) rules regarding carry-ons, take special care. First, be sure that whatever medication you must carry with you meets the TSA's guidelines. As a precaution, it's probably a good idea to have with you a letter from your child's doctor describing the medication. This might be especially handy if your child's medication comes in a liquid form and the amount exceeds the TSA's limit for carry-ons.

- While traveling generally, figure out the amount you will need for the whole trip. If you can, have two people in your party carry the full amount. If you cannot obtain enough of the medication to do that, split the supply between at least two people. This way, if someone's gets lost, at least you are covered for a few days.
- Find out from your doctor and your health insurance company what steps you would have to take to replace the medication if it is lost or destroyed and you are far from home.
- When you travel, be sure to keep all essential medications with you, in your handbag or another carry-on. Never pack medication in your checked luggage.
- Be sure anyone who might be giving your child his medication (babysitters, etc.) knows exactly what to do, is aware of possible side effects, and has access to your child's prescribing physician's phone number.
- Be sure that you are familiar with the signs of overdose or serious side effects.
- Keep your local poison control telephone number along with the name of the medication(s) posted prominently.

MEDICATION AT SCHOOL

Parents have different views on how much of their child's personal and medical history they are comfortable sharing with his school. You may have concerns about your child being stigmatized because he takes medication or to what degree the school personnel with access to that information will honor the confidentiality that all medical information deserves. First, remember that your child's right to privacy in schools is covered by the Family Educational Rights and

Privacy Act (FERPA), and the school nurse is obligated to observe HIPAA guidelines. No one in the school should know about your child's medication status unless they are in a position where that knowledge is necessary, and they should not be discussing it with anyone who has no reason to know.

For the sake of your child's safety, it is wise to give the school information about the type and dose of medication your child is currently taking, along with his emergency contact information, at the very least. (And be sure to update this if anything changes.) In the course of receiving emergency medical treatment, your child might be exposed to other medications or anesthesia that could produce dangerous, even lethal, complications. Anyone treating your child for any reason needs to know about any medication she takes regularly, especially psychotropics. Depending on the medication, you should probably alert your child's teacher and the school nurse about possible side effects and what to do if they develop. This is an especially important consideration if your child is beginning a trial of a new medication, no matter how good its general safety record.

There are other reasons to let your child's teacher and school nurse know about the medication. They are in a position to observe how your child is responding and also to make accommodations for him if necessary; for example, excusing him from gymnastics if his coordination is a little off or from a test if he's experiencing drowsiness. Many children behave differently at home than they do at school. A medication that seems to be reducing your child's anxiety at home may be making him a nervous wreck in school. These are things that you need to know. Ask your child's teacher for a brief daily report, especially when you are trying a new medication, dose, or schedule.

Some parents are attracted to the idea of turning their child's medication trial into a "scientific" experiment. They believe they'll get a more accurate "reading" on how the medication is working if they don't tell anyone at school about it. This is a really bad idea. First, your child's medication trial is not a research project. It's an attempt to find a solution to a serious problem that is not without risk. Everyone needs to be on the same page. When you opt to leave school personnel out of the loop, you lose an important source of information as well as a critical safety net. For example, some of the most serious side effects first appear in what seem innocuous developments: drowsiness, rashes or hives, or changes in behavior. According to Dr. Luke Tsai, "When young children take psycho-therapeutic medication, behavioral toxicity often appears before any other side effect. . . . The early emergence of behavioral side effects is a warning sign."[25] The problem with school personnel not knowing to look for behavioral signs is that children on the spectrum often have mood swings and behavioral changes as a matter of course. A careful eye is needed to note what may be a warning sign.

When teachers do not know that a child's behavior may be medication related, they may make assumptions and possibly even counterproductive changes in curricular demands, behavior management, and discipline that may not be appropriate. As Dr. James Snyder, a pediatric psychiatrist, points out, telling teachers may help them to see your son or daughter as "a child with a problem, not a 'problem child.'"

If your child will be taking medication at school, find out the school district's procedures for supplying and dispensing. Usually the school nurse will require a letter from you and/or the prescribing physician that states the name of your child, the name of the medication, and dosing instructions (how much and when). State and local board of education regulations will dictate how medication is handled in your school. School policies differ regarding how large a supply the school nurse will keep on hand, who may deliver it to the school, and so on. Follow this procedure:

- Provide the medication in a clearly labeled, child-resistant bottle with your child's name, teacher's name, and doctor's name and number, as well as the name of the medication, the dose, and the form. For example, "Klonopin, 0.5 mg (a half pill), after lunch."
- Provide a copy of any product information literature you receive.
- If you are required to send in a week's supply every Monday, for example, be sure your child's teacher is expecting it and that it does not fall into other children's hands en route to the nurse.
- If your child is able to open a child safety cap and/or the

medication is one that might be abused by your child or others, you might consider delivering it yourself personally to the school. In some places, this is required by law.

- If it's school policy to send home empty bottles for refill, you might consider requesting (backed up by a letter) that any extra doses (due to holidays, sick days) either be kept in the office for you to pick up at a later time or disposed of so that your child's bottle comes home empty.

TELLING YOUR CHILD ABOUT MEDICATION

This is a complex, sensitive area for many parents and children. Considering the increase in children taking psychotropics, surprisingly little has been written about it. When, how, and how much you tell your child will depend on many factors: your child, her level of understanding of AS and her behavior, the type of medication she'll be taking, and the circumstances under which she'll be taking it. Every situation is different, and you may wish to discuss how to proceed with your child's prescribing doctor, who, we hope, will have seen many other families through this dilemma.

Overall, it's important to discuss this issue in a way that your child will understand. This may be easier if you and your child have already discussed his problems, whether or not you have told him about his actual diagnosis. However, simply because you have never talked to your child about some of his behaviors or told him that he has AS, don't feel pressured to do it right now. Depending on your child's age and level of understanding, it may suffice to say, "I know you've been feeling very anxious lately; Dr. Ferry and I believe that this medicine might help with that."

If you are considering medication, chances are it's because your child is having difficulty. In addition to the problems related to AS, your child may be experiencing embarrassment, guilt, or shame over his feelings or behavior. It's not unusual for a child who has been acting out, having trouble relating to peers, or failing in school to feel "stupid," "dumb," "bad," or worse. The idea that faulty brain chemistry beyond our conscious control is at the root of many problems can be reassuring to parents and perhaps even older adolescents. ("It's not your fault; your brain works differently.") Younger children, however, may find that prospect more frightening.

Then there is the simple fact that your child will be taking medicine, and all but the very young realize that this is what you do when you are "sick" or "something is wrong." By this point, most children strongly suspect or know they are different, and different in ways that not everyone totally accepts. In a brief paper published in the *Journal of the American Academy of Child and Adolescent Psychiatry*, Drs. Nancy Rappaport and Peter Chubinsky wrote: "Even if the clinician has reassured the parents, children are also often apprehensive about taking medication and commonly believe that this is final proof that they are defective. Although they may not initially express these thoughts, many children will at some point call themselves 'crazy,' 'bad,' or 'stupid' as an explanation for why they are taking medication. Others may fear that they are brain-damaged. . . . Some children will obstinately reject medication rather than tolerate the daily reminder of their perceived defect."[26]

On the other hand, some children do see and feel the difference the right medication makes. Given positive cues by parents, doctors, and teachers, children can adapt to their need for medication without it adversely coloring their self-image. Sometimes the results of medication are so apparent to the child that the medication "sells itself."

So what do you say? First, it would be imprudent to present medication as something "that will make you feel better," "make schoolwork easier to handle," or "make you happier." The truth is, if this isn't the right medication for your child, she probably won't feel better. Making a promise that you cannot keep will only damage your child's trust in you and lay the groundwork for resistance to future medication trials.

Drugs and Abuse

There is also the issue of sending the right message about psychotropic medications and their legitimate uses. Parents are understandably concerned over the possible link between legitimate psychotropic medication use and the use and abuse of street drugs. Despite decades of programs to end drug abuse and alcoholism, these remain major problems across every demographic. However, we now know that treatment of psychiatric disorders may actually serve as a preventive. Dr. Timothy Wilens, author of the one book every parent considering medication should read, *Straight Talk About Psychiatric Medications for Kids*, offered this perspective on future substance abuse in a previous edition: "Up to three quarters of children or adolescents with a substance abuse problem may have a psychiatric disturbance in addition. The psychiatric conditions most often seen with substance problems in children are conduct disorder, AD/HD, oppositional defiant disorder, depression, bipolar disorder, and to a lesser extent anxiety and panic disorders. In many cases, the psychiatric problem precedes the substance problem, leading to conjecture that many children 'self-medicate' their symptoms by using substances. In addition, children with psychiatric problems may not have the foresight or inhibition it takes to resist getting involved with alcohol or drugs."[27]

Older children and adolescents with Asperger syndrome who have trouble being accepted by peers are known to be more susceptible to peer pressure while being less able to anticipate consequences. Sadly, this can make them attractive to peers who encourage behavior that is dangerous or illegal, such as drinking or street drug use.

Contrary to what some assume, correctly prescribed medications do not have the same effects on people who have the conditions they are prescribed for as they do on those who do not. Your child is not walking around "high," "in la-la land," or "out of it" if the prescription is the right one.

When you said "substance abuse," until recently most people thought of marijuana, hallucinogens, heroin, and other illicit substances. Today, a major source of abused substances is your—or your neighbor's—bathroom medicine cabinet. Kids prone to experiment with prescription drugs are savvy about who might have what. Some of the medications commonly prescribed for kids on the spectrum do have potential for abuse, though it is typically higher for people who should not be taking it. If your child is old enough to understand these issues or has exposure to typical peers who might be interested in the medications he takes, have this discussion as soon as you can. Your child should understand that while the medication he takes is safe for him because it is prescribed by a physician and closely monitored, it could be very dangerous for someone else. Your child should know that he should never share his medication with anyone else.

As your child gets older, especially if he travels in social circles with typical peers, assume that he will be exposed to illicit drugs and alcohol. Parents have a range of attitudes about "experimentation" based on their own experiences, how much of a problem it is in their community, and how much they know and trust their child. If your child is currently taking prescribed psychoactives, a lot of those considerations go out the window, simply because the risks of combining whatever he is currently taking with a substance of unknown ingredients and potency are just too high. Once your child is of legal age to drink alcohol, find out from your doctor whether one beer or glass of wine is safe. When my son turned twenty-one and asked if he could have his first beer at his birthday dinner, I told him to ask his psychiatrist. Though my son doesn't really care for alcohol that much, he still likes the idea of being able to join friends and family in a toast on special occasions or to have a single beer when hanging out with friends at a rock club. The fact is that not knowing whether drinking is safe probably would not prevent most kids from trying it, especially under the stress of peer pressure or the heightened drive to fit in that many of our kids experience. Knowing the limits can help you and your child make better, safer decisions about drinking and perhaps even save a trip to the emergency room.

WHEN CAN A CHILD BE RESPONSIBLE FOR HIS OWN MEDICATION?

The older child or young adult on medication presents some challenging issues. If you assume that she is on medication because she needs it, then you understand how important it is for her to take it. But does she? As more of our children grow up and even leave home, we must find some way to teach them to responsibly manage their own medication.

Our first suggestion is to consult your doctor, who has certainly confronted this problem before. Much will depend on your child, the type of medication he is taking (for example, its potential for overdose, abuse, or serious side effects from missed doses or sudden withdrawal), and the amount of supervision he will have. For example, if away at college, is there a student health professional, a counselor, or a trustworthy, mature friend who can check up on him if needed? If you plan to grant your child this responsibility in the near future, let your child start practicing while still under your roof. He should understand the medication he is taking and why, as well as have access to current versions of the charts and checklists on pages 289–290. Having a container divided into days of the week and times of day is also helpful. It serves as a visual reminder and also allows you and your child to see if any doses were missed.

As your child reaches later adolescence and adulthood, encourage her to take a more active role in her treatment. She should not only know and understand her condition and the medications she is taking, but she should also be speaking directly with her doctor and be included as part of your little "team" moving forward. She should follow a plan for knowing when her prescriptions need to be renewed, make her own appointments with the doctor, and arrange to fill and refill her own prescriptions at least a year or two before you expect her to leave home, go to college, or have a job.

I am surprised at how many teens and young adults are taking medication and cannot even tell you its name, much less what it's for. Sometimes these are very powerful medications with potentially serious consequences for skipped doses, overdose, or mixing with other drugs (including over-the-counter and "natural" products), highly caffeinated energy drinks, and alcohol. Don't let this be your child. Talking about medication and the reasons for taking it is not unlike talking about the other facts of life. You tailor the information to fit where your child is at developmentally. Taking medication is nothing to be ashamed of. That said, it is also personal health information that not everyone your child knows needs to have.

When Your Child Decides to Set the Agenda

For better or worse, the world is full of information, and our tech-savvy kids seem to be swimming in it. Most parents find it impossible to monitor every possible source of information their children might access. We also live in a culture that is open if somewhat confused about its attitude toward substances that change brain function or behavior.

It is important to talk with your child about medication openly and honestly. Some children are good at articulating how they feel, how they think their medication is working or not, and how they feel about being on medication. Others are not. Where family, friends, and teachers might see a "real difference in focus" when Sally is taking her Concerta, she may only feel jumpy and uncomfortable. Sometimes even a medication that "works" is not always a good fit. Kids who lack the skills to talk about their feelings in this area, or who believe—rightly or wrongly—that they will not be heard if they do, are very likely to take matters into their own hands. Without telling you or anyone else. Days, weeks, or months later parents discover a single spit-out pill in the garbage or, in the most alarming cases, a whole month's supply of antiseizure meds stashed in the back of the sock drawer. I have yet to meet a parent this has happened to who was not completely surprised. Aside from the obvious issues, there is also the feeling of betrayal and a question of when and if the child can be trusted again.

When asked why they have stopped taking their medication, these children may offer up everything from a legitimate complaint about a side effect to an unrealistic hope that stopping the medication will make them be "more like everyone else." Some children, reluctant or unable to express their feelings about not wanting to take medication, may complain of headaches, stomachaches, or vague body discomforts resulting in medication refusal. Anxious children, in particular, are more often sensitive to worrying about or actually perceiving many of the possible side effects of being on medication once they are told about them. In either case, children who decide to stop taking medication or refuse to start often have fears and misinformation. Obviously, you want to do whatever you can to correct that. Sometimes having your child speak directly to his or her doctor is helpful. It communicates that everyone respects the child as a person and is willing to listen.

More often than you might expect, children cannot grasp what their medication is doing for them because they do not really know why they are taking it. Again, helping your child to understand his diagnosis in a way that is sensitive and developmentally appropriate may help. Further, he also should know if he is taking a medication that must be tapered gradually to be safe, or in the case of some medications, ones that can *never* be stopped without medical supervision.

For older kids who decide to opt out of taking their medication, discuss with them why they are taking it and what risks they might incur if they do not. If your daughter decides to stop taking her medication for attention, be prepared to let her take a couple of tests at school and accept the consequences of her decision. If, on the other hand, your child is being treated for seizure disorder, severe depression, bipolar disorder, or another serious psychiatric disorder with heightened potential for self-harm, harm to others, or suicide, seek further professional help immediately. If your child has refused to take medication in the past or if you have a reasonable concern that it might occur again, talk with your child. If the possible consequences of your child being off medication include aggressive, threatening, violent, or self-injurious behavior that might result in your seeking emergency medical care or help from law enforcement personnel, be honest with your child about that.

GOING FORWARD, LOOKING AHEAD

While no medication can cure Asperger syndrome or address more than a few target symptoms, when the right medication attacks an especially troubling behavior, it can feel to parents like a miracle. Of course, medication alone is never the answer. Behavioral changes (yours and your child's), environmental accommodations, and other interventions all belong in the program. However, there is no denying that for a child who is anxious, depressed, self-injurious, suicidal, aggressive, violent, or explosive, simply taking the edge off can give him the space he needs to respond to everything else you do, to reclaim some self-esteem, and to focus on other things, such as school, play, and interests. It is unfortunate that so much of the discussion about children and psychotropic medication centers on "behavior management," because it shifts the focus from where it rightfully belongs: on what medication can do for your child. It is not and never should be about what medication will do for you, your family, or your child's teacher.

Adults and older adolescents with Asperger syndrome may suffer terribly from the experience of a childhood filled with confusion, misunderstanding, and rejection. No medication is a "miracle drug," but for those children for whom responsibly prescribed medication has made a real difference in their quality of life, their self-esteem, and their happiness, its place as a treatment cannot be dismissed as an "easy way out." For some, whose symptoms are severe or disabling, medication may be the only way out. If you are a friend, family member, teacher, or anyone else who knows a child who is on medication, be understanding and supportive. Respect the difficulties such children and their families face, assume that you do not know all there is to know about the case, and think carefully before offering opinions or passing along anecdotes about someone else's medication horror story or some amazing "natural" alternative. Decisions about medication are difficult and personal. If honest, many parents will admit that they find unsolicited information and advice in this area intrusive, stressful, and awkward to handle. You might first ask yourself how you fell into this discussion to begin with. If you find yourself having more than one or two "debates," consider if you might not be talking to the wrong people. Yes, all parents seek support and information from friends and others. But ultimately, this is a personal medical decision. You may feel okay letting some people know about the process and the decision you reached. After all, that is your experience. However, keep in mind that this decision is not about you: it's about your child. In a world where we should probably all be a bit more privacy-conscious, consider how much of this personal information your child might wish to have out. Or what others might conclude—correctly or incorrectly—about your child if they know she is "on meds." Remember: once information leaves our control, it's gone, "out there" forever. You can never call it back.

A medication that isn't right for your child usually reveals itself early in the trial, in intolerable side effects and/or a lack of efficacy. For reasons no one fully understands, some medications simply do not work for some people. It is important to bear in mind that just because a medication to treat, say, OCD fails, that does not mean that your child does not have OCD (or whatever condition or symptom the medication was prescribed to address).

Unfortunately, finding the right medication doesn't get you or your child home free yet. Depending on the medication your child is taking, several things could occur. He might become tolerant of the medication, requiring a higher dose, which may not be as effective or may produce other unwanted side effects. Side effects might arise months or even years after the medication was begun, necessitating a change. It is also possible that another comorbid condition could develop (such as a mood disorder, anxiety, and so on), which could make your child's current medication less effective. He may outgrow the need for one type of medication but have trouble finding a suitable replacement to address new symptoms. (Conversely, sometime in the future, he may be able to tolerate and see good results from a medication he could not tolerate before.) Finally, the medication your child is on may one day simply stop working for him. Or, as occurred in our house when the only factory producing Paxil was suddenly shut down temporarily in 2005, your supply might simply disappear. (And in this case, doctors and pharmacists were forbidden to offer patients Paxil they had on hand because the reason for closing the factory had to do with some longstanding manufacturing problem.)

For these reasons, you and your child's prescribing doctor should always be thinking one step ahead. You should be considering not only other medications and interventions but also the possibility that a particular medication is no longer necessary. Many experts suggest that periodically your child take a "medication holiday," so that you and his doctor can assess where he is developmentally and emotionally. This may not be appropriate for all children, and there are health and safety considerations to bear in mind when lowering or stopping any psychoactive medication. For instance, some studies have found that stopping a medication (such as lithium for bipolar disorder) abruptly may actually worsen the overall prognosis over the life span.

Always consult your doctor before attempting to reduce or eliminate a medication!

PSYCHOTROPIC MEDICATIONS

It is beyond our scope to provide everything you need to know about specific psychotropic medications. The pace of research and change would quickly render some more specific information obsolete. Be sure to consult the Recommended Resources listed here.

Recommended Resources

It is important that you regard any information you acquire through books and media, and especially the internet, as "secondary" to that provided by a medical doctor.

On the Web

Autism Speaks offers two essential "tool kits" for parents facing the medication question. Both were developed by the Autism Treatment Network of Autism Speaks and are free.

"Autism: Should My Child Take Medicine for Challenging Behavior?" This twenty-one-page Decision Aid is a PDF document that can be typed into and then saved and printed out. Using a series of questions, scales, and checklists, it covers all of the questions and considerations one might bring to this decision. At www .autismspeaks.org/science/resources-programs/autism-treatment -network/tools-you-can-use/medication-guide, or search at www .autismspeaks.org.

"Autism and Medication: Safe and Careful Use: A Guide for Families of Children with Autism" is essential for any parent whose child is taking psychotropic medication. It is full of helpful charts for tracking behavior, medication use, and behavior severity, as well as great tips on managing side effects (including medication-related sleep problems and weight changes) and helping kids swallow pills. At www .autismspeaks.org/news/news-item/autism-speaks-launches-autism -and-medication-tool-kit, or search at www.autismspeaks.org.

The Food and Drug Administration, at www.fda.gov, is the federal agency charged with overseeing the safety of the foods and medicines we use. The FDA should be the source of any specific information on drugs. From the home page, click on "Drugs." There you can find all of the information you would find in the *Physicians' Desk Reference* or the product information insert and more. Of special interest to parents on this page is "Orange Book Search," which leads you to information on approved generics and their equivalents. Another FDA resource that you will have to look a bit harder for is the Pediatric Labeling Information Database. Simply go to any FDA page and type its name into the search box. Here you can search medications by either trade or generic name. Any changes in labeling regarding approvals, side effects, dosage, and so on will be found.

Other trustworthy sources:

MedlinePlus, at www.nlm.nih.gov/medlineplus/druginformation.html. MedlinePlus is a service of the National Institutes of Health. It also includes information on supplements, vitamins, and over-the-counter products, as well as photographs of the products.

Physicians' Desk Reference, at www.pdr.net. Though the information here is also based on the FDA, PDR.net has photographs of the actual medications and a wealth of information.

Book

Timothy E. Wilens, *Straight Talk About Psychiatric Medications for Kids*, 3rd ed. (New York: Guilford Press, 2009). If your child is currently on prescription psychotropic medication, or if you are considering it, this comprehensive, authoritative, yet easy-to-read, informative book is a must.

Name of Medication _____

Medication Log Form

Date	Dose	Time	Child response	Side effects noted	Action, response	Doctor contact notes	Action taken

Sample

Date	Dose	Time	Child response	Side effects noted	Action, response	Doctor contact notes	Action taken
3/21	0.25 mg.	7:00 a.m.	no change, ate breakfast, went to school	Teacher: drowsiness around 9:00 a.m.	Sent to nurse; rested 15 minutes; back to class	Dr. called 3/21; said drowsiness may continue; monitor next few days, then call back.	None. As per Dr.: continue as prescribed; call again on 3/25.

Chapter 6

SPECIAL EDUCATION BASICS

YES, IT'S ANOTHER JOURNEY

For many parents, decisions about school placement, special education, and related services are the most important, most time-consuming, and potentially stressful of all. One reason, of course, is the importance of education to every child's development. But for parents of kids with ASD, there is so much to consider and so much at stake. Not surprisingly, school-related matters—even for those kids who can manage in a regular classroom in their neighborhood school—claim much of our attention. A "good year" of school, where the services fall into place, the placement works out, and the staff understands, is a real cause of celebration, and often the high-water mark to which other years are compared. For most of us, there are "good" years, semesters, and terms, and "bad" ones.

Although we do not usually think of school or special education as "interventions," in many ways, they are—when they work. What do I mean by "work"? When school and the services your child receives foster his growth academically, socially, and emotionally. Contrary to what some parents and advocates seem to believe, "effective" and "appropriate" education does not necessarily include every possible service or support in the book, nor must it always

291

be the complete menu of services and supports a parent requests. On the other hand, it is not by definition what your school district might tell you it is, what worked for other students, or what your district offers with the explanation, "This is how we do it."

When I first discovered special education, my son was halfway through kindergarten in a lovely neighborhood private preschool and early elementary school housed in a Jewish temple in our neighborhood. The very thought of him transitioning to a special education classroom in our public school district terrified me. In the course of attending a support group, I heard what I believed then was every horror story imaginable. I began with trepidation, to say the least. Now, more than fifteen years later, I'm done with special education (as a parent). With a bit more objectivity and time, I can say that Yellow Brick Road crossed paths with more good witches than wicked ones (though there were a couple of those), and brought us more good friends to travel with than flying monkeys. But I also see that it was a process of walking the road, putting one foot in front of the other, no matter what, and that takes energy, focus, and some discipline. There's no wizard to fly you and your baby home, no ruby slippers to click and dream on.

HOW IT WORKS

You cannot discuss special education without talking about special education law and the "alphabet soup" of acronyms that quickly become the shorthand second language of parents of children with special needs. Special education is governed by a host of federal, state, and local laws and regulations and then shaped by the individuals—educators, administrators, and officials—charged with carrying them out. In addition, special ed law works alongside other federal, state, and local education initiatives that may not technically "be special ed," but that have an impact on how it works for your child. Also, school districts and states sometimes experience problems with budgets, personnel, and facilities. Because, by definition, special education is tailored to the individual, there is often a wide variation in the type and quality of services and/or accommodations from student to student.

Here we present a basic overview of the role of special education in the lives of students with Asperger syndrome. In "Recommended Resources" (page 331) we list a relative handful of the hundreds of sources. Familiarize yourself with the state and local regulations that apply to your child and, whenever necessary, seek help—from another informed parent, an advocate, an advocacy organization, or an attorney who specializes in special education. If at all possible, make time to attend a conference, seminar, or talk on the subject.

It is impossible to generalize about the educational needs of children with ASDs beyond saying that each child is unique. Appropriate placements range from self-contained special education classrooms and schools dedicated to AS and/or related disorders to regular mainstream classrooms. Some students will go through their school years without ever needing to be identified officially as "a child with a disability" requiring special education and/or related services. However, even those who, academically speaking, are star students will often benefit from accommodations, special education, and/or related services.

Special education–related services that a student—even one who is academically successful—who has AS might receive include but are not limited to the following:[1]

- Speech and language therapy
- Occupational therapy
- Audiology services
- Physical therapy, adaptive physical education, or other therapies
- Recreation, including therapeutic recreation
- Orientation and mobility services
- Services from a school psychologist, counselor, or social worker
- Services from an aide or paraprofessional
- Services from a consultant knowledgeable about AS to work with your child or the school staff
- Services from a reader, scribe, typist, interpreter, or Braillist
- Medical services (for purposes of diagnosis and evaluation) and school health nurse
- Counseling and training for parents

- Resource centers
- Transportation
- Vocational education
- Assistive technology, such as voice-activated software, laptop computer, or audiobooks

In addition, a student with AS who does not qualify for special education and/or related services may need accommodations and considerations: for instance, more time to get from one class to another; an aide or fellow student to help her organize and pack the right books to bring home each afternoon; transportation in a smaller school bus; or extra time or access to a word processor for written tests.

As students near adolescence, you should look closely at what skills or support your child may need to succeed at college, in job training, or at work. Before your child leaves elementary school (yes, we said elementary school), speak with your district's special education department and start networking with parents of older students with similar needs, support groups, and local, county, and state agencies that provide services and job training for individuals with disabilities. Do not make the mistake of assuming that just because your child is on an academic track and destined (at least on paper) for the school of his choice that such programs have nothing to offer him. Find out. Your child may need an Individualized Education Plan (IEP) to access some of these services.

Also, keep your eye on the calendar. It's very important that accommodations be in place and official long before you request things like extended time for the SAT (Scholastic Achievement Test)and/ or the ACT.* That is because both the College Board, which administers the SAT, and the ACT require up-to-date documentation and will not allow for accommodations that are not already in use in high school. Colleges will also require documentation of disability and up-to-date reports. (See chapter 11 for more on college.)

Finally, if you seek accommodations at college or any other

---

*Confusingly, ACT is not an acronym for anything. Until 1996, it stood for American College Testing. Today, officially, the ACT exam and the private nonprofit company that administers it are simply ACT.

postsecondary education or training institution, know that there is no such thing as special education, an IEP, or a 504 plan out in the "real world." Yes, there are accommodations, but they are considerably fewer and do not include changes in the curriculum or the training.

IS THERE ONE "RIGHT" EDUCATION FOR STUDENTS WITH AS?

No. Although many children with AS share certain types of strengths and deficits in learning-related skills and abilities, there is no single educational "profile" for AS. In addition, it is common for people with AS to have other comorbid conditions that affect learning, such as AD/HD, OCD, or a nonverbal learning disability (NLD or NVLD). As a result, there is no single program, method, or technique that works for every student. A child with AS can be academically gifted or beset by multiple learning disabilities—or both. (See the box on page 446 on giftedness.) Most often, children with AS display a mixture of strengths and weaknesses. Jessie, who has been reading with comprehension since age three and can do long division in her head, is so severely dysgraphic that her test scores are always very low and written assignments go undone. Eric, who has an above-average IQ, has been diagnosed with dyslexia and dyscalculia (see page 75). Assessments indicate that Kevin probably would be an average to above-average student academically. However, his multiple sensory issues and difficulties with pragmatic speech make every school day torture.

Students with AS can fare well in a range of educational situations, provided, of course, that each is in the setting that best addresses his particular individual needs. Most children with AS attend their regular public schools and receive related services and accommodations (for example, extra time on tests). There are programs and schools designed to serve students with AS (and, in some cases, related disorders). Whether any of these would be better for your child depends on many factors. Suffice it to say, such programs and schools are not inherently better in every case. Don't forget to look in your own backyard—and your neighbors'. Some school districts that have one or two students who could benefit from a specially designed classroom or program may pool resources with other districts to create something that none of the districts could set up, support, or fund on its own. For example, for two years, my son, Justin, attended a special Asperger classroom in a regular public school in a neighboring school district. He and his classmates had the best of both worlds: a small learning environment tailored to their needs coupled with access to and involvement with typical peers when appropriate. No district could maintain such a classroom for one or two students, but by accepting students from several neighboring districts, this one allowed Justin and his classmates to have a highly individualized program in the least restrictive and most socially appropriate environment.

Here again, networking pays. School districts do not always advertise such programs, and you might be surprised to discover how little your district special educators know about what's going on even around the corner. You are not limited to only what your district offers. If you find a public school program that you believe might suit your child's needs and is within a reasonable distance (your local regulations may have something to say about how far or how long a child can travel), ask your special education administrator to apply to that district or program on your child's behalf. There may also be local charter school or private school options to consider.

WHAT IS SPECIAL EDUCATION?

Special education is more than extra help. According to the Individuals with Disabilities Education Act, 2004:

"Special education means specially designed instruction, at no cost to the parents, to meet the unique needs of a child with a disability, including—

(i) Instruction conducted in the classroom, in the home, in hospitals and institutions, and in other settings; and

(ii) Instruction in physical education.

(2) Special education includes each of the following, if the

services otherwise meet the requirements of paragraph (a)(1) of this section—

(i) Speech-language pathology services, or any other related service, if the service is considered special education rather than a related service under State standards;

(ii) Travel training; and

(iii) Vocational education.[2]

Prior to 1975, when Congress passed the first version of what we know today as IDEA (it was then called Public Law 94-142, the Education for All Handicapped Children Act), special education as we now know it simply did not exist. The federal government had no statutes affirming the legal right to public education for children with disabilities. These youngsters had no protection from being refused admittance to school on the grounds that they were unable to learn or would disrupt or distract teachers and other students. Where so-called special education classrooms did exist, they often segregated disabled children from their peers in classrooms that were inferior—both physically and academically—from those of nondisabled students. Just six years prior to the passage of Public Law 94-142, school authorities in North Carolina could have a parent arrested for attempting to enroll a disabled child whom the authorities had previously refused to take.[3]

In the wake of the 1954 US Supreme Court decision in *Brown* v. *Board of Education*, a movement among parents of disabled children took root. In finding that racially segregated schools could not be considered "equal" and that segregation violated students' rights to equal protection under the law, the US Supreme Court in *Brown* looked closely at the impact of segregation on students. Interestingly, the decision spoke of the public schools' crucial role in preparing students for life beyond the schoolhouse and mentioned the psychological impact of segregation on "their hearts and minds." The Court wrote: "In these days, it is doubtful that any child may reasonably be expected to succeed in life if he is denied the opportunity of an education. Such an opportunity . . . is a right which must be made available to all on equal terms."[4]

Public Law 94-142 (renamed the Individuals with Disabilities Education Act when it was reauthorized in 1990) established the right of every child to receive a "free appropriate public education." Further, it charged the individual states and local educational agencies with the responsibility for carrying it out. Over the years, IDEA has been revised, in 1990, 1997, and 2004. With each reauthorization, certain details changed, sometimes to the benefit of school districts and sometimes to the benefit of students. Suffice it to say, no one ever believes that IDEA is perfect. However, in some key aspects, it has improved, particularly with regard to issues of relevance to kids with ASD. For example, the 1997 revisions, which were published in their final form in early 1999, substantially expanded the rights and protections of parents and students, particularly in the areas of parent involvement, discipline, suspensions, and expulsions. The latest version, from 2004, includes preparing a child for "further education" as a newly stated purpose. In its "Findings" section, this version states something that many parents and educators knew too well: ". . . implementation of this title has been impeded by low expectations, and an insufficient focus on applying replicable research on proven methods of teaching and learning for children with disabilities," explaining the new requirements for "the use of scientifically based instructional practices." More specifically, it demands "scientifically based early reading programs, positive behavioral interventions and supports, and early intervening services."[5] This is a major step forward for students and also demands a lot of school districts, especially those which have gotten used to declining to specify particular interventions or methodologies in an IEP. As special education attorney Wayne Steeman points out on the Wrightslaw.com website: "School officials . . . argue that teachers should be free to use an 'eclectic approach' . . . and should not be forced to use any specific methodology."[6] Those days are over! (See "The New Focus on Evidence-Based Treatments" on page 161.)

IDEA AND CASE LAW

Although IDEA is a revolutionary, landmark piece of legislation, it is, like most laws, open to dispute. The interpretation of a specific point is determined as much by case law as by the law itself. The most recent standing decisions made within your federal circuit usually prevail. Only rulings made by the US Supreme Court apply in every US jurisdiction. Legal counsel on both sides of a dispute should always have one eye trained on ever-evolving case law.

If you reach a point where you believe that your school district is in violation of IDEA or other relevant statutes and regulations, we suggest you consult a professional advocate or an attorney who specializes in special education law before proceeding with mediation, an impartial due process hearing, or a lawsuit.

IDEA AND YOUR STATE REGULATIONS GOVERNING SPECIAL EDUCATION

In shaping special education, IDEA does not stand alone. Every state has its own department of education regulations regarding special education. State regulations must meet the requirements set forth in IDEA. A state must grant students with disabilities who qualify for special education under IDEA or under the state's own eligibility requirements what is mandated in IDEA. Your state is free to exceed IDEA in terms of procedural matters, eligibility, and services, but it cannot offer less than IDEA mandates. A state may mandate specific services not included in IDEA. In addition, an individual school district, school, or program may provide services that exceed what is required even by its state. Your state may set student-to-teacher ratios for self-contained special education classrooms at 10:1, but your local school district may decide that a ratio of 8:1 is more appropriate.

IDEA does not require that any student receive the "best" education, only one that is "appropriate." For various reasons we'll explore in this chapter, special education programs are not—and should not be—uniform. In fact, parents should always remember that the *I* in IDEA stands for "individuals" and the *I* in IEP stands for "individualized." Special education should be "custom tailored" for each and every student, not simply taken "off the rack."

While IDEA stands as the overriding law of the land, the policies and "traditions" of your state and your school district (in IDEA terms, your "local education authority," or LEA) can have a profound impact on the quality of special education your child receives.

WHAT WILL SPECIAL EDUCATION MEAN FOR YOUR CHILD?

Parents new to the world of special education often hear the well-meaning doctor, therapist, regular education teacher, friend, or family member say, "Go to your school district. You have a right to get all the services and help your child needs." That sounds great, but it betrays some common misconceptions about special education. One is that any student who is behind his peers academically, developmentally, or socially is entitled to receive services.

First, let's look at what your local school district must do, by law.

- At a parent's request, it must provide for a full assessment of a child at no cost to parents. (See chapter 2.)
- Under specific circumstances (including lack of personnel), at a parent's request, it must provide for an independent or private assessment of a child.
- It must meet with the parent to discuss the findings of the assessments and determine whether that child is eligible for special education and related services (under IDEA) or accommodations (under Section 504; see page 305).
- If your school district determines that your child is not eligible for special education and related services or accommodations, you may request an independent, impartial hearing. The same holds true if the school district finds your child eligible for accommodations without special education and related services.

Even if your child has a diagnosis or has been evaluated in the past, he can be considered for special education services only after he has been assessed by professionals qualified to administer recognized, validated tests. School districts must consider the findings of any independent evaluations your child has undergone, but it cannot make eligibility decisions based solely on them. No federal statute specifies precisely what degree of disability must be shown for eligibility under IDEA, although some states' guidelines address this in terms of degree as measured by standardized assessments (for instance, a twelve-month delay, a 33 percent delay, or a score of 1.5 or

2 standard deviations below the mean). It is imperative that parents have a basic working knowledge of the terminology and concepts behind the tests and measurements used in special education. The best source for this information is the Wrightslaw website: www .wrightslaw.com.

As important as standardized assessments are, a child's eligibility cannot be determined based on a single test or the impressions of a single evaluator, no matter how experienced. This is why IDEA requires that eligibility be determined by a multidisciplinary team. Every public school district is required by IDEA to fully evaluate any child who may need special education services "in all areas related to the suspected disability, including, if appropriate, health, vision, hearing, social and emotional status, general intelligence, academic performance, communicative status, and motor abilities."[7] In other words, your child cannot be considered having been fully evaluated if he is given only an IQ test or even a battery of tests that fails to include a speech assessment.

In addition to whatever assessments your school district plans to administer, it must also consider information from a wide range of sources: parents, teachers, doctors, and others familiar with your child as well as previous assessments. The tests administered must be given in your child's native language. They must also be valid, which means that they are the appropriate instruments for measuring specific abilities and disabilities. For example, an evaluator cannot conclude that because your child's IQ tested in the normal or above-normal range she does not have a problem with pragmatics or adaptive social skills. These tests must be administered and scored only by qualified people. Publishers of standardized assessment instruments (tests) clearly spell out in their instructions who may administer a test. If anyone else gives a test, the results are automatically invalid. Under IDEA, it is illegal for, let's say, the school's speech therapist to give your child a test that is designed to be used only by a psychologist or psychiatrist.

WHO IS ELIGIBLE?

Simply having a disability doesn't automatically entitle a student to special education under IDEA, nor does the fact that a student theoretically could "do better" with extra help obligate your school district to provide that help. Conversely, simply having an average (or higher) IQ doesn't automatically exclude a child from qualifying for services or accommodations under Section 504 or IDEA. This is important for parents of children with AS to understand, because school districts have been known to try to discourage parents from pursuing special education by telling them, in effect, "Your child is too smart for special ed." Numerous state and federal laws address the rights of disabled people. IDEA is unique, and so it is the focus of this chapter because it mandates a "free appropriate public education" (FAPE) for any child with disabilities from birth to age twenty-two who meets its eligibility requirements.

Here are two important legal definitions, from IDEA:

> Child with a Disability—The term "child with a disability" means a child—(i) with mental retardation, hearing impairments (including deafness), speech or language impairments, visual impairments (including blindness), serious emotional disturbance (hereinafter referred to as "emotional disturbance"), orthopedic impairments, autism, traumatic brain injury, other health impairments, or specific learning disabilities; and (ii) who, by reason thereof, needs special education and related services.[8]

Of interest to parents of children who have any form of ASD or other disability are these sections:

> (3)(b) Child aged 3 through 9—The term "child with a disability" for a child aged 3 through 9 (or any subset of that age range, including ages 3 through 5), may, at the discretion of the State and the local educational agency, include a child (i) experiencing developmental delays, as defined by the State and measured by appropriate diagnostic instruments and procedures, in one of the following areas: physical develop-

ment, cognitive development, communication development, social or emotional development, or adaptive development; and (ii) who, by reason thereof, needs special education and related services.[9]

(10) Specific learning disability—(i) General. Specific learning disability means a disorder in one or more of the basic psychological processes involved in understanding or in using language, spoken or written, that may manifest itself in the imperfect ability to listen, think, speak, read, write, spell, or to do mathematical calculations, including conditions such as perceptual disabilities, brain injury, minimal brain dysfunction, dyslexia, and developmental aphasia.

(ii) Disorders not included. Specific learning disability does not include learning problems that are primarily the result of visual, hearing, or motor disabilities, of intellectual disability,* of emotional disturbance, or of environmental, cultural, or economic disadvantage.[10]

Early Intervention and Preschool Services

As IDEA evolved, its coverage expanded to include special education and related services for infants and toddlers (mandated by 1991) and preschoolers ages three to five (mandated by 1994). Now that children on the spectrum are being diagnosed at earlier ages, and some are even receiving an AS diagnosis before kindergarten, early intervention (EI) and preschool services will play a larger role. If your child is under age three, discuss your concerns with your pediatrician, who can help arrange an evaluation through a state or local agency at no cost to you. Also contact your municipal, county, or state departments of health and

*Prior to October 2010, IDEA used the term "mental retardation." In October 2010, President Obama signed Rosa's Law, which requires that the term "intellectual disability" replace "mental retardation." The definitions of the old term "mental retardation" and the new "intellectual disability" are the same.

education. Every state sets its own policies regarding approved providers and costs to families. You do not access preschool services the same way you would if your child were school-aged. Your district, however, probably can direct you to the agency that will provide a full evaluation, determine eligibility and/or services, and provide those services (usually through outside agencies that specialize in this work). Infants, toddlers, and preschoolers receive services in a wide array of settings: home, early intervention classroom, family child care, hospital (inpatient), out-patient service facilities (such as an occupational therapist's office), and regular nursery school or child care settings, among others. For many children on the spectrum, EI services are provided in the home; in other words, special ed teachers and other therapists come to you. However, it is highly individualized, and where your child receives services may depend not only on his particular needs but also on what may be available. Your area may have a shortage of teachers and therapists for home work, but a very good EI center-based program or preschool, or vice versa. Depending on your child, you may be able to arrange for him to receive occupational therapy at his regular preschool or for your child's behavior analyst to work with the staff of his day care center to help him develop more appropriate play skills.

One cornerstone of both EI and preschool services is parental involvement. As with IEPs, parents have input into the development of the IFSP (Individual Family Service Plan). If your child's teachers and therapists come to your home, you will have a chance to see firsthand what is involved, and training for parents is a key component in good EI and preschool programs, regardless of where services are delivered.

If you have any concerns about your child's development, or another professional suggests that he or she does, contact your local health department, your pediatrician, and your school district right away and get this process in motion. (Even though your school district has no direct involvement in EI, someone on staff should be able to point you in the right direction.) Especially when children with AS are young, they may not always appear to be "that different" from their peers. Especially if your little one seems advanced in certain areas and has reached most developmental milestones on schedule or early, it can be difficult to fully accept that he or she needs help and, thus, tempting to stick with the regular child care, nursery school, or preschool arrangements you now have. (The usual argument for this is that it affords access to typical peers and social development.) If you find yourself confronting this dilemma, please consider EI and preschool services. For children on the spectrum, there is no doubt that earlier treatment is better than later. Despite their kind intentions, most regular nursery school and preschool teachers are not qualified to provide these children much more than tolerance and support.

IDEA has evolved. Until 1990, autism was not among the disabilities specified in IDEA. Recently, AD/HD was added to the list of disabilities, but students with conditions such as Tourette's syndrome and obsessive-compulsive disorder are not specifically mentioned. Students for whom these conditions adversely affect their ability to learn may be eligible for special education and/or related services but be classified as disabled under "serious emotional disturbance" (SED) or "other health impaired" (OHI).

SECTION 504 ACCOMMODATIONS

Sometimes the adverse effect of a disability is not considered to impede the ability to learn sufficiently to warrant an IEP even though it clearly has some impact on the student's access to regular education. Instead, the school district may offer what are commonly known as "504 accommodations," after Section 504 of the Rehabilitation Act of 1973. The resulting document that specifies the accommodations and/or services a student may receive under Section 504 is known as Section 504 Services and Accommodation Plan (or "504 plan"). The Rehabilitation Act of 1973 is a civil rights law, not an education law, designed to "empower individuals with disabilities to maximize employment, economic self-sufficiency, independence, and inclusion and integration into society."[11] Its definition of an individual with disability is far broader than IDEA's, and the rights and protections that it grants are far more limited.[12]

Renowned special education attorney Peter W. D. Wright illustrates the difference between IDEA and Section 504 in this analogy:

> A handicapped child is in a wheelchair. Under Section 504, this child shall not be discriminated against because of the disability.
>
> The child shall be provided with access to an education, to and through the schoolhouse door. However, under Section 504 there is no guarantee that this wheelchair-bound child will receive an education from which the child benefits. The child simply has access to the same education that children without disabilities receive. Now assume that the child in the wheelchair also has neurological problems that adversely affect the child's ability to learn. Under IDEA, the child with a disability that adversely affects educational performance is entitled to an education that is individually designed to meet the child's unique needs and from which the child receives educational benefit.[13]

You may be advised—by educators, doctors, friends, and others—to avoid an IEP and go for Section 504 accommodation instead. The reasoning is that in order to qualify for an IEP and the resulting special education and related services, a child must be identified (or "labeled") as a child with a disability. Some parents feel that this is stigmatizing. Others believe that a Section 504 accommodation plan is essentially "IEP lite," a nicer, less time-consuming, less exacting instrument. As one OASIS visitor posted, "I went for the 504 because I figured, why use a hammer when a chisel would do?" This may seem a reasonable approach, but only if you are fortunate enough to have a child who needs minimal accommodation (not services) and live in a school district where the chisel can do the job. However, in the end, an IEP is unquestionably the superior instrument in terms of the range of services and the rights it protects. Plus, eligibility under IDEA automatically entitles a student to protections and rights under Section 504.

Parents may also be under the common misperception that having an IEP automatically relegates a student to a special education program, such as a self-contained special ed classroom or an academic curriculum that is not as rigorous as that offered other students. This is not true. A child with an IEP can be fully mainstreamed in a regular classroom if such placement satisfies two key tenets of IDEA: the placement serves his individual educational needs, and it is the least restrictive environment (LRE). Also keep in mind that services provided, and where and how they are provided, are also considered in light of how restrictive they might be. For example, speech therapy "pushed in" to the classroom is considered less restrictive than individual "pull-out" sessions that remove the child from class; having an individual aide or paraprofessional is more restrictive than sharing an aide with another one or two students.

Even though a child may seem to require only accommodations, a full evaluation is strongly recommended for a child with or suspected of having any ASD. Though few parents or children could be said to look forward to the evaluation process, there are a few things to consider. ASD is a neurologically based disorder with a full range of possible comorbid conditions, including learning disabilities or differences in styles of learning. Some of these are blatantly apparent and may seem to have always been present; others seem to crop up only when academic or social demands tax a particular weakness. So though your child's dysgraphia may have always been apparent, his problems with pragmatics may suddenly seem more glaring when he's called on to analyze what he reads or to think more conceptually.

There are some circumstances under which 504 accommodations are recommended; for example, if a student is doing well in a regular education classroom but needs to be seated at the front of the classroom or requires extra time to complete tests because of mild problems with attention, vision, or hearing. You should know, however, that some school districts do provide special education and related services to students who are, technically speaking, eligible only under Section 504. This may be the result of state or local policies. If you have questions, consult your local autism group, a special education advocate, or a special education attorney. Daylong seminars and towers of books and legal decisions address the differences between IDEA and Section 504, and which is appropriate for your child depends entirely on your child. For example, a student with serious problems with reading comprehension might do well having a 504 plan in high school if he is attending a training program for carpentry and not planning to attend college. However, if that same student were to set his sights on going to college with a dream of practicing law one day, a wiser course might be to have an IEP to set the stage for accommodations that will probably be needed for testing and while at college. You needn't become a legal scholar, but you should know the pros and cons of each.

Probably the last basis on which to make the decision involves worries about the future impact of so-called labeling. You should know that your child's education records are protected under another federal law, the Family Educational Rights and Privacy Act (FERPA). Your child's school district is legally prohibited from disclosing any personal information about your child, including the fact that he or she was classified, has a disability, had an IEP or a 504 plan, or was deemed eligible to receive special education and related services or accommodations.

If your child is found to qualify as a child with a disability under IDEA, he is also automatically eligible for accommodations or related services under Section 504. You might then decide which course is best for your child. The reverse, however, is not true. Eligibility under 504 does not make one eligible under IDEA.

Generally speaking, you should consider an IEP if:

- Your child's requirements go beyond simple accommodations and involve services (occupational therapy, physical therapy, speech and language therapy, an aide or paraprofessional, an autism consultant or behavioral consultant, and so on).
- You believe she would benefit from a smaller-than-average class size; placement in a special education classroom, program, or school; one-on-one teaching or assistance.
- You have reason to think your child's disability may contribute to behavior that could result in disciplinary measures, such as suspension and expulsion.
- You have concerns about your child's academic abilities because she has a learning disability or because her style of learning is different, unique, or not well understood.
- You have concerns about your child's academic abilities because of AS-related difficulties with sensory integration, fine-motor skills, and/or emotional and social difficulties.

- You have reason to believe that your school district is less than cooperative, compliant, or dedicated to special education in general or to students with disorders similar to your child's.
- You have concerns regarding your child's ability to cope with attending college or postsecondary training, finding and holding a job, or living independently, which could be addressed by transition services.
- You can reasonably expect that your child *might* require accommodations for postsecondary education such as college or other professional training.

If you have any questions about whether your child would be better served or protected by an IEP or a Section 504 plan, consult a special education advocate or attorney.

A GREAT IDEA: THE IEP

The heart of IDEA is the Individualized Education Plan (IEP), which must be created for every child who is eligible to receive special education services. Although the process of determining a student's needs and formulating a written plan to provide special education and/or related services seems straightforward enough, there are many different views on how to craft the best IEP. There are a number of books on the art and science of the IEP, and we recommend that you read at least one. Although IDEA sets forth what an IEP should contain, it's up to individual states and school districts to develop their own formats. Increasingly, school districts are using commercial IEP/504 programs (IEPDirect is one) to create these documents. Early in the evaluation process, before you begin work on your child's Section 504 plan or IEP, ask your school district for a blank of the IEP form it uses so that you can familiarize yourself with the format.

Key Components of an IEP

The format and style of IEPs vary widely from school district to school district. However, there are specific components required by law. While some IEPs are highly individualized, others are "cookie-cutter" productions in every sense of the word. One school district may take pains to craft a plan specifically to a child's needs, while others choose descriptions of a child's needs from an IEP program, complete with bar codes or a standard checklist. Such packaged programs are not inherently inferior, but they can and should be "tailored" to fit your child's needs. In the end, how the IEP plan looks isn't as important as what it contains and how well it is implemented by the educators who work with your child. Here is a general overview of what you should find in your child's IEP:[14]

- A statement of your child's "present levels of academic achievement and functional performance."[15] This must come from assessments that yield objective data.
- A statement of annual goals that are "measurable" and include both academic and functional goals. The inclusion of short-term instructional objectives was eliminated in IDEA 2004 except for students who take alternate assessments.
- Specific special education and related services to be provided and a statement of the extent to which your child will participate in regular education programs.
- The dates for initiation of services and the anticipated duration of services, as well as how frequently they will be provided, where they will be provided, and by whom (by professional title or position, not by individual name).
- A statement about how the child's progress toward annual goals will be measured, how parents will be notified of the child's progress, and whether the progress is sufficient toward meeting the goal. This report is known informally as an "IEP report card" or progress report.
- All accommodations and modifications necessary for participating in regular classroom education programs.
- A statement of the least restrictive environment.

• After your child turns sixteen, the IEP must contain ". . . appropriate measurable postsecondary goals based upon age-appropriate transition assessments related to training, education, employment, and, where appropriate, independent living skills . . . and the transition services (including courses of study) needed to assist the child in reaching those goals."[16]

Understanding Goals and Objectives

In education, we speak of goals and objectives. IDEA no longer requires that annual goals be further broken down into the shorter-term objectives that reflect ongoing progress toward the larger goal. However, your school district or your state might require these. They are helpful for measuring the pace or rate of progress toward the final goal, and they help everyone—teachers, parents, and sometimes even students—know not only how the student is doing but also how successful or appropriate the program or strategy is. Extended periods with little or no progress should prompt everyone to consider the program before assuming that the problem is the student or the student's disability-related learning or behavior challenges.

Essentially, a goal takes a broader, long-range view of a student's development in a particular area. The objectives are the skills or behaviors the student must master for him to reach that goal. Goals are viewed as being long term; objectives as relatively short term. You should look to see relationships between goals and objectives: if the goal is the fruit at the top of the tree, the objectives are the rungs on the ladder your child will climb to reach it. Objectives should state clearly what your child will learn to enable him to reach his goals.

According to Robert F. Mager, whose *Preparing Instructional Objectives* is a classic on the subject, "An instructional objective is a collection of words and/or pictures and diagrams intended to let others know what you intend for your students to achieve."[17] Objectives consist of three key elements:

- Performance: what the student is expected to do (write a three-paragraph book report using correct grammar, spelling, and punctuation; or orally answer three questions about a book he has read; or write a book report that is punctuated to the best of his ability).
- Conditions: under what conditions he will do it (in class, in the cafeteria, on the playground, in speech class, in gym; every day, when requested, three times a day, ten times a day; with his teacher, classmates, staff people; and so on).
- Criteria: what constitutes acceptable performance, mastery, fluency, or completion. This can be described in terms of the task (David will cut the shapes star, square, and heart within an eighth of an inch on either side of the line) or percentage of correct answers (answer twenty daily math problems at 80 percent accuracy) or occurrences (appropriately line up going to and from lunch three days a school week; work independently without talking out for a minimum of two minutes). The objective should define what constitutes "appropriately lining up" (independently walking to line without talking out, crying, or engaging in stereotypies) or working independently (the aide is at least four feet away, the student is engaged in work). In addition, the objective should state what constitutes mastery: Achieving the stated criterion for ten days? For three days in a school week? For three consecutive days? Five consecutive school days, including one Monday? (A good way to check for retention, by the way.) While Scott probably has mastered fractions if he is correctly answering thirty questions at 90 percent accuracy every day for five days running, Kara's not talking out for two minutes over five days probably does not mean that that problem is fully under control.

All of these elements must be concrete and measurable. What does that mean? First, keep in mind that if you cannot see or observe something, you cannot measure it. If you cannot measure a behavior or performance, you cannot accurately track how a student is doing. While we may all feel comfortable with statements such as "Robert is doing much better in math" or "Sally seems to be able to read much more easily," those are not acceptable for gauging progress or for making decisions regarding educational programs or placement.

Unfortunately, experts in special education have countless horror stories about poorly written objectives and their effect. There is no way to observe or measure whether Ashley:

1. *improves* her social skills
2. *understands* borrowing when subtracting numbers
3. *comprehends* the meaning of idiomatic expressions
4. *increases* reading comprehension

However, we can determine whether Ashley does the following:

1. She independently and appropriately *greets* her teacher and a minimum of two classmates each morning with 100 percent accuracy. (Her aide observes her and tallies up greetings each morning.)
2. She *correctly answers* twenty written math problems that require borrowing at 90 percent accuracy without use of a calculator, number line, or other device. (Ashley takes a weekly written math test.)
3. She *accurately explains, orally or in writing*, the literal and the non-literal meanings of five idiomatic expressions at 80 percent accuracy after they are presented verbally and visually in speech class. (Ashley's speech teacher records Ashley's responses and tallies up her score.)
4. After reading a chapter in a fiction book at Ashley's current reading level, she *correctly answers* three questions, chosen from among these categories: a character's actions, words, motivation, or thoughts; the background or history of the setting. Where appropriate, Ashley will predict what might occur next. (Ashley receives a brief written or oral test every day after reading a chapter.)

Good objectives clearly spell out the criteria for performance: not only what the student will do but also the level of accuracy required. What constitutes acceptable performance, or criteria, really depends on what the student is learning. Eighty percent accuracy in correctly answering social studies questions is fine, but 80 percent accuracy in decoding is not. Just imagine not being able to decode every fifth word.

DEVELOPING A PARTNERSHIP WITH YOUR
SCHOOL DISTRICT

Let's consider the strengths and weaknesses of school districts and educators, particularly the administrative division responsible for special education. You may find professionals in a range of different specialties, with varying levels of understanding about ASDs. Again, there is no widely accepted profile defining what constitutes an effective program to address the needs of children with AS. The willingness and ability of your school district to accommodate your child and provide appropriate support and services depends on a range of conditions, many of which (like state funding and regulations, that year's budget, the skills of staff) are beyond its control.

Is Inclusion for Everyone?

IDEA and state special education regulations require that children with special needs be educated in the least restrictive environment (LRE). The belief that every child with the ability to learn within a regular education setting should be allowed access to it has driven the special education movement from the start. In fact, in certain quarters, it's considered politically incorrect even to suggest that some children might fare better in environments that are more structured, more sheltered, less stimulating, and less populated than a regular classroom. At the same time, educators are being pressured to move children out of special education classrooms and into the mainstream for a number of reasons: to be in compliance with state and federal regulations, to save money, to make space for other children with special needs, or to lower its percentage of special needs students being educated in more restrictive environments.

Most parents and most special education professionals view inclusion in a regular education classroom as the most desirable learning environment because it offers the most access to the general curriculum. (Unfortunately, many special education curricula are "watered down," although there is no justifiable reason why this must be so for all students.) In addition, the regular education classroom is often simply assumed to offer superior opportunities for socialization and social acceptance.

Unfortunately, for some children, the regular education classroom is a less than ideal setting, even if they can keep up academically. While it's possible to address many special needs through services and supports, schools don't always succeed in managing the environmental and social challenges these children face. When a school fails to address these issues, you must consider alternatives. Your child may need less exposure to the regular classroom, more time in smaller group settings, or home schooling. The general emotional well-being of your child should be considered first and foremost. (For more, see chapters 7, 8, and 9.)

BECOMING YOUR CHILD'S BEST ADVOCATE

It is "parent nature" to protect and defend our kids, and AS probably makes most of us more protective and more defensive than we might be otherwise. For most parents, the entire special education process is fraught with uncertainty and anxiety. School is the social world of childhood, and it may be difficult even for those who accept their child's disability to see her differences made "official." Many of us carry our own strong emotions about our school experiences, good and bad.

Although as parents we are, legally, equal partners with those responsible for our child's education, in reality many of us do not feel like equals in the process. Yes, you are the expert on your child; you may even be better informed about ASD than some of the professionals. Yet in the crucial details that make or break an IEP or Section 504 plan—assessment, placement, programs, related services, accommodations, and so on—we are novices, no matter how much we research beforehand. The process demands that parents do two seemingly contradictory things: advocate passionately for one of the people we love most in the world while dispassionately participating in a complex (and for most of us, alien) legalistic exercise.

A classic example of that tension: You want what is best for your child, but legally your school district is not required to provide it. In fact, special ed experts and advocates advise parents never to request what is "best," only what is "appropriate."

If this seems counter–"parent" intuitive, it is. However, learning to work effectively within the special education framework often demands the discipline to separate your emotions from the process. It also requires that we all step onto what I call "the reality train." The purpose of special education and related services is not to make your child's school experience as comfortable and as successful as it can possibly be, no matter what. Yes, it is true that Emilio is more "comfortable" when he can sit in class and doodle constantly while the teacher is talking. Giving Emilio a one-on-one aide, or providing him with prewritten notes or notes taken by classmates, however, might not be the best solution. And by "best," I mean a solution that increases Emilio's skills and helps prepare him for life beyond high school—not what might make his life the least stressful today. If his handwriting is slow or illegible, then another option should be explored, such as using a laptop or tablet for note taking. If he cannot listen and write simultaneously, maybe he can tape-record the lecture and make notes later, though it would be very time-consuming, especially for a high school student with an already heavy homework load. Where do you or your child foresee him going in two years? Five? Ten? What skills does he need to get there? (It's a safe bet that doodling while others talk to him is not one of those.) How can those skills be acquired, practiced, and mastered today?

Under "Recommended Resources" at the end of this chapter are books covering every aspect of special education. Depending on your experience, you may find room for one or all of them on your shelf. Here, our focus is on the "inner parent" and the attitudes and actions that inform true, effective advocacy.

Understand and deal with the system as it exists, not as you believe it should be. Entering the special education process is like joining a long, complex board game already in progress that most of the other players have played hundreds of times. Even if you come to the game having memorized the written rules, your fellow players have a great advantage in their understanding of the strategies and philosophies behind how those rules are actually applied. Unlike you, they also have the power to influence that.

If the special education process is like a game of Monopoly, how it is played will depend on where you live. Every game of Monopoly comes with a set of written rules, yet you probably had one friend who insisted that all the fines went to the Free Parking kitty, another who eliminated singles from the bank, and another who permitted loans to bankrupt players to extend the game. To read IDEA and your state regulations, it might appear that everything about special education is pretty clear-cut. It's not. After the laws and regulations are passed and on the books, governmental agencies and departments issue policy statements, clarifications, and directives. Delve deeply enough, and you will find a few exceptions to every rule.

Learn how your school district plays the game. Before you even contact your school district about eligibility evaluation, and certainly before your first meeting with them, talk to people who have had experience with your district's special education personnel. Other parents whose children are receiving services in your district are an obvious source, but also be sure to contact the following:

- Local special education advocates, advocacy organizations, and attorneys in your area. When speaking to a professional who charges for his services, state your intention, be brief, and express your appreciation for his input. You may be calling on him again.
- Local chapters of disability rights organizations, including those who represent people whose disabilities are different from your child's. Hint: autism organizations are obvious choices, but AD/HD organizations are a good place to start, since they represent a relatively large population that is routinely served in both special education and regular schools and classrooms.
- Any professionals who have treated or evaluated your child or consulted on her case.
- Any professionals you know socially who work in education.

It's a small world, and teachers, therapists, and consultants often have colleagues in other districts.

Don't be surprised to hear someone tell you that your district is not as good as it could be. If a parent or a professional offers you an emotional account of a horror story, try to focus on the facts, not the emotion. There are two sides to every story. Bear in mind that when you're talking to parent and professional advocates, special education attorneys, and other professionals, their job is dealing with difficult situations. Few people call in the experts when things are going well. Some people feel they have an obligation to prepare you for the worst-case scenario. Again, listen and file it, but don't take it to heart. There's a real danger in bringing to the process heightened suspicion and distrust before they are warranted in your case. It increases your own anxiety, diminishes your ability to think and advocate clearly, and serves no one.

On the other hand, make note of recurring themes, such as a district's or a school's tendency to miss procedural deadlines, direct students with disabilities to restrictive environments, or create one-size-fits-all, cookie-cutter IEPs. Some school districts are less than fully compliant.

Establish a relationship away from the meeting table with the key special education staff. Prior to any evaluations or meetings, ask to meet with or at least speak to the senior administrator who will be in charge of your child's case. Use this time to introduce yourself and your child. Offer to discuss your concerns about your child (*not* the special education process itself yet) and what you may have done to date to address them, such as consulting specialists, pursuing independent evaluations and diagnosis, and any therapeutic interventions you have initiated, including things you do at home on your own (using charts, schedules, or Social Stories, for instance). Ask the professional if she has any questions. She probably will. Offer a *succinct* history of your child's experiences in school and school-like settings, at home, and in other settings (playdates, church or temple, dance class, sports activities). Do not air old grievances or complaints. Be sure to give equal time to the positive as well as the negative.

Believe it or not, while your child is unique, his diagnosis and his history related to ASD probably are not. Most professionals in this field have seen many children who share your kid's problems with peers on the playground, odd or quirky special interests, and difficulties handling noise. In my experience from both sides of the table, you can assume that the professionals involved want to get to know you and your child. But they are most interested in the aspects of your child that are relevant to what occurs in school. Also, these days, most professionals in school districts do not have an endless supply of time, and what they do have is limited by a schedule that's pretty inflexible.

Send the right message. Remember that one of your goals in having this conversation and all of your dealings with your district is to convey that you are a reasonable, capable, informed, and committed parent. Try to send the right message. Even if you know that your child's last teacher was incompetent or that the inflexibility of the three nursery schools he attended contributed to his being asked to leave them all, be judicious and impersonal without deflecting blame on either your child or yourself. You may say, "Everyone at the last school agreed that David probably needs to have a teacher with special education training," not "His last teacher didn't have a clue about ASD." Or: "The nursery schools Alexis attended weren't structured to accommodate a child with her behavioral issues," not "There were other kids in those schools who were real brats, but they just wanted to get rid of Alexis because she required more attention." Remember: you are talking to educators, most of whom are hardworking, dedicated professionals who receive much less support and respect than they deserve. When you complain about past teachers and staff, no matter how well and supportively your audience responds, I can guarantee you in that in the back of at least one listener's mind will arise questions about how cooperative and fair you will be when it comes to them. Don't go there.

Be careful that the explanations you offer for your child don't sound defensive. Some professionals who work with children with disabilities reflexively view as "denial" a parent's insistence that behaviors have broader explanations or that the child has strengths in addition to weaknesses. Be clear in acknowledging that your child has or may have a problem. To do otherwise is to give your school district the impression that you are uncomfortable facing your child's disabilities and may be satisfied with less help than your child may need or be eligible to receive.

Even if you have specific ideas about placement, objectives, and educational methodology for your child, keep them to yourself until all the evaluations are complete and you've had a chance to consider the possibilities the school district offers. Unless you've been through the special education process before, chances are you may not be aware of the full range of available options. A program you think would be great may have just closed or changed direction. A program you never heard of may have just opened up. You may be encouraged by a special education administrator to look at different classrooms, perhaps even different schools, before a placement decision is made. On the positive side, you'll have at least an image of each place and some sense of what it's like beforehand.

On the negative side, at least for some parents considering more restrictive settings (self-contained special education classrooms, out-of-district placements, specialized schools, and so forth), is the realization that your child may require such help or that his classmates may also have some degree of disability. You are not less of a parent for secretly wishing that your child didn't have to be there. Acknowledge your feelings, but try to see the situation objectively. Focus on what a particular program or setting offers, not what it doesn't. At the same time, communicate to the special education staff and teachers that you view special placements as stops along the line to a more inclusionary setting, if that's possible or desirable for your child. Special education should function as a greenhouse, a place to shelter and nurture children as they gain skills, not a warehouse.

Which will be the best decision for your child? There is no one-size-fits-all solution. Yes, in the best of all possible worlds, children with ASDs would find a comfortable place where they were truly learning in a regular classroom or a less restrictive environment. And, of course, there are many experts out there who advocate just—and only—that. But remember: no one whose book you're reading or whose conference you attend knows your child or what your local district's resources might be. Is your child with special needs better off in a regular classroom where he is completely dependent on an aide and socially isolated from classmates because there is no school psychologist available to create a social skills curriculum for your child and the class? Or are his immediate and long-term needs better served in a smaller classroom where he can do more things independently and have more structured opportunities to interact with classmates? Ideally, the members of your IEP team will be able to answer all your questions and discuss the pros and cons of each possible choice. Bear in mind throughout that nothing said or done is ever etched in stone. Until the evaluations are complete and your child has spent a reasonable amount of time receiving special education and related services, no one truly knows what's most appropriate for him.

Another word of warning: as much as we would all like to see our children included and their deficits overlooked, be judicious about how you express this. Parents who trumpet their absolute belief that their child must be mainstreamed or "really doesn't have that big a problem" play nicely into the hands of school districts that are more than happy to do less than what your child needs. Don't let anyone "flatter" your child out of services (as in "He's too smart for the resource room" or "She's too high-functioning for ABA"). If you are distressed or appalled by the possibility that your child might "be special ed," keep that to yourself, too. School districts have been known to dissuade parents from seeking expensive (for the district) special education and services by playing to parents' fears of stigmatization. One parent told us of a school psychologist who warned her away from a self-contained kindergarten class she felt would be perfect for her daughter by saying, "You don't want her in with those kids. They're all doped up on meds." Another was dissuaded from seeking an IEP by several committee members who mentioned numerous times that to be eligible, her daughter would have to be "labeled."

Be a professional parent. Regard your involvement in your child's education much the same way you would a business, and your relationship with the school district as a business partnership.

- Take the time to learn the laws, regulations, and school policies that apply to your child to the extent necessary. You don't have to become a legal expert, but you should

understand your basic rights and obligations as well as those
of the school district. It's a two-way street.

- Obtain, organize, and update your child's school, medical,
and other relevant records. Request a full set of your child's
school records from your school district. Keep these (along
with report cards, written communications with teachers and
the district, copies of evaluations and other reports, copies of
IEPs, notes and tape transcripts from meetings, and anything
else you believe is important) in a readily accessible file.
Under IDEA, your school district is obligated to provide you
with a full and complete set of your child's records. It may
charge you a reasonable fee for photocopying. However, if
you cannot afford the fee, your district must provide you the
copies free of charge. Also know that you have the right to
have included in your child's file your written objections,
corrections, and clarifications to anything you find therein.

- Get into the habit of writing letters. A letter not only
communicates, it becomes part of your child's official
record. Contemporaneous accounts of events are invaluable,
especially if you find yourself pursuing mediation, an
impartial hearing, or a lawsuit down the road. Write to
express concerns and ask questions. Write to restate what
was said during a recent telephone call or conversation.
Write to clarify your position, follow up, and confirm that
promised services are being delivered. Familiarize yourself
with the basic writing guidelines for "A Letter to a Stranger,"
which you can find at the Wrightslaw website (www
.wrightslaw.com). The premise of the "Letter to a Stranger"
is that you'll use your letters to put down in writing the
key facts and events in your child's school history in such
a way that the reader will consider you a fair, rational, and
knowledgeable parent. Needless to say, letters that are sharply
worded, confrontational, insulting, or accusatory don't make
the grade. (Granted, you might feel great writing them; if so,
write them and then throw them away.)

- What about email? It's quick to write, is delivered instantly,
and can be copied and shared virtually around the world
with a keystroke. These are all pretty good reasons why you

should think twice about using it to communicate anything important, state a complaint, or address anything that you might reasonably expect to take a turn requiring more expert legal help in the future.

- Take notes during any telephone conversation you have about your child. Note the name of the person to whom you spoke, the date, the time, and the gist of the conversation, then include a brief summary of the conversation in a follow-up letter.

- If possible, try not to attend meetings alone, unless you are comfortable doing so. We encourage the participation of fathers not only for the obvious reasons but for the fact (alas, sexist but true) that the paternal presence has been known to color the tone of meetings in a positive way. There is nothing wrong with bringing your friend or your mother, but it might be better to choose someone who can be more than simply a witness. Depending on your situation, another parent who has experience with special education, a lay or professional advocate, or, if the going gets rough, a special education attorney might be better choices.

- Approach any meeting with your school district, especially IEP meetings, like a business meeting. Come prepared and on time. (In the busier seasons, school districts often schedule meetings back to back.) If you think you will need extra time, request it when you make the appointment. Be sure you leave with a record of what was said, either by having someone along taking notes for you or, preferably, by tape-recording the meeting. (And don't forget to transcribe it immediately, lest you forget an important point or have additional questions.) The saying about good fences making good neighbors also applies to meetings that everyone knows are being recorded. Everyone tends to speak more thoughtfully. Be sure that you fully understand what your district proposes for your child and precisely how it plans to implement that program. For example, who will be providing speech therapy—when, where, and how often? Also, be sure that you understand the district's reasoning behind all of its decisions—those in your favor and those that are not. Finally, never feel pressured to agree to anything about which you're uncomfortable. *If you have reservations about anything in your child's IEP, don't sign or agree to it.* Inform your school district that you need a few days to consider its recommendations and ask to schedule another meeting. And, of course, follow it up within a few days with a letter outlining your understanding of what took place in that meeting.

- Remember, your child's IEP is not a "package deal." You have the right to accept some components and reject others. It is a good idea to spell out in writing which parts of the IEP you accept and which you are rejecting.
- Your child may be eligible to receive services during the summer vacation. Ask your district about extended school year (ESY) services.
- Join your local Special Education PTA (SEPTA) or other support or advocacy organization, if available. These not only can be excellent sources of information, they can also provide a sense of community and understanding.
- Study up on the art of negotiation. Wrightslaw has some good suggestions along this line.
- Attend a conference or presentation on special education. These are offered by school districts, state agencies, private agencies, nonprofit organizations, parent groups, and others. Pete Wright and Pam Darr Wright are deservedly famous for their Special Ed Bootcamp seminars, which they present around the country. Visit the Wrightslaw website, www.wrightslaw.com, and find out when they will be in your area.

WHEN PROBLEMS ARISE

In the best of circumstances, with accurate information and the best intentions, parents and educators can disagree. When you believe that your child's education could be improved by a particular teaching method or access to a specific service, it can be difficult to hear that your school district disagrees or that your child is deemed ineligible. When the IEP you so carefully crafted hasn't been read or implemented by the third week of school or when you continue to see the outbursts you know could be curtailed or eliminated by basic behavioral techniques the teacher "doesn't believe in," it may be difficult to maintain your "professional parent" cool. Another potential trouble spot is the provision of special education or related services over the summer vacation.

You may have other parents, your spouse, and your friends encouraging you to go after your district, make a big stink, and "show them." The latest outrage may be the first or it may be just the last in a long history, and parents easily fall into a cycle of replaying past injustices, great and small.

Righteous anger is a powerful feeling and, to be honest, can be a refreshing break from the doubt, uncertainty, and anxiety many of us experience at times. But the sense of empowerment you feel is a false one. You may believe that your case and your cause are as unique as your child, when the truth is that educators have seen this all before. Part of being a good special education professional is maintaining a caring yet neutral demeanor. Parents who routinely become extremely emotional, make threats, become verbally abusive, or attempt to dominate the proceedings probably will not get the "rise" out of professionals they would like. Some interpret this as professionals being callous and uncaring. No doubt there are some who are, but more often than not, the professionals are just being professional. The fact is that parents have a far greater investment in these outcomes than anyone else. And, besides, imagine your next district meeting with your child's teacher verbally abusing you or your chairperson pounding on the table. (If that happens, by all means, get legal help. That behavior from professionals is unacceptable.)

TRY TO WORK IT OUT

Ultimately, many decisions about accommodations, special education, and/or related services sometimes boil down to judgment calls. It may well be impossible for a parent to know the true reason why a child is being denied a one-on-one aide in a mainstream classroom, for example. You may be told it is because an aide is not warranted for your child, or that an aide would foster more dependence rather than independence, or that the presence of an aide would stigmatize your child in the eyes of her peers. Every single one of those arguments might be true. That still does not necessarily mean that you are wrong to request an aide or that your child would not benefit from having one.

Your school district must give you prior written notice of its decision, and that should include an explanation of the decision. Bearing in mind that there may be cases in which those objections would be correct, ask your school district to explain the decision in terms of your child specifically. A reasonable explanation of a decision not to hire a one-on-one aide for Sam might be: "In Sam's basic academic subjects, he's been doing above-average work without extra help, but we do see the anxiety and related behaviors at less structured times, such as lunch and recess. We believe he warrants closer supervision or a quiet place to go to, if he wishes, during those times only." In contrast, "We find aides often create more problems for the children than they solve" or "This isn't how we do things" are not reasonable explanations, because they don't address your child's unique, individual needs. You might request that your district provide a service on a limited, "trial" basis—for example, an individual aide or paraprofessional for six or twelve weeks—with clearly defined criteria for measuring progress or need and a firm date for future review.

You may never know what invisible (to parents, at least) factors may be shaping your child's education. In the case of an aide or paraprofessional, it may be district resistance to hiring additional personnel, or a classroom teacher's reluctance to accommodate a child with special needs, or her refusal to add supervising the aide to her duties, or the long list of other parents making the same request who have been denied and probably will restate their demands when they learn that your child got the aide. You may be told by your school district that it has had "bad experiences" with aides, because "good people are hard to find" or because "there is always a lot of turnover." That may well be true. However, a district's past failure to provide aides with better training and better wages, or to treat them as important members of the education team, does not excuse it from the obligation to provide a suitable aide for your child today.

In these situations, arguing from a moral or ethical perspective about what is "right" or "best" for your child is often ineffective. Pointing out your district's policy shortcomings may not help, either. The people you are talking to don't set the budgets or write the rules. They may be as unhappy with some of the conditions in your district as you are. But you will never know this, and it's impolite to ask. In the best of all worlds, your child's education should not become a battleground (although you should not let that discourage you from taking up the cause in letters to your board of education, superintendent, local elected representatives, and local support organizations). Keep your focus trained on the needs of your child and encourage your school district to do the same by asking (repeatedly, if necessary) for the reasoning behind the decisions.

In every exchange with your school district, try to bring something to the table: input from other professionals who know your child, information on a behavioral approach that worked, new findings about ASD that may play a role in your child's problems, or informative books, articles, or tapes. Be knowledgeable, but avoid giving the impression that you're a know-it-all. Carol Gray, the creator of Social Stories, suggests that parents try to avoid stating the problem and offering the solution in the same conversation. Some teachers and educators may feel self-conscious or embarrassed that they do not have the same information you do. As I learned personally shortly after this book was published in 2001, not everybody at the special ed table appreciates a smarty-pants. So even if it is true that you have some knowledge or expertise your child's team might benefit from, try to be cool about it. Unless you have worked inside a school yourself, it is impossible to know how complex and demanding the job is and the dozens of factors that easily render what you consider a "simple" fix something much more difficult.

BE REALISTIC ABOUT WHAT YOU—AND THE LAW—CAN AND CANNOT DO

Perhaps in the future, our legislators will see fit to make states, school districts, and educators fully and immediately accountable for the quality of education our children receive. At the moment, when it comes to individual students, oversight and accountability are not what they should be. The rewards for a school district's conscientiously following the law, adopting the most effective methods, and providing the education from which our children can derive the most benefit accrue to children and parents, not school personnel. In fact, there may well be budgetary and other pressures that work as disincentives to your school district's doing its job as well as you believe it could and should.

At the same time, school districts know very well how slowly the procedural wheels turn. The penalties school districts, schools, and educators theoretically face for failing to meet their obligations to an individual are rare and distant. Though every parent has the right to a fair and impartial due process hearing (and you may represent yourself, as some parents do), special education professionals know that relatively few parents have the resources to pursue it for all but the most egregious violations. Some subtly and not-so-subtly let it be known that activist advocate parents are not smiled upon and that professional advocates and special education attorneys create an "adversarial" atmosphere. (What is often conveniently overlooked is which side struck the adversarial pose that got you to this point to begin with.) This is why school districts don't always respond automatically to parental threats of reporting procedural violations or pursuing legal action the way a poorly run department store jumps when you threaten to contact the Better Business Bureau. The percentage of parents who actually do follow through is relatively low.

Your goal, then, should be to take charge and steer your child's journey through what one author calls "the special education maze" with an eye to avoiding whatever problems you can and responding rationally but assertively to the first signs of trouble. The wheels of bureaucracy turn slowly, and it may be weeks or months before changes can be put in place. In the interest of maintaining a good relationship with teachers and their district, parents may feel uncomfortable pressing for quick responses or pursuing a matter on the next administrative level up. At the other end of the spectrum are parents who believe it's best to resolve matters quickly. They have no qualms about reporting problems to state and federal authorities or calling in a professional advocate or special education attorney early on. Neither approach is right or wrong. How you choose to deal with your school district will be influenced by your child, your school district, the problem at hand, and your own personality.

WHEN TO CONSIDER GETTING HELP

Most parents think of getting outside help only after they believe they have exhausted all of their options or have become too emotionally overwrought to be effective. In fact, you may consider bringing in a professional advocate or special education attorney at any point in the process. Some parents think of advocates and attorneys as a last resort, but other parents find it helpful to have them on their team from the beginning. Contrary to the belief that advocates and attorneys "create" an adversarial environment, in fact, their presence may help prevent the situations that demand such a posture later on. For some parents, using an advocate or attorney is simply a matter of practicality, because they lack the time, the energy, or the inclination to be as effective an advocate as they believe their child deserves. Also, you can learn a lot from a professional advocate or attorney, and this can improve your own advocacy skills in the future.

To find an advocate or attorney, ask around for references. Special education attorneys are rare in some parts of the country, and you may find a lay advocate who has had extensive experience dealing with your school district. If, however, you have reason to think you may be pursuing an impartial hearing or other legal action, consult a special education attorney as early as possible. With any luck, doing so might force a reconsideration of the problem by everyone and possibly make such action unnecessary.

Before hiring anyone, be sure you understand and agree not only on the nuts and bolts of fees and scheduling, but also on the advocate's attitude toward the process and your school district. One parent we know consulted an attorney who advised her that the best way for her to obtain one special service by winning at a future impartial hearing was to "reject the entire IEP"—despite the fact that the IEP was satisfactory in every other aspect. Further, that IEP allowed for her daughter's placement in the perfect AS program in a private school. Had she followed that attorney's advice, she might have won the sought-after service (probably months later), but her daughter certainly would have lost her place in the very small and in-demand program. Remember, whomever you hire will be speaking for you and acting on your behalf. Just because you have hired someone to speak for you does not absolve you of your responsibility to know what is going on. If anything, that responsibility may even increase. If you have questions or problems concerning how an advocate or attorney sees your case, your district, or a strategy, feel free to consult with another advocate or attorney for a second opinion, if possible.

HOW YOU CAN MAKE A DIFFERENCE

Now for some good news. Schools—public, private, charter—across the country are meeting the challenge of educating children with AS. Parents can and do make a difference.

Closest to home, if you have a kind thing to say about any of your child's teachers, aides, therapists, or other school personnel, say it. Be sure that your district superintendent, building principal, board of education, special education administrator, and anyone else in a position to help, support, or promote those who have helped your child know all about it. Write letters, arrange a brief meeting, even consider standing up and speaking for three minutes at your next open school board meeting. When special education works well, everyone needs to know. More informally, the occasional note, a bouquet cut from your garden, a batch of cookies, or a special favor from you never hurts, either.

What else can make a difference? An active (and, some would say, activist) local parent organization —preferably one that includes you; administrators and teachers who are willing to learn about ASD and try new, evidence-based approaches; and parents who have the savvy to truly be their child's best advocate and who recognize when they need outside help. Ultimately, the success of your child's educational program depends on teamwork. Taking an active role in your child's education also means taking the time to develop relationships with teachers, therapists, administrators, and others who know your child. For additional information on dealing with ASD in the classroom, see chapter 9.

Recommended Resources

Peter W. D. Wright and Pamela Darr Wright, *Wrightslaw: Special Education Law* (Hartfield, VA: Harbor House Law Press, 1999) and *From Emotions to Advocacy: The Special Education Survival Guide*, 2d ed. (Hartfield, VA: Harbor House Law Press, 2006).

Council of Parent Attorneys and Advocates (COPAA), http://www.copaa.net.

Diane Twachtman-Cullen and Jennifer Twachtman-Bassett, *The IEP from A to Z: How to Create Meaningful and Measurable Goals and Objectives*, 2d ed. (San Francisco: Jossey-Bass, 2011).

Wrightslaw, www.wrightslaw.com.

Part Three

The Whole Child

SO now you're the ringmaster of a three- (and sometimes six- or ten-) ring circus. In one ring is the school district you struggle to train to toe the line. How easily that goes depends on whether you inherited the dancing bears or the man-eating lions. In another, you (we hope with some professional help) are facing the day-to-day (sometimes moment-to-moment) challenges with the flexibility of a contortionist and the aplomb of the world's greatest magician (all the while making a mental note to start working on your mind-reading skills). In the next, you juggle the competing demands each day brings. Some days you're catching the cream pies; others the flaming swords. Meanwhile, high on that tightrope, under the spotlight, with all eyes on him, your child is inching ahead. You hold your breath as he fitfully stops, teeters, and even takes a step back. But then you hold your heart as he glides for a while with grace and confidence. Sometimes he falls. Through it all, though, you never stop looking up, and you never let go of the net.

Until now, we've concentrated on the different "rings" the AS circus plays in. Now we turn our attention to the practical issues of parenting its "star": the child with AS. It may seem an obvious point, but how we help our kids manage emotional, social, and educational challenges is perhaps even more important than the other interventions they receive. We are, for now, the constant, and these years provide infinite opportunities for the "teachable moments" that can make such a difference in how our children understand, respond to, and cope with not only themselves but also the world.

Perhaps equally important, how well we parents learn to anticipate and handle the many difficult moments of our children's lives helps us, too. Unraveling the small knots saves your personal resources for bigger tangles. Ironically, it is in understanding your child, accepting her limitations, and applying basic "Asperger sense" and sensitivity that you—and she— make the first crucial steps forward.

The Essential Meditations

"I can make a difference." The parent-teacher conference, the birthday party, the supermarket, inside your own home—is there no end to the many opportunities we share for having our parental self-esteem crushed? (This is a rhetorical question; please don't start counting.) To survive, and for your child to thrive, you have to have faith in your ability as a parent. No one is as interested, as concerned, or as invested in your child as you are.

"My child with AS is my child first." Especially in the time immediately following diagnosis, you may worry that you're seeing or responding to your child's AS first and the child himself second. Even at those times when it feels as if "addressing the AS" is consuming every moment, stop and remember your child for the person that he is, not the disability or the diagnosis that he has. Make a conscious effort every day to look for and celebrate the humor, the wisdom, the joy, the affection, and the fresh worldview that is your child's gift to you.

"My child will grow up." Time passes for everyone—much more quickly than you will ever imagine. Although it is likely that his development will be uneven and he may not always seem to keep pace with his same-age peers, your child will mature—intellectually, emotionally, and socially, as well as physically. With support, he will become more patient, more thoughtful, more responsible, more capable, more independent—in other words, more grown-up—than he is today.

"My child will have his own dreams." We all have hopes for our children, but their dreams are their own to pursue. Your job today is not to build a dream, but to set the stage—emotionally and socially—for your child to meet his own dream.

"My child will find her tribe." Socially, your child's world may be very different from what you accept or value. After a certain point, accepting your child also means accepting some of her important life choices.

"I am a capable parent and person, but I am not perfect." No one is perfect. The fact that you're facing extraordinary challenges doesn't automatically bestow upon you boundless patience and infallible judgment. (But if it's true that "practice makes perfect," you may be getting closer to perfection than you think.) Don't undermine what you realistically can do by not forgiving yourself for what you cannot.

"It is never too late for my child." Rather than anguish over how late your child was diagnosed, learned to ride a bicycle, or showed an interest in making friends, look ahead. Although AS may have placed your child on a different route, with a different schedule and different stops, he is still on the journey, and it is not all one-way. There is no time limit on when he can acquire skills, abilities, and understanding. Early intervention is not the only intervention. We are all capable of learning throughout our lifetimes. People with AS are no different.

"It's okay to be sad, angry, afraid, apprehensive, or uncertain." You and your child will have bad days and rough patches. There will be times you will curse this disorder and everything it brings. And there will be times when that is the only healthy, rational response. You are not a "better" person for denying those feelings or a "worse" person for wishing that life would be easier for your child. Also, don't be afraid to validate these feelings in your child. Respect his feelings.

"It is never too late for me, either." Change is always possible. Depending on who you are, you can learn to be more patient with your child and/or less patient with the pace of her progress, or more organized with your paperwork but less of a housework perfectionist if it means spending more time with friends for a well-deserved break. Just because you have given every free hour to the cause for five years does not obligate you to continue. Nor does your having remained more on the sidelines until now mean it's too late to jump in. You will grow, too. The degree of control and assurance of safety you needed when your baby was five probably will not be appropriate or healthy when he is fifteen.

"I can change the world, if only a little bit at a time." Through simply loving and supporting that remarkable, unique person who is your child, you have already begun. Everything you do for your child and every contact you make on his behalf has the potential to make a difference not only for him but for those families who come after you. When you advocate for him, you advocate for everyone. Without even realizing it, you and your child will change the world.

"I am not alone, and neither is my child." There are thousands upon thousands of children and adults who are diagnosed with Asperger syndrome and ASD. This community is here for you and for your child. It truly understands. It knows things about living with ASD that even the world's greatest experts cannot fathom (and, in my personal opinion, shares that information in a much more colorful and interesting way). That community needs you as much as you need it.

"My child and I are sharing a journey that he will finish on his own." Parenting a child with ASD often shifts many of us into a "control" drive that it's hard to shift out of. It is hard to imagine a time when your involvement in your child's life might be not only undesirable and possibly counterproductive but also impossible. Embrace independence as your—and your child's—ultimate goal.

Chapter 7

YOUR CHILD'S EMOTIONAL LIFE

MANY people with AS will experience what would best be described as "emotional difficulties." We use this term with some trepidation, since too often people who don't understand AS assume that it's simply an "emotional problem." When we talk about emotional difficulties, challenges, and problems, we are speaking of those that seem to arise from the AS itself (such as difficulty regulating or modulating behavior, low frustration tolerance, or rage) and those that develop in part as a response to the challenges of AS (depression, anxiety, low self-esteem, social isolation, and so on).

Although social difficulties often prompt concern, the first bell ringers many parents, family members, friends, educators, and doctors notice are problems with self-regulation, frustration tolerance, and extreme or unusual expressions of anger, sadness, confusion, depression, or anxiety. In most cases, the child behaves in a manner that is considered "immature" for his age or "out of proportion" to the circumstances.

The ability of the person with AS to learn to understand and appropriately express powerful emotions is the cornerstone of several other important life skills. Socialization, maintaining friendships, and interacting with others in school and, later, at work all depend on learning to recognize, self-monitor, and modulate emotional responses. Ironically, by the time many parents reach the point of diagnosis, their child may have developed a repertoire of emotional responses that create obstacles to effective discipline, socialization, education, and therapy. These difficult behaviors also have the potential to give our kids an unfair reputation as lazy, stubborn, spoiled, rude, selfish, self-centered, or attention seeking. Such labels—spoken or unspoken—can take an inestimable toll on our kids' self-esteem. They can also have an adverse impact on how we feel about ourselves as their parents.

As parents, we spend more time with and exert a greater, more consistent influence over our children than anyone else. Ultimately, teaching our children to cope with their emotions falls to us, no matter how many other professionals we rely on. To some extent, virtually every moment is "a teachable moment," an opportunity to explicate and illuminate the world our children can find so confusing.

FACTORS THAT MAY CONTRIBUTE TO EMOTIONAL DIFFICULTIES

Developmentally related emotional immaturity. For various reasons, children with Asperger syndrome appear to be less socially mature than their chronological age would suggest. Generally, it is believed that children with AS are, on average, about three years "behind" in terms of social and emotional development. One team of experts contends that between ages nine and nineteen, a child with AS has the emotional maturity of someone two thirds his age. (For example, a nine-year-old has the maturity of a six-year-old.) Compared to same-age peers, they may seem more naive, more emotionally volatile, and less in control of themselves. Those whose problems with motor planning, motor skills, executive function, central coherence, and other abilities go unrecognized may develop a dependence on others for the most basic activities (such as getting dressed, bathing, finding things, and so on). Children with autism spectrum disorders often don't let parents know that they no longer need assistance the way typically developing children do. For example, most typical children will hit a phase where they revel in taking off their own clothes, which signals to parents that they can begin teaching dressing and undressing, and helping them to another stage of independence. However, a child with AS who has motor skills deficits usually cannot remove her own clothing spontaneously, therefore "missing" the chance to develop an important, independence-building skill in a developmentally appropriate time frame. Concurrently, in the absence of this important signal, her parents miss out on a chance to nurture that independence by stepping back. Years of well-intentioned "help" can result in so-called learned helplessness or prompt dependence and an unhealthy over-dependence on the prompting, direction, reminding, nagging, and presence of others. When combined with low frustration tolerance and AS's hallmark avoidance of the new, novel, or untried, prompt dependence can result in a child who seems unable to do much for himself and is "unwilling" to try.

Low frustration tolerance. Particularly as they grow older and realize that others are more capable, our kids can become frustrated and angry struggling over zippers, handwriting, and basically just knowing what to do or where to go.

Low tolerance for "boredom." As many observers have noted, kids with ASDs generally seem "drawn" to screens—computers, TVs, iPads, smart phones. For reasons not fully explored, kids with ASDs seem to find moments of waiting, of "not having anything to do," of being asked to attend to anything that is less than dazzling or personally highly reinforcing, difficult to endure. Alas, the real world is made up of many such moments, and learning to cope with them politely is essential.

Is It Time to Rethink Your Child's "Relationship" with Screens?

Probably.

As many observers, including Temple Grandin, have noted, kids with ASDs seem to have an affinity for screens—on computers, on smart phones, on gaming consoles, on portable devices of all stripes—that meets *and* exceeds the "e-addiction" too many of us accept as part of our oh-so-busy online lives. Let's be honest: *most* of us could exercise a little more restraint when it comes to grabbing the smart phone every time it tweets or reflexively checking our email every time our laptops *ping*.

For too many kids with ASDs, screens are a quick fix: they keep them amused, out of trouble, engaged, and sometimes even learning something (though the educational value of screen time in general is highly, highly overrated). Ten years ago, video games were viewed as a great social opportunity: if my kid liked to play a video game and the kid down the street liked the same video game, we had the start of the perfect playdate. Computers offered activities that dovetailed beautifully with many AS kids' interests and abilities.

But there is a darker side, the results of which seep into real-world life, too. Every moment your child engages with a screen is a moment free of social responsibility, demands, anxieties, risks, or disappointments. It is also free of opportunities for social growth, positive interactions in real time with real people in the real world. (Which, by the way, is where most of us will be living for the foreseeable future.) For many with ASDs, it is a very comfortable, easy place to be. Most of the things that kids do on screen are engaging, interesting, and highly reinforcing—from looking up special interests to posting on Facebook and playing online games (sometimes adult online games that include gambling) and viewing pornography.

Yes, I said pornography. Do you really believe that a kid who has been living on a computer several hours a day *can't* do this? As Joan Rivers would say, "Grow up." As renowned authority on ASDs, adolescence, and sex education Dr. Peter Gerhardt points out, there is a "porn version" of every special interest you can imagine, including anime,

Magic: The Gathering, Transformers, Pokémon, dinosaurs, Lego, Teenage Mutant Ninja Turtles, My Little Pony, and Thomas the Tank Engine. This is known as Rule 34: if it exists, there is pornography of it. (See chapter 10 for further discussion of sexuality.)

Behaviorally speaking, we know exactly what keeps someone returning to and repeating a behavior. The "sticky" apples of internet, game, and social media design fall straight from B. F. Skinner's tree. Reinforced behavior is repeated, and behavior that is reinforced "instantly" and predictably, and requires the least effort, is far more likely to occur again than behavior that requires more effort and/or offers less or less-valued reinforcement, on a delayed or unpredictable schedule. Apply that equation when you compare what many kids "put into" and "get out of" engagement with screens compared to engagement with people. It's easy to see why screens too often win. Ironically, the loser in all of this is your child.

Although some might argue that it is fashionable to appear occupied with your phone or your screen, such engagement in actual or potentially social situations literally puts you "someplace else." You are unavailable. You are obviously less interested in anyone else in the here and now than whatever you've got going on "out there." How better to promote the impression that our kids are "aloof," "rude," and "uninterested"? It's interesting that most of us would object to anyone else drawing a conclusion like that about our kids. And yet many of us send our kids out into the world with a "prop" seemingly designed not only to create precisely those "wrong" impressions but also to place a ceiling on how much real social engagement can occur. As long as your child carries a "portal" to the e-world in his pocket, there will always be an instant, easy alternative to engagement, to "boredom"—to anything that is less than absolutely thrilling.

The real irony here is that while your child is sitting in a high school or college classroom, at a restaurant with coworkers, or on what might be a first date and twiddling on his screen, he misses a lot—most crucially, the negative responses from the people around him to his electronic residency in his own private Idaho. In my professional experience, the kid's innocent responses when you do bring it to his attention—"I didn't notice that it bothered her," "I didn't realize you were talking to me," "I missed what the question was"—do little to encourage future tolerance, especially from peers, teachers, professors, bosses, coworkers, and others who might not completely understand AS but are making an effort to be accepting and kind.

Difficulty beginning and ending activity or behavior. People with AS often struggle with two "bookend" difficulties: starting and stopping any activity that requires you to recognize when to begin and when to end. And that could apply to almost anything and encompass academics, social skills, self-help skills, and just about anything else one would do on purpose. Some of the initiation problems may lie with deficits in executive functioning and the inability to plan steps of something like gathering all the books and notebooks for tonight's homework. Over time, a child may become so used to making mistakes in carrying out the simplest activities, such as getting a snack from the refrigerator or getting the right materials on her desk for the test, that she may fall into the habit of not even trying or performing tasks with a lack of mastery and fluency and/or an unacceptable number of errors. As a result, she needs more prompting. At the other end, it's hard for people with AS to quit an activity at the appropriate time. Part of this is probably related to difficulties with transitions or change, and children who are obsessive, compulsive, anxious, or perfectionistic may have additional difficulty recognizing when "enough is enough."

Deficits in theory of mind. Not only do people with AS have problems with "automatically" understanding that other people have thoughts, feelings, and desires that are different from their own, they are often at a loss as to what constitutes a correct response in a given situation.

In their essential *Teaching Children with Autism to Mind-Read*, Patricia Howlin, Simon Baron-Cohen, and Julie Hadwin state, "Mindblindness has far wider implications for development than experimental studies alone might indicate. Such difficulties continue to affect social and communicative functions well into adult life." They then list ten affected areas:

1. Insensitivity to other people's feelings
2. Inability to take into account what other people know
3. Inability to negotiate friendships by reading and responding to intentions
4. Inability to read the listener's level of interest in one's speech
5. Inability to detect a speaker's intended meaning
6. Inability to anticipate what others might think of one's actions
7. Inability to understand misunderstandings
8. Inability to deceive or understand deceptions
9. Inability to understand the reasons behind people's actions
10. Inability to understand "unwritten rules" or conventions[1]

Deficits in central coherence. According to educational psychologists Val Cumine and Julia Leach and teacher Gill Stevenson (authors of *Asperger Syndrome: A Practical Guide for Teachers*), central coherence is "the tendency to draw together diverse information to construct a higher-level meaning in context."[2] Neurotypical people get the "bigger picture" without thinking. Without any conscious effort, you know that the real meaning of words and events derives from their context. You probably know that when the movie hero's love interest says she's going to "slip into something more comfortable," it has an entirely different meaning than when your mother says it coming through the door after a long day of work. The words are the same, but the context—and thus the meaning—is different. That essential contextual information is what many people with AS cannot recognize without a great deal of training and concentration.

In every situation, your brain automatically sorts and prioritizes incoming information, so that when someone on the street screams at you, "Look out!" you don't stop to note the color of his shoes. You understand automatically what's important and which details you must attend to in order to understand. If two people are talking, you listen to what they say but you also note their nonverbal language, how they respond to each other, and so on. You don't focus on the Coke machine behind them or the fact that today is Thursday and your dog has a vet appointment. Someone with Asperger syndrome, however, might do just that.

Problems with central coherence are believed to manifest in such behaviors as insistence on sameness and routines, perseverations, obsessions, and, oddly enough, the development of special abilities. Sometimes a child with AS will seem to hear only part of what you said, focusing on a word with particular meaning to him to the exclusion of all else. If you say, "We may have time to go look at the model trains after dinner," your child may hear that as meaning that you are going to look at model trains now.

Deficits in executive functioning. As discussed earlier (see page 50), executive function (EF) is essentially the ability to "prepare for and execute complex behavior, including planning, inhibition, mental flexibility, and mental representation of tasks and goals."[3] EF deficits are also at the core of the motor planning difficulties many people with AS have, as well as problems with understanding emotion and imitating the behavior of others and engaging in pretend play.

Self-consciousness, embarrassment, fear of making mistakes. Sooner or later, a person with AS begins to notice that he is different from his peers. Typically, this occurs in early adolescence, but it can happen far earlier. Children who are prone to emotional outbursts, social faux pas, teasing, bullying, or ridicule may realize this sooner. Unfortunately, many people consider people with AS "aloof," "oblivious," or "absentminded" and assume that they simply don't notice the behavior of others. As most parents can attest, that is hardly true. The pain and humiliation children with AS feel are acute and real. Unaddressed, they can lead to further avoidance of potentially difficult situations, anxiety, depression, misplaced anger, and other problems.

Difficulty with attribution. How we perceive, respond to, and later think about our experiences plays a significant role in how we see ourselves and the world. Attribution is a fairly complex psychological concept that, in its simplest terms, describes our ability to understand "the causal judgments that individuals use to explain events that happen to themselves as well as social and physical domains of life . . . Such causal attributions are frequently answers to 'why' questions."[4] No doubt, how you perceive and make sense of, for instance, the rowdy adolescent who accidentally bumped into you on the line in the supermarket or the teacher who chose to confer the special privilege of caring for the class pet Tommy Turtle over the holiday to another classmate, determines how you feel about what occurred and how you feel about yourself.

If you have functional theory of mind, you can be annoyed at the rambunctious kid who bumps into you in the supermarket while knowing somehow not to become too upset. This kind of thing rarely happens, and it had nothing to do with you personally. You can figure out from observing that kid for ten seconds that he would have bumped into anyone; you just happened to be standing there. Similarly with Tommy Turtle. Most neurotypicals would not have failed to notice that Danielle, who will be Tommy's guardian over the break, has seemed a bit sad lately because her pet frog Herman died. They would not have difficulty understanding why Danielle is getting Tommy this time. They would know that it has nothing to do with them, nor does it mean that they will never be chosen to care for Tommy in the future.

But what would these situations—and the hundreds like them we make attributions about every day—be like for a child with AS? Theory-of-mind deficits can and do result in major errors in attribution. If you cannot accurately assess the kid on line at the supermarket, what would stop you from believing that he chose you and you alone to bump into? Or that his intent was not to hurt or to anger you? Or that if he bumped into you, who is to say someone else might not do it? Or that he will do the same thing if he sees you again? When you cannot assume another person's perspective, make even a decent guess as to his or her possible motives, or take in the many circumstances that might contribute to a given situation, you are left with just the observable facts. Your interpretation of the situation cannot help but be in some way flawed. When people with AS act out on flawed assumptions—in this example, say, expressing anger toward or even shoving the bumping boy—problems can arise.

First, it is important to understand the different domains of attribution. We can view events or situations in terms of their causality (internal or external), control (stable, unchanging over time; or unstable, changing over time), and generality (global, whose effects are broad and influence many things; or specific, related only to a narrow, specific area). When you view causality as internal, you operate from the premise that you can exert control over a situation. Conversely, when you view causality as external, you assume that you exert no influence. When you view control as stable, there is no hope of change; what occurred yesterday will occur today and tomorrow as well. When you see it as unstable, there is the chance that situations might change. Just because this kid bumped you in the supermarket does not mean he or anyone else will bump you again. Finally, a global sense of generality means the rainstorm this morning that canceled the softball game has ruined the whole day. If you look at it more specifically, the rain ruined the softball game. Period. Neither way is right or wrong. What constitutes a healthy, appropriate response depends almost entirely on the situation. It's probably a good idea to regard the weather or your boss's whims as beyond your control. But it would be detrimental to your ability to function if you viewed keeping the car gassed up, getting to school on time, or seeing the dentist regularly in the same light.

Studies of typical children have demonstrated a strong relationship between attributional style and self-esteem, academic achievement, perceived loneliness, social success, and goal-directed behavior after failure, or the willingness to persist, to try again. So-called attributional abnormalities are also related to depression, anxiety, and paranoia. We know that people with Asperger syndrome make flawed attributions, for many reasons: lack of social understanding, problems with central coherence, deficits in theory of mind.

Dr. Brenda Smith Myles, who has made landmark contributions to our understanding of children with AS, and her colleagues have studied attribution in students with AS. They found among thirty-three adolescents with AS a relationship between having depressive symptoms and attributing "social failure to their ability and the sum of their ability and effort."[5] The authors write, "An internal explanation or taking responsibility for negative events is associated with a loss of self-esteem."[6]

Manners Deficits: Can Your Child Afford to Appear "Rude"?

The real world—be it college, career training, a job, or anyplace else our kids want and deserve to be—is more comfortable with and understanding of autism than it is of what looks like rudeness. After all, no one can help having ASD. But after a certain point, being rude looks too much like a choice. And let's be honest: some kids on the spectrum do not just "appear to be" rude, they really are. Sometimes it's a by-product of AS-related social deficits; sometimes it's a response to recognizing that peers behave similarly and that it's considered cool; sometimes it's a combination of the two. It's probably fine to display less than great manners if you have the social acumen to know when it's safe to do so, and, most important, if you can talk your way out of trouble.

As our kids get older and move further out into the world, being rude or being perceived as being rude (and, honestly, what's the difference in terms of the bad impression it makes?) evolves from a forgivable "side effect" of ASD to a precursor or setting event for social situations that can get out of hand too easily. What's a parent to do? First, teach manners. That means saying "please" and "thank you," learning to listen or at least behave as if you are listening, holding doors open when it's expected, and so on. Explain it, model it, expect it, and then acknowledge and reward it when you see it. Every time. This isn't rocket science.

When Asperger syndrome was "new," behaviors and comments that others might consider rude were explained in terms of why they occurred: the lack of theory of mind, the inability to consider how someone else might feel, the difficulty inhibiting responses, the faulty "filter" between thoughts and words, and that superhuman yet naive capacity for brutal honesty.

Temple Grandin has been outspoken on this topic, because she views the pervasive lack of basic manners as a major stumbling block for many with ASDs who but for this deficit would have more opportunities in their lives. In 2006 she remarked during an interview on National Public Radio, "People have to learn social skills. I mean, I had to learn social skills, like being in a play. And this is one advantage that being a child of the fifties was. All children in the fifties were taught manners, they were taught to say please and thank you, they were taught not to be rude. And I'm seeing some problems today where somebody's losing a job because they made fun of a fat lady that couldn't fit in the elevator. I mean, that was the sort of thing that, when I was eight years old, my mother made it very clear to me that that was not okay to say that kind of stuff."

It's interesting that Grandin brought up the fat lady, because the little kid with Asperger syndrome who points and loudly comments on how fat (or whatever) someone is has been the light, funny moment in more Asperger syndrome conference presentations than I can count. Yet what the well-intentioned speakers leave out—and parents would rather not consider—is what happens in Act Two: when the lady, or her spouse, child, or friend says something back; or other unpleasant consequences—that your child might not understand any better than he understands the social faux pas that got him into this mess to start with—ensue.

When Temple Grandin talks of being a child of the fifties and being taught manners in a clear, direct way, she describes perfectly what some of our kids could benefit from today. Manners can be learned, and with concrete direction, kids can also learn to understand what is okay to say—when, where, and to whom. It really boils down to a task of discrimination with clear "always/never" rules. (Exceptions and other situations that move or blur the lines should wait for later, when you know your child is old enough to understand.)

One approach I've found helpful for a range of kids consists of three quick questions and a yes/no "flow chart" decision-making process.

1. *Is my comment about another person?*
   Yes. Say nothing. Go to number 2.

2. *Is my comment complimentary, supportive, or kind?*
   No. Stop. Say nothing. Keep it to yourself, share at home, or write it in a journal at home.
   Yes. Go to number 3.

3. *Would I feel okay if someone said this about me?*
   No. Stop.
   Yes. It's probably okay to say.

When teaching manners, it's rarely sufficient to frame things in terms of "How do you think she would feel if . . . ?" because the root of this problem is that how another person might feel often lies beyond your child's ability to imagine. Rather, be direct and clear:

"When you say that someone is fat/ugly/stupid and so on, it does not matter whether it is true. That kind of remark can make someone feel hurt or very angry. It might also make him or her want to say or do something back to you to express that hurt or anger."

"You are a good person. When you say that someone is fat/ugly/stupid and so on, your behavior tells people that you might not be the nice person you really are."

"Good manners are a way for people to see some of the best things about you: that you are caring and kind."

To paraphrase Blanche DuBois from *A Streetcar Named Desire*, in some ways, our kids are likely to be dependent on the kindness of strangers to some extent, just as we all are from time to time. Good manners are an essential social skill that everyone needs.

CREATING STRUCTURE AT HOME

Having regular daily routines for things such as meals, homework, and bedtime can have a positive emotional impact on a child with ASD. Ironically, many of us find that, prediagnosis, we've developed "antiroutines." Many children with AS never got the knack of putting themselves to sleep as babies, so we end up with an eleven-year-old who falls asleep wherever, whenever, if ever. Homework, another common battleground, may be put off, avoided, or abandoned because parents and children alike succumb to anxiety and frustration. Ironclad resolutions to leave on time for school, work, and other appointments are blown to dust by unpredictable and inexplicable responses to transition. And so on. Especially before parents learn to understand their child's AS-related behaviors, family routines suffer from stress and unpredictability.

We've heard from parents who prefer not to set routines because it simply doesn't fit their lifestyle. They may believe that their kid should have greater latitude in making his own choices or is "happier doing his own thing"—even if that means staying up past midnight on school nights playing video games, skipping meals, or neglecting basic hygiene. Some reason that because their child is subject to so much structure in school, she needs or deserves a break from routine. In fact, people with AS usually benefit from routines. Generally, they need more predictability, structure, and certainty, not less. For children who have difficulty conceptualizing time, as many people with AS do, set routines can serve as "landmarks" (before dinner, after homework).

Another way parents can provide structure is by being consistent about household rules. Even if you felt stifled by your own parents' rules as a child, bear in mind that for the child with AS, consistency means less stress and confusion. For parents who feel they spend more time than they like watching, instructing, and correcting their children, basic rules can help to reduce the need to monitor.

Children with ASD often find comfort in rules. Having rules for everyday activities—say, dirty clothes go immediately into the hamper, not on the floor, before bath time—eliminates the occasions when your child will have to wonder what to do next. Each time he puts his clothes in the hamper, it is one more opportunity to praise, one less occasion to correct, reprimand, remind, or scold.

Rules about behaviors can present a little more of a challenge because children with AS may have difficulty understanding how to handle inconsistency. Many families find that trouble often starts with the "this time only" exception to an otherwise ironclad rule: perhaps jumping on the bed, riding the scooter without a helmet, or walking the dog without his leash. Whereas typical children might be able to see the bigger picture and how circumstances and judgment may make it okay to bend or break a rule now and then, a child with AS might see it differently. Once you break that rule, the genie may be out of the bottle, and you may find it difficult to put it back. To minimize confusion at my house, I applied the "always/ never standard" for most situations. In other words, if it's okay to eat pizza in the den, it should always be okay; if it's not okay to eat pizza in the den, it should never be okay.

This worked fine when Justin was little, but as he got older, he needed to practice exercising good judgment, making decisions, and dealing with the consequences. It had to become his job (not

Mom's or Dad's) to ask himself, *What kind of food is okay to eat in the den? Where in the den should I eat it? What should I do if I make a mess?* (He has to clean up any mess he makes.) It's time to change the pizza rule. Of course, there will always be exceptions, but sticking to a set of rules for most everyday matters will greatly reduce the number of situations open to debate and misunderstanding.

USING LISTS, VISUAL STRATEGIES, ACTIVITY SCHEDULES, AND OTHER "REMINDERS"

Deciding to have rules and routines is great. The problem sometimes arises when a child with AS knows there is a rule or routine but lacks the organizational skill or initiative to follow through. Some parents and teachers resist the idea of making lists, visuals, or activity schedules for children with AS. They mistakenly assume that these are really only for children with more difficulties and fewer cognitive strengths. That's simply not so (I write as I remember to check my calendar for next week on my iPhone). One characteristic that is almost "universal" to every ASD is difficulty recognizing and attending to appropriate, relevant cues. Most of us without an ASD depend on a countless array of environmental prompts and reminders to get us through our day, so that we are basically responding to a series of elaborate cascades of cues for such seemingly simple activities as getting ready for school or making dinner.

We know that people across the spectrum tend to underattend to or miss relevant cues and to focus on irrelevant ones instead. For children with AS, problems with executive functioning, possible attention deficits, anxiety, and central auditory processing issues—the list goes on and on—can turn the simple "It's time for your shower" into nothing short of an attempt on Everest. Sometimes the problem is not that our kids don't know what to do; they do. They may not know precisely how, or in what order, or what to do now after they have done whatever came before. Or they may need to have a clearer, more concrete picture of the sequence of events than they can generate internally.

An activity schedule is "a set of pictures or words that cues someone to engage in a sequence of activities . . . Depending on the child, the activity schedule can be very detailed—breaking a task into all of its separate parts—or it can be very general, using one picture or symbol [or in the case of students with AS, words] to cue children to perform an entire task or activity."[7] Activity schedules promote independence, because your preteen son's being able to refer to a

December

Sunday	Monday	Tuesday	Wednesday	Thursday	Friday	Saturday
1 No School	2 School	3 School	4 School	5 School	6 School	7 No School

Sunday	Monday	Tuesday	Wednesday	Thursday	Friday	Saturday
1 No School ☒ Chores ☒ Homework ☒ Social Activity ☒ Hobby ☒ Family	2 School ☒ Chores ☒ Homework ☒ Social Activity ☒ Hobby ☒ Family	3 School ☒ Chores ☒ Homework ☒ Social Activity ☒ Hobby ☒ Family	4 School ☒ Chores ☒ Homework ☒ Social Activity ☒ Hobby ☒ Family	5 School ☒ Chores ☒ Homework ☒ Social Activity ☒ Hobby ☒ Family	6 School ☒ Chores ☒ Homework ☒ Social Activity ☒ Hobby ☒ Family	7 No School ☒ Chores ☒ Homework ☒ Social Activity ☒ Hobby ☒ Family

How you design your child's calendar really depends on your child. For example, some younger kids are only interested in one week at a time (top). For others, you can turn a weekly calendar into a general to-do checklist (bottom). This weekly calendar provides a general list of the most frequent regular daily activities and includes space for writing in more specific details.

December

Sunday	Monday	Tuesday	Wednesday	Thursday	Friday	Saturday
1 No School	2 School	3 School	4 School	5 School	6 School	7 No School

Day	Date	What Kind of Day
Sunday	1	
Monday	2	
Tuesday	3	
Wednesday	4	
Thursday	5	
Friday	6	
Saturday	7	Chores

As unusual as it might sound, for some kids, it really does matter whether time moves from left to right, like a textbook timeline (above) or whether it runs from top to bottom (left). It is easy to create calendars using standard programs with basic clip art or with photos or drawings you create and import.

December

Sunday	Monday	Tuesday	Wednesday	Thursday	Friday	Saturday
1 *No School*	2 *School*	3 *School*	4 *School*	5 *School*	6 *School*	7 *No School*
8 *No School*	9 *School*	10 *School*	11 *School*	12 *School*	13 *School*	14 *No School*
15 *No School*	16 *School*	17 *School*	18 *School*	19 *School*	20 *School*	21 *No School*
22 *No School*	23 *Holiday!*	24 *Holiday!*	25 *Holiday!*	26 *Holiday!*	27 *Holiday!*	28 *No School*
29 *No School*	30 *Holiday!*	31 *Holiday!*				

You can also draw a general calendar grid (5 rows, 7 columns) with permanent marker on a dry-erase board or on laminated poster board that takes dry-erase markers.

December

Sunday	Monday	Tuesday	Wednesday	Thursday	Friday	Saturday
1 *No School*	2 *School*	3 *School*	4 *School*	5 *School*	6 *School*	7 *No School*
8 *No School*	9 *School*	10 *School*	11 *School*	12 *School*	13 *School*	14 *No School*
15 *No School*	16 *School*	17 *School*	18 *School*	19 *School*	20 *School*	21 *No School*
22 *No School*	23 *Holiday!*	24 *Holiday!*	25 *Holiday!*	26 *Holiday!*	27 *Holiday!*	28 *No School*
29 *No School*	30 *Holiday!*	31 *Holiday!*				

You and your child can have fun drawing in the symbols and/or writing the words to fill it all in. Another idea is to create and laminate a number of the pictures, symbols, or words that are bound to crop up often (like the word school *or a picture of a school bus). Then attach the soft, furry side of a Velcro dot to each. Place a matching hard, loopy Velcro dot on each of the date boxes, then place, move, and remove schedule items as you wish.*

chart listing the sequence of events that should occur during show-ering does not need you outside the bathroom door reminding him what to do or later reprimanding him because he forgot to wash his hair. In this case, you could type up a list of steps (turn on shower, wet hair, shampoo, rinse, etc.), laminate the sheet, and place it in the bathroom. For a younger child, you might draw and laminate a basic body form and number the areas to wash in order. As time goes by, and your child becomes more independent—the ultimate goal of using tools like these—you can change the list or schedule from, say, pictures to words, or from full sentences to single words. The goal is to gradually fade the cues until the routine is so well es-tablished that the activity itself provides the cues your child follows.

TANTRUMS, RAGES, AND MELTDOWNS

While not every person with AS experiences tantrums and rages, this behavior is far and away the most often cited problem behavior parents face. *Tantrum* is as apt a description as any, but it sounds ba-byish after a certain age. *Rage* is often the correct word, but many of us recoil from its connotations. "She totally melted down," "He blew up," and "He spun out of orbit" seem fit to describe anger that goes "from zero to sixty in a second," "is off the charts," and "out of control." We also have heard from parents who opt to use less descriptive, more neutral terms, such as "neurological episode" or "frustration response."

Regardless of why your child is experiencing outbursts, it is important to always remember—and to remind others—that this reaction is not as volitional or subject to the degree of self-awareness and self-control that the neurotypical person possesses. The more emotional your child with AS becomes, the less able he will be to reason, apply skills he does have, and control himself.

These outbursts are more likely to occur in situations in which the person with AS feels emotionally stressed, which may include such public settings as school, the playground, the shopping mall, the birthday party, and other environments that put his behavior "on display."

WHAT PARENTS CAN DO TO HELP WITH EMOTIONAL DIFFICULTIES

Regardless of the source of your child's emotional issue or its manifestation (crying, tantrums, withdrawal, depression, and so on), your responses must be shaped by the realities of dealing with ASD. These "realities" probably don't include "tough love"–style approaches, inflexibility, or the well-intentioned advice of anyone who doesn't understand AS (including family members, professionals, friends, neighbors, and strangers). One of the biggest challenges for many parents is that the best, "ASD-correct" response often demands from us qualities like patience, reason, and perseverance, plus the emotional distance to maintain them. These may be sorely tested at the height of your child's meltdown, no matter how well you understand the disorder.

Difficult as it may be, you must train your focus on managing the outburst itself, *not* on addressing its causes, the manner in which your child is expressing himself, or expressing your disapproval or distress over the event. This is a tall order for those of us who would feel oddly unparentlike if asked to dispense a Band-Aid without the accompanying "How many times have I told you not to skate without your knee pads?" After all, as parents we're practically programmed to serve up, with the best of intentions, a side order of guidance, correction, advice, admonition, or warning with every dish of help, instruction, or support. For typical children, this may be effective. For children with ASD, however, it may be disastrous: exacerbating tempers, fueling self-blame, and adding more confusion and anxiety to the mix.

We may feel compelled to get in that all-important "last word," but as Dr. Brenda Smith Myles and Jack Southwick, authors of *Asperger Syndrome and Difficult Moments*, perceptively point out, "It is not important to have the last word, but it is imperative that parents have the LASTING word [emphasis in original]. In this way, children will learn to understand that they can count on parents to help set boundaries for them and enforce limitations." They present four basic steps for coping with the potentially interminable debates parents and children with AS are prone to:

1. Say what you mean—mean what you say.
2. Say it only twice in a calm voice.

3. Verify the child's understanding. If the child processes information visually, you may need to choose your words carefully. Consider using icons or pictures to facilitate understanding.
4. Stop talking and take action.[8]

Although the steps are simple, following them through in the midst of a crisis isn't always so easy. The key to managing outbursts productively, so that your child emerges from the experience with more self-control and self-esteem, is first controlling your own responses. We each have different capacities for coping with emotionally charged situations. Parents who are naturally uncomfortable with confrontation, who feel it is inappropriate to express strong emotions such as anger, or who have been traumatized by physical or emotional violence may have an especially difficult time dealing with rage. If you have problems maintaining self-control on a fairly consistent basis or if you find yourself avoiding the issue (and letting your child become increasingly out of control), consider seeking professional help to address your feelings. Remember, your child's sense of the world as an unpredictable place is a key component of his anxiety and possibly his outbursts. What could be more frightening than a parent out of control or unable to reestablish control? Enough said.

Here are some tips for executing the preceding steps:

1. Use as few words as possible. Pick one short sentence that tells your child what to do, and repeat it twice, as above. For example, instead of "I can't believe you are standing here shouting at the top of your lungs in the store," simply say, "Take my hand and walk with me to the car." Repeat. Say nothing else until the direction is followed. Sometimes having a concrete direction to follow is the first step out of the tantrum.
2. Keep your voice tone what I describe as "bright neutral." You want to extract any trace of emotion that signals your distress, anger, impatience, and so on. However, you don't want to sound like a robot. This is not always easy, but try practicing in front of a mirror. In your mind, picture and

hear the voice of someone you identify as cool, calm, and unflappable. Your goal is to be able to give a direction in a tone that communicates, "You have done what I am asking you to do a hundred times before, and I have absolutely no doubt that you will do it now." Use this tone and hold on to that thought even if—especially if—not a word of it is true.

NURTURING AND SUPPORTING A HEALTHY EMOTIONAL ENVIRONMENT AT HOME

Conflict is a natural part of growing up and learning to separate from one's parents. The challenge facing parents of children with AS is that the nature of the conflict is significantly more complex. All kids need discipline and a sense of limits, and children with AS may need them even more. You probably watch your child with AS more closely; her vulnerabilities may make you quicker to intervene, to correct, to explain. Add to this your child's limitations in social understanding and emotional awareness, and it's hardly surprising that misunderstandings, arguments, and outbursts occur. When it comes to preventing and responding constructively to emotional outbursts, most of the do's are actually don'ts. Here is a list of what *not* to do:

Don't believe that tantrums and rages "come out of nowhere." They don't. If you look carefully enough, you will probably be able to identify the trigger, or antecedent, of the outburst. It may not be the same for each one, but it will usually follow a pattern that involves sensory issues and other environmental factors, anxiety, misunderstanding, social difficulties (teasing, bullying, rejection), fatigue, or stress, to name a few possibilities, or some combination of these.

Don't assume that there is nothing you can do. It's true that there is nothing you can do to stop a rage cycle in progress, but you are in control of many other important factors. You can be sure that your response serves to defuse rather than exacerbate the situation. You can remove your child to an environment or situation conducive to better control. You can study the situation for information that will help you prevent or better manage future outbursts.

Don't ignore the warning signs or the conditions that you know may prompt an outburst. The signs appear as ominously as dark clouds before a storm. Many parents will say, "I should have seen it coming." It's the late-night run to the department store, the "just one more page" of homework, the school-day morning after the midnight power surge killed every alarm clock in the house and left everyone rushing. Some kids whine, complain, repeat the same questions anxiously, or become unusually quiet. Others engage in "nervous" habits: toe tapping, finger tapping, pacing, nail biting. Their tones of voice may change; they may appear tense; they may grimace, roll their eyes, or convey their discontent through other facial expressions. There are a number of ways you can divert a tantrum before it explodes. Each child is different, and what works for one may not work for others, but try to redirect your child's attention by using humor; encouraging him to engage in something of special interest to him; gently directing him to a familiar, routine activity; or removing him from the situation in a calm, neutral way ("Let's go inside," as opposed to "Let's get away from that noisy lawn mower"). Some children respond to touch or a mutually agreed upon nonverbal "secret signal" that lets them know you know they're uncomfortable. In one family's house, this "rumbling" stage, as one expert terms it, has often been short-circuited with the simple "Do you need a hug?"

Don't respond to the behavior; respond to your child. Communicate to your child, verbally and nonverbally, that you are there for her, that her behavior will not drive you away, and that you are her ally—not her enemy—in the fight for self-control. Don't say anything about how the outburst is making *you* or others feel.

Don't use too many words. According to Dr. Fred Volkmar of the Yale Child Study Center, words are the "lifeline" through which people with AS understand the world. So it is little wonder that parents sometimes feel compelled to talk a child through a tantrum and end up making a bad situation worse. In the moment of rage, words are just more sensory static, irritating and distracting. The more you say, the more likely you are to provoke further anger and frustration. Sometimes it's best to say nothing.

Don't say what you don't mean or fail to do what you say. When you do speak, say less, but mean it more. In other words, strip your language down to the basics, and then, at the first sign of a possible storm, be prepared to act. You could respond to the classic toy store meltdown with "Okay, well, if you're going to get so upset because you don't want to share trains here at the train table, I'm afraid we're going to have to leave"—and then watch your child throw himself to the floor. Or you could simply say, "We are going now," take your child's hand, and leave the store—even if that means your nephew's birthday present is left in the shopping cart, your child is screaming bloody murder, you have to pick him up and carry him to the car, and everyone in the store is staring at you. No bargaining ("If you want to try one more time, and if you can behave, we'll stay"—honestly, how many times has that ever worked?), no cajoling ("If you stop crying now, I'll give you a cookie"), and no permitting the situation to deteriorate because you must finish shopping or you refuse to let these tantrums run your life. Someone must be in control, and it has to be you. And that's true even if it puts another part of your life out of control temporarily.

Don't expect your child to handle situations that you know are beyond him without support and an escape plan. Sometimes as parents, our wishful thinking gets the best of us. We may know that Jeremy hates hearing children singing "Happy Birthday" and that Sarah panics inside movie theaters. Yet sometimes we are persuaded to "give it another try" by our fears that they may never learn to adapt, the influence of others, and sometimes even our children's desire to do certain things. It is important to help your child expand his repertoire of life experiences. You should encourage new experiences, but treat them like "experiments" and don't burden your child unfairly with responsibility for the outcome. If Jeremy wants to attend his best friend's party, have a plan to take him for a walk outside the party room during the singing. Go over with Jeremy what's going to happen as many times as it takes, then be sure you see it through, even if it requires that you be the only guest's parent who stays for the party. If Sarah is determined to try to go to the movie all the other kids are talking about (and any indication that your child wants to be part of the crowd should be supported), try to determine what caused problems in the past. Was the sound too loud? The theater itself too large? Too crowded? Did she feel trapped because those she was with wouldn't leave at the first signs of her distress? Is she worried she may have to use the automatic hand dryer in the restroom? The list goes on and on. Be a detective and do your research.

If your child can tell you what bothered her the most, perhaps you can find a solution: a quieter theater (sometimes older neighborhood theaters that haven't been modernized with state-of-the-art sound systems are more tolerable), going at a less popular time (weekday afternoons as opposed to Saturday afternoons), wearing special earplugs, going someplace where there are paper towels (or, better yet, packing a few in her pocket), and letting her know that if she is uncomfortable, you will leave immediately. No matter what the outcome, praise your child for her courage, point out everything that she did manage to handle, and let her know that you are proud of her and willing to try again when she is. One mother we know estimates she spent over a hundred dollars over ten theater visits just buying snacks and sitting through previews before her daughter could finally manage a whole movie. But it was worth it. Most important, ask your child what she thinks would make the experience a better one next time.

Don't expect your child to read, understand, or respond appropriately to your body language or facial expression. Don't depend on nonverbal communication to carry important messages such as "I am becoming annoyed," "Your behavior is inappropriate," or "I am losing my patience." At the same time, be on guard for the negative, hurtful, or demeaning messages you may be sending through rolling your eyes, frowning, crossing your arms in front of your chest, turning away, and so on.

Don't ask rhetorical questions. This staple of many parents' crisis repertoire—"What were you thinking?" "Don't you know better?"

"Haven't I told you a dozen times?" "Don't you ever listen?" "Can't we go to the supermarket once without you making a scene?" "Can I ever finish a phone call?"—can be very threatening to a person with AS. He may feel pressured to actually answer a question that (a) has no answer, and (b) only adds to the verbal barrage.

Don't make generalizations. Statements such as "You always do this" and "You never do that" are provocative and beg to be argued—something that some of our children seem all too adept at.

Don't use sarcasm, hyperbole, or gentle teasing to make your point. Even people with AS who can understand your real meaning when they're relaxed may not be able to do so when they're upset.

Don't issue ultimatums or say you will do something that you cannot or will not follow through on immediately. Ultimatums such as "If you don't stop screaming, I'll leave the room" may be effective if your child has not been swept away by a full-blown outburst and is simply in the habit of yelling to get your attention. (Remember, always determine the purpose of your child's behavior before deciding how you will address it.) Under "non-rage" conditions, there's nothing wrong with teaching the art of negotiation: "If you can sit quietly through the rest of your sister's recital, you can have some extra time on the Game Boy." Once your child has lost self-control, however, any "deal" that demands he control what he obviously cannot will only add to his already overwhelming stress and anxiety. In fact, the prospect of future unpleasant consequences may make it harder for him to regain control, not easier. The other consideration is that you might end up accidentally reinforcing behavior you do not wish to encourage.

Focus only on the present moment and the issue at hand. Disconnect your child's present behavior from the past or the future. Neither he nor you can control either, and recalling past "failures" or predicting future ones undermines your child's ability to regain control and his self-esteem.

Don't teach, preach, or explain until your child is safely out of crisis. Practically speaking, it's a waste of breath, because your child simply will not be able to take it in and process it in any useful way. Extra verbiage only adds to the "noise" and the stress of an already difficult situation. Later, when your child has recovered and is in a calm, receptive mood—and that may be fifteen minutes later or days hence—revisit the situation with him, propose reasonable ways that he might handle it differently next time, and let him know that he will have support if he needs it.

Don't outnumber and overwhelm your child. If you can keep your crisis interaction to a one-on-one exchange, so much the better. Sometimes parents and family members can develop a good "tag team" strategy that plays to their strengths. Mom may be good at weathering the outburst calmly as Dad delivers the recovery hugs. Since there may be times when you need backup (the other parent, a family member, a friend), be sure ahead of time that everyone understands the rules of engagement. It's not unusual for a child to re-explode when third or fourth parties, well meaning though they may be, toss in their two cents by repeating what you may have already said, asking their own questions, or attempting otherwise to help. One mother told us of a time that her upset child cried, "I hate myself!" This prompted his grandmother to scold, "No, you don't! What a terrible thing to say! It breaks my heart to hear you talk like that." This only sent the child spinning further out of control. Sometimes a person with AS simply cannot handle being spoken to by even one person, much less a chorus. If you see that someone else's involvement is causing distress, use a silent signal or simply say "I am handling this. Please leave." Do not explain, debate, or argue then, but later do make sure that everyone understands how to respond in the future.

Anyone in the room who is not talking should take ten steps back. Literally. Sometimes even when everybody is not talking to an upset child, they all hover around him. This can be uncomfortable or irritating. Make a rule: if you are not actively managing the problem, take ten steps back.

Don't let your words or actions have any point or goal beyond helping your child regain his emotional equilibrium without feeling guilty, "bad," or in any way diminished in your eyes or his own. When it's over, be supportive and loving. Try to arrange for him to have some quiet downtime, be alone, or do something he finds relaxing. Let him know that you understand how difficult it is for him. Although it may feel strange to offer compliments on your child's behavior during a meltdown, if there is any way in which your child has exhibited improved self-control—say, by not using foul language, by letting someone know he was feeling stressed before the outburst, by not hitting or throwing things, by regaining control more quickly—praise him explicitly and generously.

Give your child an opportunity to repair whatever he can of the situation. If that means apologizing to someone later, do that. If it means returning to a place to complete unfinished business, do that. Be sure to show your child that even in the aftermath of a difficult moment, there is a "way back," and that feelings or opinions about her have not been irreparably damaged.

Respect your child; let him save face. Sometimes it is impossible to repair the damage. This might have nothing to do with your child but, rather, with another person's attitude about things or the rules. Sometimes there is simply no tolerance for outbursts, inappropriate language, or unpredictable behavior. You may sense that while your child is welcome to apologize or to return, the response will not be forgiving or fair. Sometimes it may be best to steer your child in a different direction.

What to Do in Case of a Personal Crisis

Unfortunately, despite everyone's best efforts, children with ASD some-times reach a point of emotional crisis. This can be due to severe de-pression, anxiety, or another disorder; adverse reaction to prescribed psychotropic medication or alcohol or illicit drugs; or a tantrum or rage cycle that has gone far out of control. Other crises may occur because a child is experiencing suicidal or violent thoughts and impulses, which he may attempt to act upon.

According to a study published in 2012, children with ASD be-tween ages three and seventeen are nine times more likely to access the emergency room for psychiatric reasons than are those without ASD. The risk of hospitalization for psychiatric or severe behavior problems increases with age. Among the characteristics that make a person under age eighteen with ASD more likely to be hospitalized are a diagnosis of Asperger syndrome or autistic disorder; late diagnosis; and/or the pres-ence of a comorbid psychiatric condition such as AD/HD, depression, or OCD.[9]

For the parent of a child with AS, it's easy to feel that no one—not even the professionals—understands how to handle the disorder. As a result, some parents are reluctant to seek emergency medical help or the aid of law enforcement to help bring a rapidly deteriorating situ-ation under control. Sometimes a crisis arises out of another crisis: for instance, a child runs away and hides during a house fire because he's afraid of sirens, or bolts from an emergency medical technician despite the fact that he is bleeding profusely from a cut.

Fortunately, first responders, hospital staff, and other community helpers are much more knowledgeable about ASD than they were in the past. Organizations such as Autism Speaks, the Organization for Autism Research, and federal, state, and county agencies publish brochures, tip sheets, articles, and even PowerPoint presentations and full reports on their respective websites. Every child is different, and the resources in your community are different as well. So while we cannot offer a one-size-fits-all step-by-step guide, here are general guidelines for coping with crisis.

Be honest and realistic. Your child's behavior could result in a situation with high risk of physical or psychological harm to your child, yourself, or someone else. If your child presents with troubling, unusual symptoms or behaviors you do not understand, or if you have not sought professional help to address the problems that seem to be worsening or seem to potentially have more serious consequences, your risk could be greater.

Be prepared. The first thing you should do after closing this book is find out what is available in your community in terms of mental health, crisis, and other services.

Before the crisis, establish a relationship with a psychologist, psychiatrist, or physician in your community who is knowledgeable about your child. This way you will have a professional who can speak for your child in the event that other medical professionals or law enforcement personnel become involved.

Educate your local law enforcement officials about the fact that you have a child with an ASD and guide them to the resources available. (See also "Encounters with Law Enforcement and Other Authorities," page 489.) Before the crisis, pay a personal visit to your local police precinct and ask to speak with someone there about your child and AS.

Dennis Debbaudt, the father of a child with autism and a private investigator who is an authority on law enforcement issues and ASDs, also recommends that parents and adults with ASDs consider carrying with them at all times a small card, which you can type up and have laminated, that includes the following information:

the person's name,
the diagnosis and its basic symptoms and behaviors,
medications he may be taking,
your names and numbers as well as those of his doctors and school
    personnel who are familiar with him, and
particular sensitivities or extreme reactions (panic when touched, fear
    of sirens, and the like).

It should also indicate that people with AS may have difficulty understanding their legal rights, and that if arrested, your youngster must be protected from the general jail population. Teach your child that if he is approached by a law enforcement officer, firefighter, emergency medical technician, or other community helper, he should immediately tell the person that he has Asperger syndrome (or other ASD) and/or ask permission to hand that person the card. In some cases, it might be more helpful to use the word *autism* instead. Most community workers know what that is. It's possible that they may not consider Asperger syndrome as "serious" a problem.

Before the crisis, contact the local chapter of the Autism Society of America, any other autism- or mental health–related support group, and your local mental health department. Some organizations, institutions, and government offices can provide crisis teams of personnel especially trained to deal with people in psychiatric crisis. Some of these teams can come to your home or wherever the person in crisis is. Some of them can help you, for example, get someone to the hospital or doctor. Find out if such an organization exists in your community, contact them, and talk to someone on staff about your child. Find out when they are available, what services they provide, and if there is anything you must do to be eligible to receive their help. Some autism-specific crisis teams are funded through government grants and may treat only individuals who meet certain eligibility requirements.

Find out from your child's doctor the name of another doctor who could talk to authorities or medical personnel in the event that he himself is unavailable.

Find out which organizations and hospitals in your area have knowledgeable personnel on staff in the event that your child's doctor isn't available. You might want to contact the head of a local children's hospital or the pediatric department of a local mental health center, then speak with someone about your child and whether he or she would be willing to respond to other medical and law enforcement personnel in the event of an emergency.

Find out if your hospital has a staffed pediatric emergency room, pediatric psychiatric emergency room, and pediatric psychiatric department. If it does not, find one that does, if you can. It is not unusual for children with ASD in psychiatric crisis to spend some time in the hospital afterward.

During a crisis, keep calm and call for help the moment you sense the situation is veering out of control. If it is possible and safe, try to make contact with the local mental health center, your child's doctor, or a representative from a local autism or mental health organization before dialing 911. Try to have someone at your side who will be able to work as a liaison between your child and law enforcement or medical staff, if the need arises.

Some localities offer 911 identification systems, so that if you do need to call 911, those responding will be notified that your child has an autism spectrum disorder. If your community has such a system, have your child's condition entered today.

Always keep on your person or with you a brief written description of your child's condition, medication he may be taking, and situations or behaviors that may cause him to react adversely. Remember, you may not have an opportunity to discuss these points clearly in an emergency situation.

If your child is removed from your home or from school, try to accompany him and explain his disorder and its ramifications to everyone directly involved in his care. Be very vocal and clear about the fact that your child's ASD and related conditions may place him at high risk for an adverse reaction to psychotropic medication. Before anyone tries to "give him something to calm him down," demand that he or she first contact your child's doctor or another physician familiar with the disorder. This is especially important if he is currently taking or has recently taken psychotropic medications—both prescription and illicit.

If your child is held in a hospital under psychiatric observation, impress the need—with the help of your child's doctor, therapist,

369

or teacher—to make the environment as therapeutic as possible. Dr. Brenda Smith Myles suggests that familiar teachers can play an important role by spending time with the child and being part of the treatment team. In some settings, however, this is not possible. Some hospitals have their own teachers on staff, who are specially trained and work closely with your child's teacher to maintain his education during his stay. Also, sometimes visitors to such facilities are limited to family.

If your child is arrested, contact agencies and organizations for support and for referrals to attorneys who specialize in handling such cases. Again, your child's doctor should be involved, as should anyone who knows your child and can explain his behavior.

If you know that your child has a history of violent, self-injurious, or suicidal behavior; has made verbal or written threats against others; or has engaged in other behavior that could result in arrest (for instance, illicit drug or alcohol use, vandalism, property damage, theft, driving without a license, and so on), you should have an attorney already.

If you have a personal attorney, make sure that he is aware of your child's disability. It is better that your lawyer or someone in his or her firm be educated about Asperger syndrome before a crisis occurs.

Consider enrolling with MedicAlert. It's simple: by paying an annual membership fee and providing your child's health information, your child receives an inconspicuous personal item—a bracelet, pendant, wristband, dog tag, watch, shoe tag, and so on—that contains basic contact information (child's name, list of medical or psychiatric conditions, allergies, medications) plus the MedicAlert ID number that health care or law enforcement personnel can give at the service's toll-free, twenty-four-hour number to obtain more details. Once a medical professional contacts MedicAlert, a detailed form that you and your child's doctor fill out and submit to MedicAlert is relayed immediately. You can contact MedicAlert at www.medicalert.org or 888-633-4298.

HOW TO INCREASE YOUR
CHILD'S EMOTIONAL AWARENESS

Most people who don't have AS paint their emotional self-portraits and landscapes from a full palette. Not only can we automatically access dozens if not hundreds of shades of happiness, sadness, anger, joy, disappointment, fear, and surprise (to name only a few emotional states), but we can mix them and qualify them in infinite combinations to precisely describe our experience to ourselves and to others. Most of us understand the concept of having mixed feelings. We can be thrilled at the prospect of a new job yet reluctant to leave coworkers who have become friends. We are able to hold in our minds responses that, on the surface, seem to be in conflict, like the classic "love/hate" relationship.

In comparison, people with AS seem to have a far more limited emotional spectrum, with most of the shades concentrated at either end and few representing degrees of feeling that fall in between. The relationship between two conflicting emotions is more often than not an either/or proposition. As a result, the child with AS may respond to situations and people in ways that seem extreme, out of proportion, or inappropriately intense. Though no one has determined precisely why this occurs, experts agree that helping people with AS learn to recognize, understand, modulate, and express their emotions more appropriately is crucial.

Look for teachable moments every day, no matter where you are or what you are doing. There are many ways to teach a child with AS about emotion and to expand his emotional palette. Social Stories and Comic Strip Conversations, as well as social skills training and cognitive behavior therapy, can all help. Using pictures, photographs, and a mirror, you can teach your child not only how to read the facial expressions and gestures of others but how to mimic them appropriately. Through role-playing and watching and discussing videos, movies, or television programs, you can increase your child's understanding of tone of voice and body language, as well as broaden his understanding of how others think, feel, and may be expected to act. For children who have difficulty modulating their responses, creating an "emotion scale" that uses objects, symbols, numbers, or words to convey different degrees of, say, happiness or frustration can be very helpful.

Henry's Anger-mometer

Children with Asperger syndrome often have difficulty identifying, modulating, and expressing their feelings in a manner that is appropriate to a given situation. Devices like this anger scale can make the idea that there are different levels of any emotion concrete for children. It can also help them identify the conditions that warrant one degree of intensity as opposed to another.

Condition	How Angry Am I?	It Would Be Smart To (Choose all that you need!)
Red	I feel like hitting someone or something or running away.	Ask for time out in a safe place right now.
Orange	I feel like screaming or calling someone a bad name.	Ask for help right now. Take deep breaths.
Yellow	I felt like screaming for a moment, but I feel less angry now. I'm still thinking about it.	Sit down and try to remain quiet.
Green	I wish it didn't happen, but it won't ruin my day.	Tell someone how I feel right now.
Blue	All calm. I was annoyed for a minute, but it's over. I'm okay now.	Talk about it later. Ask to talk with Mom or Dad. Draw a comic strip or write a Social Story with someone now. Draw a comic strip or write a Social Story with someone later. Think about my dog Bert. Think about my favorite movies. Imagine resting safely in my underground secret laboratory (my bedroom).

Be your child's "emotional guide." Get into the habit of narrating and explaining your own emotional and social behavior. Telling a child who is inconsolable over the restaurant being out of chocolate mousse that he is "overreacting" teaches him nothing. However, you can use your own disappointment in a similar situation to teach. Instead of ordering blueberry pie when the waiter tells you the mousse is gone, let your child know what you're thinking. You might say to your child in an upbeat tone, "I was looking forward to the chocolate mousse, so I'm a little disappointed, but I'm glad they have blueberry pie. I like that, too. Sometimes restaurants and stores run out of things we want and we get the chance to have something else that we like. I know I'll get to have the mousse some other time."

Let your child know when you, too, are faced with situations that he finds problematic, such as handling a change in plans, disappointment, or misunderstandings. Expressing anger inappropriately is a common problem for children with AS. Beyond the obvious—not modeling behavior you don't want your child to copy, like slamming down the phone or shouting—you can narrate the thoughts, feelings, and decisions that help you handle your own reactions. "I'm sorry that your sister broke that special plate, but I know it was an accident. She said she was sorry, so I know that she feels bad about dropping it. Sometimes accidents happen to people even when they're being very careful. I wish the plate hadn't broken, but I'm not upset about it."

Remember the importance of generalization and how difficult it is for many of our children to carry over skills from one environment or situation to another. Your child may be learning a range of skills in different areas: how to greet friends in socialization, how to organize himself for work in school, how to tie his shoes in OT. Still, he needs you to help him learn to use them in the real world. Stay on top of what he is being taught and find out from his teachers, doctors, therapists, and others what you can do to help him practice his new skills and apply them more widely. Never underestimate the reinforcing power of basic, everyday activities. For a child with problems with visual discrimination, that could mean being given the "job" of finding his favorite flavor of ice cream in the supermarket freezer. A youngster with fine-motor issues can get a lot of practice just opening food packaging while you cook dinner or by buttoning his little sister's coat after he buttons his own.

Teach independence—which is the true root of lasting self-esteem—at every opportunity. Hard as it may be, resolve never to do for your child what she can do for herself, even if that means taking three minutes to put on a pair of socks or ten minutes to set the table. Do whatever you must to help your child become more self-reliant. Give your child ample opportunities to practice making decisions, dealing with consequences, and managing emotions.

When faced with a difficult situation, run down a mental checklist and determine how your child views the situation and what specific deficit or deficits might be at work. If the problem is executive function, then you need to focus on organization. If the social misunderstanding arises from an erroneous attribution, get out paper and the markers and draw that Comic Strip Conversation.

Is your child anxious about the changes in the school calendar that December brings? Make a calendar like the one on page 355. If there are questions about where Mom will be on the upcoming business trip, visit websites that might show the hotel where she will be staying or some of the places she will be going. Show your child that she has Mom's phone numbers and can reach her. Make a tentative schedule for calling her or plan to send an email to her every day she is away. Write a Social Story explaining why moms make business trips, stressing that she will be available and she will come home.

A FINAL WORD

It is not always easy to set clear priorities when it comes to addressing the many issues related to AS. However, regardless of how much your child may need this service or that treatment, your first priority should always be his mental health and emotional well-being. Free your child from the worries, anxieties, fears, and difficulties that you can. Teach him to understand, to cope with, and to compensate for those you cannot. Show him through your words and your actions that you not only love him, but also respect him, enjoy him, and value him. Let him know that he is a person who deserves the respect and the affection of others. Help him to build a foundation of self-esteem and confidence from which he can one day venture into the world on his own.

Chapter 8

YOUR CHILD IN THE SOCIAL REALM

ULTIMATELY, for all children and adults with AS, social skills and social difficulties will have a profound effect on virtually every aspect of their lives. When most of us think of social skills, we think in terms of our child learning to get along with others and to have personal relationships. In addition, social ability colors virtually every other experience. We have heard from many parents of children with AS and adults with AS whose opportunities for satisfying, meaningful education, employment, and recreation are often severely undermined by their poor social skills. Social skills difficulties have other repercussions. They make our children more vulnerable to those who would take advantage of them or do them harm; they render our children open to upsetting, even dangerous "misunderstandings"; and they make it easier for them to retreat from even positive, rewarding social interactions and relationships. According to Dr. Tony Attwood and Carol Gray, "A . . . study examined the perceived quality of life of high-functioning adults with autism and Asperger Syndrome, and only one variable, 'hours spent with friends,' was able to significantly predict the scores on any of the quality-of-life measures. These adults valued and desired friendships more than anything in their lives, yet few had the ability to maintain acquaintances, let alone friends."[1]

Clearly, children with AS need specific, explicit instruction in developing social skills. Participation in structured social skills group training and one-on-one cognitive behavior therapy can be extremely valuable, as can using tools such as Social Stories, Comic Strip Conversations, visual strategies, and theory-of-mind exercises. More than anything, however, our children need practice in social skills across the broadest range of experiences and situations possible. We must aggressively capitalize on every opportunity to teach, reinforce, practice, and increase our child's social ability.

That sounds great, right? However, when it comes to teaching someone social skills, most neurotypical people find themselves at a loss. We can figure out how to teach a child how to read, ride a bike, or tie his shoes, because these are skills we ourselves were taught by someone else or that we learned by observing others. There were certain steps involved, seemingly natural abilities already in place, prerequisite skills we developed from infancy on, because we could observe the behavior of others and apply our native theory of mind to understanding what we saw. Then we tapped these to develop ever more complex and sophisticated skills. Most of us feel, understandably, that social skills came naturally, and, in a sense, they did. If asked to explain what you observed that led you to assume that your best friend was reluctant to discuss her latest date, or how you figured out that the telephone solicitor's promise of a free Caribbean cruise was a scam, you would probably say, "I could just tell." But how? You probably don't know how you know, or if you do, you would need a few minutes to explain it.

Our minds automatically take apart every life experience and "file" its components—the thoughts, actions, emotions, and attitudes of ourselves and of others—for future use. Even more important, and remarkable, these components can be recombined in infinite combinations. We can apply what we learned about the bully on the elementary school playground to dealing with our boss, or apply our experience of being a child to the experience of raising a child, or apply our feelings of grief to comfort another. Or we can call upon information learned outside our own direct experiences to guide our responses. Even if we have never encountered the specific situation—for example, attending a religious ceremony that is different from our religion—we are able to draw on information we have read or heard about to help us know what to do. Even more important, we are able to look around the room and see how others are responding and adjust our behavior, attitude, tone of voice, facial expression, body language, and the words we use and how we say them accordingly.

To varying degrees, people with AS lack the ability to generalize, so that what is observed and retained (which may be limited to begin with) remains a discrete, unique event, the social and emotional components of which are not always broken down nor retrievable in "pieces" ready to be "reformulated" into a strategy for a future situation. In cooking terms, it would be like amassing a pantry Martha Stewart would envy, yet being unable to conceive of using the flour, sugar, eggs, milk, butter, vanilla, baking powder, and salt in anything but a particular sugar cookie recipe. In contrast, those of us with more typical social abilities whip those same ingredients into countless varieties of cookies, not to mention sweet rolls, cakes, and muffins.

A SPECIAL CHALLENGE FOR PARENTS

Since the social skills arena is usually the one in which our children's differences and deficiencies are the most glaringly obvious to others, if not to us, we—and our kids—may harbor painful memories of their social failures. At a certain age, children may also be reluctant to venture into social spheres that have been difficult for them. One mother we know says, "As much as I believe Sam could benefit from spending time on a quiet playground with a few good friends, we have such a history of 'disasters' there, he avoids it. And, if I'm honest, I admit that I'm secretly relieved. Just recalling the looks we got from other parents and kids, and the terrible meltdowns Sam had there through the years is enough to make me cry even today."

Encouraging children to participate in building social skills isn't always easy, and it's not hard to understand why. For someone with AS, it's difficult, frustrating work. It demands that he think and behave in ways that might be counter to his natural social instincts, and that alone can provoke anxiety. Most of all, though, the process of practicing social skills may be, from your child's point of view, a high-risk, low-reward venture. Just as more social exposure increases the chances for success, it also increases the opportunities for misunderstanding, embarrassment, and rejection. While it's never too late for a person with AS to benefit from social skills training, older children may be more resistant to starting therapy than younger ones are.

Though most parents can understand the need for expanding a child's social repertoire, some feel conflicted. As one father observed, "My twelve-year-old daughter says that she doesn't want or need friends. She says that she prefers to be alone. Part of me sympathizes with her and agrees that maybe this is just who she is. Another part of me, however, is always looking ahead and wondering, Does she prefer to be alone because it's so hard to be around other people? Or does she really want to have a friend or two but is afraid of trying?" Again, the familiar question arises: Is AS something to have or someone to be?

It is not uncommon for a child to be truly not interested in socializing with peers and then one day—typically in adolescence—to wake up and desire to have friends and to do the things they do. At the risk of stating the obvious, kids do grow up. Even if your ten-year-old's attitudes and tastes seem set in stone today, it's probably safe to assume that he will not feel exactly the same about most things as he does today. As kids enter their teens and meet peers outside school, they sometimes blossom. Meeting new people who have no memory of your kindergarten meltdowns or your emotional withdrawal in middle school presents a truly fresh start. (In fact, the chance to "start from scratch" socially is the one thing kids consider valuable about doing volunteer work, having a job, or starting college or job training.)

Also consider that your child's ambivalence toward engaging with peers might have been shaped by a host of factors: anxiety, depression, difficulty understanding the "hidden rules," lack of practice being among others, or the absence of one peer who is interested in him. Any one—or all—of those could change, thus making the first steps in this journey not only possible but desirable.

Teaching a child with AS about social skills requires a clear-eyed assessment of where he stands today. Understanding why your seven-year-old dominates the few playdates he has or why your preteen cannot talk to his peers without talking *at* them is useful only insofar as it leads you to the most appropriate intervention. If you find yourself saying, "Well, that's just the way she is" or "She has AS, and that's part of it," remember that "the way she is" without intervention may not be the way she "is" at all. It may be the only way she knows how to be *at present*. Social skills are learned.

SOCIAL SKILLS: THE BASICS

For most parents, the greatest advantage of a child's developing social skills is the ability to participate comfortably among peers and, they hope, to have and to become a friend. Though there are many components of what we term *social skills* (see chapter 4), and educational and therapeutic interventions should all involve some degree of social skills training, here we will focus on what parents can do.

Reinforcing Social Skills in Daily Life

In addition to Social Stories, Comic Strip Conversations, social skills training, and cognitive behavior therapy (all discussed in depth in chapter 4), there are other tools and techniques you may find helpful in building social skills.

Visual strategies. You can use drawings, calendars, charts, schedules, photo essays, and other visual tools to "show" as well as tell. For example, you might use a circle to indicate which people in your child's life are "close family," "family," "close friends," "friends," "neighbors," and "strangers," and describe what types of greetings, physical contact, or topics for opening conversation are appropriate for each.

Playing board games. Board games are fun and can provide good practice in basic social skills such as turn taking, listening, observing cues (for instance, whose turn it is to roll the dice), planning, and motor planning, among others. Cooperative games, as opposed to competitive games, require that two or more players work together toward a common goal. On the other hand, learning to win and learning to lose gracefully are extremely important skills, too.

Movies, videos, television programs. Movies and TV programs—particularly those on DVD or video, which can be paused, stopped, rewound, and repeated—can be used to draw your child's attention to and discuss many social skills–related topics. For younger children, programs such as *Sesame Street*, and old favorites such as *Mr. Rogers' Neighborhood*, *Blue's Clues*, and *Thomas the Tank Engine*, as well as films such as the *Toy Story* series, and others offer ample fodder for discussions about understanding the behavior, feelings, and thoughts of others. Because the narrative is often simple and the characters' facial expressions exaggerated, children with AS may find them easier to follow. For older children, just about anything that is not excessively stimulating, violent, or otherwise inappropriate may be rich with discussion possibilities.

Reruns of programs such as *Third Rock from the Sun*, *The Beverly Hillbillies*, *Mork and Mindy*, *Mr. Bean*, *My Favorite Martian*, and similar "fish out of water" comedies base their humor on the premise that the characters lack necessary social skills for the environment in which they find themselves. Not surprisingly, people with AS are often drawn to fictional characters struggling to understand an "alien" culture: Mr. Spock from the original *Star Trek* and Data from *Star Trek: The Next Generation*, as well as characters from other classic science-fiction TV series such as *Doctor Who*, *Babylon 5*, *Star Wars*, *Hitchhiker's Guide to the Galaxy*, *The Prisoner* (the original), and others. The current flood of movies and television series about comic book superheroes (*Smallville*, *The Justice League*, *Teen Titans*, *Spider-Man*, *X-Men*) often depict characters whose specialness is a double-edged sword and who work hard to make sense of the mere mortals whose world they must share. The Harry Potter movies (and books) provide many examples of characters who are not what they seem or whose motives are questionable. You can watch or read along and ask your child what makes him think that Gilderoy Lockhart is not really brave or Professor Snape is not really pleased to see Harry back at Hogwarts. Beyond discussing the obvious (the plot, the characters), you can also draw your child's attention to and talk about what a character means when he shrugs his shoulders or the different ways in which different characters greet each other. You can explore questions surrounding a character's thoughts, motivations, and feelings. How can you tell someone is lying? Why do you think she did that? What is that character "saying" without talking? What might happen next?

If possible, seek out videos and DVDs that touch on or include something of your child's special interest. Documentaries on even the most technical subjects, such as the development of the jet fighter or the history of the personal computer, usually have some human interest angle worked in. You can talk about what those involved in developing technology thought or felt about what they were doing.

Mirror work; audio and video recording. In a safe, relaxed atmosphere, working with your child in front of a mirror or recording and playing back his voice and/or image can help him get a sense of how he appears and sounds to others. With practice, children can be taught to modulate their voices and use an appropriate style of speech. You might practice how to say "no" to a friend's offer of ice cream, your brother's daring you to jump on the new couch, or a stranger's inappropriate advance. You can also teach and practice appropriate facial expressions, such as accompanying most greetings with a smile or using gestures appropriately with and without words. There is one "yuck" face appropriate at Grandmother's when the brussels sprouts get passed around that is quite different from the one you make when your brother puts ketchup on your ice cream. There is one hello for friends in church, another for those same friends out on the playground; one "I'm sorry" for accidentally breaking Mom's favorite vase, and something quite different for your teacher whose father passed away.

Mirror work and recording are also good for learning to express and interpret the different meanings of the same sentence when you change the volume, cadence, tone of voice, stress, and facial expression. For instance:

I didn't know you wanted the red apple today.
Meaning: You are mistaken. You didn't tell me that you wanted the red apple today.

I **didn't know** you wanted the red apple today.
Meaning: I really didn't know you wanted the red apple today; I'm not lying.

I didn't know **you** wanted the red apple today.
Meaning: I'm sorry I gave it to Suzy. I didn't know you wanted it.

I didn't know you **wanted** the red apple today.
Meaning: I didn't think you cared whether you got the red apple or not.

I didn't know you wanted the **red** apple today.
Meaning: I thought a green apple or a yellow apple would be okay; you didn't tell me the apple had to be red.

I didn't know you wanted the red **apple** today.
Meaning: I thought you wanted the red grapefruit or the red pear.

I didn't know you wanted the red apple **today.**
Meaning: I planned to go grocery shopping tomorrow; you didn't tell me that you wanted it for today.

Regular comic strips, comic books, and graphic novels. Because they tell a story with visuals as well as words, comic strips, comic books, and graphic novels can also be used in teaching some social skills. Unlike movies and television programs, comics have the ability to show what a character is thinking and saying and doing in the same "frozen" frame. Obviously, some comics are more suited to this than others, depending on your child's age, reading ability, interests, and so on. If your child has anger management issues, you might steer clear of comics that contain violence or feature characters whose behavior you do not want to see imitated. I have used *Batman* comic books from the 1940s and 1950s to help my son understand the relationship among thought, word, and action because they are graphically less impressionistic and less violent than later versions. (Another added benefit: a surprisingly rich vocabulary and the frequent use of colorful appositives—something people with AS have trouble with—such as "mirthful menace," "killer clown," "grim jester," along with "villain," "criminal," and "nemesis," for the Joker.)

Novels, short stories, some journalistic accounts. Both fiction and nonfiction can be used as springboards for discussions about emotions, thoughts, feelings, and beliefs. Because prose usually lacks accompanying visuals, it may not be accessible to all children. However, for children who have sound comprehension skills, any well-told story can be explored in terms of perspective taking and point of view, the relationship between what characters mean and what they say, what they think and what they do, and so on. Reading aloud stories that are rich in dialogue and "acting out" the lines is another way to sharpen speech skills, particularly when it comes to tone of voice, stress, and volume. For younger children, you can contrast the imperious attitude and voice of Yertle the Turtle to the growing frustration of the otherwise mild-mannered Mack in *Yertle the Turtle*, or use the Mr. and Miss Books series (*Mr. Silly, Mr. Grumpy, Mr. Sad*). For older kids, characters in Harry Potter books, Judy Blume books, the Wayside School series, the Encyclopedia Brown series (there's always a bully and a good guy), and the Boxcar Children are good choices.

Music. Good music of any genre can inspire emotions and thoughts. If your child likes music, view it as another platform from which to launch discussions about feelings and ideas. If it's instrumental music, explore what your child thinks the music is "saying" or what story it's "telling." If the music has lyrics, talk about what the song is saying, how it says it, what the singer may be thinking or feeling. Is it the same as the words she sings? Or is it different? How can you tell? If you can, try presenting your child with two different versions of the same song and talk about what makes them sound and "feel" different. Or take a simple song your child knows well and ask him to sing or hum it "happy," "angry," "disappointed," or "scared," even if the words don't fit.

Helping others. Kids with AS tend to receive more adult attention in the form of reminding, prompting, and assisting than typical kids their age do. As a result, they may lack opportunities to be the person providing the help instead. When we help others, it's a guaranteed positive social exchange. It gives us an opportunity to be valued and to feel appreciated. Whether your child is doing chores around the house or your middle schooler is volunteering with you at the local food pantry, helping others brings a wealth of benefits to your child.

BREAKING DOWN BASIC SOCIAL BARRIERS

All the world is a stage, and we are all players. While great minds ponder the many meanings Shakespeare intended, for parents of children with Asperger syndrome, it really boils down to scripts and rehearsal. It may take a highly structured approach to teach certain social skills. However, once your child begins to get it, you should work equally hard at helping him learn to generalize what he has learned and apply it to many different situations.

Most of us recognize the need to prompt and prepare children for events outside the daily routine: birthday parties, vacations, doctor's appointments, the first day of school. Beyond giving a general rundown of what will happen, it's equally important to talk about where and when the event will occur, who may be there, and who your child can go to if he has a question or needs help, and any specific concern your child may have. (Does the place have a restroom? An alarm system in case of fire? Food? A water fountain?) Be sure to ask specifically, "Is there anything you feel you need to know about the party?" You may be surprised by what you hear. One mother told us that her son Zack avoided birthday parties through the third grade. She assumed the noise and commotion were simply too much for him. One day he said, "I would like to go to Kari's party, but I hate pepperoni." It took his mother a few minutes to make the connection. When he was five, they served pepperoni pizza at the last party he attended, and since then, he has assumed that all birthday parties serve pepperoni pizza—and that he has to eat it. No wonder the Social Stories his mother wrote and the explanations she offered him about balloons, clowns, candles, and kids screaming "Happy Birthday" hadn't worked.

When you prepare your child to go somewhere, keep details

that are subject to change general. Say "Many of your classmates will be at David's party," rather than "Joey and Sam will be there," or "The party will end sometime between four and five o'clock," rather than "The party ends precisely at four."

Once again, we turn to our old and constant friend, the teachable moment. A mother who often took her daughter Cindy out for lunch started with teaching her how to ask the waitress for the check—which requires looking for the waitress, politely signaling to get her attention, requesting the check, *please*, and saying "Thank you" (being sure to do so while making eye contact). Once Cindy mastered that, her mother taught her how to order in a restaurant. Again, it was a great mini-lesson in watching another person for the cues that signal "your turn," listening for and responding to questions about the order, saying "Thank you," and so on.

Cindy became a favorite at one restaurant, with staff and strangers commenting on how polite and well mannered she was. That became a lesson in recognizing, accepting, and acknowledging compliments. One day her mother was pleasantly surprised to hear Cindy say to the waitress, "Thanksgiving is next week. Are you going to spend it with your family?"

"Why, yes," the waitress replied. "How about you?"

"Oh, I'm going to my grandmother's. She makes pumpkin pie. Do you like pumpkin pie?"

"I sure do."

"Okay." Then after a few seconds of silence, Cindy looked up again and chirped, "Have a nice Thanksgiving!"

"You, too."

Once Cindy became comfortable with the "restaurant routine," her mother helped her adapt it to the doughnut shop, the pizza parlor, the bakery, the ice cream store, and the fast-food place—each of which presented its own variations on the basic theme. Next on Mom's agenda: paying for the food, waiting for change, saying "Thank you" again; after that, counting out the money and checking the change.

BULLYING AND TEASING

People with AS and related disorders are even more likely to be targets of teasing, harassment, and bullying of both a verbal and physical nature. As parents, we had long suspected as much, but with the recent focus on the subject, we now have real studies that confirm what many of us, sadly, knew too well all along: kids with autism are more likely to be bullied. Further, because of difficulties with recall, language, expressing emotions, and knowing how to get help, they are also less likely to be able to report being bullied, provide a good account of what occurred, or, in some cases, even identify their tormentor.

There is truth to the saying that there is "safety in numbers." Victims of bullying and teasing are likely to be those children on the perimeters of social groups, the loners, the children who don't fit and are perceived by their peers as being "different." There are certain times and areas where teasing and bullying are much more likely to occur—unstructured and less closely supervised times at school such as lunch, recess, in school hallways, in bathrooms, in locker rooms, and on the bus; anywhere your child might be perceived by his attacker as "alone" or without help. For example, some students find the walk to and from school the worst time of day. Too often school districts take the position that what happens "off school property" is not their responsibility. These are the times when most children with AS face the greatest challenges socially and are the most vulnerable.

Too often teachers, family members, and friends seem to believe that children with AS will learn appropriate social behavior if they find themselves shunned or teased by other children. One mother reported that when she told her son's teacher about an incident in which a bully called her son a "retard" and pushed him on the playground, the teacher first refused to believe the incident had occurred, then added, "Well, your son *is* different and it bothers the other children." Other parents have reported numerous occasions in which the response to their complaints about teasing have amounted to blaming the child with AS for "bringing it on himself" by essentially being who he is. None of these responses is acceptable—from children or adults—or should go unchallenged.

When bullying and teasing are not stopped, the child with AS may be provoked to respond in kind or be forced to defend himself physically. Unfortunately, the chances are good that the person(s) provoking your child are socially savvy enough to "hide their tracks," so that all a teacher or other witness sees is your child responding, not the provocation he is responding to. The child with AS who does fight back may be viewed as the aggressor and not the victim. And, even if justified, his response might be more intense— louder, more forceful, more prolonged—and less discreet than that of another kid (namely, the kid who would not get caught).

In today's school climate of "zero tolerance," a child who in frustration does fight back or act out risks suspension, expulsion, and perhaps even involvement of law enforcement officials (see the box titled "Zero-Tolerance Policies in Schools," page 418). Although some experts contend that zero-tolerance policies do not increase safety, they seem to be here to stay. When older children are bullied in junior high and high school, quite often the bullying goes unreported, out of fear that "telling" will make the abuse worse.

We know of families who have opted to homeschool rather than continue to subject their children to constant harassment from bullies. While incidents of both verbal and physical bullying occur at all grade levels, parents of children with AS report that incidents seem to peak during the junior high school years. This is not to say that bullying stops in high school, but parents report that it's much more likely that their teen is teased and rejected than physically attacked.

Unfortunately, bullying and teasing aren't confined to peers. All too often, children and adults with ASDs are subjected to teasing and harassment from adults, teachers, coaches, friends, and family members who persist with the misguided belief that they can embarrass or shame someone into "acting normal." Siblings of children with disabilities are often teased as well.

It is *imperative* that our children and their siblings be protected from both physical and emotional abuse from anyone. The good news is that around the country awareness about bullying has increased dramatically. The bad news, of course, is that these developments were prompted by a seemingly never-ending series of news items about children and teens whose suicides or violent rampages were preceded by bullying.

Bullying and Teasing: How Parents Can Help

We urge all parents to have an IEP or Section 504 plan in place that specifically recognizes that a child with limited social skills and other disabilities may be especially vulnerable to teasing and bullying and that addresses how bullying and teasing will be handled. This statement should also include forms of cyberbullying, such as texting to your child's cell phone, sending emails, and engaging through social media.

- Be aware of where and when bullying is most likely to occur. Make sure that there is proper supervision during recess and lunch, before and after school, between classes, and in areas such as hallways, playgrounds, restrooms, locker rooms, and on the bus.
- Know that social media (Facebook, Twitter, and so on—there are new formats, services, and sites cropping up weekly) provide a platform for bullying behavior that not only defies the laws of space and time—they put your child within the bully's "reach," no matter where she is—but that often elude the laws of criminal behavior, too. Unfortunately, in most areas, law enforcement and laws currently on the books have not yet caught up with this relatively new form of harassment and intimidation.
- Through the ability to copy, share, forward, and blog, the cyberbully is often reinforced by an "audience" for his behavior potentially a hundred times larger than the biggest crowd he could attract on the playground or at the bus stop. Experts agree: whether peers are active, enthusiastic participants, or scared, silent bystanders, their presence and interest embolden the bully. It is no coincidence that cyberbullying is often cited in cases where victims attempted or committed suicide.
- Document incidents of bullying and report them to school officials. Remind your school district personnel—orally and in writing—that an atmosphere of harassment constitutes a violation of your child's right to a free appropriate public education. Make it clear the first time you contact them that you will pursue the matter as far as necessary.

- If your school district is unresponsive or unable to protect your child, report incidents to local law enforcement officials. We know of several families who discovered that the harassment did not stop until they involved the police. This may not be the best first response, but if your child is in danger, you may have no choice. Also keep in mind that a police car pulling up in front of a bully's house makes an impression on his parents that notes and calls from school alone might not.
- Call a lawyer who specializes in special education law. Your child is being teased and harassed because of his disability, and the school's failure to protect your child may constitute a form of discrimination.
- Be aware that bullying may be happening to siblings of your child with AS. They may be too frightened or embarrassed to tell you. Be very clear with all of your children: teasing and bullying are not acceptable, and you can and will protect them.
- Carefully weigh what you teach your child about how to handle teasing and bullying. A number of books on the market outline how to "bully-proof" your child, but these tactics may be ineffective for our children, who may not have the skills to carry them off. Social skills training often addresses this very issue, teaching skills such as the right "comeback," how to find help, and ways to behave that may discourage bullying. Be aware that among certain groups, ignoring bullying behavior—something some bullying programs and well-meaning advisors promote—can be interpreted as the ultimate sign of disrespect and a provocation.

THE BASIC SOCIAL SKILLS

Different experts have different opinions of what constitutes a basic social skills repertoire. Unfortunately, there are few widely available, basic resources that outline a comprehensive step-by-step program for teaching social skills. (See "Recommended Resources" on page 239.) You'll doubtless devise a program using a number of different interventions. You can help your child most, however, by looking through "Asperger eyes" at every conceivable social opportunity and finding a way to make the world make sense to her and, equally, help her to be better understood by the world.

A good place to start is assessing your child's current level of social ability. Dr. Tony Attwood and Carol Gray list the following behaviors as crucial components of effective social interaction or, as they term them, "friendship skills":

Friendship Skills

1. Entry skills
2. Assistance
3. Compliments
4. Criticism
5. Accepting suggestions
6. Reciprocity and sharing
7. Conflict resolution
8. Monitoring and listening
9. Empathy
10. Avoiding and ending

Entry Skills: Learning How to Join In

When it comes to approaching other children, or responding to another child's approach, many children with AS don't know where to begin. You can see their discomfort as they remain on the sidelines of the action, fail to pick up on the invitations (verbal and nonverbal) to join, or seem to ignore a peer who expresses an interest in them or what they're doing. This inability to connect stops the action before it even has a chance to start. A child who doesn't respond to social overtures may be viewed as rude or uninterested.

How parents can help. Chances are, there are situations in which your child joins in or invites others to join him. For many children with AS, that may occur only at home, with family. If that's the case, talk with your child, perhaps using a Social Story or a Comic

390

Strip Conversation, about what he's doing right. For example, "I notice that when you see your little sister Jasmine doing something you want to do, you first get her attention by saying 'Hi, Jasmine,' or 'Excuse me, Jasmine,' and then you ask her if you can color, too. That's a friendly thing to do. You can also say those same things to your cousins, and kids at school, no matter what they're doing."

Sometimes people with AS simply miss the social cues, partly because they don't recognize them and they pass by quickly. For children who are more literal minded, hearing someone say, "Do you play ball?" "Are you a good catcher?" "We're short a few guys today," or "I haven't seen you here before" doesn't sound anything like "Would you like to join our game?" Be sure that when you consider the social situations your child may encounter, you cover other possible verbal cues. For some kids with AS, "Cake?" "Are you hungry?" "Got room in that tummy for dessert?" or "Do you like cake?" don't automatically translate into "Would you like a piece of cake?"

Through looking at pictures, watching videos, or drawing a Comic Strip Conversation, you can stop time, so to speak, and spend minutes pointing out and explaining the dozens of ways in which a few seconds' communication said, "Welcome. Would you like to play?" With the help of friends and family members, you can "stage" situations so that your child can practice his skills.

Assistance: Learning How to Ask for and Offer Help

Children with AS aren't always aware that someone else may know or be able to do something that they do not. This may prevent them from seeking assistance from others. Because a child with AS may not be able to read the "signs" that someone else needs help—an expression of confusion, frustration, sadness, crying, and so on—he also misses opportunities to offer help. Seeking and providing help are basic social exchanges that we use to do everything from asking strangers for directions to starting a conversation that sparks a friendship.

How parents can help. Remind your child when he can or should ask others for help. Identify for him the types of people in different situations who may be helpful: in the doctor's office, the nurse; in the store, the clerk; at the movies, the cashier, the usher, the ticket taker, the snack bar attendant. Teach a number of possible "opening lines"—"Excuse me. I was wondering if you could help me?" "Can you help me, please?"—as well as the appropriate tone of voice, posture, gestures, and so on. Some people with AS worry that they will "look stupid" to others. Remind your child that asking for help is always a smart thing to do.

As for teaching your child how to offer assistance, focus on the signals that indicate someone needs help. Using various visual media—photographs, videos, mirror, video recording—point out to your child the signs that someone might want assistance: everything from a polite "Excuse me" to a scream for help. Teach your child to respond appropriately and talk about what constitutes a friendly, helpful response. Discuss those situations in which he should seek out help in turn (a playmate getting hurt, an emergency) and how he would go about that (shouting, finding and telling an adult).

Around the house and out in the world with your child, ask for more help than you really need. In some situations where your meaning will be clear, pause and look at your child expectantly. If he doesn't get it right away, offer a cue: "I'm standing here at the kitchen sink and my hands are wet. What could you get for me, please?" My son learned to open doors for others simply by my stopping dead in my tracks on our way into every store, restaurant, movie theater, and so on that we went to. No talking, no nagging. You would be happily surprised at how many strangers complimented him on his great manners. He sure was!

Unfortunately, peers and adults who seek to take advantage often initiate their contact with a request for help. Studies have shown that even typical older children who have been well trained to recognize "stranger danger" will respond to a child molester's plea for help: for example, to help him find his lost puppy. Teaching any child how to distinguish a legitimate, friendly request from a dangerous one is difficult. You might begin by explaining that while it's good to help certain people in certain situations (classmates in school or at play, or an adult you know), there are other times when "helping" isn't appropriate. It's easy enough to tell your child never to help anyone do anything that is dangerous or wrong, yet it may be impossible for her, in the moment, to recognize the potential danger. Using a Social Story format, a list, or a chart, you might outline the types of help different people might ask them for, how they would act, and what it's okay to help with: sister putting on her skates, the postman asking you to carry in the family's mail, your friend asking you to help him finish his Lego castle. Then you might talk about the types of people and requests for help that are never okay: someone asking you to keep a secret, a stranger asking you to go someplace with him or her, anyone asking to let them touch you or asking you to touch them. Obviously, it gets tricky, because, statistically, children are taken advantage of and abused by people they know far more commonly than by strangers. And how do you make it clear that it's a good thing to keep the secret about Mom's birthday party but not a good thing to keep the one about the beer the school bully tried to coax him to drink? Unfortunately, there are no hard-and-fast rules. Just keep talking about, teaching, and demonstrating it whenever you can.

Compliments: Learning How to Offer Them and Accept Them

The inability to offer and graciously receive compliments shuts down another bridge to initiating and maintaining social relationships. A child who doesn't acknowledge compliments may appear snobbish, aloof, or simply mean. We may wonder why it's so difficult for our children to give (and sometimes receive) compliments, when it seems, on the surface at least, to be such a simple act. However, in her *Gray's Guide to Compliments*, Carol Gray explains that there are three types of compliments: on appearance; on skills, talents, and efforts; and on personality. The basic compliment involves two people (the sender and the recipient) and three parts: (1) noticing, (2) paying a compliment, and (3) the response.

Breaking down a compliment into steps is a good way to help our children learn how to make them. Compliments serve many social functions beyond the obvious. We usually think of a compliment as a means of showing someone that we like or care about them, but a compliment can also be a means of acknowledging someone's efforts, shoring up his confidence, cheering him up, taking the edge off a disagreement, or repairing a social faux pas.

People with AS may not automatically recognize situations that call for compliments, or they may not understand the point of telling someone something they "already know." As one eight-year-old observed, "My dad knows I like his cinnamon toast because I eat it. Why do I have to tell him again?" By the same token, they may not recognize the true intention—the unspoken communication—behind a compliment they receive. "I *know* this is a cool shirt," one young teenager said, "so why is she telling me?" It has been noted that people with AS may respond to compliments by appearing visibly uncomfortable, giving too little acknowledgment, or ignoring them altogether.

How parents can help. Be generous and specific in compliments you pay to your child; express your appreciation through your gestures as well as your words. You may even want to tell your child why you are complimenting him while you're at it, since for some people with AS the "why" of compliments is not always clear. "Good job not shouting in the car" is just not as good as "I really like the way you sat quietly during the car ride. I know it's not always easy for you, and I know you tried very hard. I appreciate the extra effort you put into that. It made it a pleasant ride for everyone."

In their important article "The Discovery of 'Aspie' Criteria," Carol Gray and Tony Attwood remind us that when we compliment our kids, it's best to note those qualities and accomplishments they value. A child who values his intelligence may very well appreciate a compliment on how smart he is over a compliment on how well he sat down during the test, even though you may feel that the good behavior is the greater accomplishment. They suggest mentioning the talent itself when you acknowledge social achievements. For example: "How smart of you to remember to raise your hand when you needed to ask a question."[2]

The types of compliments that may be more meaningful for your child may change over time. For quite a while now, I've gotten a lot of mileage out of telling Justin how his socially appropriate behaviors are "cool" and "like what a teenager would do." That worked when he had a small circle of friendly preteen and teenage family friends, sitters, and acquaintances (camp counselors, social skills group helpers, and so on) he admired. As he got older and began thinking about girls, "Girls really appreciate that," and, conversely, "That would turn a lot of girls off" worked, too. For older teenagers, letting them know that what they've done is something a teacher or a boss would appreciate doesn't hurt, either.

Talk to your child about compliments, explaining that they do seem illogical sometimes, but they are a way to let others know that we care about them and appreciate them. Stress that paying and receiving compliments is a friendly and smart thing to do, because most people like to receive and give compliments. Remind your child that even if something is "obvious" to a person with AS, those of us who do not have AS have a "problem," in that we often need to be told certain things we already know (that my dress is pretty) or that may or may not be entirely true (that it looks great on me) in this particular, illogical, redundant way. And then point out occasions to compliment, and prompt your child, if necessary, to practice the art.

Criticism: Learning How to Understand and Respond to It

This is a difficult issue for children with AS for many reasons. Because of a lack of social understanding, a person with AS may criticize another person unintentionally, usually as a result of being blatantly honest. A child with AS may tell his chess-playing friend, "That was a dumb move," whereas a typical child might suggest, "Are you sure that's the move you want to make?" or "Did you see this move?" As discussed previously, children with AS usually have not built up an arsenal of social "sweeteners" (asking questions, making suggestions, using less highly charged words) with which to blunt or disguise a critical remark. Nor do they always know what *not* to say. For those who like rules, old saws such as "If you can't say something nice about someone, don't say anything" can be helpful.

As objects of criticism—or what they perceive to be criticism—

kids on the spectrum can be extremely sensitive. Some have a lot of difficulty interpreting a difference of opinion as anything but a criticism of them personally. The supposed esteem-saving value of such parental standbys as "I'm not upset with you, I'm upset with your behavior," may not be as clear or as effective as you might hope. As parents, we feel that part of this is due to the fact that most children with AS are the recipients of so much help, intervention, correction, reminding, prompting, and discussion about what they say and do that they reach a point of overload. Although it may seem obvious that we and others are just trying to help, most children past a certain age understand that no one "helps" or tries to "fix" what isn't wrong, broken, or could stand improvement. Problems with pragmatics and reading social cues may also cause a child with AS to see criticism in innocuous comments. Ten-year-old Peter became furious when his friend said, "Bet you can't beat me at Wii today." Instead of interpreting it as a friendly invitation to play a video game, Peter took it literally and as an insult.

Parents frequently mention that in addition to having difficulty telling the difference between a friendly suggestion and criticism, their children often seem to misinterpret the volume of the speaker's voice. Numerous times when I was speaking to my son in a completely calm voice, he responded, "Quit yelling at me!"

Learning to handle criticism takes on additional importance as our kids enter their teens. Those who intend to pursue part-time jobs while in school, begin career training, go to college, or get a job after graduation need to learn to understand criticism in even greater complexity. In the world beyond school, you encounter a number of people who have the right and in some cases an obligation to point out your shortcomings. These are called bosses, job coaches, professors, instructors, and sometimes customers, co-workers, and classmates. As kids get older, they may require explicit instruction and a good deal of practice to develop the knack for hearing legitimate criticism and responding to it appropriately.

How parents can help. First, monitor how much criticism your child receives and over what. Criticism laced with hyperbole, sarcasm, anger, and coldness is never appropriate. If you don't do so already, get in the habit of offering necessary criticism in a caring, constructive way that protects your child's self-esteem. Model accepting criticism, too: "You know, your father's right. I should have put the garbage out last night after dinner. I said that I would, so I can understand why he's a little annoyed."

Explain to your child and model what constitutes acceptable criticism and what does not. Help her to distinguish between criticism of something someone does or thinks and criticism of who they are (which is a very sensitive point for many with AS). Rather than saying, "Don't tell your friend Greg you think *The Hunger Games* is stupid!" expand the concept and offer alternatives. "It's okay not to like what Greg likes. Everybody likes different things. Friends just have to like each other; they don't have to like everything the other friend likes. One way to be a good friend is to tell Greg that *The Hunger Games* isn't your kind of movie and that you'd rather watch something you both like. Or you can take turns watching the movies you each like."

Pay attention to the role of pragmatics in "misinterpretations" and work on making your child aware of the many ways in which people say the same things. Also teach him to recognize criticism that is unacceptable, personal, and intended to hurt.

Avoid the tendency to overexplain or repeat yourself. Give your child time to absorb the suggestion before you start talking again. Keep your suggestions clear, short, and to the point.

Learning How to Accept Suggestions

Being able to listen to, consider, and adopt other ways of doing things is a crucial skill, from the playground to the boardroom. Children with AS may have three different challenges in learning how to accept suggestions. One is that they may be interested only in doing things their way. Those who are particularly locked into strict, ritualistic patterns of play may become upset at any suggestion that something be done differently. The second problem arises when a child interprets a suggestion of an alternate activity or way of doing something as a personal criticism. A third possible problem is the belief some of our kids have that there is only one "right" way to do something or that there is a "rule" that applies and supersedes any other approach. Although holding fast to the "one right way" position can come across as snobbism or worse, it is often the result of your child's inability to generalize or improvise. Another point to consider is that sticking fast to "the one way" is a good hedge against unpredictability and, in some cases, failure.

How parents can help. Model flexibility by soliciting suggestions from your child and compliment him when you accept one: "Hmm, do you think we should drive home the long way or take the highway?" You might say, "I really like to take the highway because it's faster, but your idea to take the long way home is a good one. Look at all the great trees and gardens we get to see. I'm glad I listened to you. That was a great suggestion. Thank you." If your child has problems accepting suggestions from others, make a point of practicing them in low-stakes situations that you know he isn't sensitive about or that can be fun (dessert-first dinners, extra TV or video time, for instance). The point is to show your child that suggestions can have good outcomes. When you think about it, many things that don't appear to be suggestions can be dressed up to look like them for the sake of practice. Instead of saying "You can have an extra cookie," try, "May I make a suggestion? How about another cookie?"

Prior to playdates and other social occasions, remind your child that we can do only what we want to do when we are alone but that being with friends and others means we have to take turns. If you can anticipate a friend's interests, talk with your child about some of the possibilities ahead: "You know, Dan really likes your toy robot. He may ask to play with it," or "If you want to play with trains and Dan wants to build a tent in the den, we could make the train run in and out of the tent and pretend it's a secret cave. What do you think of that?"

When your child does accept suggestions and demonstrates flexibility in play, praise her specifically and generously, pointing out how much fun both she and her friend had. Also focus on teaching your child how to rephrase his requests and demands in the form of suggestions, as well as how to adopt the appropriate tone of voice. Remind him that just like him, people prefer to be told something in a nice, friendly way.

At the same time, teach your child to understand a bit about why a friend might want to do things *his* way. Sometimes letting a friend have his way is the nice thing to do.

Learning to Share and to Reciprocate

Most people would name sharing—of time, ideas, activities, objects, interests—as the essential foundation of friendship or membership. However, many children with AS experience the social world differently, so they're limited in their ability to derive the full emotional, social, and cognitive benefit of what they do experience. Among the AS-related problems that may affect a child's ability to interact with others are one-sided conversational style (usually related to the special interest); lack of spontaneous curiosity about or interest in the thoughts, feelings, and behavior of others; aversion to new or novel situations and activities; insistence on sameness and routine; and difficulty understanding the purpose of "small talk" and other social exchanges that do not seem "logical."

How parents can help. Using Social Stories, pre–social event prompting, and postevent review and encouragement, explicitly explain to your child what constitutes appropriate behavior. If there is a behavior that you consider inappropriate, discuss why (in terms of how it would make the other person feel if, for example, "you sat alone in the corner and read your *Titanic* books"), and in what situations that behavior would be appropriate ("in your room before bedtime"). Point out to your child any and every time someone shares something with him—be it a joke, a smile, or a cupcake— and don't forget about yourself, family members, teachers, friends, and others.

You might consider substituting words such as *share, trade, exchange,* and *cooperate* for some of the less descriptive terms we usually use. For example, rather than "I'm going to tell you what happened when I took Sparky to the vet today," say "I'm going to share with you what happened with Sparky at the vet today. I know you care about Sparky and would like to know." Or instead of "I see you're reading a book about Cheap Trick. What do you think?" try posing questions that will lead to others (not "yes," "no," or "I don't know") and giving answers in which you model an appropriate response (such as answers with "because" clauses). You might say, "I like Cheap Trick, too. Let's trade thoughts. I'll ask you a question, and then you ask me one. What's your favorite Cheap Trick song?"

"'Surrender.' What's your favorite song?" (Prompting may be required for some children to ask the question: "It's your turn to ask me a question," "I want to share my thoughts with you, but I can't if you don't ask me.")

"It makes me feel good that you asked [smile]. Thank you for asking. I like 'Surrender,' and I also like the theme song to *The Colbert Report* because of the guitar sound. Why do you like 'Surrender'?"

"I like 'Surrender' because it's about having parents who are cool. I also like the guitars on it."

"Hmm. I guess we both like guitars."

One way parents can help their children is by gently imposing limitations on common AS conversational styles that make reciprocity impossible. Setting rules for special interest talk and activity is an important one. It would be unfair, however, to limit talk among those who share the special interest. But even then, your child should learn the socially appropriate way to discuss the special interest and any other topic.

Try to restrict special interest talk to two times a day, for no more than five to ten minutes each time, and only after the completion of specific chores (for instance, being ready for school in the morning, setting the dinner table). You can expand this time as a reward for good behavior or other accomplishments, though you should never reduce or take it away as punishment. One family has also built into the special interest exchange other social skills practice:

- Asking a listener if it's a good time to talk about it (and handling delays and refusals appropriately), as opposed to simply launching in;
- Pausing to answer the listener's questions and responding to the listener's comments, which greatly reduces the run-on, one-sided nature of the talk;
- Noticing and observing the listener's cues that it's time to wind it up (the listener breaking eye contact, humming,

crossing his arms in front of his chest, distractedly saying, "uh-huh").

When the child fails to pick up on the cues, parents should verbally draw his attention to them: "I'm looking away and humming. That's how I'm letting you know that I would like to talk about something else." In this case, long-winded, seemingly endless monologues have gotten shorter as the parents give their most enthusiastic praise for "a good ending."

When it comes to sharing objects, time, or a third party's attention, children with AS may act immaturely for their age. Here again, the solution is making your child aware of the value of sharing in terms of how it makes others feel, and reassuring him that he isn't "losing" anything. This is sometimes a difficult concept because some children with AS see things in black and white and may be limited by certain play and behavior "rituals." Tony Attwood has identified this as the "Frank Sinatra syndrome" because everything has to be "my way."

Eight-year-old Eddie was extremely possessive of his favorite toys (a toy airport, airplanes, and related things) and was distressed when anyone interfered with his play. After a series of playdates in his home that ended in full-blown tantrums over his friend's playing with "his" toys, his mother wisely arranged for playdates in other children's homes (with her present). After each, she would remind her son that someone had shared with him and talk to him about how good it felt. She also realized that Eddie was worried that his play guest would abscond with his toys, so she reminded him many times that while he did get to play with Joey's Nintendo DS, he didn't take it home with him; Joey still had it. When Eddie was ready to have guests at his home, his mother removed the toys he was most possessive of, leaving him and his friend a large selection of "neutral" toys. If Eddie asked about his airplanes, she would offer him two—one for him and one for his friend—on the condition that they take turns sharing. Once Eddie's guest left, his mother reminded him that no one had taken his toys and that he also had fun playing with other things. As Eddie got older and began to treasure his playdates, his mother would include him in the planning and ask, "Tell me which toys you think you will have a hard time sharing. I don't want them to spoil your great playdate with Jordan."

Eventually Eddie felt secure enough that he could share his favorite toys and even play with them in different ways.

One mother found that "formalizing" her daughter's role in the playdate has been helpful. She is officially "the hostess" and now very much enjoys being told she was "an excellent hostess" and specifically why. Another unexpected benefit is that it has paved the way for discussions about the role of a host and that of a guest, and how they are different. (For starters, the rules of the house you are in prevail.)

Learning to Avoid, Recognize, and Resolve Conflicts

Conflict resolution, a skill that rarely comes naturally to any of us, is essential for people with AS. Their social deficits place them at increased risk for misunderstandings while at the same time leaving them with few, if any, effective strategies for avoiding conflict or resolving it appropriately. Every one of the "Friendship Skills" listed on page 390 should be considered an essential component of a conflict resolution "program."

Two of the more socially stigmatizing aspects of AS are the inability to consider different opinions or ways of doing things and the inability to express disagreement in a socially appropriate manner. Unfortunately, these deficits are too often read by others as stubbornness, arrogance, hostility, or worse. People with AS sometimes perceive personal criticism or rejection where none is intended. They may have difficulty seeing the difference between a disagreement with their idea and a dislike of them personally. One mother recalled her daughter Caroline becoming angry when a playmate declined to share in her daughter's favorite snack. Even though her friend said she just wasn't hungry, Caroline felt rejected and hurt. Another mom discovered her twelve-year-old son, Tom, screaming at his younger brother, Carl, because Carl wanted to watch a favorite television program. Even though Tom had no intentions of watching television himself, he was angry because he felt his brother's choice was "stupid," which he continued repeating long after he had made his point. When his mother suggested that Tom go watch what he wanted in a different room, he refused. The argument was not about who had control of the TV but about Tom's intense response to Carl having a difference of opinion.

How parents can help. First, realize that your child isn't trying to be difficult, argumentative, or unlikable. Whenever possible, even when his behavior is unacceptable, stay focused on resolving the conflict and modeling behavior conducive to achieving that goal. The moment when your child feels most misunderstood and under attack isn't the best time to forcefully impose your own views. Also remember that most people with AS consider their intelligence to be one of their greatest strengths and, like all of us, may use their opinions to demonstrate how smart they are. We find it revealing that one child we know automatically assumes that anyone who disagrees with him considers him "stupid."

Whenever possible, point out when you or others disagree appropriately. Discuss in clear, explicit detail why one person might disagree and what that means ("Different people think different things") and what that doesn't mean ("that someone dislikes you personally"). Reassure your child that you can disagree with someone else and still like him or her, and that even people who love each other very much disagree now and then. Most marriages and partnerships offer a treasure trove of compromise examples: Dad likes chicken, and Mom prefers fish; Dad watches science fiction, Mom is into sports; Dad rides his motorcycle, and Mom thinks it's dangerous. When your child or someone else reaches a compromise, point it out, label it, and talk about the consequences. "Dad wanted us to go see a spy thriller, and I wanted to see a love story. But instead of arguing or being upset with each other, we compromised: Dad gets to pick the movie this week, and I get to pick the movie next week. Even though I probably won't like Dad's movie, and he probably won't like mine, we'll have a good time because we're together."

If your child is younger or socially immature, you might consider reducing or eliminating videos, music, television programs, movies, or video games that promote inappropriate conflict resolution styles or in which characters express disagreement with personal attacks on others, rage, or violence. Point out when people do the right thing, and encourage your child by praising even the smallest compromises in a way that the disagreement is not forgotten. Rather than just saying "That was very fair and friendly of you to compromise and let your sister watch *Beauty and the Beast*," you might add, "even though I know you don't like that video."

If your child tends to respond to conflicts inappropriately, don't deny his feelings but teach him better ways of expressing them. These can range from basic rules, such as "no shouting, throwing things, or hitting," to a structured program geared toward teaching him to monitor and control his emotions through relaxation techniques, cognitive behavior therapy, and so on.

Learning to Notice the Behaviors of Others and Oneself

For various reasons, some children with AS frequently fail to pay attention to what goes on around them; nor are they aware of the messages they send to others through their behavior, words, and body language.

How parents can help. Gently and sensitively draw your child's attention to what other people do and say. Help him become, as Dr. Temple Grandin—a woman with autism—describes herself, "an anthropologist from Mars." In the British documentary *My Crazy Life with Asperger Syndrome*, a young teen with AS sits with a neurotypical friend in the center of their town and studies passersby. Which two are a couple? Which are just friends? Or strangers? Or probably brother and sister? How do you tell?

The idea behind people watching is not only to see what social behavior looks like and begin to "decode" what it means. It is also to help kids to tune in to those around them, including people they do not know and will probably never see again. Generally, this is more easily accomplished by older children and adults than by younger children. Even so, it takes a great deal of constant practice and gentle reminding by parents and other "socio-cultural guides."

Learning to Respond to Others
in an Appropriate Way

It may seem that the rules are fairly clear-cut: you comfort some-one who is crying, you smile back when a stranger smiles at you. But if you begin to look closely at just a handful of common situations, you appreciate how much more complex the rules really are. You may put your arm around someone who is crying if you know her well, but that response would be inappropriate for a stranger. Since the ability to empathize depends so much on having theory of mind, "teaching" empathy is one of the harder challenges parents face. How do you teach someone to care? How do you teach a person with AS how to decide the appropriate course of action?

How parents can help. Use techniques such as Social Stories and explicit teaching for which types of behavior are acceptable and expected in different situations. Look at the world through your child's eyes and try to break down for him the unspoken rules of so-cial behavior. Always bear in mind your child's penchant for taking things literally, and be sure that you teach in such a way that allows for exceptions. It is important to teach your child not only what is expected in a given situation but also why, what it means, how it makes others feel, and so on. Eight-year-old Chrissie's best friend's grandmother had passed away a few weeks earlier, so before their next playdate, Chrissie's mother said, "Lisa's grandmother died, and she feels very sad about it. When you see her, remember to say 'I'm sorry to hear that your grandmother passed away.'"

Chrissie looked perplexed and then asked, "Why am I saying I'm sorry? I didn't do anything wrong. I didn't do anything to make her grandmother die."

Chrissie's mother considered for a moment and then said, "Sometimes we tell someone we care about 'I'm sorry' when some-thing happens that makes them sad or unhappy. You're right: some-times you say 'I'm sorry' to apologize for something you did. But there are other times, like when someone passes away or somebody gets hurt, when we say 'I'm sorry' as another way of saying 'I wish this bad thing didn't happen to you, because you are my friend.' This tells Lisa that you care about her and hope that she feels better. When you say that to Lisa, it will make her feel glad that you care."

Narrate your own socially appropriate empathetic behavior and that of others, in real life as well as in movies, books, and so on. This is particularly important if your child seems to miss or misunderstand the "point" of doing favors, being courteous, or saying or doing things (as in the case of Chrissie) that, to them, seem illogical. After a major snowstorm, a thirteen-year-old boy was confused as to why his father was shoveling the walk of an elderly neighbor, because "Dad said shoveling snow is a big pain in the neck, and he hates it." His mother explained what it meant to be a good neighbor and reminded her son of the many ways in which the neighbors had helped him in the past (by feeding his fish when the family was on vacation and bringing over cake on his birthday). When Dad was all finished, Mom made a point of prompting him to explain that even though he didn't care for shoveling, it made him feel good when the neighbors said thank you.

When discussing a past mistake (and Comic Strip Conversations can come in handy here), try to be understanding and gentle. Rather than criticize, walk your child through understanding not so much "what was wrong" as how his behavior made others think, feel, or act. Help him to understand the possible alternatives in a given situation and recognize when to ask for help. Until your child can be reasonably expected to respond appropriately, prompt him and prepare him ahead of time, especially when it comes to "high-stakes" situations such as weddings, funerals, social events, and any situation where the rules of behavior and/or the other people involved may be less flexible and forgiving of mistakes.

If your child does commit an embarrassing faux pas, remind him that everyone makes mistakes sometimes (be sure to tell him about a few of your own) and be supportive. Also try to have in place a good backup plan so that he is not put at social risk unnecessarily. If, for example, you must attend the big family reunion, have a babysitter on call or a friend or relative who has agreed beforehand to take him to a quiet place for a short time while you fulfill your social obligation. Allow him to bring his Game Boy (sound off) or a book, keep a snack or two in your bag, and ignore anyone who feels you are "coddling" him.

Learning How to Avoid and End Social Interaction

Just as children with AS must be taught explicitly how to join or initiate a social exchange, they also need instruction on how to "leave the scene" appropriately. Another related skill is understanding how to let others know that you prefer to be left alone without coming off as rude. We all appreciate the value of first impressions, but final impressions can be equally lasting.

How parents can help. Respect your child's feelings about the people with whom he wishes to interact. Teach him the verbal and nonverbal ways to let another person know that it's time for him to go, a conversation has run its course, or he has no interest in an exchange. Model and practice spotting the other person's cues, finding the correct opening, making eye contact, and using the right words. Left to their own devices, children with AS sometimes appear to give short shrift to leave-takings and declining conversation. More than a few parents have noticed that even the beloved grandparents who may not be seen again for another year get the same perfunctory "Bye" as the mailman.

Social interactions such as excusing oneself, saying good-bye, or telling someone you cannot talk to her right now all have special rules. When we follow these rules and say these things in a polite and friendly way, we remind people that we care about them even though we're going to do something else or prefer to be alone. Teach your child appropriate expressions to use—"I'm sorry, but I have to go home now," "Excuse me, but I'm going to spend some time in my room," and so on—especially if your child tends to question why he just can't get up and leave. A friend remembers a New Year's Eve party at which her son (age nine at the time) quietly pulled the hostess aside and said very politely, "I sometimes get overwhelmed at large parties. Is there a room where I can read my book?" The hostess was charmed and delighted at his request, offered the den, and asked him if he would mind her joining him if *she* got "overwhelmed." While some would criticize this kind of behavior as being antisocial, look closely and you can see that her son demonstrated a number of positive, essential skills. (1) He realized when he was in danger of becoming overwhelmed and figured out how he could avoid that. Also, (2) he took the initiative of approaching the hostess politely, (3) explained his problem (self-advocacy), and (4) asked for help.

Model the appropriate behavior and talk about it with your child. Help your child develop a repertoire of exit lines for a wide range of situations.

The Real-World Social Dangers of Online Social Media

When the internet was new (I mean, as in pre-Facebook and other social media days), the opportunities to "meet" and exchange ideas with others who shared interests—from literally anyplace in the world—seemed a gift from the heavens. Those exchanges took a bit of effort to find and were either one-to-one or as part of an email list, discussion group, or message board. Most of these tended to be made up of relatively small groups of like-minded people. Those who disagreed—the "haters," the "trolls"—were quickly and easily dispatched. These were true communities in the fullest sense, not a collection of "friends of friends of friends of friends" ad infinitum. One half-baked comment did not reach thousands of people—most of whom you don't know at all—in seconds. It was new and exciting and had its own risks, but it was saner, slower, and much easier to control than what kids face today.

Social media sites have much to recommend them, but they also pose social risks that are new, widespread, and enduring in ways that most adults do not fully understand or feel that they can control. As mentioned earlier, social media has also emerged as a weapon of choice for bullies and others. Another problem is the absolute loss of privacy, regardless of what social media sites claim or how many intricate instructions they offer to bolster users' false sense of security.

For kids with typical ASD deficits in social understanding, inferencing, theory of mind, and emotional self-regulation, social media poses other serious risks. As any adult who has misinterpreted and responded to a post knows well, hitting the Send button in haste often results in scrambling to repair the damage, explain yourself, and then worry about who saw your post and what they will think. How we have come to see a medium that demands careful, mature social judgment and offers virtually no margin for social error as a risk-free social tool for our kids is baffling.

It's easy to see why kids with social challenges love social media. The appeal of instantly collecting a "friend" with the click of a mouse is understandably irresistible. Unfortunately, many kids get into serious trouble with social media and find themselves in situations— ranging from misunderstandings among friends to attention from law enforcement—that can and should be prevented.

Here are some suggested ground rules for keeping your child safe.

- Even if you never plan to post a single status update or link to a video starring a cute cat, do join the social media site your child is interested in. Spend some time there, look around, and carefully read the fine print regarding privacy policies and terms of service.
- Understand how privacy settings work on the site. Set them so that her posts stay among "friends" and are never "public." Facebook, along with others, has proved less than trustworthy when it comes to what it means by *privacy*, and keeping up with its many changes in formatting and privacy settings takes effort.
- Take the time to identify each friend as, in Facebook terms, "friend," "acquaintance," or "public." It's easier if your child is only friending and posting to people who truly are her friends.
- Nothing on the internet is "private." Ever. Anything that anyone posts on the internet should be considered public and "out there" forever. This is also true of services that claim that posted messages or pictures "disappear" after time. The truth is, they don't. Talk to your child clearly and often about the risks of revealing information and set firm guidelines about what kinds of topics are off-limits. Your child might feel that she has a right to post to friends on Facebook about, say, how upset she is that her sister was pulled over for speeding. It is your responsibility to be sure that she understands that that is private information

that could be damaging to her sister if seen by others (employers, friends, parents of friends, college admissions staff, your auto insurance agent) or discussed by others, online or in the real world.

- You should be included among your child's friends and have access to viewing his page at any time. Make this a deal-breaker. Your virtual presence is an additional, essential reminder that information posted on social media is neither a diary entry nor part of a private conversation. It is public. Out there. Forever. If you are having qualms about this, just think: Do you allow people you don't know in your house when you are not there? Or even if you are? Do you allow your child to have deep personal conversations with or to get into a car with strangers? Didn't think so.

- Friends on social media should be friends in the real world. You can define the terms of "friend" however you wish, but I would suggest someone your child has had a conversation with in the real world.

- You and your child should have a list of topics that are okay to discuss online and topics that are strictly off-limits. Again, you make the rules, but some topics you might consider as off-limits would be anything about another person, positive or negative (maybe Jimmy does not want everyone to know he is the county Magic: The Gathering champ); anything related to politics, religion, or sex; and anything that your child would not want his grandparents or clergyman to see.

- You and your child should have a list of what words and terms are inappropriate to use. Obviously, curse words and hate speech are out. But also think about the words that seem to have sneaked into mainstream entertainment media—"blows," "sucks," "bitch," and "retard"—and many older kids' conversation (beyond adult ears, obviously). At worst, words like these can still offend; at the least, they can make a bad impression on, say, a future employer or the college admissions staff.

- Friends who post inappropriate comments, engage in bullying, or are mean to your child or anyone else should be unfriended immediately. Explain to your child why this is necessary. Leave the door open to reengage with that friend in the future if his or her behavior improves.

- Your child should be limited to a specific number of posts per friend per day. Social media makes it way too easy to contact repeatedly, which is often interpreted as stalking.

- If your child is posting links, or sharing, be sure that the shares and links are safe and appropriate.

- If something that happens in the real world or on social media upsets, confuses, or troubles your child, he should log off immediately. Strong emotions compromise everyone's judgment, but for kids who are not fully aware of the "hidden curriculum" and who do not do well reading between the lines, an angry, emotional post can be the start of a nightmare. In our zero-tolerance world, it takes only one phone call from the concerned recipient of a post or a parent to set into motion a process that brings the police, the courts, your school district, various mental health professionals, and others into your lives.

- Social media is sexual predator heaven. People with ASDs—boys and girls, regardless of age, regardless of cognitive ability, regardless of social ability—are at significantly higher risk for sexual abuse. See chapter 10.

- Arrangements for parties, get-togethers, and social outings should not be posted on social media, unless you're okay with a hundred kids you don't know knocking on your door. Nor should there be posts about family schedules, vacations, work being done on the house, or anything else that could help someone take advantage of that information, such as criminals.

SIX WAYS TO SET UP YOUR CHILD FOR SUCCESS

1. As much as possible, direct your child to situations that show off his strengths, not those that expose his weaknesses. For virtually every social activity, there is an alternative. It would be unwise, perhaps even cruel, to send a boy with motor skills deficits to try out for the basketball team or demand that your sensorily challenged daughter attend her sister's birthday pool party "just like everyone else" at the noisy indoor public pool. In fact, that boy would probably do well and derive great benefit from one-on-one activities such as weight training, private or small-group lessons in martial arts, bowling, and other individual sports. Your daughter can celebrate her sister's birthday in a manner that is more comfortable for her. Perhaps she can skip the pool portion of the festivities and arrive in time for dancing and cake.

2. Understand and respect your child's social limitations. I've come to believe that we are each born with a "social battery" that only lasts for as long as it can. When all the lights on your child's "emotional dashboard" light up, there's probably little you can do except turn off the engine and head for someplace quiet to recharge. Over time, your child can build up some endurance and travel farther, longer. But until that day comes, getting out while the gettin's good is probably a good idea.

For some kids with AS, a social situation with fewer social demands and a clear beginning and end is ideal. For some kids, a movie and pizza afterward provide a chance for companionship without their constantly having to listen to, look at, and respond to someone else. Seeing the movie together gives them a shared experience that both probably will be eager to talk about afterward. If your child can handle an hourlong playdate but invariably melts down after that, then make sure the playdate runs only about an hour. Better yet, resolve beforehand that the playdate will end *immediately* at the first sign that your child (or another) is unable to maintain control. That may mean accompanying him to his room while his guest gets ready to go without the standard long, polite good-byes at the door; or, if you are at someone else's house, leaving carrying your child's jacket in your hands. Or even better than that: if experience has taught you that the end of the first hour is when the trouble starts, start your good-byes ten minutes before. Don't let the fact that things are going so well undermine your good judgment. Many parents can tell you from experience that those last extra ten minutes can spell the difference between social success and social disaster.

3. Go out of your way to create a social setting in your home. Creating social opportunities for a child with AS can be time-consuming, frustrating, and difficult. The reality is that you'll probably spend far more time hosting other children than your guests' parents do. However, creating a controlled social environment for your child has the potential to be very rewarding, with benefits that could pay off over his lifetime. As much as possible, try to make your home the place where other children feel welcome and like to come play. If you can, offer to have other children over after school regularly for a self-limiting, short, and usually manageable playdate. I have seen my son grow socially because I invited over "friend candidates" on a regular basis, which allowed him and his guest a chance to get to know each other. Don't forget to involve children who are a little bit older as well as those who are a little younger. Sometimes a child with AS is more comfortable with someone not exactly his own age. Try to keep expanding your pool of potential playmates. So-called rent-a-friends ("friends" in name only) are a good idea for younger children. However, they may not be as easy to come by once children grow old enough to choose their own playmates. For one thing, depending on the one friend who suddenly stops coming over can be heartbreaking. One caveat: be sure other parents don't abuse your hospitality and that drop-off and pickup times are observed, for your child's sake and your own.

As kids get older, arrange more age-appropriate activities: hanging out at the mall, going to a movie, seeing a concert, watching a game, or eating out. If you are lucky, other parents will offer to pitch in with rides and supervision, where needed. If you are not, consider doing it yourself anyway. One of our favorite outings with my son and a couple of his friends was dropping them off at little rock club in Queens, while my husband and I checked out all the great Greek and Italian restaurants and bakeries nearby. Everyone had cell phones, in case they needed to reach us, but we were out of sight and they were out there on their own, like any other teens.

4. Accept your child's friendship on his or her own terms, not your—or anyone else's—idea of what friendship "should be." Your child's special interest may provide the foundation for a relationship with another who shares that interest. In fact, their social interaction may appear to be about nothing but the special interest. Some parents find this distressing; however, remember that even if your daughter and her friend talk of nothing but horses, they're still experiencing companionship and acceptance. Many parents find that special interest relationships often do grow to encompass other activities. To someone not familiar with AS, our children's friendships may seem "different," and their interaction may appear atypical (which it is), but that doesn't mean it isn't valuable or meaningful to your child.

5. The play's the thing—in more ways than one. Play and social practice are perhaps the most valuable experiences you can give your child. Rehearse, practice, prompt, discuss, and review to teach your child systematically the unspoken social rules. Then provide him every possible opportunity to practice, generalize, and expand his skills. That can include everything from having your daughter telephone her friend to invite her over, to corresponding with social media or email pals who share her interests. (Believe it or not, there are still pen pals.)

6. Acknowledge and reward every attempt at social sufficiency—even if it results in "failure." Don't forget that even when everything seems to go wrong, your child did do one brave, smart, and admirable thing: he tried.

Recommended Resources

See page 239 for resources specifically designed to teach social skills.

Book
Richard Lavoie, *It's So Much Work to Be Your Friend* (New York: Simon & Schuster, 2005).

Video

Last One Picked . . . First One Picked On: Learning Disabilities and Social Skills, by Richard Lavoie, a leading authority on the social, emotional, and psychological aspects of learning disorders and disabilities. With grace, insight, and humor, he offers practical solutions. This is part of the Learning Project series of acclaimed videos; all of them are worth seeing. Order through PBS at (800) 344-3337 or online, through LD OnLine, at www.ldonline.org.

Chapter 9

YOUR CHILD IN SCHOOL

THE strengths and weaknesses of many children with Asperger syndrome seem to converge most glaringly in school. Those who are academically gifted or have developed special interests that are validated in school may get their chance to shine. Unfortunately, the social, sensory, and organizational challenges of school also provide ample opportunities for even these children to experience anxiety, stress, and, sadly, failure. Students with AS who also contend with learning disabilities, comorbid disorders, emotional difficulties, or other issues may find each school day a struggle. This chapter is devoted to ensuring that the student with AS is understood and accommodated.

WHAT CAN BE GOOD ABOUT SCHOOL?

Your school district is obligated to provide an appropriate curriculum for children who are identified as gifted, talented, or exceptional, which many children with AS are.[1] School allows your child the chance to learn to interact with a range of personality types, to practice flexibility, and to grow toward greater independence. Finally, as a major training ground for socialization of all children,

417

school provides "practice" for simply learning to live among and get along with others.

WHAT CAN MAKE SCHOOL DIFFICULT FOR KIDS WITH AS

If asked to design an environment geared specifically to make a person with ASD uncomfortable, you might come up with something that looked a lot like a school. You would want an overwhelming number of peers; periods of tightly structured time alternating with periods lacking any discernible (to your child, at least) structure; regular helpings of irritating noise from bells, schoolmates, band practice, alarms, fluorescent lights, and crowded, cavernous spaces; countless distractions; a dozen or so daily transitions with a few surprises thrown in now and then; and the pièce de résistance: regularly scheduled detours into the social and/or sensory storm of recess, lunch, gym, and the bus rides to and from school. It's a wonder that so many children with AS manage to do so well. That's not to say, however, that most of our children couldn't be doing a lot better and experiencing more pleasant, less stressful days.

Zero-Tolerance Policies in Schools

The movement toward so-called zero tolerance of violence and aggression gained force in spring 1999, after two students opened fire on their classmates, killing twelve students and one teacher and wounding twenty-one before committing suicide at Columbine High School in Littleton, Colorado. Sadly, shootings and violence in our schools continue. Although it is imperative that all children be safe in school, indiscriminate application of zero-tolerance policies have placed children with AS and other neurological differences at risk for being labeled, or "profiled," as a danger to others. In some places, this has fostered a witch-hunt environment, in which hearsay and isolated incidents carry far more weight than they probably should in many cases. For example, a straight-A student with Tourette's syndrome, few friends, and a limited social life was suspended from his school a day after Columbine because a fellow student told a teacher that she "could imagine that he might commit such a crime."[2] This teen and many other students throughout the country have been subjected to interviews, reviews, suspensions, and expulsions for behaviors that fall well within the diagnostic criteria of AS and other disorders.

We mourn the loss and the pain of students victimized by school violence. The fact remains, however, that our children are far more likely to be victims of such actions than to be perpetrators. We must protect our children from becoming, in a very different way, victims of these tragedies. People with AS may respond with aggression or violence when threatened, bullied, rejected, frustrated, or otherwise provoked. They may voice the thoughts and feelings that most other children would know better than to share: "I hate you," "I'm going to blow up this school," "I hate everybody," "I'd like to kill the kid who knocked me into the locker," and so on. While these behaviors are likely related to AS, and the person is someone who responds like this under stress, they may make your child a target for zero-tolerance enforcement.

There are other things about kids with AS and ASDs that contribute to what some would call a "suspicious" profile. They may choose to wear loose clothing or wear the same clothing every day. Because of sensory issues, they may hold their bodies in such a way that they appear to be hiding something. If this same child lacks friends or has formed relationships with other children who are considered to be outside the mainstream, he could be perceived as "antisocial," a "loner."

It is very important that your child's school district be made aware of his diagnosis and that he have an IEP (and thus the disciplinary protections under IDEA) in place before something happens. (There are no special provisions regarding discipline for disability-related behaviors under Section 504.) In addition to taking the actions mentioned throughout this book to increase your child's social skills and create a positive environment in school, establish your own "zero–tolerance" policy for bullying and teasing of your child as well as inappropriate responses from teachers, administrators, and staff.

If your child does experience outbursts, be sure that their occurrences and the circumstances surrounding them are documented. Be sure that your child's doctor, therapist, or another professional familiar with him addresses the nature of his behavior in a letter to your child's teachers and principal, with copies sent to the superintendent and your board of education. If necessary, obtain written backup from an advocacy or mental health official or organization documenting the fact that your child's behavior is a direct result of his disability. Let everyone know—in writing—that, in the event he is threatened with disciplinary action, you will vigorously defend your child's legal rights.

Finally, the wisest course is preventing such incidents from occurring. Again, helping your child develop social skills and emotional control, coupled with a supportive and understanding educational environment, can go a long way toward avoiding misunderstandings and undesirable behavior. If your child's behaviors are serious or have the potential to become so, he should have a behavior intervention plan (BIP) that is based upon a functional behavior assessment (FBA). The FBA should address observable, measurable behavior, and the resulting BIP should include criteria for demonstrating effectiveness and plans for regular review and possible revision.

HOW TO WORK WITH YOUR CHILD'S SCHOOL

Keep Your Mind Open

In an ideal world, everyone responsible for teaching and guiding your child would be on precisely the same page when it came to the important decisions about your child's education. In reality, however, you must be prepared to hear differing views and consider different approaches. Depending on your age and where you live, your child's experience of school might be very much like or very, very different from your own. The recent focus on high-stakes testing, the well-publicized problems with bullying in schools, and whatever local issues are shaping your child's school experience all come into play. There is no one size that fits all. Every district, every school, every classroom has its positive aspects and those that could use a little work. And, really, what doesn't? But every parent wants "the best" for his or her child. What does that mean to you?

First, as discussed in chapter 6, that means an appropriate education for your individual child. Next, it means an environment in which your child, and all students, are safe from the threat of bullying and violence. Finally, it means an environment conducive to your child's learning and growing. And by "learning," I don't mean just what he needs to pass his finals or get good grades. I mean learning to get along with others, learning to understand himself, and learning to feel more comfortable in the world.

Yes, we parents know our children better than anyone else does. But we also need to be open to the views of the educators whose job it is to create those daily experiences that one by one eventually add up to "an education." Most of us recall with fondness that one great teacher: the one who just seemed to get our kid from day one, who went above and beyond every time. What a wonderful world it would be if our child could only have that teacher every year. Obviously, that's not possible, and it probably would not be a great idea anyway, because one thing school does offer our kids is the chance to learn to understand and work with the expectations and personalities of other people. Sometimes the teacher who seems at Meet the Teacher Night absolutely clueless about your child's condition turns out to be the most creative in terms of trying new things.

Keep Your Eyes Open, Too

Despite increased training and autism awareness, not every teacher you meet will fully understand the ramifications of autism spectrum disorder. If, for some reason, your child's teacher is unfamiliar with your child's issues and needs, offer to help. Don't assume that simply by having an IEP, a 504 plan, or other education program in place, your child's teacher will fully understand either him or AS. Take the initiative. Create a notebook for your child's teacher (and consider making a second copy to go in your child's file for others to see) that includes information about AS and the specific behaviors and issues he faces. You might use colored divider tabs and organize information under such sections as "Sensitivity to Noise," "Play Skills," "Dysgraphia," and so on. Rather than fill the notebook to the brim with every piece of information you find, pick the one or two most comprehensive and authoritative pieces. Lend educators videos and books, provide print material, and let everyone know that you are always available to talk about AS. However, try always to do so with tact and understanding.

Once your child enters middle school or high school and more teachers are involved, ask for a team meeting at the beginning of the year to introduce your child and yourself. Transitions to middle school and high school are difficult for most kids under the best of circumstances. Suddenly learning to navigate a new building and to understand and meet the different expectations of different teachers can be challenging. Be sure to make contact with guidance counselors, school psychologists, social workers, special education administrators, and others who will be working with your child.

Watch out for signs that maybe the role of ASD in your child's life might not be well understood. "Code" statements that betray a clear misunderstanding of your child and AS that you might hear include the following:

"If only he applied himself."
"He's so smart, why can't he _____?"
"Her inappropriate behaviors get in the way of her learning."
"He uses his sensitivity to noise to avoid work."
"His outbursts are nothing more than attention seeking; the more attention we give them, the worse they will get."
And, our personal all-time favorite "She simply has to get used to the noisy lunchroom/teasing/remembering to bring home her books/[you name it]."

It is imperative to establish a good relationship with your child's teacher. You can be cooperative and friendly in the classroom without undermining your effectiveness as an advocate at the IEP table. Even when you feel strongly about a matter or wish to share information, be tactful above all else. Educators may feel self-conscious because they lack, through no fault of their own, adequate training or experience in dealing with children like ours. Try to be sensitive in how you present your ideas and suggestions. Even if you are, for now, the resident "expert," be sure everyone knows that you are first and foremost a team player who is interested in helping create an environment at school that works not only for your child but for everyone: teachers and other students alike.

If you find that either your child's behaviors or learning problems in school are not responding to interventions, ask your district to bring in a consultant who specializes in ASD. Different districts work with consultants in different ways. One popular arrangement is to use the consultant as a resource for the staff. Sometimes educators find it easier to accept suggestions from a professional consultant who has a wider view of all the aspects of school than it is from a parent, whose focus is their child.

THE OASIS LETTER OF INTRODUCTION

There's a lot more to your child than what his teacher might read in his records or his IEP. Rather than leave your child's teacher to develop a relationship with him based on trial and error, introduce your child through a letter that you can copy and distribute to anyone who may need it. Be sure to send a copy to your school district and ask that it be included as part of your child's permanent records.

This letter is based on the work of OASIS's early forum members. In 1999, one of them, Elly Tucker, invited other members to contribute suggestions for a "letter of introduction" for teachers about Asperger syndrome and how it affects a particular child. This format is based on Tucker's work. The material in italics is the type of thing you might add. Feel free to add or delete sections to fit your child. You can download this form letter as a Word document from www.aspergerguide.com and tailor it to your needs.

Letter of Introduction

Dear _____,

We are the parents of _____. Our child has been diagnosed with Asperger syndrome, an autism spectrum disorder. He also has the following comorbid conditions [list them] and learning disabilities [list them]. While AS affects many aspects of behavior, it shares with autism the "core" deficits in social understanding and language. Simply put, our child sees and experiences the world differently from people who do not have AS. He may seem to "overreact at nothing" or become very emotional "for no reason." We have learned that in most instances, there is a reason for why our child responds the way he does. And it is a reason that "makes sense" once you understand AS. We have also learned that there are things we can do to help him. The first and most important is accepting that some of his behaviors are not under his control.

People with AS often have a unique and at times unusual mixture of abilities and deficits. They may appear to be more capable than they actually are. AS can affect virtually every facet of a child's academic, social, and emotional life, sometimes in ways that may be unfamiliar to you. There is no "cure" for AS, but research on the disorder and new interventions and therapies are moving ahead quickly. We will be happy to share with you whatever information we find that may be helpful to you in helping _____ have a positive, productive experience in school. Please feel free to call us anytime at [phone number] or email us at _____.

Every child with AS is unique. No two have the same pattern of behaviors, skills, or deficits. A technique or approach that worked for one child may not necessarily work for the next. Or what worked last month may not work today. In the years since our child was diagnosed, he has received the following therapies and interventions: [list]. We found [list the most effective ones] the most helpful. He is currently receiving [list other interventions]. [Add if relevant] He is taking [name of medication(s)] to address [list the behavior(s)].

- Our child's main strengths are: [list strengths]
- The praise he values most is: [list: *being told that he is bright, wise, fun to be around*].
- The most effective rewards would be: [list].
- The strongest disincentive would be: [list].

Like many people with AS, our child has special interests: [list special interests]. You may find it helpful to allow him to indulge his special interest by talking about it for a limited period of time as a reward. You may also use his interest as an instructional tool (for instance, write math story problems about trains, allow a book report on an interest-related book).

AS affects numerous areas. Below is a list of the difficulties _____ faces and what we and his other teachers and therapists have discovered works and does not work.

General Personality and Behavior

_____ is [list the positives: *warm, loving, has a great sense of humor, and so on*].

The areas in which he is most seriously challenged are: [list challenges]. We believe that these can be most effectively addressed by [list interventions and tactics that have proved successful].

Some other approaches, such as [list what does not work for your child], do not work for our child and tend to make him feel [describe adverse or undesirable behavior]. When that occurs, we find that it helps to [describe action].

Social Skills with Adults

_____ is [list the positives: *warm, loving, polite, etc.*].

The areas in which he is most seriously challenged are: [list challenges: *has difficulties following multistep directions, a tendency to ask for help with things when he does not necessarily need it, and so on*]. We believe that these can be most effectively addressed by [list interventions and tactics that have proved successful: *breaking down oral directions into short, simple steps; gently encouraging him to do those things you know he can do*].

Some other approaches, such as [list what does not work for your child: *repeating complex instructions several times; forcing him to do things he feels inept at*], do not work for our child and tend to make him feel [describe adverse or undesirable behavior:

anxious, dumb]. When that occurs, we find that it helps to [describe action: *calm and comfort him to regain control*].

Social Skills with Peers

_____ is [list the positives: *interested in other children and anxious to make friends*].

The areas in which he is most seriously challenged are: [list challenges: *his inability to join in appropriately, participate in conversations, and understand how to reciprocate*]. We believe that these can be most effectively addressed by [list interventions and tactics that have proved successful: *using Social Stories to cue and remind him of appropriate behavior; setting up situations where he can practice these new skills with other children*]. Some other approaches, such as [list what does not work for your child: *simply leaving him in a group of children on the playground to "find his way"*], do not work for our child and tend to make him feel [describe adverse or undesirable behavior: *stressed, anxious, and sad*]. When that occurs, we find that it helps to [describe action: *gently remove him from the situation and set up another experience that is "rigged" for success*].

Expressive and Receptive Language

_____ is [list the positives: *has a large vocabulary, tells interesting make-believe stories*].

The areas in which he is most seriously challenged are: [list challenges]. We believe that these can be most effectively addressed by [list interventions and tactics that have proved successful]. Some other approaches, such as [list what does not work for your child], do not work for our child and tend to make him feel [describe adverse or undesirable behavior]. When that occurs, we find that it helps to [describe action].

Auditory Processing

_____ is [list the positives: *can completely recall songs or poems he has heard only once or twice*].

The areas in which he is most seriously challenged are: [list challenges]. We believe that these can be most effectively addressed by [list interventions and tactics that have proved successful]. Some other approaches, such as [list what does not work for your child], do not work for our child and tend to make him feel [describe adverse or undesirable behavior]. When that occurs, we find that it helps to [describe action].

Sensory Issues

_____ is [list the positives].

The areas in which he is most seriously challenged are: [list challenges]. We believe that these can be most effectively addressed by [list interventions and tactics that have proved successful]. Some other approaches, such as [list what does not work for your child], do not work for our child and tend to make him feel [describe adverse or undesirable behavior]. When that occurs, we find that it helps to [describe action].

Fine- and Gross-Motor Skills

_____ is [list the positives: *almost at age level with basic living skills; he can tie his shoes, zip his jacket*].

The areas in which he is most seriously challenged are: [list challenges]. We believe that these can be most effectively addressed by [list interventions and tactics that have proved successful]. Some other approaches, such as [list what does not work for your child], do not work for our child and tend to make him feel [describe adverse or undesirable behavior]. When that occurs, we find that it helps to [describe action].

Self-Care and Hygiene

_____ is [list the positives: *independent using the bathroom*].

The areas in which he is most seriously challenged are: [list challenges]. We believe that these can be most effectively addressed by [list interventions and tactics that have proved successful]. Some other approaches, such as [list what does not work for your child], do not work for our child and tend to make him feel [describe adverse or undesirable behavior]. When that occurs, we find that it helps to [describe action].

Organizational Skills

_____ is [list the positives: *able to pack his book bag at the end of the day if prompted; sometimes able to work at his desk without prompting*].

The areas in which he is most seriously challenged are: [list challenges]. We believe that these can be most effectively addressed by [list interventions and tactics that have proved successful]. Some other approaches, such as [list what does not work for your child], do not work for our child and tend to make him feel [describe adverse or undesirable behavior]. When that occurs, we find that it helps to [describe action].

Perseverations

_____ is [list the positives: *engaging in perseverative behaviors less this year than he did last year, and is becoming aware that they are stigmatizing*].

The areas in which he is most seriously challenged are: [list challenges]. We believe that these can be most effectively addressed by [list interventions and tactics that have proved successful]. Some other approaches, such as [list what does not work for your child], do not work for our child and tend to make him feel [describe adverse or undesirable behavior]. When that occurs, we find that it helps to [describe action].

Transitions

_____ is [list the positives: *managing to handle transitions, provided he is given clear, detailed explanations of what is expected*].

The areas in which he is most seriously challenged are: [list challenges]. We believe that these can be most effectively addressed by [list interventions and tactics that have proved successful]. Some other approaches, such as [list what does not work for your child], do not work for our child and tend to make him feel [describe adverse or undesirable behavior]. When that occurs, we find that it helps to [describe action].

Changes in Routine, Surprises

_____ is [list the positives: *still uncomfortable with surprises but less likely to scream when they occur than he was a few months ago*].

The areas in which he is most seriously challenged are: [list challenges]. We believe that these can be most effectively addressed by [list interventions and tactics that have proved successful]. Some other approaches, such as [list what does not work for your child], do not work for our child and tend to make him feel [describe adverse or undesirable behavior]. When that occurs, we find that it helps to [describe action].

Eye Contact, Gaze Modulation

_____ is [list the positives: *making as much eye contact as he comfortably can right now*].

The areas in which he is most seriously challenged are: [list challenges]. We believe that these can be most effectively addressed by [list interventions and tactics that have proved successful]. Some other approaches, such as [list what does not work for your child], do not work for our child and tend to make him feel [describe adverse or undesirable behavior]. When that occurs, we find that it helps to [describe action].

[Add any other information you feel is important.]

Sincerely,
[your name]

CLASSROOM STRATEGIES FOR DEALING WITH ASD

IF THE STUDENT	TRY THIS:
Gets "stuck" on a question or problem and cannot work on sheets or tests "out of order."	Remind him that in most cases, it does not matter what order the questions are presented in.

Offer explicit instruction and practice in skipping hard questions, completing easier ones, and then returning to the hard ones.

Practice these strategies when the stakes are lower—i.e., homework as opposed to during an actual test.

Offer questions or problems that are not numbered individually and in random order. |
| Makes irrelevant, off-topic comments; interrupts others; talks over others. | If possible, ignore irrelevant, off-topic comments.

Remind the student to wait before speaking.

Offer explicit direction for recognizing when it is okay to speak (e.g., the other person stops speaking; there are a couple of seconds of no one else talking).

Use Comic Strip Conversations to illustrate what it "looks like" when too many people talk at once. |

Exhibits off-task behavior and seems to have difficulty staying on task.	Consider environmental factors: student's proximity to busy spots like the pencil sharpener, or visually distracting spots like right next to the classroom door, a window, or a computer monitor. Also take an honest look at seating. While it's convenient to place all of the students who need extra attention together, consider "surrounding" a distractible student with good models instead. When prompting attention, opt for nonverbal gestural prompts rather than spoken prompts. Nonverbal gestural prompts—such as tapping the worksheet lightly, pointing to the board or the teacher speaking, or turning the book to the correct page—draw less attention and are not as distracting to some students as spoken reminders.
Forgets assignments, loses materials, cannot seem to get organized.	Remember that there are often neurological issues underlying problems with executive function. Have the student use—and the staff check—a daily agenda or to-do list. Expect the student to collect all the books, notebooks, and other materials needed for homework but also be sure to double-check. Praise the student for what he did assemble, even if it was not complete. Work with parents and the student to devise an organizational system that is simple and works for him. Help the student establish "one place for everything" that is to go home.

Seems "paralyzed" when faced with a task that requires multiple steps and planning.	Before the student begins, even if the steps are few or "simple," have someone assist him in writing them all down. If specific materials will be required, include that, too. Stand by to offer assistance with an eye to catching mistakes before too much time passes or the student gets too far into the assignment.
Has difficulty maintaining a comfortable posture at his desk without leaning.	Before repeatedly offering verbal reminders to "sit up," check the work area. Is the desk or table and chair a good fit ergonomically for the student? Do his feet rest comfortably on the floor? Is the desk at the proper height for efficient, comfortable writing? Consider requesting a consult from the school occupational therapist. Does the student keep a clear desk? Is the desk overcrowded with unneeded materials? Does he position paper correctly for writing comfortably?
Never or rarely raises his hand or participates in class.	Do not let that stop you from calling on him, but limit to questions you are certain he can answer correctly. Praise his raising his hand even if you did not call on him. For pair and small-group work, place student with classmates who are friendly but not overwhelming. Praise participation specifically, even if the answer offered is incorrect. The first few times the student raises his hand, be sure to call on him.

| Seems to take "too much time" to answer questions or respond. | Determine if the student needs extra time to formulate a response; if so, wait patiently and consider teaching the student some polite "holding phrases" such as "Let me see," "That's a good question," or "That's interesting."

If the problem lies with language processing, *do not* restate the question in a different way. Instead ask, "Would you like me to repeat that?" If so, repeat the question exactly as posed originally.

For some people with ASDs, a significantly reworded question is like a brand-new question, which starts a brand-new "processing" period. |

A CONSULTANT MOM'S TOP TIPS FOR TEACHERS

As a parent, I always gave my son's teachers articles and books (all colorfully highlighted) to help them understand AS and, I hoped, him better. While many of the ideas shared were useful, too many required extra time, materials, and effort—all things few teachers have much of these days. As a consultant who spends a lot of time sitting in classrooms and working with educators, it's clear that teachers need a tool kit of strategies that are always available (that is, do not require a special chart, piece of software, or materials). Teachers teach and manage their classrooms largely by talking to their students. I've found that by simply changing specific aspects of *how* they talk to students with ASDs, teachers can address attention, behavior, and learning issues, and, in many cases, head them off before they develop into problems or difficult moments for our kids.

Make directions and expectations crystal clear. In as few words as possible, state what you want, what the end product should look like, and—to the extent feasible—where the information or "supplies" can be found. It's better to ask for "a one-paragraph description of the space shuttle based on what you read on page ninety-four" than to say "give me a brief statement based on your reading about the space shuttle."

Be positive, and by that I don't mean just look happy. Use positive statements when you give directions: "Please sit down" is better than "This isn't the time to be standing." "Take out your paper, your pencil, and your blue social studies folder" increases your student's chances of delivering much better than does "Get ready for social studies."

Be sure that any praise, direction, or redirection is behavior specific: that is, it names or references specific behavior in terms that are concrete and clear. Try to use the old general generics like "Great work," and "Good job" sparingly. Go instead for "Great job adding those numbers," or "I like the way you numbered your spelling list right down the margin." When giving directions, "Erase this number and try to add these two numbers again" is better than "Fix this."

When speaking to the student, be no more than arm's length away, and then check for understanding by asking the student to repeat what you just said. Asking, "Do you understand?" does not count, because many students with AS either will not know what they don't know (in other words, they might believe that they understand when they don't), or they might be self-conscious about admitting they don't understand.

Teach your student to ask for help. Remember that kids on the spectrum do not always recognize that they need help, and sometimes even if they do, problems with theory of mind might make it hard for them to imagine that anyone else knows something that they do not. As a result, they might not ask for help. Monitor and hover—observe discreetly. When it looks as if help might be needed, do not simply begin assisting. Instead, narrate the process: "I noticed you paused here. Let me know if you need help." This prompts the child to notice what's happening in her work, and it also sets her up to volley back with a request for help. Students who never need to ask for help (because an adult is always swooping in) or who need only provide a yes or a no to "Do you need help?" never learn to take the initiative and make the request themselves. This is the first step in self-advocacy.

Keep in touch. Just as kids on the spectrum do not always notice when they are doing the wrong thing, they typically do not always notice when they are doing the right thing, either. Be prepared to provide a "behavioral compass" by giving feedback that is frequent, explicit, and clear.

That goes for parents and guardians, too. Not learning of a problem in school until days or weeks after it first appeared is a top pet peeve for parents and a common "trust buster." Do not worry that you will upset a parent with bad news; odds are, most of us have dealt with worse before. And if it is truly bad news, most parents know the value of addressing it as quickly and effectively as possible. Hearing about a "crisis" that they find out actually has a long history they knew nothing about puts parents in an awkward—and don't be surprised to find out, unhappy—position. First, it gives the impression that the school takes seriously issues that are important for the student only when they become problems for the school. Second, what about all those days their child came home and reported having a good day or that "nothing" happened in school?

Sometimes a fresh approach to a school day standby, like homework, can make all the difference for a student with AS.

Homework on weekends? Yep. When kids with AS come home from school, they are often tired. Because of the stress of juggling the dual curriculum or the fact that homework sometimes cannot begin until after dinner, it's easy to see why in many households, this is the most unpleasant part of the day. Consider making certain assignments for the following week available on Friday. For example, spelling words, reading assignments, and other homework that the student can complete in small "chunks" over the weekend does a couple of good things. First, it keeps your student in touch with the material. Second, it can reduce each weeknight homework session by ten to twenty minutes. Sure, it doesn't sound like much, but many parents will attest that it's the last minutes that are the most difficult.

Evaluate the classroom environment for distractions. Remember that for many kids on the spectrum, "sifting through" the countless stimuli in the environment and then instinctively focusing on the relevant cues is very difficult or requires so much effort that doing so becomes a distraction itself. Preferential seating, a desk and chair that "fits," writing implements that are comfortable and require the least effort to use, space to spread out, and so on can make a huge difference.

Set up the environment to make the student as independent and self-reliant as possible. If the student is physically capable of, say, getting up and retrieving his own textbook off the shelf or organizing his own desk, let him do it. Consider accepting that some things might not be as perfect as you would like for the sake of independence. For example, a less than perfectly folded letter done without help provides a better learning experience than your student observing another person doing the folding for him.

The teacher's contribution to a child's social and emotional growth is inestimable. That said, teachers who do not have a lot of experience with ASDs do not always recognize how they might help. Talk with colleagues who know the student, and find out what works and what does not. If the student consistently seeks you and other adults out to talk to and seems to ignore peers, take every opportunity to "set up" the conversation and pop it over the net to a receptive peer. Whenever possible, set up the student to "shine." Do not neglect to ask the student a question because you're sure he knows the answer; the social practice of simply raising one's hand and speaking up in class for some can be valuable.

Have a clear idea of what your student is expected to be doing during downtimes, such as between classroom activities, during snack time, transitioning in hallways, or just plain waiting. Where possible, shoot for the standard of behavior expected of other students. Be prepared to offer explicit directions for what behavior is expected and positively reinforce when expectations are met. Do not permit these unstructured moments to become a "stage" for this student's inappropriate, stigmatizing, or interfering behavior.

Step into the role of social director. Do keep your eyes open for classmates who show an appropriate interest in or affinity for this child. Also be on the lookout for classmates who might not be so nice or who engage in bullying, however subtle. Do not expect your student with ASD always to be able to recognize that he is being treated unkindly or bullied, much less to tell you about it.

THE SCHOOL-HOME CONNECTION: KEEPING THE LINES OF COMMUNICATION OPEN

Consistency is crucial to a child with AS. While it's unreasonable to expect that you and your child's teacher will handle every situation exactly the same way, your child will benefit greatly if you and those at school agree on major issues. How to manage high-stakes situations such as emotional meltdowns, misbehavior, and social issues tops that list. A teacher who persists in trying to stop a meltdown, for instance, or forces a child out on the playground every day despite obvious signs of stress must be persuaded to adopt strategies that are effective.

The key is, obviously, communication. Make it your first priority to see that the teacher understands AS and how it affects your child. Next, propose (and insist, if necessary) that you and the teacher exchange a notebook, checklist, or some other written update of your elementary school child's day. Checklists are often preferred, since for many teachers, time is at a premium, and they have other children to teach. For kids in middle school and high school, try to have a "go-to" person—school psychologist, social worker, homeroom teacher, guidance counselor, or administrator—your child and you can go to first with questions or issues.

It is impossible to track every behavior of the day. To make the data you or your child's teacher collect and analyze meaningful, follow these guidelines:

1. Be specific. Target behaviors (having tantrums, pushing in line, greeting teacher and peers each morning, hitting other students, bringing in homework) that you can observe and count, not states of mind, moods, or attitudes you cannot. For example, you can count how many times Nina bangs her fist on the table. You cannot count or measure any dimension of Nina "feeling angry."

2. If you are concerned with a mood, attitude, or state of mind, identify behaviors that might be indicative of it and document the behavior. For instance, rather than rate Neil's anxiety on a scale of 1 to 5, if you know that higher anxiety tends to bring about more tantrums, count the tantrums.

3. Define your terms so that you and your child's teacher are talking about the same thing. Let's take the tantrum. What will define the tantrum? Your child raising his voice, complaining or whining or crying loudly, hitting objects or people, getting out of his chair, falling to the floor, running out of the classroom—these could all be parts of tantrum behavior. Specify what defines a tantrum and agree with your child's teacher to count only that. So, for example, a tantrum has to include loud complaining, or whining, or crying *and* refusal to return to his seat; your child should not be scored as having a tantrum if he's annoyed and muttering under his breath while he sits in his seat. An appropriate greeting might be defined as follows: "Independently and at a volume a listener can hear clearly, Neil will initiate a brief greeting (Good morning, Hi, Good day, Hello, or whatever) to a peer that includes a least one second of eye contact." A silent wave or a mumbled "hi" won't cut it.

4. Choose behaviors that have a clear beginning and an end.

5. Pinpoint specific times to observe the behavior. It would be impossible for Tali's teacher to chase behind her and count up every time she greets anyone over the course of a school day. But her teacher or an aide can watch Tali for the first three minutes after she's entered the classroom and track whom she greets and how.

6. How much data do you need? If Tali's just learning to greet others, every day for a week or two would establish whether

she's mastered the skill. After that, you might want her teacher to observe her once a week until it's clear that she's got it.

7. What will you do with it? Make a simple chart, like the one shown on page 441. (Or, if you are handy with a spreadsheet program such as Excel, you can create something a bit fancier.) What does it tell you? We can see that for Neil, tantrums are significantly more common on Wednesday than on any other day. Now the "detective work" begins.

Using Data to Monitor Behavior and Behavior Intervention Plans

It is not unusual for kids with ASDs to exhibit behaviors that are inappropriate in a given situation, that interfere with learning, that create disruptions, or that have the potential to create a risk of harm to oneself or to others. Failure to address serious problems can result in anything from fewer opportunities to make friends to a change in educational placement. For this reason, it is imperative not only that problem behaviors be addressed quickly and effectively, but that any discussion—no matter how "early" or "tentative"—regarding changes in educational placement, medication, or other interventions or services be based on real, quantitative data, not simply anecdotal records (though these also have their place) and the recollections or impressions of others. Increasingly, school staff and other professionals are approaching problem behaviors not as simply something we should learn to accept and live with because a child has an ASD, but are instead looking for the function of the behavior and then creating behavior intervention plans (BIPs) to address them. Be aware: some professionals believe that any strategy patched together in the hope of addressing a specific behavior constitutes a real BIP. It doesn't. At the heart of an effective BIP—or at the very least, one that has some reasonable chance of succeeding—is an understanding of the function of the behavior. And for that, you need someone with experience and training to conduct a functional behavior assessment, or FBA.

Neil is a second-grade student who has a history of tantrum behavior. What is a "tantrum"? Most of us would agree that it depends on whom you ask. But that should not be acceptable when there is a reason for data being collected. To count and analyze the frequency of Neil's tantrums, the first thing everyone needs is a solid definition of the observable behaviors that, taken together, we define as "tantrum." This is the only way to be sure that everyone who records data agrees on what they see and count. Our definition for Neil, for this particular behavior, at this particular time is as follows:

"A tantrum is defined as Neil refusing to follow a direction followed by crying with visible tears and/or loud verbal vocal protests that last more than 30 seconds each *and* include getting up out of his seat and refusing to follow a direction to sit down."

Obviously, this definition would not capture tantrum behavior for another child. In fact, there may be no other child on earth for whom this exact definition fits. That's because this definition is based on what has been observed before and what behaviors occur most frequently together for this child. In Neil's case, verbal protests like, "I hate doing math" or "This stinks!" have been observed to pass quickly. However, for Neil, the consistent behavior that is always followed by the most intense protests, crying, and attempts to escape the classroom begin with his leaving his seat.

Another reason to have a precise definition of observable behaviors is that Neil, like most youngsters, at one time or another probably engages in a repertoire of behaviors that adults might prefer that he not. For example, when his keyboard in computer lab froze, Neil might have pushed his chair back and yelled, "Hey! This stinks!" Or when someone cut him off in the cafeteria line and called him a "baby," he might have cried a few tears. While these individual behaviors form pieces of the tantrum definition, they are not tantrums as "tantrum" is defined for Neil, for this BIP. Neither of these incidents should be recorded as tantrums. One common downfall of BIPs is the failure to set clear definitions and parameters of the behavior of interest. As a result, everyone taking data counts or doesn't count behavior based on their own personal ideas of what a tantrum looks like or their own personal opinions about what types of behavior Neil should or should not be engaging in. On the other hand, some people will observe a series of behaviors that fit the definition to a tee, but they might choose not to record a given incident because, for example, they understand why Neil would refuse to do his math: it's his worst subject. I have even encountered staff who will stop counting because they believe that a child such as Neil having so many tantrums "looks bad" or that parents will be upset.

Neil's Weekday Tantrums, October

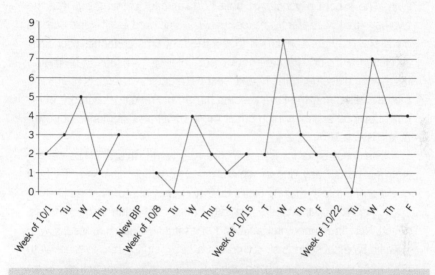

The data graphed here—and any data deemed worth collecting should also be worth graphing and sharing with others, especially parents—track the daily frequency of tantrums for one week before a new BIP was implemented and for three weeks after. Assume that a functional behavior assessment occurred, but let's assume for the sake of argument that the BIP implemented had some flaws. After three weeks of implementation, Neil's parents meet with his teacher and other staff to discuss how things are going. When presented with the preceding graph at the meeting, Neil's mother is surprised. "I have several days of getting notes home saying that Neil has had a great day or that he had no tantrums. I thought things were improving." Neil's teacher and school psychologist explain that, yes, things are better on some days and point out that two of the last fifteen school days were tantrum-free. However, when Neil's parents look at the graph carefully, they notice two important things: First, Neil's tantrums consistently "spike" on

Wednesday—the day he has two pull-outs for services and music class, which is uncomfortable for him due to hearing sensitivity. Second, and perhaps more important, Neil's weekly number of tantrums decreased the first week of the BIP, but the number rose to seventeen for the past two weeks. Even though that's only three more than the fourteen that occurred the week before the BIP began, it still indicates that the current BIP is ineffective. And, in fact, the Wednesday "spikes" remain high. The school psychologist politely disagrees, pointing out that the two days that were "tantrum-free" show "some progress." Neil's parents disagree. They are concerned that if the tantrums continue, especially as Neil grows older, it might not be possible for his needs to be met in his current placement: the regular second-grade class. Neil is bright and friendly. His parents believe keeping him in his regular classroom in his neighborhood school, which offers more social and academic opportunities, is crucial.

Like most behavior issues in the real world, this one has several "moving parts," any one of which, or all of which, or none of which might play a role in making Neil's tantrum behavior more or less likely to occur. For Neil's parents, the first, most obvious problem is music class, which Neil finds uncomfortable and stressful. He has had issues with specific types of sounds since he was a baby. Urging him to "stick with it"—as his teachers have been doing to date—has never worked to reduce his anxiety about sound. So Neil's parents convince the school to remove him temporarily from music. Second, they question the wisdom of scheduling two pull-outs on a single day for a child who is still learning to transition easily. The school agrees and moves one pull-out session to a different day. On page 443 are the data for the next two weeks with only a schedule change and a suspension of the previous BIP:

The reduction in the frequency of Neil's tantrums is clear. Not only are there significantly fewer tantrums on Wednesdays (just 2 and 0 compared to 8 and 7 the previous two weeks), but there are fewer instances on the other days, too. From weekly totals of 14, 8, 17, and 17, we have 7 and 3 for the past two weeks. Plus, an added "bonus": four days out of ten with no tantrum at all. This is an example of why it's so important to focus not only on what a child does in terms of problem behavior, but also to look carefully at environmental factors that form the

Neil's Weekday Tantrums, October–November

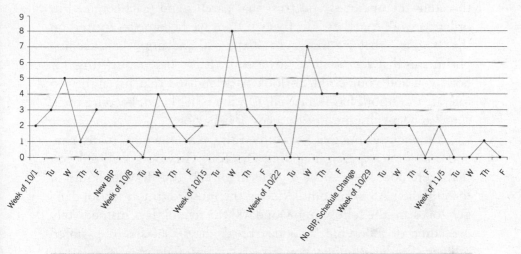

"backdrop," such as activities or classes, scheduling, and other considerations. Going forward, the team at school should implement a revised BIP to address the tantrums that continue to occur. By reducing the frequency of tantrums through schedule changes, Neil's parents and the team might have a clearer view of the function of—and the most effective possible interventions for dealing with—the tantrums that remain.

Because the source of our children's difficulties and behaviors can be so mysterious, always keep your child's teacher posted on changes at home, changes in schedule—anything that may be upsetting to your child. This includes the obvious ones (changes in medication, illness, family crisis) and seemingly less important things (an unsuccessful weekend playdate, an after-school dental appointment, concern over the fact that music class has been moved to right before lunch instead of right after). Children with AS can become troubled over things most people wouldn't even notice.

Keeping specific data over a period of time can help you see where your child is making progress and where he needs some extra help. We've heard from too many parents who learned that their child was having a problem only after it had reached crisis proportions. This lack of communication not only deprives the student of the chance to benefit from effective, timely intervention, but also threatens the openness and trust that parents and teachers need in order to work together effectively. Often we become so fixated on the "biggies" that we lose sight of the real and important accomplishments that accrue slowly over time. It can be encouraging, for both you and your child, to look back and see that his ability to tolerate transitions has improved. On the other hand, keeping track can also help you pinpoint patterns of behavior.

Although no one has yet studied this phenomenon, many parents and some experts, including Dr. Tony Attwood, will tell you that there does seem to be a pattern, an ebb and flow, to some of the common AS symptoms. Among the most common school danger zones are the following: Mondays; the school days immediately preceding or following a holiday break; days that are interrupted by special events (holiday concerts, field days, field trips, special assemblies, and so on); and days when there is a substitute teacher or aide. This, of course, is in addition to the run-of-the-mill school stressors: quizzes, tests, and projects, not to mention fire drills and other sensory assaults.

Unfortunately, many parents and teachers view home-school communication as the *Bad News Daily*. Of course, you need to know when things go wrong, but it's equally important to be aware of what goes right, and to encourage the teacher to focus on those positives, too. Considering how difficult many of our children find it to tell us what they did in school, saying, "I see that you've been asking for help instead of getting upset. That's the smart thing to do. You're doing a wonderful job," might be a good opener. Besides, our children can never receive enough specific praise for their accomplishments and their efforts.

You need to know what goes on in school, particularly if it's been a rough day. For many children with AS, school-related stress and anxiety don't end when the bell rings. If your child hasn't had the best day, you should know and plan accordingly, perhaps postponing the dreaded haircut, reducing the homework load (talk with your child's teacher about doing this), or rescheduling a playdate.

HOW MUCH HELP?

As we've said, it's impossible to generalize about the best educational placement for a child with AS. Different children need different things, and some children with AS need the help of a one-on-one paraprofessional, or aide. (These terms are used differently in different areas of the country; here I'm using the word *aide*.) Unfortunately, in some school districts, aides function merely as in-class babysitters. There are so many ways in which a well-trained "para pro," as autism and education expert Diane Twachtman-Cullen terms them, can help a student with AS not only develop academically, emotionally, and socially but also learn to gain independence.

It's in your child's interest for you to initiate and maintain a relationship with his aide. If your child requires such support, you can assume that it may not be the easiest job. Anything that you can do to help the aide to better understand your child will probably be appreciated. (If it's not, you should talk with his teacher and consider requesting another.) When things go well, be sure that you let your child's aide know that you appreciate her work, and let others—your child's teacher, special education administration, and even your school superintendent and board of education—know it, too. Remember, many school district policies are created out of default or a lack of positive input. If your child's aide has helped facilitate his progress, write a letter outlining specifically what has improved and the aide's role in making that happen. You may be doing other parents whose children require the same level of help a big favor by offering evidence that one-on-one intervention for children with AS is effective.

If your school district doesn't routinely include aides in meetings related to IEP and 504 plan development, encourage it to do so. If the aide cannot attend, ask that she write up a report of her observations of your child, including challenges, progress, strategies (effective and ineffective), and so on.

Although this sounds counterintuitive, the ultimate goal in providing a student with individualized support like an aide is to foster the skills that will render this level of assistance unnecessary. Especially when everyone feels that your child is doing great with an aide, there should be regularly and carefully scheduled "holidays"—

maybe just fifteen minutes or a whole period or even a whole day—when data can be collected on how well she does on her own. At some point, especially as kids enter their middle school and especially high school years, they feel that the aide's presence sets them apart. And it does. Research on the attitudes of children toward classmates who had different types of assistance or special equipment (wheelchair, personal aide, etc.) found that children are more likely to approach a child with obvious medical equipment than a child with an adult aide. Older students who decide to shrug off the aide often find themselves in a precarious position if they have not yet developed the skills to work without one. Be prepared: One day your child will write a check for independence. It's your job—and your child's aide's job—to be sure that he has the skills in the bank to cover it.

And a special note to parents who foresee their child attending college. An individual personal assistant is not a regular accommodation that colleges are required to provide. (For more on college, see chapter 11.)

AS and Giftedness

To most people *gifted* merely means exceptionally intelligent (usually an above-average measurable IQ) and/or talented. Contemporary definitions of these students also recognize other traits, including creativity, leadership, and a specific talent in practically any field of endeavor. Giftedness is also evidenced in abilities to manipulate abstract symbol systems (dance or music notation, mathematics, and so forth); acquire, retain, and discern associations among quantities of information; solve problems in novel ways; and exercise sound judgment. For the *highly gifted* (IQ at or above 145), researchers have identified other qualities: intense curiosity, perfectionism, difficulty conforming to the way others think, and precocious concern with moral and existential matters, among them.[3]

The challenges and the joys of being gifted or raising a gifted child are quite complex and not always well understood by educators and other professionals. You might be surprised to learn, for example, that between 10 percent and 20 percent of high school dropouts are intellectually gifted, and 40 percent of those who graduate in the top 5 percent of their high school class do not complete college.[4] One possible explanation for these statistics is that learning disabilities are as common among the gifted as they are among other students. Studies have demonstrated that gifted students with conditions such as AD/HD are often underdiagnosed and, because of their giftedness, fail to qualify for extra help, special education, or related services.[5] Another is that the psychological and emotional experience of giftedness brings its own challenges.

Children who are intellectually gifted often present with asynchronous development. That means that a child can "appear to be many ages at once," according to author Stephanie Tolan—eight (his chronological age) on his bicycle, but fifteen in algebra class and two when sharing a cookie with a sibling.[6] Further, gifted children experience an internal reality that is very different from that of their peers. The brilliance, the creativity, the achievement that we see are only the external products of an internal reality we probably cannot imagine, and which without the proper understanding and support can foster emotional and social problems.

Intuitively, we all seem to know or suspect that gifted children have emotional difficulties. But why? Tolan writes, "Often the products of gifted children's special mental capacities are valued while the traits that come with those capacities are not. For example, winning an essay contest on the dangers of global warming may get a student lots of attention and praise, while her intense emotional reaction to the threat technology poses to the planet . . . may be considered excessive, overly dramatic, even neurotic . . . Writing a winning essay is deemed not only okay, but admirable; being the sort of person she had to be to write it may not be considered okay."[7]

Remember that so far we are discussing neurotypical gifted individuals. When you add AS (and other comorbid conditions) to the gifted mix, certain strengths (intensity, concentration, focus, tendency toward nonconformity, highly developed moral sense), and weaknesses (disparities between chronological age and social and emotional maturity) can increase exponentially. A child who is twice exceptional (or thrice or four or five times exceptional) needs the benefit of specialized attention, individualized educational programs, and emotional support to reach his or her potential. There is no federal law protecting the rights of gifted students, despite their clearly different and urgent needs. Most, but not all, states have mandates requiring special services for gifted and talented children. Unfortunately, in absence of a federal mandate like IDEA, when education funding gets tight or school districts find themselves having to meet the requirements of other mandates, gifted programs often suffer. After all, some would say—wrongly—gifted students "don't really need help."

Despite research that demonstrates gifted students' need to be educated with their academic peers,[8] many of them are being pulled back into mainstream classrooms, like too many students, swept away in the tide of inclusion. There they may be assigned to helping less able students instead of using the time to pursue a curriculum that challenges them. Current research dispels many of the myths about gifted children: their parents are not more aggressive about pushing them, they benefit from accelerated placement in "ability-grouped" classrooms, and they do not report having lower social self-perception than others their age.

According to Dr. Tony Attwood, many people with AS already have a heightened sense of right and wrong. We know that sometimes kids with AS have difficulty accepting what they perceive as unfairness. Unlike most typical peers, they might have difficulty letting go of thoughts about a mass tragedy in another part of the world or the ongoing social, political, or environmental crises most of us hear about every day and then put out of our minds. Attwood points out, "Having advanced intellectual maturity can be associated with a relatively high level of moral development and ideals. The young child with Asperger's syndrome then becomes extremely distressed in situations of injustice . . ."[9] He also notes "the increased anxiety associated with advanced intellectual ability," which a child with Asperger syndrome might not have the emotional maturity or coping strategies to handle comfortably.

If your child with AS has been identified as gifted, learn all that you can about the issues surrounding this exceptionality. Most important, however, do not allow your child's intellectual abilities to exempt him from any special education, services, or supports he may need. Giftedness does not "cancel out" your child's preexisting needs because of AS, learning disability, emotional issues, or social challenges. It only complicates them. If anything, your child will need more individualized attention and support to reach his potential, not less.

LUNCH AND RECESS: WELCOME TO THE JUNGLE

For many students with Asperger syndrome, some parts of the school day are easier to negotiate than others. The most common areas of difficulty are the unstructured activities—namely, recess, lunch, and the school bus ride—when sensory overload, social confusion, and anxiety can become overwhelming. Depending on how your child's school handles things, these may be prime settings for tantrums, meltdowns, and other inappropriate behavior—the social ramifications of which are only magnified by it being witnessed by the student's peers. If your child indicates that these activities are difficult for him, or if his behavior—before, during, and after—suggests that this may be the case, work with his teacher to create alternatives. Quiet free time inside spent reading, playing, or working on the computer can take the place of recess. Lunch can be spent with a small, supervised group. It may be very informal or an opportunity to provide a structured social skills experience.

PHYSICAL EDUCATION CLASSES

While many neurotypical children find gym class a welcome release from the academics and look forward to the games, activities, and the social aspects of physical education, the opposite is often true for children with Asperger syndrome. Gym class is an environment that showcases his weaknesses rather than his strengths. From a sensory perspective, the noisy atmosphere of the gym and the piercing sound of the coach's whistle can be painful to a child who experiences auditory difficulties. The smell of the locker room and the sensation of changing clothing and showering can easily overwhelm a child with AS. A child who struggles with shoelaces and buttons will take longer to change into gym clothes than his peers and may find himself late for class.

While there are exceptions, most children with Asperger syndrome are to some extent clumsy and have difficulty with both small- and large-motor planning issues. They may not run fast, catch, or throw well. They may struggle with playing as part of a team, and often find games such as basketball, baseball, and dodgeball extremely difficult. We often forget that what many of us loved about physical education and team sports is exactly what makes them so challenging for kids with AS: the social component. Think back to your own days on the court, in the field, or staring down your tetherball or foursquare opponent on the blacktop. What did you say to each other? Little or nothing; you communicated nonverbally, for the most part, using everything from simple glances and gestures to elaborate play-calling gestures. In addition, many children with Asperger syndrome do not do well with competition and have difficulty with winning and losing. Because of problems with making realistic attributions, they may blame themselves or others for things that happen in a game that are beyond their control. And unless your child's teammates—and their opponents—are exceptionally sensitive, mature, and well versed in sportsmanship, any player's errors will not go unnoticed. For some would-be team players with AS, these factors combine to make even the prospect of team sports unappealing, to put it mildly.

Although educators almost automatically mainstream children with AS for gym, even if most of their other classes are in special education or related services, this may not be the best idea. Unlike, say, a science class, phys ed has its own social rules. Children who are not athletically inclined easily become the objects of teasing and taunting by other children and, unfortunately, sometimes by the gym teachers themselves. The combination of sensory overload, lack of athletic ability, and all too often being the object of teasing can have a devastating effect on the self-esteem of a child with Asperger syndrome. Adapted physical education (APE) can help address many of these issues.

Some parents have persuaded their school districts to grant their child credit for regular, documented participation in health or fitness activities outside school. If your child is having a particularly difficult time with physical education in school, or your school just doesn't seem to get it, find out if your child could substitute a couple of weekly sessions working out, swimming, or taking exercise classes at your local Y, community center, college, or private health club. Some of these places offer special programs for individuals with disabilities. You might also find local instructors in martial arts, dance, archery, bowling, or other nonteam activities that your child might enjoy. Don't give up on finding a Little League or other team that would welcome and work with your child.

THE SCHOOL BUS

If your child experiences negative reactions to time on the school bus, look carefully at what factors might be changed to make the trip more enjoyable. One solution is riding on a smaller bus, which, theoretically at least, might result in a quieter, shorter, and better supervised trip. You might request that your child be given special seating (at the front of the bus rather than in the back), or an aide or matron, or that the bus route be altered so that he spends the least possible amount of time in transit. Arranging a small car pool with children your child feels comfortable with may be another option. It's quicker and quieter and provides a low-stress opportunity for informal socialization. Other parents drive their child to and from school. One mother feels that the ride to school provides her child with a more gradual transition between home and school. "I learn a lot in those fifteen minutes about how he feels, what may be bothering him," one mother told us. "It gives me a chance to get in a little pep talk or correct some misconception he has about the day ahead. If necessary, I can also give his teacher a heads-up. I like to think of the ride home as 'the decompression zone.' If he had a problem, he gets it all off his chest before we pull into the driveway, and we can start the afternoon on a fresh page."

THE HOMEWORK QUESTION

In the spring of 2000, Dr. Tony Attwood posted a paper on his website posing the question that many parents and teachers were asking themselves: "Should children with autistic spectrum disorder be exempted from doing homework?" As Dr. Attwood points out, for many children with AS, the "stress and mental exhaustion" of coping throughout the school day, as well as cognitive difficulties, may render homework an exercise counterproductive to both the student's emotional well-being and his academic progress. Emotionally, some children with AS need to separate school from home. They need the school day to have a clear and precise ending. If the child has other challenges that affect his cognitive abilities, the prospect of tackling additional schoolwork when tired may prompt refusal, defiance, tantrums, and other avoidant behaviors. Parents may also find homework a difficult, frustrating experience.

"The worst feeling in the world for me," one mother told us, "is sitting there and watching him struggle to write, and erase, and write, and erase, and write the same letter over and over. I want to grab the pencil myself and break it, or do the work for him, or throw it all out the window. Rather than be upset when he melts down, I find myself marveling that he stuck with it as long as he did."

With the ever-increasing emphasis on academic achievement, most parents, particularly those whose children have other learning disabilities, may be reluctant to forgo this opportunity to squeeze in a little more learning. Dr. Attwood suggests that parents do all they can to create a pleasant homework environment. It should be quiet, free of distractions, and follow, to the extent possible, strategies that have been successful in class, such as the use of a timer, frequent breaks, incentives, praise, and ample, undistracted supervision. Many parents find it best to make homework part of a strict routine, so that children know what to expect.

Teachers can help by providing explicit instructions for both the student and the parent regarding what is expected. If you're unsure about some aspect of your child's homework, contact his teacher as soon as possible. If your child's teacher won't respond to phone calls or emails off-hours, arrange for your child to have extended deadlines so that he can stop working on an assignment he does not understand. If homework is difficult for your child, ask your teacher to use it for reviewing material rather than teaching new material.

If you and your child's teacher have tried everything and your child is still having problems, you must then consider whether the negative repercussions may be outweighing any potential benefit. We say "potential" because several studies have questioned the academic value of homework, particularly for children in elementary school. For children who are chronically frustrated by learning disabilities, it isn't unreasonable to wonder what is gained from insisting that they engage in an exercise that undermines their self-esteem and creates negative feelings about school and learning. Be honest with your child's teacher. What is the point of a specific homework assignment? Is he learning something new (as when he reads a book for a class book report), or is he just practicing an acquired skill? Perhaps you can reach some agreement about what types of homework must be done and which are optional. If Kate can answer the first twenty of fifty algebra problems correctly, does she really need to do the other thirty? If it's possible, you might also ask if your child could work on homework during recess times, unless he would prefer to join his classmates and take a break.

EXTRACURRICULAR ACTIVITIES: SOMETIMES MORE IS BETTER

When your child struggles with school, for whatever reason, it is easy to overlook some of the opportunities for learning, socialization, and a sense of belonging that can come from extracurricular activities. Especially in middle school and high school—where choices range from sports to robotics, special issues clubs such as SADD (Students Against Destructive Decisions) to volunteer work—extracurriculars can offer kids with AS a chance to shine in ways that are not so obvious in class. Some kids who positively hate gym, for example, happily take up archery after school. These activities also allow your child's classmates to get to know him in a different light.

WHEN SCHOOL IS JUST TOO MUCH

With the appropriate accommodations and interventions, most children will find a school placement that works for them. Even then, however, it's not unusual for some students with AS to need a break from school. During periods of particularly intense stress or difficulty, some children benefit from an extra day away from school. (If possible, you should get your child's work in advance so she can complete it at home.) Discuss this issue with your child's teacher.

For a small minority of students with AS, school is nothing short of torture. Even with the seemingly appropriate programs, services, and interventions in place, there are students who simply cannot cope comfortably with the stress of school. And by "cope comfortably," we don't mean just holding it together until they can fall apart after school. Sometimes the stress in combination with other conditions, such as depression, anxiety, and obsessive-compulsive disorder, creates serious problems. Or the stress can even cause anxiety, depression, OCD, and other psychiatric disorders. For this small group of people with AS, the esteem-shattering experience of school—whether the result of emotional stress, social failure, teasing or bullying, academic difficulties, or anything else—is not unlike war, and the experience may profoundly affect them for years hence. In fact, some adults with AS do suffer a form of posttraumatic stress syndrome as a result of their school experiences.

You must learn to recognize when enough is enough—when your child has reached a point where his current academic placement poses a threat to his current and future well-being. Alternate school placement—to a smaller classroom, a smaller school, or a school that specializes in autism-related disabilities, the gifted and talented, or children with specific behavioral and emotional issues—may be appropriate. We've heard from a number of parents who, often in the wake of their child's emotional crisis, opt for home schooling, with good results. If your child is emotionally or psychologically unable to attend school, he should be provided with a home tutor. Fortunately, relatively few parents face these options. Because there are matters of law involved, consult with a local advocacy group or a special education advocate or attorney if you're considering these courses. Protect your child. Know and exercise your rights. Be especially careful if you are contemplating voluntarily removing your child from his current placement and enrolling him in a school or home schooling program for which you will seek reimbursement from your school district. There are specific steps and procedures you must follow to protect your child's rights. Speak with a special education attorney before you act.

Home Schooling

You may decide that the best and most appropriate educational environment for your child is home schooling. Perhaps the situation at school is so desperate that the child cannot function in the school environment, or perhaps you're an advocate of home schooling to begin with.

One great concern is whether a child with AS will have access to social opportunities if removed from the school environment. But as one mother stated, the "social interactions that my son was involved in were so detrimental to his self-esteem that no contact with other children would be better than continued contact with bullies." The quantity and quality of this boy's social interactions actually increased because the mother was able to protect him from the bullying at school, and he was able to interact with other children in her home schooling network. In many ways, she felt she was much more able to help her son learn appropriate social behavior due to her involvement and support.

Most homeschoolers belong to networks in which they have contact with other children of a variety of ages. They may meet a couple times a week for gym (at a local YMCA or other community center) or other activities. Home schooling provides opportunities for a child who has sensory issues or gets tired or overwhelmed easily to work in a quiet environment. Those who struggle with OCD, attention difficulties, or other issues and may not be able to succeed in a classroom situation can learn at their own pace. Home schooling takes a tremendous amount of time and dedication, and it is not for all families and children. But those who have used this method feel that it offers their children the best opportunities for successful learning and socialization. Again, if your child is eligible for or receiving special education or related services, be sure you are fully aware of your rights and responsibilities *before* you withdraw your child from his current placement. We strongly suggest consulting an attorney or advocate.

Something to Think About

Can a child with ASD get everything he needs from school? Some thought-provoking research suggests that the answer might well be no. Ironically, while many kids with AS can handle the regular school curriculum academically, such a course of study may not be meeting other important needs. In fact, according to one authority, "Placement in regular education may inadvertently widen the gap in higher-functioning children if the teaching focus on traditional academics overshadows teaching other social and self-care skills these children need."[10] Dr. Ami Klin points out that as such children grow older, instruction in adaptive skills should, in fact, be intensified. This was among the conclusions of a 2007 study that explored the adaptive skills of higher-functioning individuals between ages seven and eighteen with autism spectrum disorders. Despite an average full-scale IQ of 99.4, age-equivalent scores on the Vineland Adaptive Behavior Scales in the areas of play/leisure, daily living, personal, and domestic ranged from 5.1 years to 6.9 years, a finding that Klin and colleagues describe as "worrisome." They also call attention to "the need to prioritize adaptive skill instruction as its own goal in intervention."[11]

THE OLDER STUDENT

As students enter their teens, most parents' thoughts turn to life after high school. Whether that means college, special job training, or employment depends on numerous factors. Most students with AS will require special support through the years when most other students require significantly less.

Plan ahead, bearing in mind that the special education, related services, and supports your child has received in school under IDEA end when he either graduates from high school or turns twenty-two. IDEA requires that IEP meetings and IEPs written when a student is age sixteen or older provide specific information on transition services. If you believe that your child may need extra time to prepare for life after high school, IDEA provides that transition can be discussed and planned for earlier. See pages 498–500, "Transition Planning."

It is your school district's responsibility to provide transition services. If, for some reason, your committee on special education concludes that your child does not require some or all transition services, that information must be included in the IEP. Transition is part of the IEP and must address three areas: instruction, community experiences, and employment and/or other postschool living objectives.[12] Transition planning should address daily living skills, if needed.

Note that the purpose of transition is to help prepare the student for a wide range of post-school activities, including college. Don't let your school district persuade you that your college-bound child is "too smart" to benefit from transition services. Among special education experts and advocates, transition services often get low marks because they're not always sufficiently individualized, intensive, or creative. If you can locate a public or private organization or agency that specializes in providing such training in your area, make an appointment. Your state office for individuals with developmental disabilities or a local autism advocacy group can probably make recommendations. It may be the best way to learn what really can be done, as opposed to what your school district usually does. People with AS may require very specialized training and preparation for independence. Insist that your school district call in outside professionals if you feel it's necessary.

If college is an option, first read chapter 11 for more information. Then be prepared to do a lot of research. Just as there is no one school placement appropriate for every student with AS, there are no guidelines for finding the right college beyond the obvious: support, understanding, and accommodations. We've heard from many parents of adults with AS who look back and regret that their child did not receive the training in social skills, emotional self-management, and daily living skills that would have supported success in higher education or a job. One development we are very pleased to see is the slow but steady growth in post-secondary programs that recognize and support the student with ASD.

While the needs of an elementary school student may be radically different from those of the high school student, the primary goal for all students with AS is that their educational environment allows for both academic and social development. Even if your child wasn't diagnosed early or didn't require services in previous years, it's never too late to initiate supports at school or to make changes in the educational environment.

SELECTED RESOURCES FOR TEACHERS

We consider this list the "AS/ASD library" we wish every school serving our kids had (and every educator read). Most of these books are written especially for and by educators.

Tony Attwood, *The Complete Guide to Asperger's Syndrome* (London: Jessica Kingsley, 2007).

E. Amanda Boutot and Brenda Smith Myles, *Autism Spectrum Disorders: Foundations, Characteristics, and Effective Strategies* (Upper Saddle River, NJ: Pearson, 2011).

Catherine Faherty, *Asperger's: What Does It Mean to Me?* (Arlington, TX: Future Horizons, 2000). Note: If your child's teacher is using this book, make it clear that you do not want anyone at school informing your child of his diagnosis. (This is the first exercise in the book.)

Deborah Fein and Michelle A. Dunn, *Autism in Your Classroom: A General Educator's Guide to Students with Autism Spectrum Disorders* (Bethesda, MD: Woodbine House, 2007).

Ellen S. Heller Korin, *Asperger Syndrome: An Owner's Manual: What You, Your Parents, and Your Teachers Need to Know* (Shawnee Mission, KS: Autism Asperger Publishing, 2006) and *Asperger Syndrome: An Owner's Manual 2: For Older Adolescents and Adults* (Shawnee Mission, KS: Autism Asperger Publishing, 2007).

Diane Twachtman-Cullen, *How to Be a Para Pro: A Comprehensive Training Manual for Paraprofessionals* (Higganum, CT: Starfish Specialty Press, 2000). Though ostensibly designed to train paraprofessionals and aides, this 200-page spiral-bound book is indispensable for teachers.

Julie S. Vargas, *Behavior Analysis for Effective Teaching*, 2d ed. (New York: Routledge, 2013). Excellent, accessible source for anyone who wishes to understand more about applied behavior analysis in the classroom. A must-have for teachers.

Journals

Autism Spectrum Quarterly, edited by Diane Twachtman-Cullen, PhD. In 2004 Carol Gray's *Jenison Autism Journal* (formerly the *Morning News*) evolved into a new format. It provides ideas and examples for teachers and parents on ASD-related topics. For information, go to www.asquarterly.com.

Chapter 10

GROWING UP HEALTHY AND SAFE

FOCUS ON HEALTH

For all of the testing and studying that people with ASD have received these past twenty years, it's remarkable how little attention has been paid to the physical aspects of autism. Sure, ASD is a neurological disorder, but it also has an effect on general physical health. Now that increasing numbers of youngsters on the spectrum are entering adulthood, growing older, and living more fully within their communities, their unique health needs are receiving some long overdue attention. Although researchers track some interesting, eye-opening trends, it's the so-called little things—such as poor physical and dental hygiene, limited diets, and not enough physical activity—that we are learning can also present significant health risks over time.[1] While we recognize that how we feel physically can have a profound effect on how well we function cognitively, emotionally, and socially, science is just now playing catch-up in exploring these connections for people with ASDs. The good news is that there are things that parents can do to improve our kids' physical health and well-being, and these changes can also set the stage for progress in other important areas, such as learning and behavior. The connection between a high-carb, low-fiber diet and the myriad stomach and GI problems common to people with ASDs rings strongly of common sense, as do inadequate tooth brushing and serious dental problems, and insufficient sleep and behavior problems.

As our children grow up, they also encounter health concerns and risks that we as parents are less able to control. And, because many of our kids have been socially and developmentally out of the loop and behind for so long, we may lose track of how close they are to puberty and the changes and challenges it brings. It's probably safe to say that no parent is really ready to start talking to his or her child about relationships and sexuality, HIV and pregnancy prevention, sexual abuse, and the dangers of alcohol and illicit drug use. But these discussions take on a clearly different tone when it comes to our kids. More on that later.

SELF-HELP AND SELF-CARE

Good health begins at home with regular daily routines that help kids stay healthy. Regardless of measurable IQ, kids with AS are often behind same-age peers when it comes to basic hygiene and self-care.[2] When they are little, it is easy to help them—say, by brushing their teeth, washing their hair, or monitoring them in the shower or bath—or to overlook various personal preferences about using deodorant, washing their hair frequently enough, keeping their nails clipped and clean, and so on. Ironically, children who are more severely affected by their autism often receive direct instruction in these areas as part of their education. Kids with ASDs such as AS often "skip" those types of interventions and find themselves, appropriately, in less restrictive educational settings where these matters are viewed solely as the parents' problem.

In an informal online survey on adaptive daily living skills conducted for *The Parents' Guide to Teaching Kids with Asperger Syndrome and Similar ASDs Real-Life Skills for Independence*, the one hundred parent respondents indicated that most of their children with ASDs were typically two to three years behind in acquiring basic skills, such as dressing and undressing, brushing or combing hair, and showering or bathing independently. In most cases, the problem with managing personal care is the result of one or a combination of the following factors:

- Executive function deficits
- Sensory sensitivity to substances, materials, or the environment
- Poor imitation skills
- Fine- and/or gross-motor deficits

So let's take Bobby brushing his teeth. He might have a problem with planning and executing the steps of the task (get the toothbrush, open the toothpaste, squeeze out just enough, and so forth), or he might not like the taste or the texture of the toothpaste, or he might not be able to learn simply by watching someone else demonstrate these steps. Another possibility is that his motor deficits make it difficult to apply the correct amount of pressure while brushing and to hold the brush at the right angle, and so on (and on, and on).

Deficits in self-care skills can have far-reaching consequences. On the home front, parents get tired of needing to remind, supervise, and nag, especially when the kid is older. At some point, having Mom or Dad help with wiping, washing hair in the shower, or shaving just isn't right for anyone. Peers and others can be less than welcoming or kind to someone whom they perceive as not clean or unkempt. Finally, deficits in these areas can have profound ripple effects on everything from your child being able to go to that first sleepover to her being hired for that dream job.

Teaching Self-Care Skills

Teaching these skills presents a number of unique problems. For one thing, kids cannot always see exactly what they are supposed to be doing; this is the case with brushing teeth, wiping, and other grooming tasks.

1. Job one is to identify where the roadblocks lie and try to find workarounds that help your child to perform the skill as independently as possible. If it's an executive function problem that involves difficulty

organizing, prioritizing, remembering, focusing, or staying on track, think of visuals, lists, and other prompts to help your child gather everything he needs before he starts and then to follow the steps. If it's a sensory problem, that means maybe finding a soap that smells and feels right or a toothpaste that tastes okay. For the child whose imitation or motor skills get in the way, model, teach, and practice. Repeat.

2. Get over the idea that these skills are "simple." They are not. And if your child has not met a self-care milestone he should have, understand that even a basic skill might be very difficult for him.

3. Set up clear routines and rules, and avoid making exceptions. The more routine self-care becomes, the more easily your child can learn and the more independent he can be.

4. Explicit, direct instruction may be required, even if your child is academically advanced. Mastering self-help skills is different from acing long division.

5. At the beginning, use intensive prompts to help ensure error-free practice. For tasks such as washing hands, brushing teeth, and combing hair, that usually means starting out with hand-over-hand prompting (which is placing your hand lightly over your child's and guiding hers through the motions), which you fade gradually as your child masters each step.

6. While your child is learning, follow the same steps exactly every time. This will help kids whose executive function skills and motor planning aren't so hot to develop motor memory of the task.

7. Practice, practice, practice the task "outside the moment." By that I mean, don't expect your kid to become adept at brushing his teeth if his only practice occurs when he brushes in the course of the day. For many of our kids, the practice time is rushed. (The bus is coming!) And what parent can possibly supervise every time? No wonder they can develop sloppy habits, do the job halfway, or not at all. Instead, set aside time when you will practice the full task or any step that needs work. You will have a lot more success isolating and practicing a "trouble step" (say, figuring out how much shampoo or conditioner to use) if you dedicate some time to that alone. Stand at the bathroom sink and measure out the product ten times in a row.

Practice hand drying two or three times in a row until the job's truly done.

8. Practice to acquire the skill and then practice some more to gain fluency. *Fluency* is a word you will be hearing more in the coming years, because skills that are not fluent—that is, performed correctly, easily, and quickly—are easily interrupted, practiced incompletely, and even forgotten. Fluency has been shown to be a hedge against distraction and frustration, as well as a solid support for those with executive function issues. The goal of teaching self-help skills to fluency is, essentially, to put them on autopilot. Fluent skills require less thought, less planning, and less effort.

9. Choose the right teaching tool for the job. Social Stories, visual schedules, checklists, and instructional videos are effective, in their place. None of these really gives your child the opportunity to perform the task, and for that reason alone, they should not be used by themselves. For instance, a Social Story can explain *why* deodorant is a good idea, and a visual schedule or checklist can remind your child *where* in the morning routine it fits (after the shower, not before), and an illustration or video can demonstrate *how* to apply it so it does its job. But nothing truly teaches the skill like your child's actually doing it.

For more, see *The Parents' Guide to Teaching Kids with Asperger Syndrome and Similar ASDs Real-Life Skills for Independence.*

HYGIENE: THE BASICS

By age five, your child should be totally independent in meeting his toileting needs, brushing his teeth, drying himself with a towel, and blowing and wiping his nose. By age six, hair brushing should be on its way, if not perfect.[3] As kids grow older, the skills they need increase and have a way of letting everyone know that it's time they get addressed: skin breakouts, oilier hair, increased sweat, various types of hair to shave, and puberty-related hygiene concerns (menstruation for girls and daytime emissions for boys). For many parents, it's the nearing or the arrival of puberty that throws a harsh light not only on the new skills that will need acquiring but also on whatever skills are currently missing or not up to par.

Take an honest inventory of where your child is in this area. It is never too late to start teaching skills or improving skills. Talk with your child openly about what your concerns are and why they should be addressed. If your child is older, speak frankly about the possible implications of poor hygiene as they relate to him. If your kid replies that he does not really care what others think, recast your argument to help him understand the impact the impression he makes might have on a future employer, admissions officer, or friend.

EATING NUTRITIOUSLY

Childhood obesity is a serious health problem everywhere, but those with ASD are at especially high risk, and the problem starts early. According to a recent study of children whose average age was just under four years, 30 percent of children with ASD were obese, compared with 10 percent of the general population that age.[4] The risk appears greater for children who are more severely affected and less for those with AS-type profiles. However, given the typical low rates of physical activity and preference for more sedentary activities, our kids are at greater risk. In addition, some of the commonly prescribed psychoactive medications (for example, the SSRIs and especially the neuroleptics, among others) can have weight gain as a side effect. The risks of being overweight are well known by now, and we also know that people who are overweight in childhood are at increased risk of having problems with weight for the rest of their lives. Further, poor nutrition and/or overeating can be contributing factors to stomach and toileting problems. (See page 472.)

Most of us know which foods are healthy and which are not. For many parents, the problem lies in the limited range of foods our kids enjoy because of sensory preferences regarding taste, texture, smell, color, and so on. One popular solution is to substitute the high-fat, high-sugar snacks for something healthier. However, eating is also a behavior, and we know that you improve the odds that the substitute will be accepted if it shares at least something in common with the food it's meant to replace. For example, there is nothing about a raw carrot stick that is anything like an oatmeal cookie in terms of taste, texture, and what junk-food designers call "mouth feel." However, there is some nice crossover between an oatmeal cookie and a healthier granola bar, or between a regular potato chip and a chip made of pita, or popcorn, or other puffed grain (provided it's got the same crunch, snap, and salt level). Now more than ever, even the average grocery store offers healthy alternatives to popular, less healthy foods.

Instead of focusing on what your child is choosing to eat and entering into debates and negotiations about it, start by changing the environment. One of the best things we ever did was simply not bring certain tempting foods into the house, especially things like cookies and chips that we were all eating without much thought. I made a deal with my son: no snacks or sweets in the house, but he could choose a special treat that we would get out once a week. Yes, he still got to eat something probably not so healthy, but this approach did move desserts from the everyday snack category into the occasional treat, where they rightfully belong. It also gave some social skills practice for behavior in restaurants.

For many kids, the texture and taste of vegetables is a particular problem. Again, there are more options. First, even if your child rejected, say, string beans at ages three, four, five, and six, you should still present them periodically. Don't make a big deal out of it, but encourage your child to take a nibble. Most parents can tell when the reaction says, "Just don't really care for" or "Intolerable!" If there is a real sensory hypersensitivity, you might choose to let it go, provided your child is eating well enough otherwise. There is nothing wrong with adding some pureed or finely chopped vegetables to soups, sauces, or other foods. One parent I know slipped probably about a pound of finely chopped spinach into a pasta sauce served over baked ziti. No one in the family knew the difference. Kids on the spectrum tend to fall at the extreme ends on the taste scale. Either it's bagel, noodle, white-bread bland or it's chili, chocolate, and citrus-sour *pow!* with not much in between. If your child goes for the most exciting stuff, consider using sauces or condiments to liven up vegetables or meats that are tolerable but not that interesting.

If your child has a limited repertoire that is made up largely of packaged products, such as macaroni and cheese, ramen noodles, frozen pizza, or chicken nuggets, gradually move toward healthier alternatives. Often these foods appeal to the basic evolutionary preference for salt, sugar, and fat. Foods that combine all three—take the classic fast-food burger with that sugary bun and special sauce— hit a neurological bull's-eye. It's no wonder that people keep coming back for more. Again, do some exploring. Introduce foods that are similar but healthier: a less fattening mac and cheese, a lower-sodium ramen noodle, a more nutritious pizza, a chicken nugget that is more chicken and less fat and salt.

Some recent studies have found that kids with Asperger syndrome and similar profiles are also at increased risk for being underweight[5] and even developing eating disorders such as anorexia nervosa[6] (a psychiatric disorder characterized by extremely restricted food intake and obsessive behavior related to eating and body image) and, to a lesser extent, bulimia nervosa (a psychiatric disorder in which one either vomits or exercises excessively to eliminate calories ingested). If you suspect that your child is not getting the nutrition she needs or that she may have an eating disorder, seek medical help immediately. Anorexia nervosa is a difficult condition to treat successfully, and it has the highest fatality rate of any psychiatric disorder.

BEING ACTIVE

Everyone needs regular physical activity to be healthy, and kids need it especially. Now we know that kids with ASDs derive even greater benefits. A number of recent studies reveal that in following programs that included regular physical exercise, kids with ASD showed decreases in a wide range of interfering behaviors and symptoms, including aggression, stereotypal behaviors, and off-task behavior. On the plus side were increases in on-task behavior, appropriate motor behavior, and academic engagement.[7] Vigorous exercise appears to confer more benefits than less demanding activities.[8] Further, the right exercise program can increase upper and lower body strength, abdominal strength, flexibility, and balance.[9]

Many kids with ASD have what OTs and PTs refer to as *low tone*. At they grow taller, you may see a looser gait, slumping while sitting, or difficulty maintaining a posture that makes it easy, for example, to write comfortably or execute movements in a logical, productive, and efficient manner.

A child's ability to participate with peers in physical activities— even if that means just being able to hold up one's end in a game of catch or join others biking or skateboarding—has long been over looked as a pathway to social skills. While experts tend to guide parents away from team sports for kids with ASDs, some kids thrive when the right team, right coach, and right sport come together. Challenger Little League, which is part of the national Little League organization, has chapters and teams all over the country. Many community teams welcome kids with disabilities, either on their regular teams or on special teams. While archery, swimming and diving, martial arts, ice skating, track and field, bowling, biking, dance, and other individual, nonteam-oriented sports are an obvi- ous choice for many of our kids, they provide opportunities for social interaction with peers, even though there is not a team in the usual sense.

For some students, adaptive physical education is the appropriate choice. Adaptive PE classes are conducted by specially trained teach- ers and work on developing the basic physical skills required for par- ticipation. Such a class can be a good alternative for children who have extreme difficulties with coordination, balance, and physical performance generally. However, chances are the class will be very small and the other students will have a wide range of physical and cognitive ability. While it may be a good fit in terms of your child's physical needs, some kids, especially as they grow older, find place- ment in such classes stigmatizing, or they may lack the social judg- ment not to express impatience with their less capable classmates.

True, there is a lot about our daily lives that seems to conspire against our kids getting the good half-hour to hour of physical ac- tivity they need. In many schools, recess and/or physical education class are reduced in frequency and length if not eliminated alto- gether. Since children with AS can have both physical and social challenges that interfere with their full participation in either, the exercise benefit might be minimal to nonexistent. Add to that their seemingly natural inclination toward the sedentary world of computers, computer games, and viewing, it's easy to see how easily fitness slips away.

You can take some steps to turn the tide in the right direction. First, there are many good reasons to consider limiting screen time (see page 342), and here is another. If your child is spending a lot of time sitting, schedule in some "up" time: say, after an hour of sitting, ten minutes walking on a treadmill or doing chores around the house before returning to pixel land. Second, if you have exercise equipment in your home, work it into your child's schedule. Perhaps begin by using it as a break during homework. (Think behaviorally: that will probably be more palatable than using it as a break between video games.) Finally, if you have serious concerns about your child's fitness, consider having him join a gym or signing up with a personal trainer. Good personal trainers are often experts at motivation; they have to be. If your kid and his trainer have a good rapport, you can let the trainer do some of the cajoling and prompting about eating and exercise habits. The individual attention makes for a much more efficient and intensive workout than what is probably possible at home or in school, where a lot of gym class consists of standing and waiting for classmates to do their thing.

GETTING ENOUGH SLEEP

It's hardly news that most Americans do not get enough sleep. However, some good recent studies point out that not only are kids with ASD particularly prone to having a range of sleep disorders, but the impact of sleep disorders can be more serious.[10] Prior studies had found benefits of adequate sleep that included better social relatedness, reduced insistence on sameness,[11] and reduced problem behaviors.[12] In a 2007 study that compared children with AS and typical control subjects, those with AS were found to be twice as likely to get less sleep and five times as likely to have trouble falling asleep.[13] Another study from around the same time also found longer nighttime awakenings and earlier wake times for kids with AS and so-called high-functioning autism profiles.[14]

For various reasons, kids these days tend to stay up later. Many older students have hours of homework, and parents find it difficult not to allow some downtime after the homework is done before bed. The daily routines of most families have rendered time after dinner anything but relaxing. Parents are often busy with work brought home, getting things ready for the next day, or doing cooking and housework. Another problem is that some of the before-bed activities our kids choose—video games, online chatting, television viewing, and so on—are known to encourage wakefulness and thus make it even more difficult to fall asleep, because they are so mentally stimulating.

- If your child is having sleep problems, first survey his environment and make changes where needed. Are the bed and pillows comfy? Is there enough light or darkness, depending on your child's preference?
- See if homework can be reduced or some of it shifted to the weekends, so it does not end so late.
- Limit screen time so that screens are off at least an hour or so before bedtime.
- Try to limit fluid intake in the couple of hours before bedtime if nighttime waking to use the bathroom is a problem.
- Speak to your child's doctor about a trial of melatonin, an over-the-counter hormonal supplement that some people find helps with sleep.
- Be sure your child is getting some physical exercise every day. For some kids, exercise before bed helps them sleep; for others, it keeps them awake. You know your child best.
- Establish nighttime routines for your child. A story or time spent talking with a parent at bedtime can be relaxing. A shower or bath, and maybe some time to read might also help her to fall asleep.
- Consider some nighttime routines for everyone in the house. It's difficult for kids to fall asleep sometimes if they know that a sibling or parent is up watching TV or playing on the Wii. Consider recording and watching your favorite late-night show some other time. If you have a big issue to discuss with your child, try to address it some other time.

- Get everything ready for the next morning. Try to be sure your child goes to sleep with everything needed in the backpack, clothes picked out, and so on.

If difficulties persist, talk to your doctor to rule out any medical issues.

TUMMY AND TOILETING PROBLEMS

For reasons not clearly understood, people with ASDs receive more medical care for gastrointestinal problems than their same-age peers across the life span.[15] There are several possible reasons for this, including the following:

- an unvaried diet high in processed carbs, sugars, or fats but low in fresh fruits, vegetables, and whole grains;
- routines or habits around toileting that result in constipation, diarrhea, or both;
- incomplete or inadequate toilet training that results in the development of unhealthy routines or habits, such as:
  - able to use the restroom only at a particular time of day (for example, can have bowel movements only at night before bedtime);
  - able to use the restroom only in particular places (for example, only at home or Grandma's house, but never at school, at a friend's house, or at the movie theater);
  - able to use the restroom only if the "right" toilet tissue, wet wipes, soap, and so on, are available;
  - able to use the restroom only if also able to engage in specific behavior chains that may not be appropriate or safe or possible in settings outside the home (for example, must talk while using toilet, must remove pants completely, must shower or bathe afterward, and so on).

Where to start? If this is an area of concern, first speak with your child's pediatrician and request a referral to a pediatric GI specialist. You want to rule out the possibility that there might be a food allergy or sensitivity, or other physical issue. Some kids have sluggish GI tracts due to lack of physical activity; others might benefit from a change in diet or the introduction of a mild fiber supplement or laxative. Check with your doctor first, though. If the problem turns out to be more behaviorally based, consider consulting a behavior analyst or a psychologist who understands behavior analysis. It is highly doubtful that a more psychoanalytic, Freudian view of toileting issues will help much. An ethical behavior analyst or psychologist should not proceed without medical clearance. If the professional you contact offers to move forward without this, move on. Any intervention should be evidence based, and all decisions should be based on collected data.

Using the Restroom Is Also a Social Skill

Dr. Peter Gerhardt and others point out one serious flaw in how some boys with ASD learn to use the restroom: their teachers are women. The problem with this becomes abundantly clear when women are presented with a diagram of a row of urinals in a public men's room showing which are currently occupied. When asked, "Which one should your male student choose?" many women have a hard time seeing why it matters. After all, for women, socialization does not stop at the restroom door. Even though we may have never met anyone else there, we remark on the conditions of the room; we compliment one another on appearance or the behavior of children. We will pass a needed tissue or other personal item under the stall door to a stranger if she asks.

The social scene at the urinal wall could not be more different. For one thing, men do not talk to one another during this activity. They do not look at one another, and, whenever possible, they choose a urinal that offers the buffer of at least one unoccupied "station" between themselves and the next guy. There is a strict code regarding how the pants are opened and how much of the body is exposed.

Whatever the social norms for public restroom use are in your area, your child should know them. They should also know that engaging with strangers in a semisecluded location like a public restroom should be done with caution. Your child should not be afraid to use a restroom, but he or she should know how to behave. First, be clear and specific about which common comments and behaviors are appropriate ("How do you turn on the water here?" "Is that dispenser also empty?" and so on) and which are not (requests for personal information, touching). Second, your child should know that certain behaviors in a public restroom are just not acceptable: masturbation, self-talk, spending excessive time grooming, removing more clothing than necessary, dawdling or hanging out, and so on. Even if this permitted at home, it is essential that you instill the concept of "right time, right place" and "wrong time, wrong place."

It's safe to say that most of us have our own preferences when it comes to personal care matters like this. And, yes, there are perfectly neurotypical people who would never use a public restroom, no matter what. So it's easy to see how many of us slip into overlooking and accommodating a child's "preferences" in this area. However, it is essential that you take a hard look at any behavior that occurs at home; picture it in the middle school gym restroom, in the public restroom at the local mall, or at an acquaintance's home; and then consider the reasonable outcome. Yes, people can "understand" autism. But a teenage boy who cannot urinate standing without dropping his pants or a girl who cannot attend to her personal needs without audibly "talking her way through it" place themselves in danger of being misunderstood and ridiculed (at the least) and possibly becoming the target of frightened bystanders and even law enforcement in more public settings.

THE DOCTOR'S OFFICE

There is much about a visit to the doctor's office that a child with AS might not like: the smell; the noise of other children in the waiting room; the prospect of a shot or blood draw; that stiff, crinkly paper on the exam table. Alas, regular doctor visits cannot be avoided, so it's wise to do whatever you can to increase your child's coping skills.

For some kids, the problem with going to the doctor traces back to that one unpleasant experience that they just cannot seem to get over. A number of good books about going to the doctor feature familiar characters (for example, *Sesame Street*, *Arthur*, *Mister Rogers*, and others). If your child is open to it, you can also try incorporating some doctor's office role-play, using family members, stuffed animals, or dolls. Let your child be the doctor or the patient, or switch parts.

Taking the Stress Out of Visits to the Doctor or Dentist

1. Make sure that your doctor or dentist knows of your child's ASD and how it affects your child's behavior.
2. If possible, visit the office ahead of time. Let your child see the waiting room and maybe meet the doctor without any exams or procedures taking place. Stop by and say hello. Maybe sit for a few minutes with a favorite toy in the waiting room. Take home a sheet of that exam table paper and just play with it.
3. Find out what will be on the "agenda" for the appointment. If no shot is scheduled, tell your child that right away; it might alleviate one unnecessary worry. However, if a vaccination is going to be given, you might want to let your child know a couple of days ahead of time—or not. For some kids, knowing all of the details ahead reduces anxiety, but for some others, it makes it worse. You know your child best.
4. If a shot will be given or blood will be drawn, ask your doctor or dentist about any steps you can take beforehand to reduce discomfort. Desensitizing the skin by applying the topical anesthetic cream Emla (lidocaine and prilocaine) before needle sticks is a well-established protocol in many hospitals. You will have to arrange this with the doctor beforehand, since Emla requires a prescription and must be applied before the visit.
5. If possible, schedule the visit for when your child is fresh and alert and has time to relax afterward.

6. Ask your doctor if you can send a fax or an email a day or more ahead of the visit outlining your concerns. Especially if your child's reaction to being at the doctor's demands most of your attention, it might be easier for everyone if your doctor has an idea of the issue before seeing your child.

7. If your doctor has concerns or needs to discuss something with you, try to arrange beforehand for the discussion to occur out of earshot of your child. Perhaps bring along an older sibling, friend, or family member to watch your child while you and the doctor or dentist speak privately.

DENTAL CARE

Did you know that dental emergencies are one of the leading causes of visits to the emergency room for kids with ASDs?[16] There are several reasons why. Many of our kids engage in behaviors, usually when they are younger, that set the stage for dental problems later on: chewing on nonfood items, bruxism (or teeth clenching), placing nonfood items in their mouths. In the United States, snacking is a way of life, and many of our kids do so at home and at school. For those who receive some edibles as reinforcers, these may involve candy, juice, dried fruit, or other items that are sugary or sticky—bad news for teeth.

Due to sensory and/or motor skills problems, many kids do not perform or cooperate with the daily dental basics well enough to make them effective in preventing cavities and other problems. And then for a variety of reasons, many of them also avoid the dentist or do not receive the degree of care they probably should. Granted, there is much about being in a dentist's office that can be difficult for a youngster with AS: the bright light, the unique office smells, having to lie back in the chair (a position that stresses some people due to the perceived loss of control), the discomfort of holding your mouth open, having that plastic bitewing tab in your mouth for X-rays, the sound and feel of the drill, and that shot. The list does indeed go on and on. Finally, once a parent or child has a traumatic experience at the dentist's, it becomes easy to delay routine or follow-up care, thus sometimes setting off the process that ends up in the ER or back in the dentist's chair.

The first, most obvious step is to teach your child to brush thoroughly and as often as warranted. Be especially insistent about this during school hours, too. Especially in the younger grades, kids have a morning snack, lunch, and then an afternoon snack. In addition, teachers and therapists might offer small treats—the Hershey's Kiss for great work in speech, a cookie at the end of OT—and not too many weeks pass without a classroom holiday celebration or a classmate's birthday party.

Some children with ASD also develop unusual eating behaviors that can contribute to cavities and other dental problems. For example, some children "pocket" food in their cheeks and do not swallow completely. Others go about with a box or cup of juice at hand almost constantly. Yet others might be taking medication that sets the stage for tooth decay by either reducing salivation or being high in sugar (a concern with liquid medicines).[17]

The next step is to help your child learn to tolerate the dentist visit. If she has had a difficult time in the past or is unusually anxious about the dentist, consider bringing in a behavior analyst to develop a desensitization program. Look for dentists who specialize in pediatrics and/or children with disabilities. If possible, arrange for your child to drop in at the dentist's for a dry run: maybe just sit in the dentist's chair or practice spitting out water into that little sink.

EMOTIONAL AND MENTAL HEALTH ISSUES

Depression and Anxiety

For various reasons, adolescents are at increased risk for anxiety, depression, and other disorders. Some psychiatric disorders make their first appearance in the teen years. For people with AS, simply the fact of being an adolescent can exacerbate existing problems or create new ones. A teen is at a much greater risk for developing psychiatric disorders than a ten-year-old simply because of more time spent with less adult supervision, coupled with access to alcohol, illicit drugs, cars, and sex. The opportunities for and risks of acting out are so much higher.

Know the signs of depression and anxiety. (See pages 65 and 67.) If you have any concerns about your child's behavior or mood, see a psychologist or psychiatrist, preferably one who specializes in children *and* in ASD. If your teen has depression, something that is not at all uncommon for neurotypical teens and very common for teens with AS, please discuss it with your teen's physician. If your teen has never taken medication and finds that she is having increasing difficulties that cannot be managed by other methods (such as therapy, environmental changes, relaxation exercises), you may want to discuss the possibility of medication with your child's pediatrician or psychiatrist. Both anxiety and depression are risk factors for self-injury or suicide. Dr. Tony Attwood describes what he calls a "suicide attack," in which a person with AS makes "a spur-of-the-moment decision to make a dramatic end to life."[18] In many cases, that person showed no "signs" anyone recognized. Attwood points out that something as seemingly minor as having made a mistake or having been teased can precede an impulsive act. It's also important to keep in mind that for some youngsters with AS, the stressors known to contribute to suicidal thoughts, plans, and actions are too familiar: social isolation, bullying, depression, anxiety, and inability to see "a way out" of current problems.

If your child with AS is currently taking psychotropic prescription medicine but is still experiencing increased anxiety, depression, or behavioral problems, see your doctor. Adolescence brings hormonal changes and growth spurts that may require adjusting dosages or switching medications.

UNDERSTANDING RELATIONSHIPS AND SEXUALITY

The teen years are a time when most young adults become interested in forming intimate relationships, but for those with AS, such relationships are not easily formed. Those interested in dating may find that they lack the skills to play the dating game. Knowing whether someone likes you, knowing how to approach someone in a way that lets her know that you like her (but without being inappropriately forward), finding the courage to ask someone out, and handling rejection if she says no—these have the power to prompt anxiety, fear, embarrassment, and pure mortification in even the most socially adept. For people with AS, they can present an emotional and social minefield.

In relationships, it's important to learn to read signals and pay attention to the other person's likes and dislikes. Perhaps there are a few who sail through this gracefully, but for most teens, it is definitely a learning process. Teens with Asperger syndrome may feel particularly lonely as they see their peers become involved in dating relationships. They may make awkward attempts and develop crushes, only to be disappointed.

Remember that before pursuing a romantic relationship, your child should have experience with having and being a friend. Friendship skills are the foundation of more serious, intimate relationships. Youngsters who do not acquire at least a basic repertoire in this area will probably encounter more difficulty in this vastly more complex arena.

If your son or daughter wants to have a relationship and it isn't working out, try to be as understanding as possible. Encourage your teen to participate in activities where he's likely to meet other teens who share similar interests: after-school clubs and activities, volunteer work in your community, and so on. Remind your teen that not everyone dates in high school, and that most people are interested in many other people before they find the "right one." Reassure your teen that there is no time limit on when people begin dating, and that while it may not seem so right now, most people don't find a true, serious relationship until they're in their twenties or older.

If your son or daughter does begin dating, you and your child may have to consider whether to tell the boyfriend or girlfriend about the AS diagnosis. This decision can be particularly difficult if peers at school are unaware of it. The boy or girl your child is dating may well realize that something is different but may blame themselves or your child for behaviors that are a result of AS. Although many teenage dating relationships are short-lived and some end dramatically, it may be wise to limit the information shared until you're sure where the relationship is going.

You'll want to assure your child that someday he or she may

find someone special who will love and care for them and appreciate them as they are. Yet at the same time, you may secretly wonder
if this is true. You may waver between wanting to encourage your
child to take the initiative and ask someone out and wanting to
protect him or her from rejection and disappointment. Perhaps the
best approach is to offer suggestions gently and always be there, no
matter what the outcome.

Kids with ASDs do grow up, and faster than you expect. Further, we live in a culture that historically views people with disabilities as lacking the drives and interests all normal, healthy people
have. Where other parents seem programmed to be constantly looking forward into an endless horizon, many of us take the diagnosis,
construct a protective fence, and then fail to imagine a day when
our child will have the desire and the means to knock it down. And
yet that day usually does arrive, and often sooner than we expect.
This brings us to sex.

What Your Child Needs to Know About Sexuality:
The Essentials

Although studies have found that parents of adolescents with ASD
express grave concern over matters related to sexuality (how it will
be expressed, whether the child will be a victim of sexual abuse,
whether the child has the potential to become or be perceived as
a sexual offender), most of the research on sexuality for this group
is limited and relatively new. What we do know, however, should
have parents running, not walking, to find local resources that can
help their children better understand relationships and sexuality, as
well as pregnancy and HIV prevention, and ways to avoid sexual
abuse. Contact your local autism organization; your state, county,
and local departments of health and disabilities; and any university
or hospital where people with ASDs are treated or ASDs are being
researched.

First, sexual abuse is a problem for everyone. Current estimates
place the rate at 6 percent to 10 percent for men and 16 percent to
23 percent for women.[19] Keep in mind that these estimates pertain
to the general population, not just people with ASDs. The statis-

tics on sexual abuse are hard to come by, because even cognitively adept people with AS do not always recognize and/or report such incidents. One study of 156 children with ASD (including AS) and an average age of just eleven and a half found that 12 percent had experienced at least one incident of sexual abuse and an additional 4 percent were victims of both sexual and physical abuse.[20] Many experts agree that the actual rates are almost certainly significantly higher.

It is important for parents to be aware that every child with an ASD is at increased risk of sexual abuse. According to Dr. Stephen Edelson, among the many risk factors particular to people with ASDs are difficulty detecting deception, trouble discriminating safe and unsafe people and situations, and problems recognizing when and knowing how to ask for help. Kids who need help to complete personal tasks, such as showering, dressing, and toileting, are also at increased risk for abuse. Some youngsters might have gathered from their learning experience that it is always better to follow directions or that refusing to do something an adult tells you to do is "bad." For someone with ASD, these lessons might become easily overgeneralized, and so that person can have a difficult time recognizing the moment when it is right not to cooperate. We know that some people with AS are inclined to be strict rule followers, sometimes to the extreme. That makes it all the more important to offer them highly explicit and direct instruction on recognizing situations when it is right to break certain rules.

While it is true that people with ASD are more likely to be victims of sexual offenders than to be perpetrators, they are no less likely than the general population to be offenders. It is possible to develop a special interest of a sexual nature. People with ASDs whose general social skills repertoire is weak are susceptible to having their behavior misinterpreted as something it is not. Familiar examples include the stare that is perceived as threatening, the frank compliment that is perceived as too forward, and the romantic persistence that is perceived—and sometimes is—just plain stalking. Individuals with AS might also have difficulty discriminating public from private behavior. For example, an adolescent who is told that he can masturbate only in the bathroom might understandably generalize that social rule to *any* bathroom, including the one in the gym locker room at school, at the shopping mall, and at work. Needless to say, the consequences could be devastating. Public exposure can happen when someone with AS is egged on by more socially adept peers or when it occurs to the person with AS that this might be "funny." In one study, the authors hypothesized that a large percentage of sexual offenses of this type committed by people with AS were the result of peer pressure combined with a lack of social understanding on the perpetrator's part.

What All Kids Need to Learn About Sex and Relationships

Unfortunately, we are just beginning to understand what people with ASDs require in terms of learning about sex and relationships. According to Dr. Peter Gerhardt and others,[21] these are the basics of what your child should know and approximately when.

Elementary School and Preschool

- differences between genders
- the concept of public versus private
- the concept of good touch versus bad touch
- when to tell and/or ask for help

Elementary School

- The basics of puberty should be taught well in advance of its arrival.
- masturbation

Middle School and Beyond

- puberty
- hygiene

- independent use of bathroom
- physical attraction
- values
- laws
- safe sex
- pregnancy

It's Never Too Early to Start Talking

Long before the issue of dating arises, it is imperative that both boys and girls with AS are educated about issues concerning sexuality—including sexual abuse, contraception, safer sex (to prevent transmission of HIV and other sexually transmitted diseases), and date or acquaintance rape. Remember, children with Asperger syndrome reach puberty at the same age as typical children, but they may be more confused and unprepared for the changes occurring in their bodies. Parents wonder if their children, who tend to take things literally, will misinterpret sex education information. Considering that schools are introducing discussion of these matters at increasingly younger ages, you would do well to start talking about sexuality early and often, in terms that your child understands.

When it comes to sex, many of us are accustomed to using a wide and ever-broadening choice of terms and expressions that are not really concrete and that may be confusing for youngsters with ASD. For example, we know that "sleeping together" means "having intercourse." For many of our kids, it will just mean sleeping together. So ditch the birds and the bees (which have absolutely nothing to do with sex) and any other "unofficial" terminology that may be comfortable for you or in vogue. Use the "real" medical terms, even though that might feel a bit awkward. If you think of how we talk about sexuality and consider the concrete, literal meanings of many of the words commonly used, you can understand how confusing and troubling they might be to a child with AS, particularly those who think more visually. As an extremely literally minded child, I recall my amazement when in third grade I learned from a friend with older brothers that a cat and a rooster—by other names, of course—were somehow involved. At some point, however, your child should also learn what those other terms are and which are okay to use and when.

Most high school health classes cover many of these topics, but there has been some discussion as to whether this is the best environment for a student with AS to learn about and discuss these issues. Classes taught using a social skills/group discussion format may create awkward situations for a teen with AS. Some adolescents with AS can be literal and ask or answer questions in a way that might elicit teasing. Students harassed one teen with AS after he told the members of his health class that he was "not interested in girls" and thought dating was "a waste of time." He was simply telling the truth as he saw it, not making a statement about his sexual orientation.

Contact your local autism or Asperger syndrome organization, university or university hospital, or therapy practice that specializes in treating people with AS. There is an increasing need for sex education for people all across the spectrum, and programs are cropping up. For example, on Long Island, the Cody Center for Autism and Developmental Disabilities at Stony Brook Children's Hospital has offered individually designed programs on relationships and sexuality for individuals on the spectrum as young as nine. The Unitarian Universalist Church offers a sexuality education program, Our Whole Lives (OWL), which receives high marks from autism professionals.

A pervasive lack of social skills can result in difficult situations for young men and women who don't engage in the full complement of culturally accepted gender-specific behaviors. Young women who dress for comfort and take a casual approach to grooming, and young men who aren't into sports or avidly pursuing girls, may be labeled "gay." However, the teasing and harassment that usually happen to both boys and girls is generally based not on true sexual orientation but on how teens with AS are perceived by their peers. Of course, individuals with AS, as in the general population, can be gay, straight, or bisexual. They can also be gender dysphoric (feeling that they were born into the wrong gender body), and some have undergone treatment and become transgender. They might also choose to be celibate and not pursue romantic or sexual relationships.

ILLICIT DRUGS AND ALCOHOL

Illicit use of drugs and alcohol poses problems and risks for all kids. However, for people with AS, these risks are multiplied. The social disability makes our kids easy marks for those who would take advantage of them—by asking them to "hold" or sell drugs or steal beer from a store, for example. Peer groups that are heavily involved in such illicit activities tend not to be as picky as some groups you might prefer your child associate with. Our children with AS may be more readily accepted by them. We are all well aware of the role of peer pressure in teenage drinking and drugging. However, peer pressure takes on a whole new meaning and a lot more force when directed at a young person with AS who may be even more desperate to fit in and lack the social savvy to fully appreciate all aspects of a situation.

Our teens will be exposed to drugs and underage drinking just as other teens are, so it's important to discuss these issues early and often. What do you say? Once again, the research is not in yet, but common sense tells us that we can do several things to help our kids steer clear of problems:

- Use to your advantage the AS tendency to see moral issues in terms of black and white. Tell your child that drugs and underage drinking are illegal (possibly leading to arrest, going to jail) and dangerous (addiction, overdose, alcohol poisoning, etc.). Explain that drugs and underage drinking are not good for anyone and that a true friend would never pressure you to place yourself at risk.
- Although the typical teenager may scoff at the idea that drinking or doing drugs is "stupid" or makes people "look dumb" and do embarrassing things, a teen with AS may accept those as compelling reasons to abstain.
- Explain how drugs and underage drinking can impair people's judgment, making them attractive prey to bullies

and others who would take advantage of them sexually or otherwise, and making it all too easy for them to be caught in bad situations.

- Establish and reiterate rules of behavior, such as not visiting anyone's home or hanging out where there is no adult supervision; immediately leaving any situation in which drugs or alcohol are used; telling you or another adult of peers' drug or alcohol use; never holding or transporting drugs or alcohol, no matter who asks you to do it.

- Build a network of friends and activities to counter the boredom, lack of supervision, and peer pressure that often precede alcohol and drug use.

- Make sure that your teen knows how to respond if he is offered alcohol or drugs and that he knows to leave any situation where they're being used. In this case, "Just say no" might be the most direct approach. It's certainly the simplest.

- Be sure that your teen knows how to respond to law enforcement officials and other authority figures, particularly if alcohol or drugs are present.

A special note for parents who may have experimented with drugs in the past or who use alcohol or drugs now: Whether or not you personally agree with a hard-line "Just say no" approach, that is the only sound advice to give your child. A "Do as I say, not as I do" position may be confusing, and recounting your own past experiences (though arguably helpful with typical kids in helping them relate to Mom and Dad) may simply complicate and cloud the issue for the teen with AS.

Some parents of children with AS worry that the use of prescription psychotropic medication will lead to drug abuse. In fact, children whose serious emotional and psychological problems are not treated with therapy or medication, or whose treatments have not been effective, are at the highest risk for underage drinking and illicit drug use. The fact that drinking and illicit drug use serve the function of "self-medicating" is well established among both pediatric and adult populations. If anything, prescription psychotropic medication, when used correctly, may actually reduce your child's risk of experimenting with alcohol and street drugs.

Warning: If your child is currently taking any prescription psy-chotropic medication, she should understand that the interaction with alcohol or other drugs may cause adverse reactions, including sudden death. If you suspect that your child who is taking medica-tion may be experimenting with alcohol or drugs, or is at high risk of doing so, speak with your child's prescribing doctor immediately.

DRIVING AND GETTING AROUND

Can a young person with AS learn to drive? Get a license? Become a safe driver? All of that is possible, but recent studies[22] identify the characteristics shared by kids with AS/HFA who learn to drive:

- Age seventeen and older
- Enrolled in full-time regular education
- Plans to attend college
- Has a history of holding a paying job
- Has a parent who has taught another teen to drive
- Has had driving-related goals on his or her IEP

Though two thirds of older teens with AS/HFA say they plan to drive, there are some real challenges that should be considered. One study, for example, found that individuals with ASD were less likely to recognize hazards involving people (as opposed to those that involved objects), and they were generally slower to respond to *any* hazard.[23]

Driving is a highly social enterprise in that as drivers we make split-second decisions based on what we perceive to be the inten-tions of our fellow motorists. In many ways, driving, even alone in your car, requires that we attend consistently to the behavior of other drivers and accurately predict how they might respond. If asked, you might be hard pressed to explain exactly how you know that the driver in the yellow car will probably try to cut you off or that the driver in the blue car will let you change lanes in front of him to make your exit. Somehow you "just know."

The most obvious obstacle to safe driving is the trouble that many young people with AS have in doing more than one thing at a time and quickly shifting focus from one second to the next. Teens and young adults who do not have their temper under control, who are prone to rages or aggression, who are extremely easily distracted, or who become easily flustered or frustrated by circumstances beyond anyone's control should delay getting behind the wheel. On the positive side, most AS individuals are fairly rule oriented and abide by the law. But the negative side of this is that they may adhere to every rule too strictly in every situation. As any experienced driver can tell you, there are times when you must pull off on the shoulder (no matter what the sign says) or not proceed through the intersection (even when your light flashes green). Kids with AS are also probably less likely to drink and drive, blast loud music, or show off for their friends. That said, driving can be very challenging for anyone, and your child may not receive his license until years after his peers do.

Is My Child Ready to Drive? Ask an Expert

Many state and local agencies that serve the disabled offer driver evaluations. There your child will be screened for skills such as attention, ability to shift focus, reflexes, and so on. You will then receive a report outlining your child's strengths and weaknesses and have a clearer, objective idea of how well prepared your youngster is to drive. One well-known program, the Adapted Driver Training Program at the Henry Viscardi Center of Long Island, has been teaching people with a wide range of disabilities, including ASDs, to drive for more than forty years.

You can find a certified driver rehabilitation specialist in your area by visiting the Association for Driver Rehabilitation Specialists at www.aded.org. The organization also offers a helpful two-page overview of common areas that might be of concern: "Asperger's Syndrome and High Functioning Autism (AS/HFA)" at www.driver-ed.org/files/Fact%20Sheets/Asperger_Autism%2003182013.pdf.

A great general source of information comes from the Children's Hospital of Philadelphia's Teen Driver Source (www.teendriversource.org).

For those who do drive, here are some tips:

First, practice, practice, and more practice is essential. Driving is all about looking for and responding to the unexpected. Be sure that your child has massive amounts of supervised practice so that the act of driving comes more naturally, and he can focus his attention on the road. To reduce distractions, opt for an automatic as opposed to a manual transmission, keep the car in good repair, and be sure your child always has a cell phone programmed with every conceivably important phone number he may need.

Set some rules for driving. Number one, the cell phone should be off. Period. Change radio stations and CDs only when the car is stopped. And he is to have no friends in the car without your prior permission.

Make sure your teen knows the most basic rules of car safety: how to get off the road and park safely in the event of mechanical trouble, whom to call, where to wait until help arrives, and so on. Also drill him on what to do if he's involved in an accident. He should know whom to call immediately and be able to produce all the required insurance documents and see those of the other driver, too. He should not admit to any wrongdoing and know how to talk appropriately to the police. (See the following section.)

ENCOUNTERS WITH LAW ENFORCEMENT AND OTHER AUTHORITIES

Because of their Asperger syndrome, children and young adults may run into unforeseen misunderstandings and difficulties when dealing with law enforcement officers and other authorities. There is no research indicating that people with AS are more likely to be involved in illegal activity. However, parents should take seriously the risk that having such a pervasive social disability poses. People with AS are at greater risk for being victims of any kind of crime: for being "misled" into situations they cannot foresee or understand (including illegal or suspicious activity), for being coerced or forced to take part in illegal activity, and so on. Despite the fact that many people with AS are rule abiding to a T, they often lack the social sophistication to fully appreciate the possible implications of a particular action or to foresee how certain types of behavior may look to others: for example, standing outside the public restroom in a park at night or following a woman walking down the street too closely.

We have heard of cases from around the country where a person with AS was left holding the bag, so to speak, after being taken in by more savvy companions who then convincingly denied any involvement. In these cases, peer pressure, a need to feel accepted, and a lack of social understanding conspired to create the setup. In other cases, a person with AS reacted aggressively or violently after being attacked, provoked, or overwhelmed. Here again, the real perpetrators could stage it in such a way that their claims of innocence were believed.

Sometimes a person with AS finds himself in trouble based solely on the way he responds to a police officer or other authority. By their very nature, people with AS can sometimes "look suspicious" even when innocent. A teenage boy who walks through a store wearing an oversized coat (because of sensory issues) and clutching his arms close to his body (because of unusual posture) could appear to be shoplifting. He may not know how to respond in the expected way to the store manager or security guard's "Hey, what have you got in there?" Rather than assume a friendly demeanor, make eye contact, volunteer to open his coat, and apologize for any misunderstanding, he may reply, "My arms," start walking or running away, or panic—each of which may exacerbate the situation. Under stress, he may exhibit tics, become echolalic, start talking to himself, scream, or behave in other ways that give the impression he is unstable, dangerous, or under the influence of drugs or alcohol. If approached, touched, or restrained, he may become more agitated and even violent out of panic and fear. Consequently, this misinterpreted behavior may incur the use of force.

People with AS can seem uncooperative or threatening by virtue of their body language or how they respond to routine questions. Dr. Brenda Smith Myles gave the example of a man stopped for speeding. When the police officer asked, "Do you know how fast you were going?" the man replied simply, "Yes." The fact is, he did know how fast he was going, so he was telling the truth and answering the officer's question. However, most of us recognize that in dealing with police officers and other authorities, the "right" answer is not always the literal truth. Even young kids know that when a policeman pulls you over, the first thing you want to convey is respect for his authority. In this context, the plain, unvarnished truth takes on an edge of flippant sarcasm that most law enforcement personnel would consider disrespectful at the very least.

If a person with AS is the victim of or witness to a crime, he or she may not be a good witness. The trauma of the incident coupled with difficulties in recognizing faces or noticing details may make him unable to describe perpetrators—what they looked like, what they did, or what they said. Sometimes law enforcement officials mistakenly assume that no crime was committed or that the person may be "covering up" for someone else.

Finally, most people with AS—even those with average IQs and above—don't understand their legal rights. They may interpret what is said to them literally or not understand the ramifications of what they say or do. In one case we know of, a man with autism confessed to a crime he did not commit because he wanted the interview to end. He believed that if he "did what the police wanted," they would let him go home.

Dennis Debbaudt is a former police detective and the father of a young man with ASD. He is also creator of the website Autism Risk & Safety Management (www.autismriskmanagement.com) and a true pioneer in recognizing the real-life risks people with ASD face every day. He believes that law enforcement personnel need to be educated about the behaviors and needs of people with ASDs. For example, he says, there are ways to interview individuals with autism that will make it possible for them to provide the right information if stopped by police. In addition to training law enforcement personnel and first responders around the world, Debbaudt has also published a number of great books and videos on a wide range of topics.

There is a lot you can do to protect your child. Here are some suggestions:

1. Take the first steps to make your local police, fire, emergency, and other helping personnel aware of autism and AS. Present them with information about Dennis Debbaudt's work. Get

your local and national AS-related organizations to press this issue.

2. Educate your child about police and fire safety. Many communities sponsor programs such as Safety Town or school visits from firefighters and police officers, who talk about how to respond in emergencies. Ask your school district to work with your local police department and fire department to develop a program designed for children with disabilities. If that isn't possible, consider setting one up through your local support group. Invite police officers, firefighters, and EMT personnel to meet your children and give a short presentation about the issues facing people with ASDs. Be sure to offer print material as well.

3. Design a wallet-sized card, which you can have laminated, that identifies your child as a person with Asperger syndrome. (See page 367.)

4. Teach your child the proper way to respond to police, fire department, and EMT personnel. Keep in mind that these encounters may include sirens and other troubling noises.

Think about the rules our kids are taught, especially when it comes to more sensitive, grown-up issues, such as drinking and sex. We might teach them that drinking is illegal (before a certain age) and probably not the best thing to be doing to excess at any age. But we often forget to teach the "hidden curriculum" of these situations. Again, the hidden curriculum is "out there" in the atmosphere. What most typical kids don't pick up from family or friends, they glean through media and other sources. And, again, our kids are usually, to some degree, out of that loop. Things can get complicated when your kid's interpretation of a rule ("It's okay to drink at twenty-one") is acted upon without the benefit of other rules or customs that usually don't get taught: namely, that you don't walk down the street in broad daylight drinking from a can of beer.

AVOIDING COMMON INJURIES AROUND THE HOUSE AND ELSEWHERE

Because of problems with physical coordination and a less-than-vigilant awareness of their environment, kids with ASDs are at higher risk than other children to be injured in accidents.[24] Most accidents occur in the home or in the course of routine activities. A couple of experiences really brought this home for me: teaching my son to bake bread and observing teens with ASDs in shop class.

For parents of kids who have problems with coordination and fine- and gross-motor skills and other difficulties maneuvering through the physical world, simple chores can be extremely difficult. That awkward grasp on the scissors, the super-forceful mashing of baked potato with a fork, and the tendency to walk over rather than around objects might not seem like serious issues when they are little and under someone's constant care. However, as our kids grow older, these problems can result in unsafe situations. Try that awkward grasp with a sharp knife, the heavy hand with a razor, or the obliviousness to the environment with a flooded kitchen floor, and you have the perfect setup for an injury.

Whenever you are teaching your child a skill or working with her on a basic chore, think about the safety aspects. This may require a special effort on your part, since, for many of us, this kind of information is "just common sense." Once again, we take for granted all the ways we assimilate information and regulate our responses without even thinking about most of it. Things may be different for your child—a little different when it comes to some things and maybe a lot different when it comes to others.

WHERE IT ALL COMES TOGETHER—OR FALLS APART: THE "HOME ALONE TEST"

Dr. Peter Gerhardt identifies three crucial qualities that all young adults need: choice, control, and competence. He describes a scenario that never fails to leave most parents thinking, to say the least. He calls it the "Home Alone Test."

Essentially, here's Dr. Gerhardt's test: Imagine that your child is left alone with someone to care for him while you are halfway around the world. Something happens that prevents your timely return, and the person you were depending on cannot stay with your child, either. Now he or she is truly home alone. At this point, I ask parents to just revisit their average day and then ask themselves, "Is my child able to . . ."

- Call someone for help?
- Buy and cook food?
- Keep the house locked and secure?
- Turn on the alarm system, turn off the alarm system, react appropriately if the siren sounds?
- Call the police or fire department?
- Cross a street by himself?
- Treat a minor cut or burn?
- Call 911 for a health emergency?
- Respond to a kitchen fire?
- Respond to a toilet or sink overflowing or a broken pipe?
- Turn the heat in the house on, off, up, down?
- Shut off the power or the water to the house?
- Know when to answer the door and when not to?
- Know how to answer the telephone and what information to offer to whom?
- Know when prescriptions need to be refilled and whom to call for that purpose?
- Have and use a health insurance card?
- Know the names of his doctors?

This list, obviously, could go on forever. So how do you teach all of this? Here are some tips:

- Start today.
- Spend a day or two taking note of everything you do in the course of a day to keep yourself and your family safe and comfortable.
- When your child is around, narrate your thoughts and actions as you, say, check out the washing machine when it makes that crazy banging noise or check the stove before

leaving the house. Talk about what you are doing, what you are looking for, why it matters, and what you would do if you discovered a different result. For example, "The washing machine was banging, so I rearranged the clothes more evenly. I turned it back on again, and it was fine. But if it had kept making the noise, I would probably call the repairman. Something might be wrong with the machine that I cannot fix."

- Hold real safety drills. In addition to knowing what to do in case of fire or other emergency, your child should also know how to answer the front door or dial 911. Teach by demonstrating and, again, talking through it whenever it happens.
- Think about the OT issues: body position, coordination, eye–hand coordination, and fine- and gross-motor skills when it comes to common chores. For example, in the midst of a bread-baking phase, I started really thinking about how to use an oven safely, and then I spent what turned into a surprising amount of time demonstrating and/or narrating how to put on the oven mitts, where to stand to open the oven door, how to make sure the oven door was open all the way and flat (so it doesn't spring up and touch your arm), how to gently pull out the rack, and why you pull out the rack and not just the hot dish or baking sheets, why to be sure there's a safe "landing area" on the table or counter for a hot dish, and so on.
- Take an account of all the things you do for your child that he could probably do for himself. There is no reason why an adolescent cannot hand the receptionist at the doctor's office his insurance card and maybe even fill out some forms, at least partially, with your help to start. Teens should learn to call in requests for prescription renewals. Younger ones should be able to tell you when they are out of clean socks.
- Be sure your child knows how to swim.

Being safe in the world—at home, at school, on the street, in a car, anywhere—is possible only when your child has acquired the necessary skills. We tend to focus on the more esoteric social and emotional aspects of AS, but safety skills really come down to learning basic facts, practicing basic skills (such as putting on a Band-Aid, making the right phone call), and having someone help you to practice using good judgment when the moment comes. That's something only a parent can do.

Chapter 11

LIFE AFTER HIGH SCHOOL

WHEN THE UNIVERSE SHIFTS AGAIN

What would you consider a "successful outcome" for your child? It's a good question, because despite the impressive gains in knowledge and improvements in education and interventions, individuals with ASD continue to have poorer outcomes in adulthood than do others with disabilities. For example, the rate of underemployment or unemployment for people with ASDs has been estimated at 90 percent or higher.[1] Men and women with ASDs across the spectrum are less likely to have friends, be involved in romantic relationships, or have children. Although ASD symptoms can become less noticeable or troublesome over time, no one is cured; autism does not ever just "go away."[2] No matter how bright, gifted, talented, or diligent your child is, chances are good that he or she will require a great deal of support for much longer than the typical teen.

So it is essential that you begin thinking forward once your child enters middle school. Time goes by more quickly than you expect, and the middle school and high school years typically reveal more about your child's strengths and challenges, especially as they pertain to choosing a path after school. Rather than focus on the goal that you hope your child can reach, familiarize yourself with some of the alternative pathways. Yes, your child is college material, but maybe not beginning right after graduation. Sure, your daughter loves animals, but the veterinary assistant training program that your school district would have had to underwrite before she graduated now costs you several thousand dollars for her to attend as an adult. And do not overlook job training programs. A certain percentage of all students decide that college just is not right for them at this time. Sometimes this is due to their ASD, but sometimes it is for the same reasons that prompt other students toward the same decision: they aren't sure about their future, cannot afford it, or just are not strong enough academically to go forward comfortably. And then there are those who decide that college might never be the right choice and who wish to follow their dreams in other fields where a college degree is not needed.

TRANSITION PLANNING

It is no secret that transition planning for students with disabilities traditionally has been one of the weakest aspects of special education. Fortunately, the revisions introduced in IDEA 2004 seek to address these deficiencies in several ways. For one thing, the very definition of *transition services* was expanded and improved. The new words are underlined.

> (34) Transition services. The term "transition services" means a coordinated set of activities for a child with a disability that—
>
> (A) is designed <u>to be a results-oriented process, that is focused on improving the academic and functional achievement of the child with a disability to facilitate the child's</u> movement from school to post-school activities, including post-secondary education, vocational education, integrated employment (including supported employment), continuing and adult education, adults services, independent living, or community participation;
>
> (B) <u>is based on the individual child's needs</u>, taking into account the child's strengths, preferences, and interests . . .[3]

Under the previous version of IDEA (IDEA 1997), IEPs were required to include "a statement of transition services needs" beginning when the student was fourteen years of age, and then, when the child reached age sixteen, "a statement of needed transition services." With IDEA 2004, the requirement at age fourteen was eliminated. However, that does not mean that you should not begin thinking about transition before your child reaches sixteen, the age at which IDEA now requires transition planning to be part of the IEP. By the time your child reaches middle school, you should know well the types of skills—executive function, reading comprehension, handwriting, social and emotional, and so on—that she may need to be successful outside of the classroom. If it's a skill that's needed out in the world, then it's probably a necessary skill in the classroom, too. There is no reason why a younger child's IEP goals should not address them, at any age.

The first IEP your child receives after he turns sixteen must now include:

> appropriate measurable postsecondary goals based upon age-appropriate transition assessments related to training, education, employment, and, where appropriate, independent living skills . . . and the transition services (including courses of study needed to assist the child in reaching these goals).[4]

These goals, like all IEP goals, must be updated annually, and your child's progress toward meeting them must be assessed and reported on regularly. These goals must be revised if there is "any *lack of expected progress.*"[5]

It is never too early to start talking with your child and planning for the future. Although it is the least well studied and statistically the least well executed task of special education, transition is probably the most important. Your child's transition plan might entail spending part of the school day in a job training program, internship, or volunteer position. It can also include arranging his class schedule to allow for a later graduation or receiving instruction in basic daily living skills necessary to succeed at work or in college, such as travel training, driver's education, and personal finance.

Although schools have made tremendous progress in most areas, the requirements for transition before IDEA 2004 were frustratingly vague—and, not surprisingly, schools responded accordingly. There was also the misperception that for kids with ASD, having great grades was "enough." It's not. By definition—and now, thanks to IDEA 2004, by design—transition planning defies cookie-cutter, "this is how we do it" solutions. Forget "one size fits all."

Prepare to do much of the research and much of the legwork on your own. Do not be surprised to find that some members of your district team do not have all of the answers. One of the tragic flaws in our education and services systems for people with any disability is that whereas parents envision their child's progress occurring along one long, unbroken road, the services she receives—from early intervention through college or employment supports—really exist as islands linked by bridges. Most "islanders" know little about the customs of the natives on the island on either side of them. To date, our current education and disability services approach is specialized, by age, grade, disability, or degree of disability. Not every professional at the school district level has the breadth of knowledge of transition and postgraduation options that many of our kids require.

SELF-DETERMINATION AND SELF-ADVOCACY GO TOGETHER

You may hear the terms *self-determination* and *self-advocacy* more as your child nears adulthood. They are sometimes used interchangeably, but they are not the same thing. Since we are familiar with the concept of advocacy and therefore familiar with the advocating on behalf of our kids, the realization that someday soon your child will have to advocate for himself (and, most important, by himself) comes as a jolt. But let's take it back a couple of steps first. We parents know that to advocate effectively for our child, we have had to know our child and know his diagnosis and all that it entails. Similarly, for your child to advocate for himself effectively and independently, he too needs to know himself, his diagnosis, and how it affects him. He should also be aware of which strategies or accommodations are helpful to him and which are not.

Parents who have chosen to avoid discussing the diagnosis with their child or who have opted for "softer" terminology to spare feelings might want to reconsider this approach going forward. Teenagers do not need to have every technical detail about their ASD (and other conditions), but they do need to know and be able to describe the following to others who need to know: (1) the name of their diagnosis or learning disorder, (2) how it affects them, and (3) what they need to be successful in a given setting. Without this knowledge, self-determination is incomplete and self-advocacy inadequate beyond the schoolhouse doors. At some point in a child's life, knowing that he "has" something such as AS might make things difficult for him. However, as he comes closer to adulthood, not knowing can make things more difficult and stressful than they need to be, and sometimes even impossible.

Knowing oneself is key to *self-determination*. There are some technical descriptions of self-determination, but basically it is what it sounds like: a person's ability to have input in making decisions with "minimal influence from outside sources."[6] Important aspects of self-determination are the ability to self-regulate, to function autonomously, to initiate and respond to events, and to have some understanding of oneself (self-realization). Self-advocacy is the ability to recognize, understand, and explain one's needs to another person and then to take appropriate actions to ensure that those needs are met. Though self-determination is never mentioned in IDEA 2004, transition planning as described therein clearly requires that the student exercise self-determination.

Another reason it is important for your child to understand the diagnosis and how it affects him is that it will help him make better decisions when it comes to disclosing his disability, applying for accommodations at college, and seeking and using appropriate assistance. For a variety of reasons, a large percentage of college students who are entitled to receive accommodations do not access them, sometimes to their detriment. In some cases, students are choosing not to appear "different" from their peers, which is understandable. However, in others, students are rejecting accommodations because they do not fully understand why they need them; and, especially if they have been successful in high school, they might not fully appreciate how the special education, accommodations, and assistance they received contributed to that success. There are students entering college who do not know that they have had an IEP and students applying for jobs that require intensive contact with the public who do not understand why such work might be difficult for them. One wonders how anyone could expect a positive outcome from either situation.

School is the ideal environment for teaching your child to advocate for herself. Consider having your child attend her 504 plan or IEP meetings, even if only for five minutes, to hear all the good news from her teachers and therapists. Once your child hits his teens, at the latest, explain what these meetings are about, why he receives the services and accommodations that he does, and what you are all—including him—working toward. There might always be portions of the meeting that take place without your child present, but by sixteen, he should be involved in discussions related to planning services and setting goals. Talk to your child before the meeting about what will be discussed. If the committee proposes that, based on recent grades, extra time on tests should be eliminated or reduced, your child should explain from his perspective why he agrees or disagrees. Of course, you are still there as his advocate, but encourage him to put in his two cents. On a daily basis, encourage your child to speak up (appropriately, of course) to say, "I need more time to complete this test," "The noise from outside is distracting me," or "I didn't catch everything you said. Could you please repeat the question?"

Teaching self-advocacy is teaching independence. Starting early allows your child time to get used to expressing her need for assistance without embarrassment or shame. It also allows her to understand her limitations and her skills, which in itself can be empowering.

GOING À LA CARTE

Although you have probably been thinking about how things will be when your child grows up and ventures out into the world beyond high school, chances are that your ideas about what to do and how to plan are less concrete than you would like. The good news: it's not just you. The bad news: it's not just you, either. That's because transition planning for kids with ASDs remains one of the least understood and most inadequately addressed areas.

In my personal experience, I found that life before my son graduated high school was like dining at a local restaurant. I knew the staff and the buffet menu pretty well. Maybe there weren't as many of some dishes as I would like, and sometimes the servings were less than desired, but we had a regular, predictable reservation, we always got a seat, my son had a legally protected right to be there, and there were several layers of "management"—from the district special ed director to the US Department of Education—I could complain to if the service wasn't good. And one more thing: the dinner was free. Once my son graduated high school, we entered the world of adulthood. Instead of a regularly scheduled reservation, I was handed a list of "restaurants"—brochures and applications about community colleges, universities, job training, and support programs (Social Security Disability Insurance, Medicaid, state disability eligibility, supported housing, and other programs). Many of these may be agencies you have either never heard of, or if you have, you've assumed that their services were available to those with different learning profiles or diagnoses than your child's. Most parents are absolutely baffled when they hear "Medicaid" uttered in the context of job training and other programs for young adults with ASD. But if your child is not going to college from high school or does not have a job, and he qualifies, a good portion of the programs he might benefit from in the meantime are funded by Medicaid. Who knew?

So now, instead of sitting down to a full meal served at the same table, I was getting everything à la carte, with each course from a different restaurant, with different eligibility criteria and billing policies. Some of the courses are still free, but only under very specific conditions. Most must be paid for by parents or by some combination of parents and governmental agencies. Further, with the exception of Social Security Disability Insurance and Medicaid (if one qualifies), your child has no legal right to any of them. Unlike your local school district, which must accommodate every child with a disability, the institutions and agencies you deal with going forward "have" to do substantially less. Though your young adult still has rights to access and accommodation, he should not expect to be given the same degree of modification he might have received throughout secondary school. Even more important for some students, most of these other agencies, programs, colleges, and schools are under no obligation to tolerate disruptive or inappropriate behaviors even if they are related to the disability.

At the same time, once your child reaches the age of majority (in most states, eighteen), your right and ability to intervene on his behalf diminish or disappear completely. Unless you have legal guardianship over your young adult child or you have his express written permission, you cannot talk to his professors or his doctor about how he's doing or make important legal, medical, or financial decisions on his behalf. For parents who are accustomed to regarding their child's development as a collaborative effort based on communication, this comes as something of a shock. Even those parents who understand these changes intellectually often take some time to feel fully at ease with the sudden loss of involvement and control.

THE COUNTDOWN BEGINS: ENSURING SERVICES AND PROTECTIONS

Teens diagnosed as children with AS or some other disability covered under IDEA should have an IEP that includes plans for transition (see page 456) and any services and accommodations they require today *and* may be reasonably expected to require in their postgraduation endeavors. (Remember that students who have a 504 plan are not entitled to transition services, and for some parents, this may be another good reason to see to it that your child is classified and has an IEP.) If your child has a later diagnosis or has made it through thus far without a 504 plan or an IEP, keep in mind that in middle school and in high school, your child's need can change enough to create a new need or increased need for accommodations and/or special education and related services. For example, in New York, the "double whammy" of new Common Core standards and extensive revisions to state graduation requirements has created an environment that some students with ASD find more demanding and stressful. Across the country, parents, students, and teachers, regardless of what they think of education reforms, recognize that the pressure is on and the stakes are higher for everyone.

It has always been the case that a certain percentage of kids with

ASD manage the early years of school without help. One widely accepted explanation was that the shift in the later elementary years from the concrete (which many of our kids manage with ease) to the abstract was the problem. Typically, these students discover upon entering middle school or high school that either they cannot continue learning with the level of ease or success that they are used to or they simply cannot cope. The aforementioned changes in standards—which also has produced changes in the way teachers teach and in the way that students are evaluated—have not been discussed much in terms of their impact on our kids as "transitions" to something unfamiliar, but I'm confident that many parents can attest to their effects.

If your middle school or high school student is struggling or stressed and does not an IEP have currently in place (or, if appropriate, a 504 plan), we strongly suggest you consider initiating one now. Fortunately, there is no age limit on when a student can be evaluated and provided special education, related services, or accommodations—provided that he has not graduated from high school or reached the age of twenty-two. Either of those two events terminates eligibility under IDEA. You may meet resistance from your school district, which may take the position that your child has been doing "well enough" thus far without services or accommodations. Keep in mind that services and accommodations are based on *current* need. The fact that a student didn't seem to need special education, services, or accommodations yesterday has no bearing whatsoever on what he needs—and is entitled to receive—today. For some of our kids, their needs will change or increase simply because the demands of school have changed.

PROTECTING ACCOMMODATIONS
IN THE FUTURE

Sometimes, school districts and parents find ways to provide what you might call "invisible" supports and accommodations. These are not official or on paper anywhere; they're just what those who work with a student have learned to do to make things run more smoothly and help your child be more successful. Maybe the teacher lets Patrick take his tests at a desk way in the back of the room, behind a tall bookcase, because it's quieter. Or the classroom aide in Melanie's middle school class has been writing down the notes off the Smart Board in geography for her because she falls behind sometimes. Or Levi's teacher gives him extra time on algebra tests because, she says, "I know he knows the material, and I hate to see him stress." What's wrong with these pictures?

While it is very kind of everyone to go out of his or her way to make your child comfortable and successful, if a youngster truly needs help, then it needs to be official for two basic reasons: One, the support, accommodation, special education, or related service must be provided and monitored in a professional, consistent manner. Second, if the problems require this degree of attention now, what does this bode for the future? And what skills should your child be learning in order to reduce or eliminate the need for such help? It's very considerate of Melanie's aide to write the notes—but she shouldn't. Melanie should either learn to take notes herself and/or identify some compensatory strategy or accommodation that does not involve having another person doing the work for her. And, news flash: do not expect one-on-one personal attention past high school. And even before then, always be ready to prepare your child for the day *she* decides that she doesn't want individualized assistance in class because it's stigmatizing or annoying, or she would like "to be like everybody else."

Equally important—and perhaps even more important for many of our college-bound kids—you must plan ahead if it is reasonable to assume that your youngster will require accommodations in testing for AP placement, the PSAT, the SAT, the ACT, or college or job training. Students who take either the SAT or the ACT must plan far in advance for testing accommodations.[7] The College Board, which administers the SAT, requires seven weeks to render a decision after all documentation is received, for example. Both companies require specific detailed documentation of disability and previous accommodations. It is difficult to make the case that a student with no current documented services or accommodations "suddenly" requires them now. On the other hand, the College Board web page also states that "a prior history of accommodation without documentation of current need and consistent use, does not necessarily demonstrate eligibility for accommodation(s) on College Board tests."[8] So you might want to consider carefully if you should toss away any current accommodations just because your child—for whatever reason—opts not to use them. Remember: you can keep accommodations on the IEP or 504 plan and your child can choose not to use them. It is not unusual for a student to use accommodations selectively; he might need that extra time to write essays in English but breeze through a math test. You can expect that to be the case in college, too. It is also important to remember that neither the College Board nor the ACT grant accommodations on the basis of diagnosis alone. In fact, the College Board's web page on accommodations states, "Not all students with Autism Spectrum disorders require accommodations on a College Board test."[9]

GOING TO COLLEGE

Colleges and universities are relative newcomers to serving students with ASD. Even colleges that served or provided accommodations to students with disabilities in the past may have little experience with students like our kids. Sure, there have been students with ASD attending for decades, but they were typically not identified accurately, and the services and accommodations were hit-or-miss, if they existed at all. Today, students with disabilities in general have more protections and more options than in the past. However, it is important for you and your child to understand that postsecondary education differs dramatically from all that comes before it. First— and this is a big surprise to many students and not a few parents— there is no legal right to education, public or private, after your child graduates high school. IDEA and the protections and rights it affords students end at the diploma. Further—another surprise— there is not equivalent legislation that "picks up" where IDEA ends.

Colleges and universities serving students with special needs fall into one of three unofficial categories: those that provide only the accommodations required by law (more on that later); those described as providing "coordinated services" (that is, they have staff trained in disabilities and offer special classes or tutors); and full special education colleges that offer modified course work and trained staff. There may be about one hundred schools that fall into the last category.[10] Special education colleges are each unique, so the following discussion is limited to the vast majority of two-year and four-year colleges.

What to Expect: Differences in the Law

Obviously, college is different from high school, but most families are not prepared for just how different and, most important, why. Basically, the intent of the law that covered your child with an IEP was to provide a free, appropriate public education from which your child benefited (thus the *Individualized* in Individualized Education Plan). That could have included special education and related services, modified curriculum, accommodations, modified standards (such as not counting spelling or grammatical errors in grading essays), and behavioral standards and disciplinary procedures that must take into account the disability. The main law that pertains to most students attending most colleges and universities is the Americans with Disabilities Act (ADA) of 1990. It applies to all Americans with disabilities in all public facilities. While it prohibits discrimination based on disability, it *does not require free, appropriate public education*. It does require "appropriate adjustments," or accommodations that do not require significant or fundamental alterations or changes to the course, program, activity, or curriculum.

Colleges and universities are required only to provide "reasonable accommodations" to students who otherwise qualify for admission. Another way of saying this is that colleges and universities do not fashion accommodations or make changes in their programs or courses to enable an applicant who would otherwise not qualify for admission. They offer accommodations to ensure that students with disabilities who do qualify for admissions are not denied access to education because of their disability.

Accommodations might include the following:

- A separate location on campus for taking a test (but not taking the test at home, with an open book and notes).
- Receiving a copy of class notes taken by another student (but

not being provided an individual assistant to take notes or being given the notes by the professor).

- Extra time to complete the same test everyone else in the class takes (but not receiving different questions or differently worded questions or fewer multiple-choice question options than others have).
- Providing a student with impaired vision a special monitor in a computer graphics class (but not waiving the course requirement that students produce work on the computer).

To what degree the accommodations available in college will benefit your child depends on what services and accommodations your child received before—and his skill set. The general advice is to apply for and to use all the accommodations granted for at least the first semester before deciding which to decline.

Applying for and Using Accommodations

Unlike in schooling up until now, no law requires that colleges and universities actively seek to identify students with disabilities. The onus falls on students to come forward, identify themselves, apply for accommodations, and then present their documentation of the accommodations granted to each professor and work out the details. One very important point that many parents and students miss is that you do not *request* accommodations, you *apply for* them. The college then decides which it deems appropriate. And a helpful hint for parents: please allow your child to be as independent as possible in this endeavor. Yes, colleges do expect and understand working with students with disabilities. But the emphasis is on working with students, not working with their parents. At a college fair I attended a few years ago, the director of a highly regarded college program for students with developmental disabilities was describing his program and the criteria for admissions. When he mentioned that he and his staff take note of students who turn to their parents for help to answer questions directed at them, you could hear quiet gasps from the audience. He went on to explain that such students' lack of independence and seeming inability to handle basic interview questions does not bode well for success in college. Unlike your school district, where your child might have been known since childhood, on the college or university campus, your child is a young adult, an independent person, and as such is expected to be responsible for himself. In addition, as discussed previously, once your child reaches the age of majority, unless she has signed a waiver, the college staff cannot contact you legally except in case of emergency. And missed classes, failing grades, and social problems do not constitute emergencies.

Another big difference is that your child's professors will know of his disability and need for accommodations only if he tells them. Your child should also know that while it's necessary to disclose the diagnosis for the purposes of obtaining accommodations through the college disabilities office, he does not need to disclose his diagnosis to his professors in order to use the accommodations. If your child chooses not to notify his professors of his accommodations, no one will intervene with your child or contact you. This is a dramatic difference from how things were in school, where everyone working with your child was made aware of his needs and was legally obligated to meet them.

Each college or university sets its own policies and procedures, but generally speaking, here is how the process works: Every campus has an office in charge of special services; these are easily located on the college's website. There you will find a list of the college's policies, requirements for application for accommodations, a list of the types of accommodations offered, and any deadlines. Typically, these applications call for a substantial amount of documentation, so be prepared; ideally, you should check the websites of any college you are considering, just so you have an idea. Some, for example, might require a written report from a physician, which might take several weeks to arrange or obtain. Plan ahead and definitely have on hand:

- A copy of the most recent IEP or 504 plan.
- A copy of the most recent psychological or psycho-educational evaluation.
- A written diagnosis or report from a professional qualified to diagnose (psychologist, psychiatrist, MD).
- Other information or documentation the college requires.

Another tip for parents: Be sure that your child knows what these documents are and what they contain. You would be surprised how many young adults do not know that these documents even exist, much less what they say. Remember that once your child reaches the age of majority, he has the right to see all of his records, including any reports written by doctors and other professionals. Some of these will contain information that your child either is not aware of or might consider upsetting or disturbing. Ideally, you should review with your child anything that he will be voluntarily entrusting to anyone else, such as a special services administrator. After all, he is a young adult now. If, for example, he is troubled by passages in a social history or doctor's report that refer to *what he considers* embarrassing or stigmatizing, he should be permitted and encouraged to speak with the author of the report about removing or rephrasing those sections. Whatever you do, please be sure that your child does not first discover his diagnosis when he glances at a doctor's report as he's handing it to his special services counselor.

After reviewing all of the documentation and perhaps speaking with your child, the special services office will then notify your child about the accommodations it determines are appropriate. The office issues what is commonly referred to as an "accommodations letter," which the student should keep with him at all times on campus. Whether your child decides to make multiple copies of the letter or carry one copy (some people have them laminated) depends on him and the school's policy. Once the student has the letter, it is his responsibility to approach each professor separately to agree upon a time for him to present his letter and discuss how accommodations will be provided for that class. Ideally, this takes place before classes start or at the beginning or end of the first class. Be sure that your child knows how to approach the professor politely and discreetly, and that she has an idea of what she is going to say. Your child should also know, again, that she need not disclose her diagnosis— not even if the professor asks point-blank—if she chooses not to. She will still receive the approved accommodations. Keep in mind that different professors might have different ways of providing the accommodations. Students who need a high degree of consistency should be prepared for the possibility that preferential seating might mean the seat in the first row closest to the window in math, but the middle seat at a semicircular conference table in ethics.

The Decision to Use Accommodations:
The Student Takes Charge

When, where, and how to use accommodations is entirely up to your child. Unfortunately, some students are anxious to leave high school and their identity as disabled behind. They may refuse to apply for accommodations (you might not be able to make application on your child's behalf or without his or her permission) or refuse to use the accommodations once they are received. Your youngster might require specific instruction about what accommodations are and how college works. For example, after a lifetime of dealing with teachers who just seemed to know about their needs, some students have difficulty understanding that professors will not "just know" and that they are responsible for enlightening them. Some students, because of poor social skills or nervousness, find even approaching a professor overwhelming.

Long before the first day of class, your child should understand the process and his responsibilities. If you need to script it, rehearse it, role-play it—whatever it takes, do it. Notifying professors about accommodations should not be delayed. Terms move quickly. The schedules for withdrawing from a class that just isn't working out are firm and generally unforgiving. This is true not only in terms of the F or the "Incomplete" received, but also in terms of the percentage of tuition that could have been refunded with an earlier, official withdrawal from the course. Informing a professor about accommodations after the first bad grade or failed test should never be considered a possible "out." Though individual professors may make exceptions, it is entirely up to their personal discretion. In most instances, even the college cannot intervene. Your child should walk onto the campus with the understanding that there are no "do-overs" in college and that negotiation over disappointing grades is not an option.

The expert consensus here is that a student coming into college with accommodations should use them fully, at least for the first semester. If she is satisfied with her work and her grades, then she might consider using the accommodations more selectively. For example, testing in a separate location might not be as necessary in a class of fifteen on the quiet side of campus as it would be in a lecture hall seating up to one hundred. Or, having another student make a copy of his notes available might be a helpful accommodation in physics, where a visual learner picks up more from what he sees and struggles to look and write simultaneously. However, the same student might discover that his music theory teacher creates PowerPoints that the class downloads through Blackboard before class, eliminating the need to write much during the lecture.

THE SOCIAL AND EMOTIONAL
CHALLENGES OF COLLEGE

The transition to college is challenging for every student, even those without learning and other disabilities. Whether your child has breezed through school academically or struggled mightily, the truth is that academics are only part of the college experience. Further, in terms of your child's success at college, his ability to function socially and emotionally is equally if not more important. It is prudent for parents to assess their child's social and emotional status and to expect that with the transition to college, anxiety, depression, Tourette's syndrome and tics, AD/HD, and other comorbid conditions may be exacerbated due to stress.

If your child has a history of social, emotional, and behavioral issues, you and your child should be aware of how college differs from school in responding to related problems. The first is that, unlike in school, colleges and universities have no legal obligation to consider a student's disability when it comes to violations of the code of conduct. Once your child is accepted to a college, you should read and review the entire code with him and be sure that he understands exactly what it says about things such as behavior, smoking, alcohol and drug use, cell phones and electronics, academic honesty (read: cheating and plagiarism), attendance, and so on. Especially if your child has behavioral issues or tends to respond in ways that others might reasonably perceive as threatening, aggressive, stalking, or harassment, he should understand that he will be held to the same standards as everyone else. Freshmen are sometimes surprised to learn that the consequences for violations of some college rules are serious and can include expulsion. In some matters, such as academic honesty, professors might have full autonomy in determining whether cheating or plagiarism has occurred. Sometimes students accustomed to receiving multiple warnings about inappropriate behavior, or whose behavior did not generate as harsh a consequence as it would have without IEP protections, cannot comprehend how dramatically different the new rules—and potential consequences—are.

Some students have trouble adjusting to things such as the longer length of time they may be required to sit in a class (one to two hours as opposed to fifty minutes in a high school period), the relative lack of personal involvement of professors compared to high school teachers, the sometimes new responsibility they have to know when they need to take a break for a few minutes or to ask for extra help. Many of the behaviors that were acceptable or tolerated in high school might be viewed differently in college. For instance, some students are used to raising their hands the moment a question pops into their heads. However, in college, many professors plan their lectures carefully and expect students to wait until the end of the lecture to ask questions. Plus, often the question from slide one has an answer on slide three. At the other extreme are students who are used to never raising their hands and who might never have been encouraged or taught to do so because the high school staff knew that they didn't like to talk too much or that "they know the answer." Things are different in college. In many classes, especially larger ones, the only way a professor gets to know a student at all is by how she takes part in the class. Young people on the spectrum may require explicit guidelines on when to participate in class, how often, what to say, and what not to say.

Going to college often means the chance to meet new people (which many kids on the spectrum point to as a plus). With a larger social "pool" to choose from, and a wide range of clubs and activities, it might be easier to find others who share interests. College also represents a great opportunity to start fresh, to make a new impression, to learn about oneself. Like most other students, our kids will have their own dreams about attending college, some of which may be unrealistic. If your child has to be reminded not to wear the same T-shirt six days in a row or your daughter has never learned to prepare a simple meal, going away to school will probably not be a positive experience. Even if it results in short-term disappointment for your child, you should be prepared to set him up for success, and that might mean doing some things differently from what you planned originally or differently from what everyone else seems to be doing. That might mean fewer classes than a traditional full load the first semester or two. That might mean attending a community college or a college closer to home. That might mean living at home for a semester before moving into the dorms. It could also mean attending a school hundreds of miles away because of its reputation serving kids likes yours. As with any decision about college, it comes down to a question of fit.

Some children with Asperger syndrome will not attend a traditional college, for any number of reasons. The rise in universities offering online courses and degrees may be an option for some. Others may prefer to pursue an interest or begin work in a field for which a college education is not necessary, though training may be involved. Contact your state department of education and find out what is available in terms of vocational training, which has come to encompass everything from culinary arts and computer programming to health care and jet engine repair. Inquire in your community about businesses or corporations that have made a commitment to hiring and supporting individuals with disabilities. Such organizations may be a good place for your child to get his or her first job experience.

WORK AND WORK EXPERIENCE

We've heard from dozens of parents whose children had brilliant academic careers yet are virtually unemployable because of lack of previous work experience and adequate social skills. Not surprisingly, the first after-school or summer job is one rite of passage many parents sidestep, for several reasons. Many of the jobs available to teens are in the service industries (fast-food worker, movie usher, camp counselor) and demand a lot of personal interaction. It's challenging to place a child with AS in a new environment where his success depends on understanding what unfamiliar people are thinking or what they might want. For others, juggling the dual curriculum of school and then navigating homework and other obligations takes them to their emotional limit.

It may not be easy to find the "perfect" job, but teens with AS can really benefit from a summer or part-time job during the school year that doesn't detract from their schoolwork or time needed to wind down from school. Although many neurotypical teens can juggle school and work, AS teens may find this extra responsibility stressful. In addition to exposing teens with AS to the real world, being employed in some capacity during the summer or school vacations can also help eliminate the "what to do in the summer" problem many of them face. By the time they reach age thirteen or fourteen, most summer camp programs are no longer appropriate. By this age, many neurotypical kids are becoming camp counselors or attending advanced skill- and sports-oriented camps. Many AS parents express their dismay at summer, when a teen's days might be spent at home and involved in few activities other than their particular special interests. Math and science summer camps or music camps appeal to a certain percentage of teens with AS. Others may participate in camps for special-needs children.

Contact your school district to discover counselors and organizations that specialize in placing people with disabilities in jobs. If possible, try to find a job for your child that will capitalize on his abilities (say, an interest in computers or music) while avoiding his disabilities (by, for example, working directly under one or two people, having limited contact with strangers). Roger Meyer, an adult with AS, wrote *Asperger Syndrome Employment Workbook: An Employment Workbook for Adults with Asperger Syndrome*. If all else fails, he suggests that you or someone in your family who works in a field of interest to your child consider asking that he be allowed to spend a day or two "on the job." When you're out with your child, point out the different kinds of jobs other people have and encourage him to find out more about occupations that may be of interest to him.

You might find that your child is eligible to receive services such as job coaching or supported employment. These services can help ease your child into the workplace by providing training and practical support, all with an eye to your child developing the skills to work independently. For some youngsters, a two-year or associate degree from a community college or the professional development division of a four-year college or university is a good choice.

Research confirms that the greatest obstacles many young people with ASD face on the job result from social and communication deficits. For many, the actual responsibilities of the job are not the issue; they have the skills the job requires. What they often do not have are the social skills to negotiate the workplace comfortably or effectively. It should be assumed that any job will require that your child interact with others—bosses, coworkers, perhaps even clients or customers. No matter what the position, employees are expected to be polite, to listen, to accept work-related comments and corrections appropriately, and to demonstrate some interest in others, even if it is just offering routine greetings or offers to assist.

Much has been written about jobs that are supposedly "ideal" for our kids. Obviously, most will seek employment in an area of interest, where that is possible. And perhaps not as obviously, your child and everyone working with him should be aware of what types of positions are probably a bad fit from the start. For some, that might include positions involving a lot of contact with customers or intense, unpredictable deadline pressure. Just as some of our kids have a more basic, less nuanced conception of social expectations, they also sometimes have an incomplete understanding of what working entails, what different professionals do, or what other employment options might be available in a given field. Exploring different careers by learning about them and even shadowing people in their jobs for a few hours can be enlightening.

THE FUTURE WITHOUT YOU

This is perhaps the hardest thing to consider for most of us: the day when we will no longer be able to be involved in our children's lives the way we are now. As much as we all wish for a long, healthy life, the fact is that the dreaded day could come at any time. What can you do today to help your child tomorrow?

- Be prepared for the unthinkable and the inevitable. None of us enjoys planning for tragedy, but our children need these arrangements made on their behalf. If you find it difficult to make the proper arrangements, simply picture your child in the temporary custody of social services personnel or other strangers who know nothing about him, or ASD, for the weeks or months it may take to establish legal custody or find him a new home. Then get to work.

• Working with an attorney who specializes in estate planning for families with children who have disabilities, write your will and set up a special-needs trust. Choose your child's guardian wisely, and be sure you have discussed it thoroughly and the person you have chosen has agreed to assume responsibility for raising your child and managing not only the trust but all aspects of your child's life. That can mean attending IEP meetings, working with state disability and Social Security offices when he is older, and so on. Because of your child's disability, you may consider setting up a trust or other arrangement through which your child's financial needs will be met without him inheriting the money directly. Laws concerning inheritance vary from state to state, so consult with a knowledgeable attorney who specializes in this area. Also, if you have reason to expect that your child will be eligible for Social Security Disability Insurance, be especially careful how any inheritance or trust is structured. (Note: Will-writing software and "form" wills will not suffice. You need a specialist to write a will that will provide for and protect a disabled child.)

• Be sure that family members and friends you can count on have copies of critical information about you and your child: the location of his school and how to get there; any medication he may be taking, the schedule, where to find it in the house, and the name of the prescribing physician as well as the pharmacy where it is filled; the names and numbers of all of your child's doctors; where to find important papers, keys to safe-deposit boxes, and other items that may be needed in the event you are incapacitated or deceased.

• If your child is old enough and you believe the disclosure would not provoke anxiety, discuss the arrangements you have made and what will occur in the event that you can no longer care for him.

- Review your will and your plans annually. Things change, sometimes dramatically. Be sure that everyone you are depending on is informed of any changes you have made.

LETTING GO WHILE HOLDING ON

Parents of teens and young adults with Asperger syndrome are often criticized by those who don't understand their need to remain deeply involved in their children's lives. Amid thousands of so-called helicopter parents, we might not be as conspicuous as we once were. Still, you can expect people who truly believe they know your son or daughter to suggest that maybe it's time to loosen the apron strings. Even if we think that's a good idea, too, many of us will anguish over by how much, when, and how. Just as many of us were judged for "hovering" over our three-year-olds and "babying" our nine-year-olds, so we may be seen as "smothering" or "coddling" our teens. The fact remains that our children may need more support, more care, and more assistance than others their age, perhaps even for the rest of their lives. As a parent of a child with AS, you have probably weathered other criticism by now. Our advice: take it on the chin, ignore it, then go on doing what you believe is best for your child today, while you are still here and have this opportunity. As difficult as it may have been to imagine for so many years, your child with AS will become an adult with AS. What does that mean? And what is the best thing you can do?

Our job as parents is not to change our children into who we would like them to be, but rather to help guide them to be the best they can be. Liane Holliday Willey writes in her book: "I know the real me, the one that truly matters, was nurtured and shaped by the lessons my mother and father taught me. The heart and soul of their parenting was simply that I take pride in my individuality, idiosyncrasies and all."[11]

Kalen Molton, an adult on the spectrum, once said, "I try to remind myself that I am a high-functioning autistic, not a low-functioning normal person, as others would have me believe."

We must light the way for others to understand our children in terms of what they are rather than what they are not and perhaps never can be. Those who choose to enumerate the many ways in which the rare lavender rose "fails" to be a classic red rose not only miss the point, they miss the beauty. Learning to see, to understand, and to appreciate every rose is an opportunity to learn something new, not only about that flower but about themselves. As we help our children to better adapt to a world that is not very good at accepting people with differences, we should remember Kalen's words. Simply in persisting through a life that is neither predictable nor easy, our children exhibit courage, resilience, and an unusual strain of hope.

Chapter 12

AFTER ALL

PARENTS of typical kids see and feel the first date, the first drink, the first kiss, the first drive alone coming. The entire culture references these rites of passage, and most parents have a number of peers, not to mention their own parents, to rely on for reassurance. Perhaps because my own son is growing up on an "alternate schedule," I've become acutely aware of how often parents of typical kids will remark about a teen's first attempt at the driving test or the possibility that a dating relationship has gotten "very serious." Other parents nod sympathetically, offer assurances, and maybe a story from their own experience. Yes, parents of typical kids have problems, too, but the culture provides a web of support and guidance.

As children with Asperger syndrome enter the teen years, they face new and different challenges, and their parents find themselves looking forward in a way that they may have subconsciously avoided until now. Before we look ahead, it's a good idea to stop for a moment, look back, and consider how far your child (and you) have come. Take an objective look at the problems and challenges facing your teen, but also remember what has been overcome and remind him and yourself of his wonderful qualities, talents, and skills.

If this time of life is difficult for most children, it is understandably more trying or challenging for those with AS. The early teenage years are typically a time when children strive to gain a measure of independence from their parents. Gradually, the opinions and approval of peers become paramount, as they find their place in a new social realm separate from their family. Most teens want desperately to fit in with their peers. Typical teens begin to explore dating and express an interest, at the very least, in sexual relationships. Adolescence can be trying for anyone, especially your child if he lacks peer support and shared social experiences.

PARENTS GROW UP, TOO

One day you realize that the boy who didn't learn to ride a two-wheeler until he was eleven and still has difficulty holding his fork properly is starting to grow facial hair. Or you notice boys at the mall looking at your daughter, who still faces challenges in reading nonverbal communications, in a very different way.

Your child's adolescence and young adulthood may also bring with them a heightened sense of your own not fitting in with parents of neurotypical kids. As children grow up and away, parents face an important rite of passage, too. Typically, they experience the bittersweetness of seeing a child grow into a life of his own. At the same time, many parents are also looking ahead at changes in their own lives, wrought by added responsibility for their own parents, retirement, career changes, and so on. Here is yet another generational journey on which we as parents may feel left behind or entirely left out. The one thing that moms and dads of children with AS may not be able to foresee is a time when there will be an empty nest or they will not be needed to the extent that they were when their children were much younger.

While our peers are worried about their children staying out too late, drinking and driving, or experimenting with sex and drugs after a school dance, parents of teens with AS may feel out of the loop. Friends may tell us that we are "lucky" to find our son happily involved in his special interest and totally unaware that the school dance was even scheduled. Be prepared for the completely ridiculous moments when you find yourself thinking, *I wish she would sneak out to see her boyfriend*, or *I wish he did complain when he couldn't have the keys to the car*. It's not because you want to place your child in danger, or because you advocate premarital sex, or because you wouldn't worry while your son was behind the wheel. It's something else. After all, that's the growing-up period most of us have lived ourselves, that we can teach from, and that we know signals the presence of important emergent abilities and drives. At the very least, we know where to go for help with those types of situations. We could commiserate with friends; we could one day look back on it and, hopefully, even smile.

While families navigating these less-charted waters have more information available to them than ever before, ultimately, each of us walks away from the books, the conferences, the piles of pages printed off the net, and still wonders, "But what does this mean for *my* child?"

It is essential for parents to have at least one good connection to the ASD or disability community, whether that is a great support group, local disabilities agency, or transition planning organization. Know the laws and regulations that relate to your child's postsecondary education and/or employment training, employment supports, options for housing, and opportunities for engagement in the community.

VOICES OF EXPERIENCE

Perhaps most important—and encouraging—are the contributions from adults diagnosed with ASD. Their stories are often painful, and their courage in sharing both the good and the bad is to be commended. In most cases, no matter how difficult their lives were, they are intent on making sure that things are better for children and teens now being diagnosed. Some local support groups have set up programs in which adults with Asperger syndrome mentor children and young adults, and quite a few online relationships have developed after parents corresponded with adults with AS who participate in online support groups.

There are adults with AS willing to offer suggestions as to how we as parents can make things better for our children and the AS community at large. However, parents and others should understand the context of their comments. In many cases, these adults were misdiagnosed or not diagnosed at all, misunderstood, and, too often, horribly mistreated. In addition to the unfortunately "usual" teasing, bullying, and loneliness, some were subjected to emotional, physical, and sexual abuse at the hands of parents, professionals, and strangers; misdiagnosis and resulting treatment that was traumatic (institutionalization, electroconvulsive therapy—previously known as shock treatment—overmedication, and mismedication); or attempts to self-medicate through alcohol and drug abuse. Because of experiences like these, some adults with AS have a profound distrust of parents, professionals, and people in general. In some cases, their anger is truly justified. It may be unrealistic to expect them ever to understand and forgive. And, to be honest, in some situations, there can be no forgiveness. As advocates for people with AS and related disorders, we have a moral obligation to raise awareness about their plight, to respect their points of view, and to refrain from imposing upon them our opinions regarding appropriate interventions and treatments for them.

Parents of children with AS are often understandably curious to learn from adults with AS. For the most part, those who make themselves available to answer questions or serve as mentors do so because they feel a sense of community with the child with AS. Some parents, however, have been taken aback and surprised when the AS advisor expresses an opinion that does not agree with theirs. A typical flash point is the subject of medication. Some adults with AS have had such bad experiences that their only advice to parents considering medication is simply "Don't." Parents and people with AS may not always agree, but it is disrespectful of those of us who do not have AS to presume to tell those who do that their views are somehow wrong. Particularly when seeking input from people with AS on matters of parenting, realize and accept the terms of engagement. Be prepared to receive input about your views; don't ask expecting endorsement or validation for them. And you need not "correct" views that don't dovetail with your own.

People with AS, particularly those who are older and more confident and have found a place for themselves in the world, are extremely proud of their independence and their differences. This is one reason why the term *Asperger syndrome* is not likely to fade away. Some have an almost reflexive aversion to anything and anyone that seems to place a higher value on conformity to social norms than on the happiness and the acceptance of the individual. Given that we neurotypicals have the ability to adopt different perspectives, should it not be *we* who bend to accommodate those who cannot? Should it always be the responsibility of those with ASD to adapt to us?

CHANGE

By offering to individuals with Asperger syndrome help in areas such as social skills training, behavior management, independence, and understanding, we are not attempting to "cure" Asperger syndrome but rather to give the children with AS the necessary tools to make choices in their lives. Everyone with Asperger syndrome should be respected and celebrated for his differences. And everyone with Asperger syndrome or any ASD should be prepared to live her life to the fullest extent possible, on her own terms.

As a mother or father of a child with ASD, you might find yourself feeling differently about the situation than you did at the start or a few or a dozen years before. While it is important for parents and others who care about someone with ASD to have the right information and access to the most helpful resources, resist the temptation to feel that you should know it all or that you are less of a good parent if you don't. Where some people find support and community among other parents facing similar issues, others walk away feeling stressed. Some of us prefer not to share personal information, while others offer their experiences because they believe someone else might benefit. Where some take heart and find hope in participating in walks, galas, and other fund-raising efforts for the cause, others consider if the time and effort might not be better spent at home or out and about with their child. There are parents who never accept the diagnosis, parents who embrace the diagnosis as long as it serves some purpose, and those who let it go and never look back once they believe that their child is on her way, wherever that may be. None of these parents is right and none is wrong. If we claim to respect individual differences, we must be willing to accept everyone's differences, even parents' in their feelings toward this aspect of their own lives.

Chances are that your feelings will change with time. One of the most involved parents I ever met realized after her daughter was an adult that reminders of their struggles were too painful. She tracked down every paper, magazine, and book with the words *autism* or *Asperger* and ceremoniously carried them to the trash. Another has been reaching out and helping younger parents come to terms and advocate for their children for more than thirty years. Each found what works for her.

Believe it or not, life does go on. In delivering challenges to your doorstep, ASD will not be alone. Nothing about having ASD in the family holds life's other trials at bay. Some of our parents will fall to chronic or terminal illness and need our care. As our siblings and friends grow older, we will want to be there for them, too, when things go wrong. There will come a day when your child's ASD is not front and center in your life, either by choice or by necessity. And, yes, there will also come the day when you yourself cannot do all of the things you want to for your child.

BUILDING TOMORROW TODAY

As we mentioned before, being the parent of a child with ASD demands that we each wear many, many hats. Some of them fit us beautifully. Others not so much. Still, we grab the right one for the occasion and do our best to wear it with conviction, if not comfort or style (or, in some cases, not the style some people would prefer). Some you get to toss away eventually, but new ones seem to pop up on the rack. You toss away your IEP meeting helmet at your child's high school graduation with either tears or a loud, triumphant "Yes!" (complete with NFL end zone victory shuffle). Suddenly, you catch something softer, thinner, and with a lot less coverage: a mini felt beret seemingly designed for a teacup puppy. Then someone informs you that this is your new gear for accompanying your child on the path to college or career training or whatever lies ahead in the realm of adult services. Yes, the battles are fewer, but that's because your rights are fewer and involvement is less. It is not because your child might need you any less.

The task today, and every day, is to do what you can to prepare your child for this day and all those ahead. We know from experience and, in some cases, research that there are steps we can take to improve our kids' lives and outcomes. Know that for most of our kids, this diagnosis is neither the beginning nor the end. While understanding the diagnosis and the role it plays in your child's life can certainly help orient you in terms of making reasonable, sound decisions, it cannot tell you as much about the future as we would all like to know. Once you have lived with it for a few years, make it a habit to look back now and then. You will probably find that your child has grown in ways you did not expect or would never have predicted. The kid with the "hopeless" (to quote one OT) fine-motor skills finds his passion in playing the guitar, the eighth-grader who seemed so lacking in empathy grows into the veterinarian's assistant with "the touch" with every animal she encounters. The young math genius decides halfway through his first year of college that he was happiest the summer he worked as his uncle's electrician apprentice. And the little boy whose dyslexia drove his education along a less academically demanding route decides at twenty-two to start working toward an associate degree in computers.

As they say, you never know. And to be honest, probably neither does anyone else. There lies the uncertainty. But most important, there lies the hope.

ACKNOWLEDGMENTS

First, thanks as always to Barb Kirby, who let me join her on the original OASIS website, and then accepted my invitation to transfer the spirit of that endeavor to writing our first book together, *The OASIS Guide to Asperger Syndrome*, and its 2005 revised edition. Now that Barb is happily pursuing other endeavors, I'm thankful for her encouragement and her trust as the little book that we raised together grows up and flies from the "web nest" that hatched it. *Viva* OASIS.

Our very first editor, Betsy Rapoport, believed in us and our book from the start. There were a few other editors through the years, and each made important contributions. Our current editor, Leah Miller, has been indispensable, offering great suggestions and encouragement throughout. The whole team at Crown deserves a big thanks for making it happen.

Special thanks to Dr. Tony Attwood and to Michael John Carley for taking the time to read and write about *Asperger Syndrome: The OASIS Guide*. Tony was the first expert I ever saw speak on AS when my son was newly diagnosed and has been a tremendous support professionally and personally. (I promise a better restaurant next time you come to New York.) Michael John Carley is a newer friend, but one whose personal integrity and willingness to fight for the concerns of teens and adults with AS has benefited countless people, including my son. An extra-special thanks, as always, to Dr. James Snyder for vetting the "Medication" chapter. Dr. Snyder was the first person I ever heard utter the words "Asperger syndrome." From that uncertain moment until today, he has been there for our family and especially Justin.

Over the years, countless other professionals have contributed thoughts, interviews, leads, and suggestions for this book, in its various incarnations. Thanks always to Jed Baker, Dr. Simon Baron-Cohen, Dr. Teresa Bolick, Dennis Debbaudt, Dr. Michelle Garcia Winner, Dr. Peter Gerhardt, Dr. Beth Glasberg, Carol Gray, Dr. Ami Klin, Dr. Bobby Newman, Dr. Brenda Smith Myles, Dr. Diane Twachtman-Cullen, and Dr. Fred R. Volkmar.

I have two careers, but I am always first a writer. I owe my entire life in book publishing to my friend, agent, and former boss at *Rolling Stone*, Sarah Lazin.

In my second, newer career, as autism consultant, behavior analyst, and clinical instructor, I am indebted to my administrators and colleagues at the Cody Center for Autism and Developmental Disabilities at Stony Brook Children's Hospital and Stony Brook University: Dr. Margaret McGovern, Dr. John Pomeroy, Dr. Dave Makowski, Marlies Brandt, Deborah Gerard, and Michael Greenberg. Thanks especially to my teachers Dr. Susan Milla and Dr. Renee Chituk.

Our families are supportive of Justin and of us in ways that cannot be counted: Bob and Rachelle Bashe, Mary Vitro and Jeff Bender, Johnetta and John Simmons, Rick and Donna Romanowski, Michelle Assoian, Patrick and Danielle Dill, and Ivan and Tasha Karmel, along with cousins Doug Vitro and his new bride Kelsey, Dmitriy Romanowski, Katie and Adam Assoian, and Alisa and Ian Karmel. A special nod to our late nephew Alex Assoian, whose special kindness to Justin is never forgotten.

Finally, closer to home, the star of this show and the reason I do any of it: our son, Justin. I can never thank you enough for your patience while we all lived with this book (though I'm sure we can work out some deals that involve *Robot Chicken*, *Futurama*, Charlie Chaplin, Hank Williams, Starbucks, and that dacquoise cake recipe from America's Test Kitchen). Justin, you are the bravest, sweetest, funniest, and most wonderful person I know. I am always proud to be your mother, and I love you. The second guy who makes our house rock is my husband, Philip Bashe, who is great at a million things, but is also an unparalleled author, editor, and colleague who has been making anything I write better for as long as I've deserved to call myself a writer. His love has made me a better person and a better mom. Being the greatest dad to the greatest kid takes smarts, heart, determination, patience, a lot of love, and, apparently, a willingness to teach yourself to play electric guitar because your son does and you think you can help him find the perfect chord. And you do. Phil, I would love you just as much if you were still a drummer.

Finally, thank you to the countless people I might never meet who take the time to learn and to make life for my son and others with ASD a little better than it might otherwise have been.

NOTES

Chapter 1. What Is Asperger Syndrome?

1. Uta Frith, "Asperger and His Syndrome," in Uta Frith, ed., *Autism and Asperger Syndrome* (Cambridge, UK: Cambridge University Press, 1991), pp. 1–36. Also: Hans Asperger, "'Autistic Psychopathy' in Childhood," Uta Frith, trans. and annot., in *Autism and Asperger Syndrome*, pp. 37–92.

2. Adam Feinstein, *A History of Autism: Conversations with the Pioneers* (Chichester, UK: Wiley-Blackwell, 2010), especially chapter 1, "Two Great Pioneers," pp. 9–36.

3. Frith, "Asperger and His Syndrome," p. 7. Descriptions of Dr. Asperger's treatments and biography from various sources, including: Feinstein, "Two Great Pioneers"; Tony Attwood, *The Complete Guide to Asperger Syndrome* (London and Philadelphia: Jessica Kingsley Publishers, 2007), especially chapter 1, "What Is Asperger Syndrome?," pp. 11–34; Maria Asperger Felder, "Foreword," in Ami Klin, Fred R. Volkmar, and Sara S. Sparrow, eds., *Asperger Syndrome* (New York: Guilford Press, 2000), pp. xi–xiii.

4. Attwood, *The Complete Guide to Asperger Syndrome*, "Preface," pp. 9–10. Also: Frith, p. 10; Feinstein, pp. 14–18.

5. Lorna Wing, "The History of Asperger Syndrome," in Eric Shopler, Gary B. Mesibov, Linda J. Kunce, eds., *Asperger Syndrome or High-Functioning Autism?* Current Issues in Autism series (New York: Plenum, 1998), pp. 11–27.

6. For more information on savantism and savantism in autism, visit Dr.

Darold A. Treffert's website: www.wisconsin/medicalsociety.org/savant/default.cfm.

7. James C. McPartland, Brian Reichow, and Fred R. Volkmar, "Sensitivity and Specificity of Proposed *DSM-5* Diagnostic Criteria for Autism Spectrum Disorder," *Journal of the American Academy of Child and Adolescent Psychiatry* 51, no. 4 (2012): 368–383.

8. American Psychiatric Association (APA), "DSM-5 Autism Spectrum Disorder Fact Sheet," 2013.

9. McPartland, Reichow, and Volkmar (2012). See also: Claudia Wallas, "A Powerful Identity, A Vanishing Diagnosis," *New York Times*, November 3, 2009; Benedict Carey, "A Tense Compromise on Defining Disorders," *New York Times*, December 10, 2012; Benedict Carey, "New Definition of Autism Will Exclude Many, Study Suggests," *New York Times*, January 19, 2012; Amy S. F. Lutz, "You Do Not Have Asperger's: What Psychiatry's New Diagnostic Manual Means for People on the Autism Spectrum," Slate, May 22, 2013, at slate.com.

10. American Psychiatric Association, "Frequently Asked Questions About DSM-5 Implementation—For Clinicians UPDATED 9/20/13" at http://www.dsm5.org/Documents/FAQ%20for%20Clinicians%209-20-13.pdf; accessed February 3, 2014.

11. National Institute of Mental Health, "Autism Spectrum Disorder," at http://www.nimh.nih.gov/statistics/1AUT_CHILD.shtml; accessed December 15, 2013.

12. Emily Singer, "Late Arrival," SFARI: Simons Foundation Autism Research Initiative, November 2, 2012, at http://sfari.org/news-and-opinion/blog/2012/late-arrival; accessed March 2013.

13. An early analysis of prevalence studies conducted between 1966 and 1984 found autism at a rate of 0.4 cases per 1,000. Between 1986 and 1997, that figure more than doubled to 1 per 1,000. In 2003, a CDC study of 987 children in Atlanta, Georgia, demonstrated that 4 per 1,000, or 1 in 250, was most likely to reflect then-current prevalence rates. In early 2004, the rate was believed to be between 1 in 166 and 1 in 250 children. In 2012, the widely accepted prevalence rate was 1 in 88. In March 2014, the prevalence rate was revised to 1 in 68. Sources: Eric Frombonne, "The Prevalence of Autism," *Journal of the American Medical Association*, 289, no. 1 (January 1, 2003): 87–89. See also: "Autism Prevalence on the Rise," a PDF chart from Autism Speaks, available at http://www.autism speaks.org/docs/Prevalence_Graph_12_18_2009.pdf. Centers for Disease Control and Prevention, "Prevalence of Autism Spectrum Disorder Among Children Aged 8 Years—Autism and Developmental Disabilities Monitoring Network, 11 Sites, United States, 2010," *Morbidity and Mortality Weekly Report*, March 28, 2014.

14. Emily Anthes, "Sibling Study Highlights Autism's Genetic Roots," SFARI: Simons Foundation Autism Research Initiative, September 12,

2013, at http://sfari.org/news-and-opinion/news/2013/sibling-study-highlights-autisms-genetic-roots; accessed September 20, 2013. See also: Noa Ben-Yizhak, Nurit Yirmiya, Ifat Seidman, Raaya Alon, Catherine Lord, and Marian Sigman, "Pragmatic Language and School-Related Linguistic Abilities in Siblings of Children with Autism," *Journal of Autism and Developmental Disabilities* 41, no. 6 (June 2011): 750–760, doi: 10.007/s10803-010-1096-6, especially Introduction for review of previous studies.

15. Peter Tanguay, "Pervasive Developmental Disorders: A 10-Year Review," *Journal of the American Academy of Child and Adolescent Psychiatry* 39, no. 9 (September 2000): 1079–1095.

16. Ami Klin and Fred Volkmar, handout to conference "Asperger Syndrome: Diagnosis, Assessment, Treatment," New York, NY, May 3, 2000.

17. For more detailed information on the OASIS survey on Special Interests, see Patricia Romanowski Bashe and Barbara L. Kirby, *The OASIS Guide to Asperger Syndrome*, 2d ed. (New York: Crown, 2005), pp. 37–42.

18. Simon Baron-Cohen, *The Facts: Autism and Asperger Syndrome* (Oxford, UK: Oxford University Press, 2008), p. 63; also chapter 5, "The Psychology of Asperger Syndrome," pp. 51–84.

19. Baron-Cohen, p. 63.

20. Ami Klin, Warren Jones, Robert T. Schultz, and Fred R. Volkmar, "The Enactive Mind—From Actions to Cognition: Lessons from Autism," in Fred R. Volkmar, Rhea Paul, Ami Klin, and Donald Cohen, eds., *Handbook of Autism and Pervasive Developmental Disorders, Vol. 1: Diagnosis, Development, Neurobiology, and Behavior* (New York: John Wiley and Sons, 2005), pp. 682–703.

21. Baron-Cohen, p. 62.

22. Virginia Hughes, "Sound Response May Explain Language Problems in Autism," SFARI: Simons Foundation Autism Research Initiative, December 8, 2008, at http://sfari.org/news-and-opinion/news/2011/sound-response-may-explain-language-problems-in-autism; accessed August 10, 2013.

23. Russo, Zecker, Trommer, Chen, and Kraus, "Effects of Background Noise on Cortical Encoding of Speech in Autism Spectrum Disorders," *Journal of Autism and Developmental Disorders* 39 (2009): 1185–1196.

24. For more detailed information on the OASIS survey on Hearing and Noise, see Romanowski Bashe and Kirby (2005), pp. 52–54.

25. Reference to 1991 Ozonoff, Rogers, and Pennington study in Sally Ozonoff and Elizabeth McMahon Griffith, "Neuropsychological Function and the External Validity of Asperger Syndrome," in *Asperger Syndrome*, Klin, Volkmar, and Sparrow, eds. (New York: Guilford Press, 2000), pp. 72–96, cited in pp. 86–87, Volkmar, Klin.

26. Emily Willingham, "Guest Blog: Cognitive Dissonance," SFARI:

Simons Foundation Autism Research Initiative, December 13, 2013, at http://sfari.org/news-and-opinion/blog/2013/guest-blog-cognitive-dissonance; accessed December 13, 2013.

Chapter 2. Getting the Diagnosis

1. Emily Simonoff, Andrew Pickles, Tony Charman et al., "Psychiatric Disorders in Children with Autism Spectrum Disorders: Prevalance, Comorbidity, and Associated Factors in a Population-Derived Sample," *Journal of the American Academy of Child and Adolescent Psychiatry* 47, no. 8 (2008): 921–929.

2. Timothy Wilens, *Straight Talk About Psychiatric Medications for Kids*, 3d ed. (New York: Guilford, 2009), p. 145. See also: National Institute of Mental Health, "NIMH Statistics: Attention Deficit/Hyperactivity Disorder Among Children," at http:www.nimh.nih.gov/statistics/1ADHD_CHILD.shtml; accessed December 30, 2013.

3. Marja-Leena Mattila, Tuula Hurtig, Helena Haapsamo et al., "Comorbid Psychiatric Disorders Associated with Asperger Syndrome/High-Functioning Autism: A Community- and Clinic-based Study," *Journal of Autism and Developmental Disorders* (2010), doi 10.1007/s10803-010-0958-2.

4. National Institute of Mental Health, "NIMH Statistics: Any Anxiety Disorder Among Children," at http://www.himh.gov/statistics/1ANYANX_child.shtml; accessed December 30, 2013.

5. Mattila, Hurtig, Haapsamo et al., "Comorbid Psychiatric Disorders Associated with Asperger Syndrome/High-Functioning Autism: A Community- and Clinic-based Study."

6. National Insitute of Mental Health, "NIMH Statistics: Obsessive-Compulsive Disorder Among Adults," at http://www.nimh.nih.gov/statistics/1OCD_ADULT.shtml; accessed December 30, 2013.

7. American Psychiatric Association, *Diagnostic and Statistical Manual of Mental Disorders, Fifth Edition (DSM-5)*, Autism Spectrum Disorder, pp. 50–59, specifically criterion B, on p. 50.

8. Wilens, *Straight Talk About Psychiatric Medications for Kids*, p. 173.

9. National Institute of Mental Health, "NIMH Statistics: Specific Phobia Among Children," at http://www.nimh.nih.gov/statistics/1SPECIFIC_CHILD.shtml; accessed December 30, 2013.

10. National Institute of Mental Health, "NIMH Statistics: Post-Traumatic Stress Disorder Among Children," at http://www.nimh.nih.gov/statistics/1AD_PTSD_CHILD.shtml; accessed December 30, 2013.

11. Roberto Canitano, "Epilepsy in Autism Spectrum Disorders," *European Child and Adolescent Psychiatry* 16, no. 1 (2007): 61–66.

12. National Institute of Mental Health, "NIMH Statistics: Dysthymic Dis-

order Among Children," at http://www.nimh.nih.gov/statistics/1DD_CHILD.shtml; accessed December 30, 2013.

13. Ibid.

14. American Academy of Child and Adolescent Psychiatry, "Facts for Families Pages: The Depressed Child," at http://www.aacap.org/AACAP/Families_and_Youth/Facts for Families; accessed March 16, 2014.

15. National Institute of Mental Health, "NIMH Statistics: Bipolar Disorder Among Children," at http://www.nimh.nih.gov/statistics/1BIPOLAR_CHILD.shtml; accessed December 30, 2013.

16. Wilens, *Straight Talk About Psychiatric Medications for Kids*, p. 168.

17. Mattila, Hurtig, Haapsamo et al., "Comorbid Psychiatric Disorders Associated with Asperger Syndrome/High-Functioning Autism: A Community- and Clinic-based Study."

18. Tourette Syndrome Association, Inc., at www.tsa-usa.org.

19. Kenneth Gadow, Carla J. DeVincent, and Deborah A. G. Drabick, "Oppositional Defiant Disorder as a Clinical Phenotype in Autism Spectrum Disorder," *Journal of Autism and Developmental Disorders* 38 (2008): 1302–1310.

20. Various sources, including Wilens, *Straight Talk About Psychiatric Medication for Kids*, p. 152, and Gadow, DeVincent, and Drabick, 1302.

21. "Myths About Dyscalculia," LDHope.com, at http://ldhope.com/resources/dyscalculia-myths/; accessed March 16, 2014.

22. International Dyslexia Association, "Just the Facts: Dyslexia Basics," at www.interdys.org; accessed March 12, 2014.

23. Ibid. See also: Sally Shaywitz, *Overcoming Dyslexia: A New and Complete Science-based Program for Reading Problems at Any Level* (New York: Knopf, 2003).

24. List abridged and adapted from Pamela B. Tanguay, "Nonverbal Learning Disabilities: What to Look For," in *Nonverbal Learning Disabilities at Home: A Parent's Guide* (London and Philadelphia: Jessica Kingsley Publishers, 2001).

25. American Academy of Pediatrics, "What Is a Developmental–Behavioral Pediatrician?" at http://www.healthychildren.org/English/family-life/health-management/pediatric-specialists/Pages/What-is-a-Developmental-Behavioral-Pediatrician.aspx; accessed August 20, 2013.

26. Roger Pierangelo and George A. Giuliani, *Assessment in Special Education: A Practical Approach* (Boston: Allyn & Bacon, 2002), p. 159.

27. Romanowski Bashe and Kirby (2005), p. 116.

Chapter 3. Acceptance Builds the Bridge to Success

1. Jennifer B. Brobst, James R. Clopton, and Susan S. Hendrick, "Parenting Children with Autism Spectrum Disorders: The Couple's Relationship,"

Focus on Autism and Developmental Disabilities 24, no. 38 (2009): 38–49, doi: 10.1177/1088357608323699. See also: Gloria K. Lee, Christopher Lopata, Martin A. Volker, Marcus L. Thomeer, Robert E. Nida, Jennifer A. Toomey, Sabrina Y. Chow, and Audrey M. Smerbeck, "Health-Related Quality of Life of Parents of Children with High-functioning Autism Spectrum Disorders," *Focus on Autism and Developmental Disabilities* 24, no. 4 (2009): 227–239, doi: 10.1177/1088357609347371; T. Epstein, J. Saltzman-Benaiah, A. O'Hare, J. C. Goll, and S. Tuck, "Associated Features of Asperger Syndrome and Their Relationship to Parenting Stress," *Child Health, Care, and Development* 34, no. 4 (2008): 503–511.

2. Jessica Gill and Pranee Liamputtong, "Being the Mother of a Child with Asperger's Syndrome: Women's Experiences of Stigma," *Health Care for Women International* 32 (2011): 708–722.

3. Miriam Liss et al., "Predictors and Correlates of Adaptive Functioning in Children with Developmental Disorders," *Journal of Autism and Developmental Disorders* 31, no. 2 (2001): 219–230.

4. Ami Klin, Celine A. Saulnier, Sara S. Sparrow, Domenic V. Cicchetti, Fred R. Volkmar, and Catherine Lord, "Social and Communication Abilities and Disabilities in Higher Functioning Individuals with Autism Spectrum Disorders: The Vineland and the ADOS," *Journal of Autism and Developmental Disorders* 37 (2007): 748–759.

5. Mats Cederlund, Bibbi Hagberg, Eva Billstedt, I. Carina Gillberg, and Christopher Gillberg, "Asperger Syndrome and Autism: A Comparative Longitudinal Follow-Up Study More than 5 Years After Original Diagnosis," *Journal of Autism and Developmental Disorders* 38 (2008): 72–85.

Chapter 4. Options and Interventions

1. Emily Willingham, "FDA Warns Consumers About Common Off-Label Autism Therapy," *Forbes*, August 23, 2013.

2. NAC, website, at http://www.nationalautismcenter.org/about/may_institute.php.

3. C. Wong, S. L. Odom, K. Hume, A. W. Cox, A. Fettig, S. Kucharczyk et al., *Evidence-Based Practices for Children, Youth, and Young Adults with Autism Spectrum Disorder* (Chapel Hill, NC: University of North Carolina, Frank Porter Graham Child Development Institute, Autism Evidence-Based Practice Review Group, 2014). Online at http://autismpdc.fpg.unc.edu/sites/autismpdc.fpg.unc.edu/files/2014_EBP_Report.pdf.

4. Author interview with Bobby Newman, circa 2000.

5. Catherine Maurice, "ABA and Us: One Parent's Reflection on Partnership and Persuasion," address to the Cambridge Center for Behavioral Studies (CCBS), Annual Board Meeting, Palm Beach, FL, November 5, 1999, at www.behavior.org; accessed May 22, 2004.

6. Author interview with Bobby Newman, circa 2000.

7. Dr. Vincent Carbone, a psychologist and Board Certified Behavior Analyst, has made important contributions to the understanding and application of applied verbal behavior (AVB). He has stated publicly that there is no such thing as a "Carbone" method and that AVB is ABA.

8. Houghton Mifflin, Earobics web page, at http:/earobics.com/solutions /programs.php.

9. Scientific Learning website, at http://www.scilearn.com/.

10. Author unknown. "CAPD Handout for Parents and Teachers," dated February 22, 1996; available on various websites. See also: Tara Parker-Pope, "Little-Known Disorder Can Take Toll on Learning," *New York Times*, April 26, 2010.

11. Sanam Sahli, "Auditory Processing Disorder in Children: Definition, Assessment and Management," *Journal of International Advanced Otology* 5, no. 1 (2009): 104–115.

12. Carol Gray, *Comic Strip Conversations: Colorful, Illustrated Interactions with Students with Autism and Related Disorders* (Arlington, TX: Future Horizons, 1993), p. 1.

13. Susan R. Leekam, Carmen Nieto, Sarah J. Libby, Lorna Wing, and Judith Gould, "Describing the Sensory Abnormalities of Children and Adults with Autism," *Journal of Autism and Developmental Disorders* 37 (2007): 894–910, especially pp. 903, 904, 907, and 908.

14. Russell Lang, Mark O'Reilly, Olive Healy, Mandy Rispoli, Helena Lydon, William Streusand, Tonya Davis, Soyeon Kang, Jeff Sigafoos, Giulia Lancioni, Robert Didden, and Sanne Giesbers, "Review: Sensory Integration Therapy for Autism Spectrum Disorders: A Systematic Review," *Research in Autism Spectrum Disorders* 6 (2012): 1004–1018. See also: Laura Geggel, "Sensory Subtypes," SFARI: Simons Foundation Autism Research Initiative, July 26, 2013, at https://sfari.org/news-and -opinion/blog/2013/sensory-subtypes; accessed August 16, 2013.

15. American Academy of Pediatrics, Section on Complementary and Integrative Medicine and the Council on Children with Disabilities, "Policy Statement: Sensory Integration Therapies for Children with Developmental and Behavioral Disorders," *Pediatrics* 129, no. 6 (2012): 1186–1189. Originally published online May 28, 2012, at doi: 10.1542/ peds.2012-0876; also available at http://pediatrics.aappublications.org /content/129/6/1186.full.html; accessed August 16, 2013.

16. National Autism Resources, "The Wilbarger Protocol: Helping People Sensitive to Touch," at http://www.nationalautismresources.com /wilbarger-protocol.html; accessed September 14, 2013. Also: OT-Innovations.com, "The Wilbarger Deep Pressure Technique (DPPT) and Oral Tactile Technique (OTT)," at www.ot-innovations.com/content /view/55/46/; accessed September 7, 2013. *These cites are provided only for documentation purposes; their inclusion does not constitute a recommendation or an endorsement of these techniques.*

17. Cincinnati Children's Hospital Medical Center, "Best Evidence State-

ment (BESt): Deep Pressure Proprioceptive Protocols to Improve Sensory Processing Skills in Children," August 24, 2009, 6 pages. Available from the Agency for Healthcare Research and Quality: http://www .guidelines.gov/content.aspx?id=15244; accessed September 14, 2013.

18. Mayo Clinic Staff and Jay L. Hoecker, MD, "Trampoline Jumping? Safe for Kids?" March 16, 2011, online at https://www.mayoclinic.com /health/trampoline-exercise/AN01570; accessed September 7, 2013.

19. Diane Twachtman-Cullen, *How to Be a Para Pro: A Comprehensive Training Manual for Paraprofessionals* (Higganum, CT: Starfish Specialty Press, 2000), p. 11.

20. Richard Lavoie, "Ask Rick," monthly column, online at LD Online, at www.ldonline.org; accessed in 2005.

21. Dorothy Scattone, "Enhancing the Conversation Skills of a Boy with Asperger's Disorder Through Social Stories and Video Modeling," *Journal of Autism and Developmental Disorders* (2007), doi: 10.1007s/10803-007-0392-2.

22. Patricia Rao, Deborah C. Beidel, and Michael J. Murray, "Social Skills Interventions for Children with Asperger's Syndrome or High-Functioning Autism: A Review and Recommendations," *Journal of Autism and Developmental Disorders* (2007), doi: 10.1007/s10803-007-0402-4.

Chapter 5. Medication

1. Daniel L. Coury, Edvokia Anagnostou, Patricia Manning-Courtney, Anny Reynolds, Lynn Cole, Robin McCoy, Agnes Whitaker, and James M. Perrin, "Use of Psychotropic Medication in Children and Adolescents with Autism Spectrum Disorders," *Pediatrics* 130, supp. 2 (2012): S69–S76.

2. Emily Simonoff, Andrew Pickles, Tony Charman et al., "Psychiatric Disorders in Children with Autism Spectrum Disorders: Prevalance, Comorbidity, and Associated Factors in a Population-Derived Sample," *Journal of the American Academy of Child and Adolescent Psychiatry* 47, no. 8 (2008): 921–929.

3. Kennedy Krieger Institute, "Children with Autism Arrive at Emergency Room in Times of Psychiatric Crisis Nine Times More Than Peers," Kennedy Krieger website, News, December 3, 2012, at http://www. kennedykrieger.org; accessed June 18, 2013. This article summarizes Luther G. Kalb, Elizabeth A. Stuart, Brian Freedman, Benjamin Zablotsky, and Roma Vasa, "Psychiatric-Related Emergency Department Visits Among Children with an Autism Spectrum Disorder," *Pediatric Emergency Care* (2012), doi: 10.1097/PEC.0b013e33182767d96.

4. Andrés Martin, David K. Patzer, and Fred R. Volkmar, "Psychopharmacological Treatment of Higher-Functioning Pervasive Developmental

Disorders," in Ami Klin, Fred R. Volkmar, and Sara S. Sparrow, eds., *Asperger Syndrome* (New York: Guilford Press, 2000), pp. 210–230; see specifically p. 214, table 7.1, "Subjects Taking Psychotopic Medications on Date of Survey."

5. National Institute of Mental Health, "The Numbers Count: Mental Health Disorders in America," at http://www.nimh.nih.gov/health/publications/the-numbers-count-mental-disorders-in-america/index.shtml#Intro; accessed December 29, 2013.

6. Richard A. Friedman, "A Dry Pipeline for Psychiatric Drugs," *New York Times,* August 20, 2013, http://www.nytimes.com/2013/08/20/health/a-dry-pipeline-for-psychiatric-drugs.html; accessed August 25, 2013.

7. National Institute of Mental Health, Science Update, "Psychotropic Medications Are Prescribed Appropriately Among US Teens, National Study Finds," December 3, 2012, summarizing K. Merikangas, J. He, J. Rapoport, B. Vitiello, and M. Olfson, "Medication Use in US Youth with Mental Disorders," *Archives of Pediatric and Adolescent Medicine,* online and ahead of print, December 3, 2012, at http://www.nimh.nih.gov/new/science-news/2012; accessed August 18, 2013. See also: K. R. Merikangas, J. He, M. Burstein, S. A. Swanson, S. Avenevoli, L. Cui, C. Benjet, K. Georgiades, and J. Swendsen, "Lifetime Prevalence of Mental Disorders in US Adolescents: Results from the National Comorbidity Study—Adolescent Supplement (NCS-A)," *Journal of the American Academy of Child and Adolescent Psychiatry* 49, no. 10 (October 2010): 980–989; US Department of Health and Human Services, *Mental Health: A Report of the Surgeon General* (Rockville, MD: US Department of Health and Human Services, Substance Abuse and Mental Health Services Administration, Center for Mental Health Services, National Institutes of Health, National Institute of Mental Health, 1999).

8. National Alliance on Mental Illness (NAMI), "Facts on Children's Mental Health in America," citing D. Shaffer and L. Craft, "Methods of Adolescent Suicide Prevention," *Journal of Clinical Psychiatry* 60, suppl. 2 (1999): 70–74; and US Department of Education, *Twenty-third Annual Report to Congress on the Implementation of the Individuals with Disabilities Education Act* (Washington, DC: US Department of Education, 2001), at http://www.nami.org; accessed August 18, 2013.

9. Pharmaceutical Research and Manufacturers of America, "Chart Pack: Biopharmaceuticals in Perspective," Spring 2013, version 3.0, p. 3, "Insurance Covers a Lower Share of Prescription Drug Costs Than of Other Medical Services," at http://www.pharma.org; accessed June 28, 2013, revised.

10. "Controversy Over Stimulant Use Among Children," *Reuters News,* January 2000.

11. American Psychiatric Association, *The Diagnostic and Statistical Manual*

of Mental Disorders, Fifth Edition (DSM-5) (Washington, DC: American Psychiatric Association, 2013), pp. 59–65.

12. US Department of Health and Human Services, *Mental Health: A Report of the Surgeon General.*

13. Mark J. Sciutto and Miriam Eisenberg, "Evaluating the Evidence for and Against the Overdiagnosis of ADHD," *Journal of Attention Disorders* 11, no. 106 (2007): 106–113.

14. Medline Plus, "Health Literacy," last updated October 28, 2013, at http://www.nlm.nih.gov/medlineplus/healthliteracy.html; accessed December 30, 2013. Jeff Nesmith, "90 Million Americans Are 'Health Illiterate,'" New York Times Syndicate, April 8, 2004, Medline-Plus; no longer available online.

15. Luke Y. Tsai, *Taking the Mystery Out of Medications in Autism/Asperger Syndrome* (Arlington, TX: Future Horizons, 2001), p. xi.

16. Drugs@FDA, FDA Approved Drug Products, Intuniv, at http://www.accessdata.fda.gov; accessed August 18, 2013.

17. FDA, New Pediatric Labeling Information Database, Risperidone, at http://www.accessdata.fda.gov; accessed August 18, 2013. See also: Adelaide S. Robb, "Managing Irritability and Aggression in Autism Spectrum Disorders in Children and Adolescents," *Developmental Disabilities Research Reviews* 16 (2010): 258–264, especially pp. 259–260.

18. Highlights of Prescribing Information, Intuniv, revised August 2009, online at http://www.accessdata.fda.gov/drugsatfda_docs/label/2009/022037lbl.pdf; accessed March 10, 2014.

19. FDA, New Pediatric Labeling Information Database, Abilify, at http://www.accessdata.fda.gov; accessed August 18, 2013.

20. FDA, New Pediatric Labeling Information Database, Zoloft, at http://www.accessdate.fda.gov; accessed August 18, 2013.

21. Alexis Jetter, "Trying to End the Guesswork in Dosing Children: A Conversation with Dianne Murphy," *New York Times*, September 12, 2000, p. F7.

22. US Food and Drug Administration, "Drugs: Drug Research and Children," last updated August 24, 2011, at http://www.fda.gov/Drugs/resourcesForYou/Consumers/ucm14365.htm; accessed August 18, 2013.

23. Ibid.

24. Despite the possible benefits of purchasing prescription medication from suppliers or pharmacies outside the United States, the FDA has long warned consumers that it cannot regulate or guarantee the safety, efficacy, or quality of these medications. Consumers who purchase medications from outside the country have received products that were counterfeit (despite product design and packaging that were indistinguishable from the real thing), expired, or contained varying amounts of the active ingredient or, in some cases, none at all. In addition, some

medications lose their potency or become dangerous to use if they are not formulated, manufactured, packaged, shipped, and stored according to manufacturer's instructions. If you have problems paying for prescription medication, visit the PhRMA (Pharmaceutical Research and Manufacturers Association) website—http://www.pharma.org—for information on how to obtain medication at reduced cost from manufacturers.

25. Tsai, *Taking the Mystery Out of Medications in Autism/Asperger Syndrome*, p. 63.

26. See Nancy Rappaport and Peter Chubinsky, "The Meaning of Psychotropic Medications for Children, Adolescents, and Their Families," *Journal of the American Academy of Child and Adolescent Psychiatry* 39, no. 9 (September 2000): 1198–1200.

27. Timothy E. Wilens, *Straight Talk About Psychiatric Medications for Kids*, p. 181.

Chapter 6. Special Education Basics

1. There are many other types of services a student might receive, depending on establishment of need and interpretation of federal, state, and local requirements. For example, some school districts might offer music therapy, auditory integration programs, or special reading programs (for example, Lindamood-Bell). It is important to note that in most cases, from a legal perspective, any one of two or more possible interventions or services might be considered sufficient to meet the student's needs.

2. Individuals with Disabilities Education Act, 2004, 20 USC 1401(29); Subpart A, Section 300.39(a).

3. For more on the history of special education law, see the one book that should have a place on every parent's bookshelf: Peter W. D. Wright and Pamela Darr Wright, *Wrightslaw: Special Education Law* (Hartfield, VA: Harbor House Law Press, 2006).

4. Wright and Wright, *Wrightslaw*, 1999 edition, p. 9.

5. IDEA 2004, 20 USC 1401(601)(c)(5)(F); Subpart A, Section 601(c)(4).

6. Wayne Steedman, "10 Tips: How to Use IDEA 2004 to Improve Education for Children with Disabilities," at www.wrightslaw.com/idea/art/10.tips.steedman.htm; accessed August 2013.

7. IDEA 2004, 20 USC 1414(b)(1)-(3), 1412(a)(6)(B); Subpart D, Section 300.304(C)(4).

8. IDEA 2004, 20 USC 1401(6012)(3); Subpart A, Section 300.8.

9. Ibid.

10. Ibid.

11. The Rehabilitation Act of 1973, 29 USC, chapter 16, Section 701(B)(1).

12. The Rehabilitation Act of 1973 defines an individual with a disability as "any person who (i) has a physcial or mental impairment which

substantially limits one or more of such person's major life activities; (ii) has a record of such an impairment; or (iii) is regarded as having such an impairment."

13. Wright and Wright, *Wrightslaw*, 2009 edition, p. 261.

14. A good overview of the IEP process is provided by Wrightslaw: "Roadmap to IDEA 2004: What You Need to Know About IEPs and IEP Meetings," at www.wrightslaw.com/idea/art/iep.roadmap.htm; accessed September 7, 2013. In addition, your state should have a free guide for parents that you can download from the state education website or that your school district can provide you.

15. IDEA 2004, 20 USC 1414(d)(1)(a); Subpart D, Section 300.320(a)(1).

16. IDEA 2004, 20 USC 1401(602); Subpart D, Section 300.320(b).

17. Robert F. Mager, *Preparing Instructional Objectives*, 3d ed. (Atlanta: Center for Effective Performance, 1997), p. 3.

Chapter 7. Your Child's Emotional Life

1. Patricia Howlin, Simon Baron-Cohen, and Julie Hadwin, *Teaching Children with Autism to Mind-Read: A Practical Guide for Teachers and Parents* (Chichester, UK: John Wiley & Sons, 1999), pp. 9–12.

2. Val Cumine, Julia Leach, and Gill Stevenson, *Asperger Syndrome: A Practical Guide for Teachers* (London: David Fulton, 1998), p. 25.

3. Sally Ozonoff and Elizabeth McMahon Griffith, "Neuropsychological Function and the External Validity of Asperger Syndrome," in Ami Klin, Fred R. Volkmar, and Sara S. Sparrow, eds., *Asperger Syndrome* (New York: Guilford Press, 2000), p. 86.

4. F. Fösterling, *Attribution Theory in Clinical Psychology* (New York: John Wiley & Sons, 1998), p. 11.

5. G. Barnhill, T. Hagiwara, B. S. Myles, R. L. Simpson, M. L. Brick, and D. Greenwald, "Parent, Teacher, and Self-Report of Problem and Adaptive Behaviors of Children and Adolescents with Asperger Syndrome," *Diagnostique* 25, no. 2 (2000): 147–167.

6. Ibid.

7. From the essential book on activity schedules, written by the women who literally invented the approach: Lynn E. Clanahan and Patricia J. Krantz, *Activity Schedules for Children with Autism: Teaching Independent Behavior*, 2d ed. (Bethesda, MD: Woodbine House, 2010), p. 3.

8. Brenda Smith Myles and Jack Southwick, *Asperger Syndrome and Difficult Moments* (Shawnee Mission, KS: Autism Asperger Publishing, 1999), p. 93.

9. D. S. Mandell, "Psychiatric Hospitalization Among Children with Autism Spectrum Disorders," *Journal of Autism and Developmental Disorders* 28 (2008): 1059–1065, doi: 10.1007/s10803-007-0481-2. See also: L. G. Kalb, E. A. Stuart, B. Freedman, B. Zablotsky, and R. Vasa, "Psychi-

atric-Related Emergency Department Visits Among Children with an Autism Spectrum Disorder," *Pediatric Emergency Care* 28, no. 12 (2012): 1269–1276, doi: 10.1097/PED.0b013e3182767d96.

Chapter 8. Your Child in the Social Realm

1. Tony Attwood and Carol Gray, "Understanding and Teaching Friendship Skills," at www.tonyattwood.com.au and other sources on the web.
2. Tony Attwood and Carol Gray, "The Discovery of 'Aspie' Criteria," *The Morning News* (1999). Also available from Tony Attwood's website: www.tonyattwood.com.au.

Chapter 9. Your Child in School

1. See chapter 6. Contrary to what you might hear, intellectual or academic ability or giftedness does not make your child ineligible for accommodations under Section 504 or for special education and related services under IDEA. There is no such thing as being "too smart" to receive special assistance, if needed.
2. Diane Toroian, "Thomas' Struggles to Cope with a Pair of Complex Disorders in a Cruel and Provoking Teenage World," *St. Louis Post-Dispatch*, August 29, 1999.
3. William L. Heward, *Exceptional Children: An Introduction to Special Education* (Upper Saddle River, NJ: Merrill, 2000), pp. 538–539.
4. Steven G. Zecker, "Underachievement and Learning Disabilities in Children Who Are Gifted," online at http://www.nldline.com/gifted_and_ld.htm; accessed January 1, 2014.
5. Maureen Neihart, "Gifted Children with Attention Deficit Hyperactivity Disorder (ADHD)," Eric EC Digest, ED482344, at http://eric.ed.gov/?id=ED482344; accessed January 1, 2014.
6. Stephanie S. Tolan, "Giftedness as Asynchronous Development," 1994, online at http://www.stephanietolan.com/gt_as_asynch.htm; accessed January 1, 2014. Also: Parents of gifted children will find much of value on Stephanie Tolan's website: www.stephanietolan.com.
7. Ibid.
8. Johns Hopkins University, Center for Talented Youth, "What We Know About Academically Talented Students" (Baltimore, MD: Johns Hopkins University, 2007), online at http://cty.jhu.edu/research/publications/whatweknow.html; accessed January 1, 2014.
9. Tony Attwood, *The Complete Guide to Asperger Syndrome* (London and Philadelphia: Jessica Kingsley Publishers, 2007), p. 254.
10. Susan Williams White, Lawrence Scahill, Ami Klin, Kathleen Koenig, and Fred R. Volkmar, "Educational Placements and Service Use Patterns

of Individuals with Autism Spectrum Disorders," *Journal of Autism and Developmental Disorders* 37 (2007): 1403–1412.

11. Ami Klin, Celine A. Saulnier, Sara S. Sparrow, Domenic V. Cicchetti, Fred R. Volkmar, and Catherine Lord, "Social and Communication Abilities and Disabilities in Higher Functioning Individuals with Autism Spectrum Disorders: The Vineland and the ADOS," *Journal of Autism and Developmental Disorders* 37 (2007): 748–759.

12. Barbara D. Bateman, "Legal Requirements for Transition Components of the IEP," at www.wrightslaw.com/info/trans.legal.bateman.htm.; accessed May 3, 2014.

Chapter 10. Growing Up Safe and Healthy

1. Laura A. Schieve, Vanessa Gonzalez, Sheree L. Boulet, Susanna N. Visser, Catherine E. Rice, Kim Van Naarden Braun, and Coleen A. Boyle, "Concurrent Medical Conditions and Health Care Use and Needs Among Children with Learning and Behavioral Developmental Disabilities," National Health Interview Survey, 2006–2010. See also: Child and Adolescent Health Measurement Initiative, "National Profile of Children with Special Health Care Needs and Autism Spectrum Disorders: Key Findings from the 2009/10/NS-CSHCN and 2007 NSCH" (Washington, DC: US Department of Health and Human Services, 2012), at www.childhealthdata.org, revised March 21, 2012; accessed June 28, 2013; Li-Ching Lee, Rebecca A. Harrington, Jen Jen Chang, and Susan L. Connors, "Increased Risk of Injury in Children with Developmental Disabilities," *Research in Developmental Disabilities* 29 (2008): 247–255, doi: 10.1016/j.ridd.2007.05.002.

2. Patricia Romanowski Bashe, *The Parents' Guide to Teaching Kids with Asperger Syndrome and Similar ASDs Real-life Skills for Independence* (New York: Crown, 2011).

3. Ibid., chapter 4, "What Should Your Child Be Doing Right Now?" includes a helpful chart listing typical skill acquisition by age.

4. Emily Singer, "In Autism, Obesity Starts Early," SFARI: Simons Foundation Autism Research Initiative, April 2, 2013, at http://sfari.org/news-and-opinion/blog/2013/in-autism-obesity-starts-early; accessed August 16, 2013.

5. Tony Attwood, *The Complete Guide to Asperger Syndrome* (London and Philadelphia: Jessica Kingsley Publishers, 2007), p. 18.

6. Ibid. See also: Shana Nichols with Gina Marie Moravcik and Samara Pulver Tetenbaum, *Girls Growing Up on the Autism Spectrum* (London and Philadelphia: Jessica Kingsley Publishers, 2009), pp. 53–54; Maia Szalavitz, "A Genetic Link Between Anorexia and Autism?," *Time*, June 19, 2009, online at www.time.com; accessed July 11, 2009.

NOTES

7. Russell Lang, Lynn Kern Koegel, Kristen Ashbaugh, April Regester, Whitney Ence, and Whitney Smith, "Physical Exercise and Individuals with Autism Spectrum Disorders: A Systematic Review," *Research in Autism Spectrum Disorders* 4 (2010): 565–576.

8. Jane E. Magnusson, Caitlin Cobham, and Rachel McLeod, "Beneficial Effects of Clinical Exercise Rehabilitation for Children and Adolescents with Autism Spectrum Disorder (ASD)," *Journal of Exercise Physiology Online* 15, no. 2 (April 2012), at http://www.asep.org/asep/asep/JEPonline April2012Jane_Magnusson.pdf; accessed August 3, 2013.

9. Ibid.

10. E. Juulia Paavonen, Kimmo Vehkalahti, Raija Vanhala, Lennart von Wendt, Taina Nieminen-von Wendt, and Eeva T. Aronen, "Sleep in Children with Asperger Syndrome," *Journal of Autism and Developmental Disorders* (2007), unpaged; accessed August 3, 2013, doi: 10/1007/ s10803-007-0360-x. See also: Hiie Allik, Jan-Olov Larsson, and Hans Smedje, "Sleep Patterns of School-age Children with Asperger Syndrome or High-Functioning Autism," *Journal of Autism and Developmental Disorders* 36 (2006): 585–595.

11. Allik et al., p. 1, citing Segawa, Katoh, Katoh, and Nomura (1992).

12. Ibid.

13. Paavonen et al., p. 1.

14. Allik et al.

15. David Wood, Allyson Hall, Tao Hou, Peter Wludyka, and Jianyi Zhang, "Continuity of Care to Prevent Emergency Room Use Among Persons with Intellectual and Developmental Disabilities," *Journal of Policy and Practice in Intellectual Disabilities* 4, no. 4 (December 2007): 219–228. See also: Schieve et al., 2011.

16. Kenneth W. Norwood Jr. and Rebecca Slayton, "Oral Health Care for Children with Developmental Disabilities," *Pediatrics* 131, no. 3 (March 2013): 614–619, doi: 10.1.1542/peds.2012-3650; accesssed August 30, 2013.

17. Ibid., p. 615.

18. Tony Attwood, *The Complete Guide to Asperger Syndrome*, p. 142.

19. Melina Sevlever, Matthew E. Roth, and Jennifer M. Gills, "Sexual Abuse and Offending in Autism Spectrum Disorders," *Sexuality and Disability* 31 (2013): 189–200. See also: Meredyth Goldberg Edelson, "Sexual Abuse of Children with Autism: Factors That Increase Risk and Interfere with Recognition of Abuse," *Disability Studies Quarterly* 30, no. 1 (Winter 2010); accessed online through http://web.ebscohost.com.libproxy, cc.stonybrook . . . March 7, 2012.

20. While these figures may seem lower than those cited previously for the population at large, keep in mind that this study looked at kids with an average age of eleven and depended on parent reports.

21. Pamela S. Wolfe, Bethany Condo, and Emily Hardaway, "Sociosexuality

Education for Persons with Autism Spectrum Disorders Using Principles of Applied Behavior Analysis," *Teaching Exceptional Children* 42, no. 1 (2009): 50–61.

22. Patty Huang, Trudy Kao, Allison E. Curry, and Dennis Durbin, "Factors Associated with Driving in Teens with Autism Spectrum Disorders," *Journal of Developmental & Behavioral Pediatrics* 33, no. 1 (2012): 70–74. See also: Association for Driver Rehabilitation Specialists (ADED), "Asperger's Syndrome and High Functioning Autism," fact sheet, at www.aded.net; Children's Hospital of Philadelphia, Teen Driver Source, "Teens with Special Needs," at http://www.teendriversource.org/stats/support_parents/detail/111; accessed September 22, 2013.

23. E. Sheppard, D. Ropar, G. Underwood, and E. van Loon, "Brief Report: Driving Hazard Perception in Autism," *Journal of Autism and Developmental Disorders* 40, no. 4 (2010): 504–508, doi: 10.1007/s10803-009-0890-5. See also: Laura Geggel, "Driving Concerns," SFARI: Simons Foundation Autism Research Initiative, March 8, 2013, at http://sfari.org/news-and-opinion/blog/2013/driving-concerns; accessed August 16, 2013.

24. L.-C. Lee, R. A. Harrington, J. J. Chang, and S. L. Connors, "Increased Risk of Injury in Children with Developmental Disabilities," *Research in Developmental Disabilities*, 29 (2008): 247-255, doi: 10.1016/j.ridd.2007.05.002.

Chapter 11. Life After School

1. Gerhardt, Lainer, "Addressing the Needs of Adolescents and Adults with Autism: A Crisis on the Horizon," *Journal of Contemporary Psychotherapy* 41, no. 37 (2011): 37–34.

2. Howlin et al., "Social Outcomes in Mid- to Later Adulthood Among Individuals Diagnosed with Autism and Average Nonverbal IQ as Children," *Journal of the American Academy of Child and Adolescent Psychiatry* 52, no. 6 (2013): 572–581.

3. IDEA 2004, 20 USC 1401(34)(A) and (B); Part 300, Subpart A, Section 300.43.

4. IDEA 2004, 20 USC 1414(d)(1)(A) and (d)(6); Part 300, Section 300.320(b)(2).

5. IDEA 2004, 20 USC 1414(d)(4)(A).

6. Malynn Kuangparichat, "Legal Rights of Young Adults with Autism: Transitioning into Mainstream Adulthood," *Widener Law Review* 16 (2010): 175–196.

7. College Board website (www.collegeboard.com) and ACT website (www.actstudent.org).

8. College Board, http://professionals.collegeboard.com; accessed August 23, 2013.

9. Ibid.
10. Sue Shellenbarger, "Finding a College That Suits Students with Special Needs," *Wall Street Journal*, September 17, 2008, http://online.wsj.com/article/SB122160388151245179.html.
11. Liane Holliday Willey, *Pretending to Be Normal* (London and Philadelphia: Jessica Kingsley Publishers, 1999), p. 117.

INDEX

ABOUT THE AUTHOR

Patty Romanowski Bashe, MSEd., BCBA, is a certified special education teacher and early intervention provider, Board Certified Behavior Analyst, and instructor of clinical pediatrics at the Cody Center for Autism and Developmental Disabilities at Stony Brook Children's Hospital, where she also serves as acting director of the graduate program in applied behavior analysis. She is the coauthor, with Barbara L. Kirby, of the first two editions of the award-winning *The OASIS Guide to Asperger Syndrome* and author of *The Parents' Guide to Teaching Kids with Asperger Syndrome and Similar ASDs Real-Life Skills for Independence* (Crown, 2011). Earlier, she was an award-winning editor and writer of more than twenty books on a range of popular subjects, including four bestselling collaborations. She lives on Long Island with her husband, the author Philip Bashe, and their son, Justin. Visit her website: www.aspergerguide.com.